CALIFORNIA EDITION

HOUGHTON MIFFLIN

Math Steps

HOUGHTON MIFFLIN

Boston • Atlanta • Dallas • Denver • Geneva, Illinois • Palo Alto • Princeton

Grateful acknowledgment is given for the contributions of

Student Book

Rosemary Theresa Barry
Karen R. Boyle
Barbara Brozman
Gary S. Bush
John E. Cassidy
Dorothy Kirk
Sharon Ann Kovalcik
Bernice Kubek
Donna Marie Kvasnok
Ann Cherney Markunas
Joanne Marie Mascha
Kathleen Mary Ogrin
Judith Ostrowski
Jeanette Mishic Polomsky
Patricia Stenger
Annabelle L. Higgins Svete

Teacher Book
Contributing Writers

Dr. Judy Curran Buck
Assistant Professor of Mathematics
Plymouth State College
Plymouth, New Hampshire

Dr. Richard Evans
Professor of Mathematics
Plymouth State College
Plymouth, New Hampshire

Dr. Mary K. Porter
Professor of Mathematics
St. Mary's College
Notre Dame, Indiana

Dr. Anne M. Raymond
Assistant Professor of Mathematics
Keene State College
Keene, New Hampshire

Stuart P. Robertson, Jr.
Education Consultant
Pelham, New Hampshire

Dr. David Rock
Associate Professor,
Mathematics Education
University of Mississippi
Oxford, Mississippi

Michelle Lynn Rock
Elementary Teacher
Oxford School District
Oxford, Mississippi

Dr. Jean M. Shaw
Professor of Elementary Education
University of Mississippi
Oxford, Mississippi

Printed in the U.S.A.

ISBN: 0-395-98013-5

9-B-05 04 03 02 01 00

Contents

UNIT 1 • TABLE OF CONTENTS

Whole Numbers

We will be using this vocabulary:

place-value system a number system in which the value of a digit depends on its position in the number

equation a mathematical sentence in which the values on both sides of the equal sign (=) are equal

standard form a customary form of a number that is written using digits

numerical expression a combination of one or more numbers and operations

algebraic expression a combination of one or more variables, numbers, and operations

Dear Family,

During the next few weeks, our math class will be learning about whole numbers. You can expect to see homework that provides practice with order of operations. Here is a sample you may want to keep handy to give help if needed.

Order of Operations

When expressions contain more than one operation, simplify by following these steps called the order of operations.

Order of Operations
1. Complete work in parentheses first.
2. Multiply and divide from left to right.
3. Add and subtract from left to right.

Simplify: $4 \times (3 + 3) - 6$

1. First work inside parentheses. $4 \times (3 + 3) - 6$

2. Multiply and divide from left. $4 \times 6 - 6$

3. Add and subtract from left to right. $24 - 6$

18

During this unit, students will need to continue practicing adding, subtracting, multiplying, and dividing whole numbers.

Sincerely,

Name ______________________________

Place Value a[nd] Expanded Notat[ion]

NDARD

In our base-ten numeration system, there are many ways to write a number such as **34,692**.

Standard Form: 34,692 **Expanded Form: 30,000 + 4,000 + 600 + 90 + 2**

Word Form: Thirty-four thousand, six hundred ninety-two

This place-value chart shows **753,241,908,458**.

The number is separated into **4** groups of **3** digits, each called **periods.** Remember to separate periods with commas.

Place-Value Chart

Billions Period			Millions Period			Thousands Period			Ones Period			
Hundreds	Tens	Ones	Hundreds	Tens	Ones	Hundreds	Tens	Ones	Hundreds	Tens	Ones	← Place Values
7	5	3	2	4	1	9	0	8	4	5	8	← Digits

← Periods

753 billion, **241** million, **908** thousand, **458** ← Short Word Form

Seven hundred fifty-three *billion,* two hundred forty-one *million,* nine hundred eight *thousand,* four hundred fifty-eight ← Word Form

Match.

1. **47,328,000** ______ a. thirty-two thousand, two hundred eight

2. **3,020,080** ______ b. forty-seven million, three hundred twenty-eight thousand

3. **3,200,008** ______ c. three million, two hundred thousand, eight

4. **32,208** ______ d. three million, twenty thousand, eighty

5. **80,800,800** ______ e. eighty million, eight hundred thousand, eight hundred

Complete.

6. **60** hundreds = ______ thousands **4** hundreds = ______ tens

7. **7** thousands = ______ hundreds **10** thousands = ______ ten thousand

8. **20** hundred thousands = ______ millions **70** thousands = ______ hundreds

9. **3,000** millions = ______ billions **10** billion = ______ millions

10. **5** million = ______ thousands **45** tens = ______ ones

STANDARD

Write the number in expanded form.

11. 2,374 = ____________________

12. 17,472 = ________________________

13. 48,607 = ____________________

14. 398,701 = ____________________________

15. 890,823 = __________________________

16. 8,560,589 = ____________________________________

Write the number in standard form.

17. eighty-seven thousand, five ____________________

18. seven thousand, two hundred fifty ____________________

19. seven hundred thousand, seventy ____________________

20. four hundred thousand, thirty ____________________

21. eight hundred thousand, eight hundred ____________________

22. six billion, sixty thousand, twelve ____________________

23. 5 million, 3 thousand, 3 ____________________

24. 250 million, 6 ____________________

Problem Solving
Reasoning

Which sentence represents an exact number? Which represents an estimated number?

25. There were **3,465,893** visitors to a company's web site.

____

26. Twenty-three million people live in the state of California.

____

Test Prep ★ Mixed Review

27 **What number comes next in this pattern?**

26, 23, 20,

A 21 **C** 18

B 19 **D** 17

28 **In the number 308,174, in what place is the 0?**

F Hundred thousands **H** Thousands

G Ten thousands **J** Hundreds

Name ______________________________

Adding and Subtracting Whole Numbers

STANDARD

Add **529 + 192**.

Before you add, round to estimate: **500 + 200 = 700.**

1. Add the ones and regroup.

$$\begin{array}{r} {\scriptstyle 1} \\ 529 \\ +192 \\ \hline 1 \end{array}$$

2. Add the tens and regroup.

$$\begin{array}{r} {\scriptstyle 1\,1} \\ 529 \\ +192 \\ \hline 21 \end{array}$$

3. Add the hundreds.

$$\begin{array}{r} {\scriptstyle 1\,1} \\ 529 \\ +192 \\ \hline 721 \end{array}$$

Use your estimate to check that your answer is reasonable.
The sum **721** is close to **700**, so the answer is reasonable.

Subtract **631 − 157**.
Before you subtract, estimate: **600 − 200 = 400.**

1. Regroup **1** ten as **10** ones and subtract the ones.

$$\begin{array}{r} {\scriptstyle 2\;11} \\ 6\,\cancel{3}\,\cancel{1} \\ -1\,5\,7 \\ \hline 4 \end{array}$$

2. Regroup **1** hundred as **10** tens and subtract the tens.

$$\begin{array}{r} {\scriptstyle 12} \\ {\scriptstyle 5\;\cancel{2}\;11} \\ \cancel{6}\,\cancel{3}\,\cancel{1} \\ -1\,5\,7 \\ \hline 7\,4 \end{array}$$

3. Subtract the hundreds.

$$\begin{array}{r} {\scriptstyle 12} \\ {\scriptstyle 5\;\cancel{2}\;11} \\ \cancel{6}\,\cancel{3}\,\cancel{1} \\ -1\,5\,7 \\ \hline 4\,7\,4 \end{array}$$

Use your estimate to check that your answer is reasonable.
The difference, **474,** is close to **400**. The answer is reasonable.

Estimate. Then add.

1.

$$\begin{array}{r} 256 \\ +142 \\ \hline \end{array} \quad \begin{array}{r} 332 \\ +247 \\ \hline \end{array} \quad \begin{array}{r} 544 \\ +303 \\ \hline \end{array} \quad \begin{array}{r} 146 \\ +252 \\ \hline \end{array} \quad \begin{array}{r} 357 \\ +122 \\ \hline \end{array} \quad \begin{array}{r} 679 \\ +314 \\ \hline \end{array} \quad \begin{array}{r} 135 \\ +264 \\ \hline \end{array} \quad \begin{array}{r} 309 \\ +274 \\ \hline \end{array}$$

2.

$$\begin{array}{r} 1,465 \\ 4,388 \\ +9,069 \\ \hline \end{array} \quad \begin{array}{r} 2,576 \\ 5,492 \\ +\ 837 \\ \hline \end{array} \quad \begin{array}{r} \$3.06 \\ 2.75 \\ +6.09 \\ \hline \end{array} \quad \begin{array}{r} \$32.75 \\ 64.80 \\ +9.59 \\ \hline \end{array} \quad \begin{array}{r} \$5.72 \\ 3.09 \\ +5.33 \\ \hline \end{array} \quad \begin{array}{r} \$56.65 \\ 4.50 \\ +19.78 \\ \hline \end{array}$$

Estimate. Then subtract.

3.

$$\begin{array}{r} 562 \\ -139 \\ \hline 423 \end{array} \quad \begin{array}{r} 450 \\ -228 \\ \hline \end{array} \quad \begin{array}{r} 937 \\ -152 \\ \hline \end{array} \quad \begin{array}{r} 649 \\ -383 \\ \hline \end{array} \quad \begin{array}{r} 707 \\ -138 \\ \hline \end{array}$$

4.

$$\begin{array}{r} 4,084 \\ -1,338 \\ \hline \end{array} \quad \begin{array}{r} 5,399 \\ -1,864 \\ \hline \end{array} \quad \begin{array}{r} 2,309 \\ -1,145 \\ \hline \end{array} \quad \begin{array}{r} 3,408 \\ -1,127 \\ \hline \end{array} \quad \begin{array}{r} \$38.96 \\ -24.79 \\ \hline \end{array}$$

STANDARD

You may need to regroup more than once before you subtract.

1. Regroup 1 thousand as 10 hundreds.

```
   3 10
  4, 9 0 2
- 2, 9 8 7
```

2. Regroup 1 hundred as 10 tens.

```
      9
   3 10 10
  4, 9 0 2
- 2, 9 8 7
```

3. Regroup 1 ten as 10 ones.

```
      9  9
   3 10 10 12
  4, 9 0 2
- 2, 9 8 7
```

4. Subtract.

```
      9  9
   3 10 10 12
  4, 9 0 2
- 2, 9 8 7
  1, 0 1 5
```

Estimate. Then subtract.

5.

```
  $72.56     $167.93     17,000     308,419     500,002
 - 47.95    - 38.45     - 2,654    - 69,999    - 84,896
```

Add or subtract.

6.

```
  7,354      780     5,467    9,000     6,341     7,390
  4,523      355     2,347        8        18       345
 +   45   +4,221    +   57    + 236    +3,460    +9,080
```

7.

```
  26,008     50,234     75,163     79,411     82,004
 -11,578    -22,166    -58,756    -45,470    -66,810
```

8.

```
  8,154     5,138     826     7,581     3,536
  7,238       782     514    -2,746    -1,268
 +4,977    +3,205    +988
```

Test Prep ★ Mixed Review

9 In 1993, about 1,179,467,000 people lived in China. How is this number written in words?

A One billion, one hundred seventy-nine million, four hundred sixty-seven thousand

B One million, one hundred seventy-nine thousand, four hundred sixty-seven

C One billion, one hundred seventy-nine million, four hundred sixty-seven

D One billion, one hundred seventy-nine thousand, four hundred sixty-seven

10 What is this number in standard form?

7,000,000 + 300,000 + 2,000 + 700 + 3

F 73,273

G 7,032,730

H 7,302,703

J 7,302,730

Name ______________________

Addition Properties and Expressions

STANDARD

Addition properties can help you find the value of an expression.

Commutative Property of Addition
Changing the order of the addends does not change the sum.

$6 + 7 = 7 + 6$
$a + b = b + a$

Associative Property of Addition
Changing the grouping of the addends does not change the sum.

$(4 + 5) + 6 = 4 + (5 + 6)$
$(a + b) + c = a + (b + c)$

Identity Property of Addition
The sum of a number and **0** is that number. $6 + 0 = 6$ $n + 0 = n$

You can use properties to make sums that are easy to add mentally.

$46 + 17 + 14 + 3$
$46 + (17 + 3) + 14$
$46 + 20 + 14$
$(46 + 14) + 20$
$60 + 20$
80

Name each property.

1. 4 + 0 = 4 ______
2. 3 + 6 = 6 + 3 ______
3. (3 + 5) + 2 = 3 + (5 + 2) ______
4. (3 + 5) + 2 = (5 + 3) + 2 ______
5. 0 + 9 = 9 ______
6. (3 + 9) + 7 = 3 + (9 + 7) ______

Use properties to complete.

7. 8 + ______ = 3 + 8   8 + (______ + 4) = (______ + 4) + 8
8. ______ + 0 = 9   (2 + 1) + 7 = 2 + (______ + 7)
9. 16 + (9 + 8) = (16 + ______) + 8   (8 + ______) + 15 = 8 + (4 + 15)
10. 3 + ______ = 9 + 3   (7 + 3) + ______ = 7 + (______ + 4)
11. 7 + ______ = 7   (8 + 6) + 9 = 9 + (8 + ______)
12. (5 + 4) + ______ = 7 + (5 + 4)   19 + 6 = 6 + ______
13. ______ + 38 = 38   (75 + 93) + 176 = 75 + (______ + 176)

Solve mentally. Find the value of the expression.

14. 36 + 15 + 5 + 4 ______   16 + 7 + 23 + 4 ______   7 + 33 + 18 + 12 ______
15. 42 + 9 + 11 + 8 ______   23 + 5 + 17 + 15 ______   36 + 22 + 14 + 18 ______
16. 29 + 12 + 11 + 38 ______   14 + 24 + 26 + 16 ______   17 + 26 + 4 + 13 ______
17. 18 + 23 + 42 + 7 ______   11 + 38 + 19 + 2 ______   31 + 42 + 9 + 8 ______
18. 17 + 26 + 24 + 23 ______   22 + 7 + 53 + 8 ______   15 + 13 + 17 + 25 ______

STANDARD

Remember, an algebraic expression contains numbers, operations, and variables. A **variable** is a letter that represents an unknown value.

If you know the value of a variable, you can **evaluate** an expression. You evaluate an expression by substituting the value for the variable and simplifying.

$x + 3$	$18 - n$	$g + h$
the sum of *x* plus 3	18 minus *n*	*g* increased by *h*

Expression:	*Value of Variable:*	*Substitute and Evaluate:*
$16 - y$	$y = 8$	$16 - y \rightarrow 16 - 8 = 8$
$d + 17$	$d = 15$	$d + 17 \rightarrow 15 + 17 = 32$

Write the meaning of each expression.

19. $s - 4$ ______ $14 + m$ ______ $b + 20$ ______ $c - x$ ______

Evaluate the expression for $v = 7$ and $t = 13$.

20. $v - 3$ ______ $t + 7$ ______ $36 + v$ ______ $114 - v$ ______

21. $26 + t$ ______ $v + t$ ______ $t - v$ ______ $t + 129$ ______

22. $t - 5$ ______ $90 - v$ ______ $89 + t$ ______ $559 + v$ ______

Quick Check

23. Write the expanded form of 182,011.

______

Find the sum.

24. $56 + 25 + 47$

25. $266 + 97 + 518$

26. $54,024 + 36,912 + 87,606$

Find the difference.

27. $1,654 - 825$

28. $5,403 - 2,516$

29. $210,050 - 75,341$

Evaluate the expression $n - 287$ for the value of n.

30. $n = 563$ ______

31. $n = 300$ ______

32. $n = 1,007$ ______

Work Space.

Name ______________________________

Solving Addition and Subtraction Equations

STANDARD

Remember, an algebraic equation contains numbers, variables, operations, and an equal sign.

$3 + x = 5$ $12 - n = 7$ $t - 4 = 24$

When you solve an algebraic equation, you need to find the value of the variable.

To solve an addition equation, use the inverse operation: Subtract the same number from each side of the equation.

Solve: $y + 6 = 9$

1. Choose the inverse operation: Subtract **6** from each side of the equation. $y + 6 = 9$; $y + 6 - 6 = 9 - 6$

Subtraction "undoes" addition. Subtraction is the inverse of addition.

2. Simplify. $y = 3$

3. Check that the solution is correct. Substitute **3** for y to find if the equation is true. $y + 6 = 9$; $3 + 6 = 9$; $9 = 9$

The equation is true, so the solution is correct.

Complete the steps to find the solution of the equation.

1. $b + 8 = 12$ $j + 9 = 18$ $m + 6 = 14$

$b + 8 -$ ____ $= 12 -$ ____ $j + 9 -$ ____ $= 18 -$ ____ $m + 6 -$ ____ $= 14 -$ ____

$b =$ ____ $j =$ ____ $m =$ ____

2. $h + 7 = 15$ $20 = k + 5$ $z + 7 = 16$

$h +$ ____ $-$ ____ $= 15 -$ ____ ____ $-$ ____ $= k + 5 - 5$ $z + 7 -$ ____ $= 16 -$ ____

$h =$ ____ ____ $= k$ $z =$ ____

Solve the equation.

3. $x + 8 = 11$ ______ $h + 8 = 24$ ______ $v + 3 = 13$ ______

4. $j + 7 = 13$ ______ $n + 6 = 18$ ______ $g + 9 = 27$ ______

5. $y + 17 = 32$ ______ $d + 26 = 40$ ______ $16 + t = 25$ ______

6. $a + 7 = 20$ ______ $8 + b = 17$ ______ $c + 15 = 31$ ______

STANDARD

You can also solve subtraction equations using inverse operations

To solve a subtraction equation, add the same number to each side of the equation.

Solve: $m - 8 = 9$

1. Choose the inverse operation. Add **8** to each side of the equation. $m - 8 = 9$, $m - 8 + 8 = 9 + 8$

2. Simplify. $m = 17$

3. Check that the solution is correct. Substitute **17** for *m* to check whether the equation is true. $m - 8 = 9$, $17 - 8 = 9$, $9 = 9$

Addition "undoes" subtraction. Addition is the inverse of subtraction.

The equation is true, so the solution is correct.

Complete the steps to find the solution of the equation.

7. $b - 6 = 1$ | $k - 8 = 7$ | $m - 5 = 13$

$b - 6 +$ ____ $=$ ____ $+$ ____ | $k -$ ____ $+$ ____ $=$ ____ $+$ ____ | $m -$ ______ $=$ ______

$b =$ ____ | $k =$ ____ | $m =$ ____

8. $h - 25 = 17$ | $n - 62 = 125$ | $100 = p - 20$

$h -$ ____ $+$ ____ $=$ ____ $+$ ____ | $n -$ ____ $+$ ____ $=$ ____ $+$ ____ | $100 +$ ____ $= p - 20 + 20$

$h =$ ____ | $n =$ ____ | ____ $= p$

Solve the equation.

9. $t - 9 = 7$ ____ $m - 6 = 23$ ____ $b - 8 = 20$ ____ $j - 10 = 16$ ____ $c - 9 = 27$ ____ $g - 19 = 37$ ____

10. $q - 18 = 15$ ____ $z - 12 = 29$ ____ $w - 32 = 32$ ____ $g - 19 = 37$ ____ $x - 15 = 100$ ____

11. $b - 75 = 9$ ____ $k - 83 = 37$ ____ $a - 16 = 20$ ____ $r - 25 = 0$ ____ $y - 123 = 45$ ____

12. $18 = n - 7$ ____ $m - 11 = 31$ ____ $d - 105 = 17$ ____ $86 = f - 10$ ____ $48 = j - 19$ ____

Name ______________________________

STANDARD

Solve the equation. First decide whether to add or subtract.

13. $x - 9 = 25$ ____ $m + 12 = 18$ ____ $k + 7 = 36$ ____ $b - 11 = 17$ ____ $n - 8 = 34$ ____

14. $w + 16 = 32$ ____ $b + 51 = 75$ ____ $q - 17 = 40$ ____ $s - 33 = 68$ ____ $x + 22 = 59$ ____

15. $r + 54 = 72$ ____ $t - 9 = 47$ ____ $g - 11 = 20$ ____ $33 = d - 5$ ____ $17 + f = 17$ ____

16. $x - 5 = 19$ ____ $13 + n = 30$ ____ $h + 17 = 42$ ____ $p - 35 = 22$ ____ $26 = 8 + v$ ____

17. $27 = e + 15$ ____ $w - 38 = 45$ ____ $125 = b + 112$ ____ $98 = t - 7$ ____ $32 + y = 83$ ____

Problem Solving Reasoning Solve.

You can think of solving an equation, such as $x + 5 = 11$, in terms of a balance scale. Each number represents a weight.

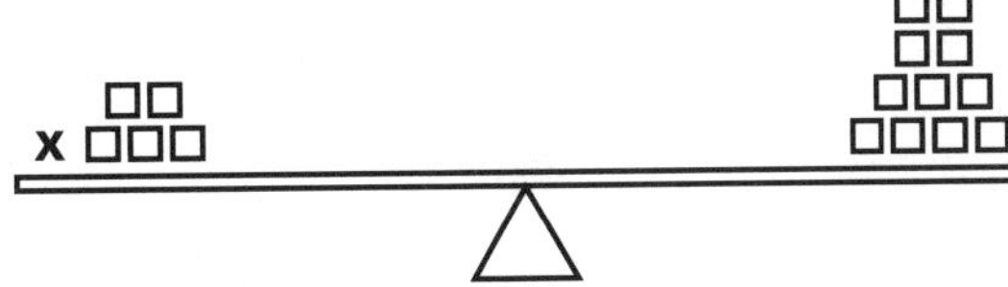

18. Could you take **3** blocks off each side and still keep the scale balanced? Explain.

____

____

19. How does removing **5** blocks help you to find the weight represented by *x*?

____

____

Test Prep ★ Mixed Review

20 What is the solution of the equation $276 + n = 276$?

A 0

B 1

C 10

D 20

21 Which number sentence goes with $97 + 5 = n$?

F $5 - N = 97$

G $97 \times 5 = N$

H $N - 5 = 97$

J $N \times 5 = 97$

STANDARD

Name ______________________________

Multiplying Whole Numbers

Sometimes when you multiply, you may need to regroup.

Multiply **6 × 583**.

Before you multiply, round to estimate. **6 × 600 = 3,600**

1. Multiply the ones. Regroup.

$$\begin{array}{r} {}^{1}\\ 583 \\ \times\ 6 \\ \hline 8 \end{array}$$

2. Multiply the tens. Add and regroup.

$$\begin{array}{r} {}^{4\ 1}\\ 583 \\ \times\ 6 \\ \hline 98 \end{array}$$

(6 × 80) + 1

3. Multiply the hundreds. Add.

$$\begin{array}{r} {}^{4\ 1}\\ 583 \\ \times\ 6 \\ \hline 3,498 \end{array}$$

(6 × 500) + 4

Use your estimate to check that your answer is reasonable.
The product **3,498** is close to **3,600**, so the answer is reasonable.

Estimate. Then multiply.

1. 623 × 7   749 × 3   658 × 2   345 × 8   985 × 5

2. 835 × 9   933 × 2   336 × 5   211 × 6   509 × 3

3. 2,531 × 8   3,819 × 5   8,537 × 3   3,841 × 6   8,362 × 9

4. 9,543 × 4   5,786 × 6   3,215 × 9   28,601 × 7   97,832 × 4

5. 95,283 × 6   236,145 × 9   7,486 × 5   6,581 × 3   2,367 × 6

6. 2,752 × 9   8,541 × 4   2,395 × 8   94,841 × 6   87,562 × 9

7. 632,658 × 7   295,611 × 2   477,403 × 4   959,312 × 3   233,361 × 9

Name ______________________________

STANDARD

These examples show how to multiply by **10**, **100**, or **1,000**.

458 × 10 = 4,580 (1 zero)	458 × 100 = 45,800 (2 zeros)	458 × 1,000 = 458,000 (3 zeros)

Multiply.

8.	275 × 1	275 × 10	275 × 100	275 × 1,000	62 × 1	62 × 10
9.	62 × 100	62 × 1,000	4,607 × 1	4,607 × 10	4,607 × 100	4,607 × 1,000
10.	380 × 10	90 × 100	206 × 100	315 × 1,000	8,072 × 10	9,300 × 100
11.	815 × 100	36 × 10	100 × 1,000	600 × 100	80 × 1,000	2,900 × 10

12.	10 × 72 = ________	10 × 56 = ________	1,000 × 39 = ________
13.	1,000 × 60 = ________	100 × 123 = ________	10 × 275 = ________
14.	100 × 98 = ________	100 × 75 = ________	100 × 90 = ________
15.	36 × 1,000 = ________	498 × 100 = ________	257 × 10 = ________
16.	10 × 85 = ________	100 × 145 = ________	1,000 × 512 = ________
17.	1,000 × 400 = ________	302 × 1,000 = ________	1,000 × 6,104 = ________

Complete.

18. Twenty nickels have the same value as **1** dollar. How many nickels have the same value as **10** dollars?

____

19. Four quarters have the same value as **1** dollar. How many quarters have the same value as **1,000** dollars?

____

20. Ten dimes have the same value as **1** dollar. How many dimes have the same value as **25** dollars?

____

21. One hundred pennies have the same value as **1** dollar. How many pennies have the same value as **100** dollars?

____

STANDARD

When you multiply by a **2**-digit number, you should estimate before you multiply.

Find: **42 × 85** First, round to estimate: **40 × 90 = 3,600**

Then find the actual product.

1. Multiply by the ones digit. Remember to regroup.

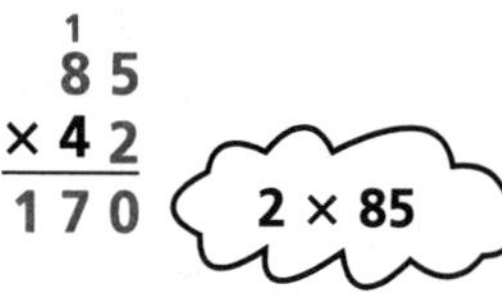

2. Multiply by the tens digit. Remember to regroup.

3. Add the partial products.

$$\begin{array}{r} 85 \\ \times 42 \\ \hline 170 \\ +340 \\ \hline 3{,}570 \end{array}$$

You do not have to write the zero.

You can use your estimate to check that your answer is reasonable. The product **3,570** is close to **3,600**, so the answer is reasonable.

Estimate. Then multiply.

22. $\begin{array}{r} 64 \\ \times 32 \\ \hline \end{array}$ $\begin{array}{r} 78 \\ \times 14 \\ \hline \end{array}$ $\begin{array}{r} 61 \\ \times 56 \\ \hline \end{array}$ $\begin{array}{r} 24 \\ \times 96 \\ \hline \end{array}$ $\begin{array}{r} 32 \\ \times 59 \\ \hline \end{array}$ $\begin{array}{r} 25 \\ \times 74 \\ \hline \end{array}$

23. $\begin{array}{r} 952 \\ \times 16 \\ \hline \end{array}$ $\begin{array}{r} 863 \\ \times 34 \\ \hline \end{array}$ $\begin{array}{r} 465 \\ \times 12 \\ \hline \end{array}$ $\begin{array}{r} 982 \\ \times 47 \\ \hline \end{array}$ $\begin{array}{r} 924 \\ \times 58 \\ \hline \end{array}$ $\begin{array}{r} 953 \\ \times 25 \\ \hline \end{array}$

24. $\begin{array}{r} 486 \\ \times 67 \\ \hline \end{array}$ $\begin{array}{r} 728 \\ \times 56 \\ \hline \end{array}$ $\begin{array}{r} 695 \\ \times 89 \\ \hline \end{array}$ $\begin{array}{r} 486 \\ \times 72 \\ \hline \end{array}$ $\begin{array}{r} 982 \\ \times 63 \\ \hline \end{array}$ $\begin{array}{r} 779 \\ \times 98 \\ \hline \end{array}$

25. $\begin{array}{r} 9{,}831 \\ \times 85 \\ \hline \end{array}$ $\begin{array}{r} 6{,}521 \\ \times 62 \\ \hline \end{array}$ $\begin{array}{r} 6{,}572 \\ \times 94 \\ \hline \end{array}$ $\begin{array}{r} 2{,}158 \\ \times 73 \\ \hline \end{array}$ $\begin{array}{r} 5{,}086 \\ \times 57 \\ \hline \end{array}$ $\begin{array}{r} 5{,}261 \\ \times 39 \\ \hline \end{array}$

Name ______________________________

Multiplying by a 3-digit number is like multiplying by a 2-digit number.

Multiply **392 × 672**.

1. Multiply by the ones digit.

```
   672
 × 394
 2,688
```

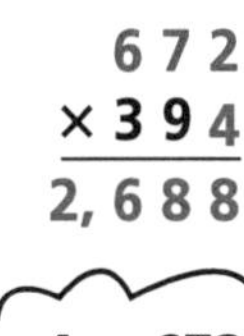

2. Multiply by the tens digit.

```
   672
 × 394
 2,688
60,48
```

90 × 672

3. Multiply by the hundreds digit.

```
    672
  × 394
  2,688
 60,48
201,6
```

4. Add the partial products.

```
    672
  × 394
  2,688
 60,48
+201,6
264,768
```

Remember to check that the answer is reasonable.

Multiply.

26.

762	503	638	4,610	3,944
× 381	× 741	× 897	× 239	× 307

Rewrite each exercise vertically. Find the product.

27. 4,050 × 89 = ____________ 396 × 66 = ____________

28. 7,430 × 365 = ____________ 8,362 × 123 = ____________

Problem Solving Reasoning Solve.

29. There are **675** students at school. If each student brings **25** pennies to school, how many pennies will there be?

____

30. There are **500** sheets of paper in one ream of paper. How many sheets of paper are there in **1,000** reams of paper?

____

Test Prep ★ Mixed Review

31 The Supreme T-Shirt Company made 3,924 shirts in the first week of May. They need 7,238 shirts. Which equation could be used to find how many more shirts they need?

A 7,238 + t = 3,924 **C** 3,924 − t = 7,238
B 3,924 + t = 7,238 **D** 3,924 + 7,238 = t

32 Mr. Singh had 375 boxes in his office. Which expression shows how many boxes he has left after he used n boxes?

F 375 + n **H** n ÷ 375
G 375 − n **J** n − 375

STANDARD

Name ______________________________

Multiplication Properties and Expressions

Knowing the properties of multiplication can help you evaluate expressions.

Identity Property of Multiplication

The product of a number and **1** is that number.

$8 \times 1 \rightarrow 8$

$n \times 1 \rightarrow n$

Zero Property of Multiplication

The product of a number and **0** is **0**.

$8 \times 0 \rightarrow 0$

$n \times 0 \rightarrow 0$

Commutative Property

Changing the order of the factors does not change the product.

$8 \times 5 = 5 \times 8$

$a \times b = b \times a$

Associative Property

Changing the grouping of the factors does not change the product.

$(4 \times 2) \times 3 = 4 \times (2 \times 3)$

$(a \times b) \times c = a \times (b \times c)$

Distributive Property

The product of a factor and a sum equals the sum of the products.

$8 \times (20 + 4) = (8 \times 20) + (8 \times 4)$
$8 \times 24 = 160 + 32$
$192 = 192$

You can use the associative and commutative properties to make products that are easy to multiply mentally.

$5 \times 7 \times 8 \times 6$
$(5 \times 8) \times (7 \times 6)$
40×42
$1{,}680$

Use the properties to complete.

1. $(2 \times 14) \times 50 = 2 \times (14 \times$ ______$)$ $5 \times (80 + 3) = (5 \times$ ______$) + (5 \times 3)$

2. $121 \times$ ______ $= 8 \times 121$ $6 \times 0 =$ ______ $8 \times$ ______ $= 8$

Identify the property.

3. $2 \times 63 = 63 \times 2$ ______________________

4. $25 \times 0 = 0$ ______________________

5. $(4 \times 2) \times 3 = 4 \times (2 \times 3)$ ______________________

Solve mentally. Use multiplication properties to help you.

6. $10 \times 7 \times 6 \times 10$ ______ $14 \times 8 \times 0 \times 5$ ______ $20 \times 4 \times 5 \times 10$ ______

7. $12 \times (11 + 3 + 6)$ ______ $32 \times 25 \times 4 \times 2$ ______ $48 \times 2 \times 0 \times 19$ ______

Name ______________________

STANDARD

Here are some ways to write multiplication expressions:

$4 \cdot 8$	$6a$	$(5)(n)$	$2(b + c)$
4 times 8	multiply 6 by *a*	5 times a number	2 times the sum of *b* and *c*

Use what you know about evaluating expressions to evaluate multiplication expressions.

Expression:	Value of Variable:	Evaluate:
$16y$	$y = 8$	$16y = 16 \times 8$ or 128

Write as an algebraic expression.

8. *n* times *m* ______

the product of 7 and *y* ______

twice the sum of *t* and 2 ______

multiply *s* by the sum of 8 and *t* ______

9. three times the difference of *p* and 6 ______

the product of 7 and the sum of *v* and *q* ______

z times 136 ______

multiply *r* times the sum of 8, 3, and *f* ______

Evaluate for $v = 7$ and $t = 9$.

10. $v \cdot 3$ ______ $(t)7$ ______ $6v$ ______ $2(t)$ ______ $5(t - v)$ ______

11. $t(v - 3)$ ______ $v(t + 3)$ ______ $2(v + t)$ ______ $16v$ ______ $t \cdot 9$ ______ $t(v - 1)$ ______

Quick Check

Write the product.

12. 88×35

13. 73×68

14. $2,476 \times 62$

15. $8,109 \times 54$

16. 903×720

17. 408×801

18. Solve.
$x + 27 = 54$ ______

19. Evaluate for $z = 23$.
$19z$ ______

Work Space.

STANDARD

Name ______________________

Dividing Whole Numbers

Review what you know about dividing with **1**-digit divisors. Try to use mental math whenever possible to find quotients such as the one below.

Divide: $7\overline{)62}$

quotient ↙

8 R6 ← remainder

divisor → $7\overline{)62}$ ← dividend

−56

6 ← remainder

Check:

8 ← divisor

× 7 ← quotient

56

+ 6 ← remainder

62 ← dividend

(quotient × divisor) + remainder = dividend

Divide. Check your answer.

1. $8\overline{)48}$ $5\overline{)45}$ $9\overline{)81}$ $4\overline{)32}$

2. $6\overline{)38}$ $2\overline{)15}$ $8\overline{)27}$ $4\overline{)31}$

3. $5\overline{)48}$ $7\overline{)52}$ $6\overline{)38}$ $8\overline{)90}$

4. $3\overline{)89}$ $2\overline{)75}$ $4\overline{)63}$ $6\overline{)90}$

5. $7\overline{)85}$ $3\overline{)54}$ $4\overline{)89}$ $2\overline{)56}$

6. $9\overline{)107}$ $3\overline{)59}$ $7\overline{)93}$ $9\overline{)200}$

Name ______________________________

STANDARD

When you divide, you may need to write zero in the quotient. Find **1,525 ÷ 3.**

First, estimate to have a sense of what the quotient will be.
Use compatible numbers to estimate.

$3\overline{)1{,}525} \rightarrow 3\overline{)1{,}500}$ with quotient 500

You know that the quotient will be about **500**.

> Compatible numbers are numbers that are easy to divide mentally. Choose numbers that are close to the actual numbers.

Now divide:

1. Divide **15** hundreds by **3** to place the first digit in the quotient.

   Think: $3\overline{)15}$

   ```
        5
    3)1,525
     -1 5
        0
   ```

2. Bring down the **2**. There are not enough tens to divide. Write a 0 in the quotient.

   ```
        5 0
    3)1,5 2 5
     -1 5↓
        0 2
   ```

3. Bring down the **5** and divide **25** ones by **3**.

   ```
        5 0 8 R1
    3)1,5 2 5
     -1 5   ↓
        0 2 5
         -2 4
            1
   ```

Remember to check the answer. Multiply the quotient by the divisor. Add the remainder to the product. The result should be the dividend.

```
  508
 ×  3
1,524
 +  1
1,525
```

Estimate. Divide. Check.

7.	$3\overline{)623}$	$4\overline{)827}$	$6\overline{)654}$	$5\overline{)539}$	$3\overline{)605}$
8.	$7\overline{)1{,}421}$	$6\overline{)1{,}624}$	$5\overline{)4{,}506}$	$5\overline{)2{,}030}$	$8\overline{)5{,}666}$
9.	$8\overline{)2{,}405}$	$7\overline{)4{,}965}$	$4\overline{)2{,}601}$	$2\overline{)1{,}634}$	$6\overline{)2{,}432}$
10.	$9\overline{)2{,}814}$	$8\overline{)3{,}872}$	$7\overline{)4{,}864}$	$3\overline{)1{,}039}$	$5\overline{)3{,}050}$

STANDARD

You can follow these steps to divide by a **2**-digit number.
Find **7,980 ÷ 32.**

1. Estimate to place the first digit in the quotient. Use rounding to estimate.

$$32\overline{)7{,}980}\quad \text{quotient: } 2$$

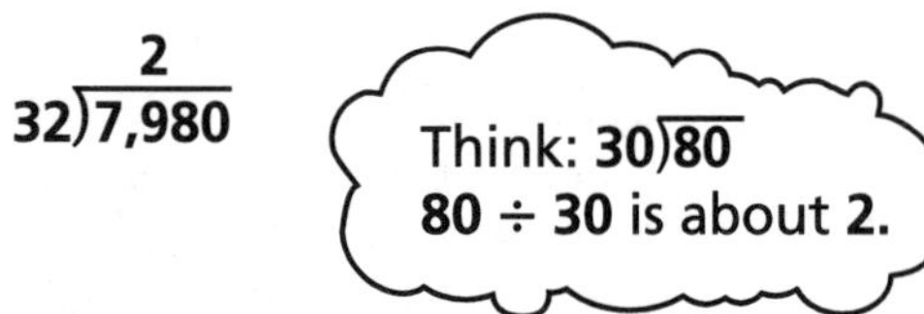

2. Multiply. Subtract. Bring down the next digit.

$$\begin{array}{r} 2 \\ 32\overline{)7{,}980} \\ -6\,4\downarrow \\ 158 \end{array}$$

3. Repeat the steps to continue dividing. Remember to write the remainder in the quotient.

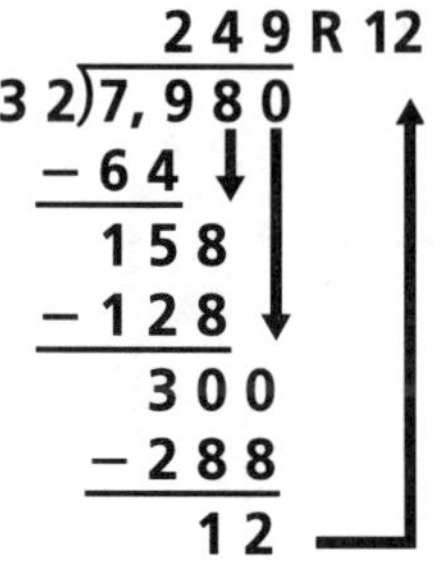

The remainder must always be less than the divisor.

4. Check the answer.

$$\begin{array}{r} 249 \\ \times\ 32 \\ \hline 498 \\ 747\ \\ \hline 7{,}968 \\ +\ 12 \\ \hline 7{,}980 \end{array}$$

Divide. Remember to check your work.

11. $56\overline{)857}$	$38\overline{)635}$	$22\overline{)8{,}329}$	$45\overline{)1{,}728}$
12. $23\overline{)4{,}670}$	$19\overline{)4{,}287}$	$68\overline{)2{,}439}$	$73\overline{)8{,}967}$
13. $48\overline{)9{,}724}$	$37\overline{)8{,}632}$	$52\overline{)2{,}647}$	$91\overline{)8{,}743}$

Name ______________________

STANDARD

Dividing by **3**-digit numbers is similar to dividing by **2**-digit numbers.

Find: 397)2,382

Estimate to place the first digit in the quotient.

Think: 400)2,400 → 6

```
        6
397 )2,382
    -2,382
         0
```

Find: 432)223,342

Estimate to place the first digit in the quotient.

Think: 400)2,000 → 5

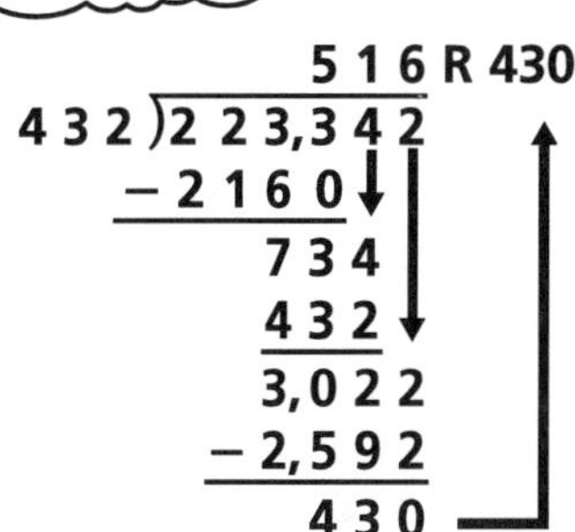

Divide and check.

14. 726)3,630 405)3,240 845)5,070 932)3,736

15. 113)94,117 256)238,920 112)82,936 305)208,317

Solve.

16. The stadium sold **650,000** tickets for a hockey game. The game was sold out. There are **130** seating sections in the stadium. Each section has the same number of seats.

How many seats are in each section? ______________

Test Prep ★ Mixed Review

17 **The Cortez family drove to a vacation spot. To get there, they traveled 467 miles the first day, 526 miles the second day, and 280 miles the third day. *About* how many miles did they drive in all?**

A 1,100 miles **C** 1,300 miles

B 1,200 miles **D** 1,400 miles

18 **A bookstore owner has boxes of books shipped to her. Each box contains 9 books. Which expression shows how many books there are in *n* boxes?**

F $9 \cdot n$ **H** $9 - n$

G $9 + n$ **J** $n \div 9$

STANDARD

Name ______________________

Order of Operations

Some expressions involve more than one operation. Follow the order of operations to simplify expressions.

Order of Operations
1. Perform operations in parentheses.
2. Multiply and divide from left to right.
3. Add and subtract from left to right.

- There are no parentheses. $12 - 6 \times 2 + 11$
- Multiply. $12 - 6 \times 2 + 11$
- Add and subtract from left to right. $12 - 12 + 11$

$0 + 11$

11

The order of operations can be used in expressions that contain variables.

Evaluate $4 + x + 3 \times 2$ for the given value of x.

First multiply. Then add.

x	$4 + x + 3 \times 2$
0	$4 + 0 + 3 \times 2 \rightarrow 10$
1	$4 + 1 + 3 \times 2 \rightarrow 11$
5	$4 + 5 + 3 \times 2 \rightarrow 15$

Simplify the expression using the order of operations.

1. $3 + 8 \times 2$ ______ $9 \times 0 + 4$ ______ $10 - 8 \div 4 + 2$ ______ $5 \times 5 + 5 \div 5$ ______

2. $6 \times 5 - 4$ ______ $10 + 2 \times 3$ ______ $8 + 8 \div 8 - 8$ ______ $7 \times 2 + 6 - 3 \div 3$ ______

Evaluate the expression for the given values.

3.

s	$6 \times s + 2 \times s$
0	
1	
2	

m	$m + 6 \div 3$
5	
10	
15	

z	$5 \times 9 - z$
9	
6	
3	

4.

d	$14 - d \div 3$
6	
12	
15	

g	$4 + 7 \times g$
3	
4	
5	

q	$3 \times q - 2 \times 7$
7	
10	
12	

Name ___________________________________

STANDARD

Parentheses and fraction bars are grouping symbols. They are used to group numbers and operations in an expression.

Perform the operation inside parentheses first.

$(4 + 6) \div 5$

$10 \div 5$

2

A fraction bar means division. It also acts as a grouping symbol.

$\frac{4 + 6}{5}$ ← Simplify the numerator first.

$\frac{10}{5}$ or 2 ← Then divide.

Simplify the expression using the order of operations.

5. $6 \times (7 - 4) + 2$ ______ $(5 + 2) \times (6 - 3)$ ______ $(15 - 4) + 2 \times (6 - 5)$ ______ $4 \div (8 - 6) \times (1 \times 9)$ ______

6. $\frac{5 - 3}{2}$ ______ $\frac{18 + 6}{6}$ ______ $\frac{8 - 2 \times 4}{9 + 7}$ ______ $\frac{4 + 1 \times 9 - 4}{3 \times (3 - 2)}$ ______

Insert parentheses to make the equation true.

7. $9 - 3 \times 3 - 2 = 6$ $16 + 5 \div 10 - 3 = 3$ $15 - 5 + 5 \times 7 - 6 = 15$

Problem Solving Reasoning

Use the order of operations to compare. Write >, <, or = in each ○.

8. $6 + 9 - 6 \div 2$ ○ $6 + (9 - 6) - 2$ $\frac{11 + 4}{4 + (5 - 4)}$ ○ $\frac{4 + (5 - 4)}{11 + 4}$

Quick Check

Find the quotient.

9. $8\overline{)960}$ **10.** $9\overline{)7{,}488}$ **11.** $23\overline{)98}$

12. $27\overline{)9{,}033}$ **13.** $59\overline{)62{,}909}$ **14.** $306\overline{)20{,}818}$

Use the order of operations to evaluate the expression.

15. $4 \cdot 8 + 8 \cdot 3 - 16$ ______ **16.** $15\,(43 - 28) - 4\,(8 + 11)$ ______

Work Space.

STANDARD

Name ______________________________

Problem Solving Application: Multi-Step Problems

Sometimes you need to use two or more steps in order to solve a problem.

Try to write simpler problems that will help you find each fact you need. Solve each simpler problem. Then use the answers to solve the original problem.

Tips to Remember:

1. Understand 2. Decide 3. Solve 4. Look back

- Think about what the problem is asking you to do. What information does the problem give you? What do you need to find out?
- Try to break the problem into parts.
- Think about the action in the problem. Is there more than one action? Which operation best represents the action– addition, subtraction, multiplication, or division?

Solve.

1. A store sold **25** T-shirts for **$10.50** each. How much profit did the store make if it paid **$52.50** for the shirts?

Think: How can you find the total sales for the T-shirts?

____

____

Answer ____________________

2. A total of **480** students went on a school trip. There were **4** adults for every **32** students. How many people went in all?

Think: How can you find how many adults went on the trip?

____

____

Answer ____________________

3. Each company truck can hold **36** crates. Each crate can hold **2** dozen bottles. How many bottles can **2** trucks hold?

____

4. A carton of apple juice holds **6** juice packs. A carton of grape juice holds **8** juice packs. How many juice packs are in **12** cartons of each?

____

5. A group of **128** people attended a meeting. Half the people were seated in the mezzanine. Fifteen people were seated in the balcony. How many people were not seated in the balcony or mezzanine?

____

6. Osamu bought two **5**-lb bags of potatoes. The apples he bought weighed **2.5** lb less than the potatoes. He also bought some fish. If the bag of groceries weighed **20** lb, how much did the fish weigh?

____

STANDARD

Solve.

7. Tomas wants to buy a bicycle that costs **$143**. He has already saved **$39**. If he saves **$8** a month, how many months will it take him to save enough money to buy it?

____

8. Erin bought a paperback book for **$2.98** and a hardcover book for **$9.98**. How much change did she get back from **$15**?

____

9. Two hundred ninety students went on a trip to the zoo. There were **98** fourth graders and **89** fifth graders. The rest were sixth graders. How many sixth graders were there?

____

10. Each of **7** tour guides took **36** of the **290** students. An eighth guide took the rest of the students. How many students did the eighth guide take?

____

11. Each day one gorilla eats **144** biscuits of monkey chow and **4** oranges. One day an attendant fed **24** oranges and some biscuits to a few gorillas. How many biscuits did he feed them?

____

12. Seventeen elephants each eat **5** loaves of special bread per day. How many total loaves do the **17** elephants eat in a **365**-day year?

____

13. The zoo gift shop purchases a gross of key chains at a wholesale price of **$15.00**. They sell the key chains for **15¢** each. How much profit does the gift shop make? **(Hint: 1** gross = **144)**

____

14. Jason wants to purchase **2** T-shirts at **$19.75** each and a hat for **$7.45**. He has **$50.00**. Does Jason have enough money?

____

Extend Your Thinking

15. Go back to problem **10**. Tell another way the **8** tour guides might have divided up the **290** students.

____

____

16. Go back to problem **11**. Describe the method you used to solve the problem.

____

____

____

17. Go back to problem **12**. Can you solve the problem another way?

____

____

18. Go back to problem **14**. Did you find an exact answer or an estimate? Explain.

____

____

____

STANDARD

Name ______________________

Using Data and Statistics

This graph shows the favorite sports of some students.

How many students chose hockey as their favorite sport?

The bar for hockey ends at the line between **100** and **150**. So, about **125** students chose hockey as their favorite sport.

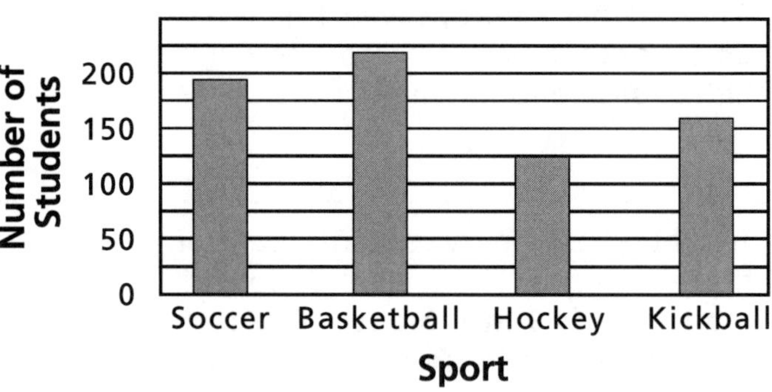

Use the bar graph to estimate the answer.

1. How many students chose kickball as their favorite sport?

____

2. Which sport did the most students choose as their favorite sport?

____

3. How many more students chose soccer than kickball as their favorite sport?

____

4. How many students chose hockey or basketball as their favorite sport?

____

To find the greatest number in a bar graph, look for the longest bar. To compare two items of data in a table, compare the digits of the two numbers. Start from the left.

River	Length (in miles)
Arkansas	1,459
Mississippi	2,340
Missouri	2,315
St. Lawrence	1,900
Yukon	1,979

Which river is longer, the Mississippi or the Missouri?

2,340
2,315

The thousands digits are the same.
The hundreds digits are the same.
In the tens digits, **4** is greater than **1**.

The Mississippi River is longer than the Missouri.

Compare the lengths of each pair of rivers using > or <.

5. Arkansas and Missouri ______ St. Lawrence and Yukon ______ Yukon and Mississippi ______

6. Write the names of the rivers in order from the longest to the shortest river.

____

Name ________________________

STANDARD

A set of data can be discussed using a single typical number, such as when you hear, "They averaged **15** miles each day." You can use the mean, median, mode, or range to summarize a set of data.

Find the range, mean, median, and mode of this data set.

Distances covered by walk-a-thon participants: **5** miles, **7** miles, **3** miles, **2** miles, **3** miles

The **range:** The difference between the greatest value (**7**) and the least value (**2**) in the data.

$7 - 2 = 5$ miles

The **mean** (or **average**): The sum of the items divided by the number of items.

$$\frac{5 + 7 + 3 + 2 + 3}{5} = \frac{20}{5} \text{ or } 4 \text{ miles}$$

The **median:** The middle number when the data are arranged from least to greatest

2 3 3 5 7

median (the middle 3)

If there are two middle numbers, use the average of the two.

The **mode:** The number that occurs most frequently

2 3 3 5 7

mode (3 3)

A data set can have more than one mode. For example, **2, 3, 3, 5, 7, 7,** has two modes; **3** and **7.** If no number occurs more frequently than the others, the data have no mode.

Find the mean, median, mode, and range of the set of data.

7. **6, 9, 7, 4, 4**

Mean ______

Median ______

Mode ______

Range ______

7, 10, 14, 23, 16

Mean ______

Median ______

Mode ______

Range ______

34, 41, 33, 41, 31

Mean ______

Median ______

Mode ______

Range ______

STANDARD

You can use a line plot to help you to organize data. This line plot shows the number of miles that **25** students walked this week. Each **X** represents the distance walked by one student.

You can count the **X**'s starting from the left to find the median.

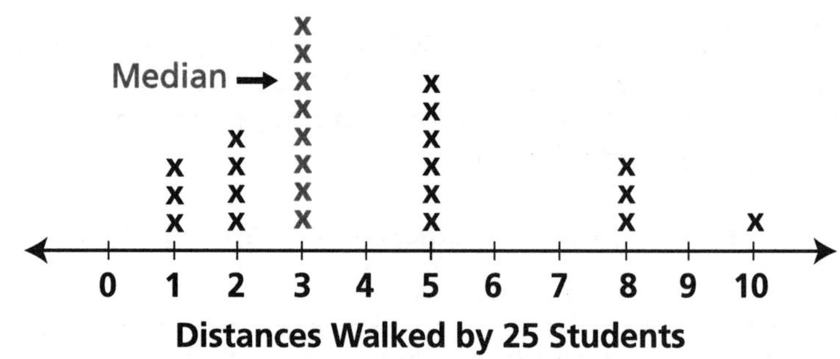

Use the line plot to answer the question.

8. How many students walked exactly **3** miles this week?

____

9. What is the greatest distance any of these students walked this week?

____

10. What distance did the greatest number of students walk this week?

____

11. Six students walked exactly the same distance. What distance did they walk?

____

Use the data set below for exercises 12–15. It lists the number of books that 12 students read last summer.

8, 10, 11, 15, 8, 6, 6, 8, 10, 9, 10, 7

12. Record the data on the line plot.

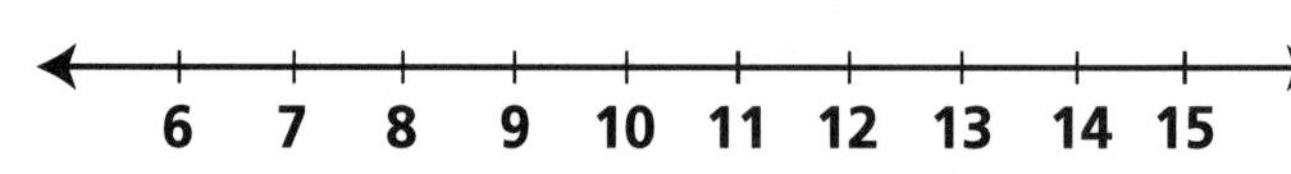

Number of Books Read

13. Find the mean, median, mode, and range.

Mean ________ Median ________

Mode ________ Range ________

14. Suppose a mistake was made when recording the data. The **15** should have been a **3**. How will this change affect the mean, median, mode, and range?

Mean ______________ Median ______________

Mode ______________ Range ______________

15. Find the new mean, median, mode, and range.

Mean ________ Median ________ Mode ________ Range ________

Name ______________________

STANDARD

Find the range of the data.

Average January Temperature of Three U.S. Cities	
City	Temperature (°F)
Roswell, NM	41.4
Concord, NH	19.9
Toledo, OH	23.1

Average April Temperature of Three U.S. Cities	
City	Temperature (°F)
Billings, MT	44.6
Denver, CO	47.4
Milwaukee, WI	44.6

16. Range ________ Range ________

Problem Solving Reasoning

Use the data to answer the questions. The yearly salaries at one company are:

$22,000 $22,500 $24,000 $31,500 $150,000

17. Find the mean, median, and mode of the data.

Mean ______

Median ______

Mode ______

18. Which of the three measures best describes the typical salary at the company? Explain.

____

____

19. Exclude the one very high item from the data. Then find the new mean, median, and mode.

Mean ______

Median ______

Mode ______

20. Which of the three measures now best describes the data? Explain your reasoning.

____

____

Test Prep ★ Mixed Review

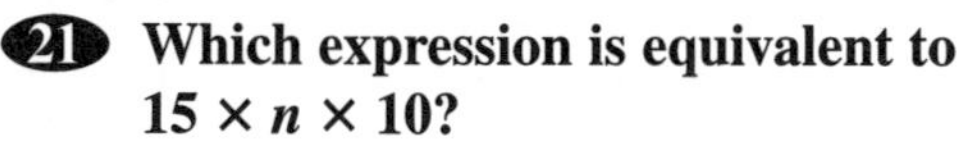

21 **Which expression is equivalent to $15 \times n \times 10$?**

A $5 + n \times 10$

B $15 \times n \div 10$

C $15 \times 10 \times n$

D $15 \times 10 \div n$

22 **Ms. Wu drove 13,500 miles last year. Which equation could be used to find the average number of miles she drove each month?**

F $d - 12 = 13{,}500$

G $2 + d = 13{,}500$

H $12d = 13{,}500$

J $d \div 12 = 13{,}500$

STANDARD

Name ______________________________

Solving Multiplication and Division Equations

To solve addition and subtraction equations, you use inverse operations. To solve multiplication equations, you also use inverse operations. The inverse of multiplying by a nonzero number is dividing by that number.

Solve: $6y = 54$

$\frac{6y}{6} = \frac{54}{6}$ Divide each side of the equation by **6**, because this is the inverse of multiplying by **6**.

$y = 9$ Simplify.

You may have been able to find the value of ***y*** mentally. This is a good way to check your work, but you also need to know how to solve equations by writing out these steps. It will help you with more difficult equations in algebra.

Complete the steps to find the solution of each equation.

1. $b \times 8 = 72$ $j \times 9 = 81$ $m \times 6 = 42$

$b \times 8 \div$ ___ $= 72 \div$ ___ $j \times 9 \div$ ___ $= 81 \div$ ___ $m \times 6 \div$ ___ $= 42 \div$ ___

$b =$ ___ $j =$ ___ $m =$ ___

2. $h \times 7 = 35$ $k \times 5 = 20$ $z \times 7 = 21$

$h \times$ ___ $\div$ ___ $= 35 \div$ ___ $k \times$ ___ $\div$ ___ $=$ ___ $\div$ ___ $z \times$ ______ $=$ ______

$h =$ ___ $k =$ ___ $z =$ ___

Solve the equation.

3. $x \times 8 = 64$ ______ $h \times 6 = 24$ ______ $v \times 3 = 12$ ______

4. $j \times 7 = 14$ ______ $n \times 6 = 48$ ______ $g \times 9 = 27$ ______

5. $y \times 7 = 28$ ______ $d \times 4 = 40$ ______ $t \times 5 = 25$ ______

6. $r \times 2 = 26$ ______ $c \times 3 = 36$ ______ $v \times 3 = 51$ ______

7. $g \times 4 = 92$ ______ $t \times 7 = 56$ ______ $b \times 2 = 82$ ______

Name ________________________________

STANDARD

You can also solve division equations using inverse operations.

$m \div 8 = 9$

$(m \div 8) \times 8 = 9 \times 8$ The inverse of dividing by **8** is multiplying by **8.** Multiply each side of the equation by **8.**

$m \div 1 = 72$ Next, simplify.

$m = 72$ The solution is **72**.

Complete the steps to find the solution of the equation.

8. $\frac{b}{4} = 16$ $k \div 8 = 7$ $\frac{m}{9} = 4$

$\frac{b}{4} \times$ ___ = ___ × ___ $(k \div$ ___ $) \times$ ___ = ___ × ___ $\frac{m}{9} \times$ _____ = _____

$b =$ ___ $k =$ ___ $m =$ ___

9. $\frac{y}{12} = 15$ $16 = n \div 24$ $25 = \frac{k}{18}$

$\frac{y}{12} \times$ ___ = 15 × ___ 16 × ___ = $(n \div 24) \times$ ___ _____ = $\frac{k}{18}$ ___

$y =$ ___ ___ $= n$ ___ $= k$

Solve the equation.

10. $t \div 9 = 7$ _____ $m \div 6 = 4$ _____ $\frac{b}{7} = 7$ _____

11. $j \div 4 = 9$ _____ $\frac{c}{5} = 10$ _____ $g \div 7 = 6$ _____

12. $\frac{w}{30} = 18$ _____ $\frac{s}{22} = 12$ _____ $\frac{p}{100} = 75$ _____

13. $\frac{t}{29} = 17$ _____ $\frac{b}{82} = 6$ _____ $\frac{k}{9} = 102$ _____

14. $\frac{r}{16} = 16$ _____ $\frac{d}{7} = 85$ _____ $\frac{n}{68} = 383$ _____

STANDARD

Name ______________________

Solve the equation. Decide whether the inverse operation is addition, subtraction, multiplication, or division.

15. $k - 25 = 17$ ______ $7x = 91$ ______ $\frac{z}{6} = 44$ ______

16. $p + 25 = 57$ ______ $q - 18 = 11$ ______ $18x = 144$ ______

17. $\frac{b}{11} = 40$ ______ $t + 45 = 83$ ______ $9h = 153$ ______

18. $37 + g = 56$ ______ $\frac{r}{33} = 4$ ______ $16 = \frac{d}{15}$ ______

19. $18j = 414$ ______ $292 = f + 167$ ______ $1{,}620 = 45m$ ______

Problem Solving Reasoning Solve.

20. What inverse operation would you use to solve **5 × *r* = 10**? Explain.

____

Quick Check

Use this table for 21–23. It shows the population (to the nearest 100 people) of four of the largest counties in the United States in 1996.

County	Population
Los Angeles	9,127,800
Orange	2,636,900
San Diego	2,655,500
Santa Clara	1,599,600

Work Space.

21. Which county has the least population? __________

22. What is the population of Santa Clara county, rounded to the nearest thousand? __________

23. What is the median population of the 4 counties? __________

Solve the equation.

24. $7x = 483$ ______ **25.** $\frac{c}{17} = 43$ ______ **26.** $\frac{k}{9} = 12 \cdot 5$ ______

Name ______________________________

Problem Solving Strategy: Write an Equation

STANDARD

In this lesson, you will write equations to solve word problems. The variable in the equation will represent the number you want to find.

You can solve the equation using inverse operations and use the solution of the equation to find the answer to the word problem.

Problem

Mr. Roberts drives at an average speed of 55 miles per hour. How many hours will it take him to drive 165 miles?

1 Understand

As you reread, ask yourself questions.

- What information do you have?

  Mr. Roberts drives an average of ______ miles per hour.

  He will drive a total of ______ miles.

- What do you need to find out?

  ____

2 Decide

Choose a method for solving.

Try the strategy Write an Equation.

- Draw a circle around the equation that can be used to represent the problem.

  $55h = 165$ $\qquad\qquad$ $55 + h = 165$

Solve

Solve the equation using inverse operations.

$55h = 165$

$55h \div 55 = 165 \div 55$

$h =$ ______ **The solution of $55h = 165$ is** ______

- **Check.** $55h = 165$

  $55 \times$ ______ $= 165$

Look back

Reread the problem. Check your answer.

Answer ______________

- Why was it important to go back and reread the problem to check your answer?

  ____

STANDARD

Solve. Use the Write an Equation strategy or any other strategy you have learned.

1. In a classroom, **17** of the **29** students are girls. How many students are boys?

Think: Which equation can be used to help solve this problem?

$17 - b = 29$ $17 + b = 29$

____

2. A shopper bought **26** items for a total of **$65.26**. What was the average cost of an item?

Think: Which equation can you use?

$26c = \$65.26$ $\frac{c}{26} = \$65.26$

____

3. One elephant weighed **11,205** pounds. A hippopotamus weighed **4,789** pounds less than the elephant. How much did the hippopotamus weigh?

____

4. Mariah is thinking of a **3**-digit number. If you round the number to the nearest ten, you get **350**. What is the least possible number it could be?

____

5. How many quarters are needed to make **$7.75**?

____

6. Sam bought **60** bagels at **$4.75** per dozen. How much did they cost?

____

7. Place parentheses in the equation to make it true.

$16 + 4 \times 3 - 1 = 24$

8. Place parentheses in the equation to make it true.

$\frac{8 + 4}{2} \times 4 - 3 = 6$

9. A bus driver drove **252** miles in **7** hours. How many miles did she average per hour?

____

10. Grace had **4** quarters, **4** nickels, and **12** pennies. She then bought a notebook for **$.95**. How much money did she have left?

____

11. A computer company produced **250** computers on Monday. On Tuesday they produced half as many. How many did they produce during the two days?

____

12. The plane holds **368** passengers. If **263** passengers already have reservations, how many more passengers can the plane hold?

____

13. An elephant eats **94** lb of plants each day. How much does it eat in a week? a month? a year?

____

14. James said that **17** more than half the **486** people are wearing sneakers. How many people are wearing sneakers?

____

Name ______________________

Unit 1 Review

1. Write seven thousand sixty in standard form. ______________________

2. Write **2,505,412** in expanded form. ______________________

3. Write **54,089** in word form. ______________________

Add, subtract, multiply, or divide.

4. $325 + 898$

5. $1{,}064 \times 36$

6. $13{,}605 - 9{,}266$

7. $132\overline{)9{,}472}$

Evaluate the expression for $n = 4$.

8. $16 - 4 \div n$ ______

9. $6 + (n - 1) \times 2$ ______

10. $n \times 6 + n \div 4$ ______

Solve the equation.

11. $b - 23 = 31$ $b =$ ______

12. $e \div 9 = 90$ $e =$ ______

13. $z \times 6 = 216$ $z =$ ______

14. $\frac{r}{5} = 25$ $r =$ ______

15. $w + 116 = 204$ $w =$ ______

16. $c - 71 = 490$ $c =$ ______

Use the precipitation table at the right.

17. Find the mean, median, mode, and range of the data.

Mean ________ Median ________

Mode ________ Range ________

18. Which of the measures in exercise 17 would be unchanged if the precipitation for Phoenix was not included in the table? Explain.

____

____

Average July Precipitation (rounded to the nearest inch)	
Anchorage, AK	2
Portland, OR	1
Phoenix, AZ	1
Denver, CO	2

Solve.

19. Leah scored 88 and 85 points on her first two math quizzes. What equation could Leah use to determine the number of points she would need to earn on her next quiz to have an average score of 90? ______________________

Name ______________________________

Cumulative Review
★ Test Prep

1 **What is missing from the empty square to complete the pattern?**

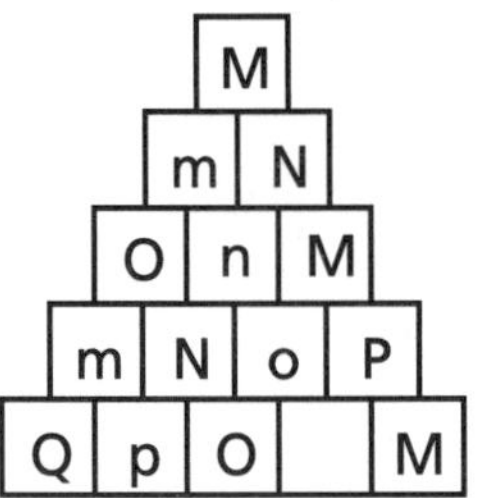

A P
B p
C N
D n

2 **Margarite withdrew $256 from her savings account. She then had $228 in the account. Which equation could be used to find how much money she started with?**

F $228 \times x = 256$
G $256 - x = 228$
H $x + 228 = 256$
J $x - 256 = 228$

3 **Ray's scores on his first four math tests were**

85, 83, 95, and 98.

What score does he need on the fifth test to have an average score of 90 on the five tests?

A 85
B 89
C 90
D 95

4 **What do you need to do to each side of this equation to solve it?**

$$y \div 22 = 651$$

F multiply by 22
G multiply by y
H divide by y
J divide by 22

5 **A theater had 85 rows. There were between 33 and 36 seats in each row. About how many seats are in the theater?**

A 2,500
B 3,000
C 3,500
D 4,000

6 **Some students counted the number of coins they had in their backpacks or purses.**

9, 7, 3, 8, 4, 5, 23, 7, 16

What is the median and mode of the data set?

F 20
G 9.1
H 6.5
J 7
K NH

7 **A fund-raiser raised $29,785 for Robinson School. There are 35 classrooms that need new equipment. How much money can the school spend for each room?**

A $951
B $851
C $850
D $841
E NH

8 **Last year the Johnson family drove 2,064 mi on their vacation to Canada. This year they drove 1,358 mi to Florida. How much farther did the Johnson family drive last year than this year?**

F 3,422 mi
G 1,706 mi
H 714 mi
J 706 mi
K NH

9 **There are 32 classrooms in a school. Fifteen of the rooms have an average of 25 students in each class. The rest have an average of 22 students. About what is the average number of students in each room?**

A less than 20
B about 21
C 22
D between 23 and 24
E 25

UNIT 2 • TABLE OF CONTENTS

Decimals

We will be using this vocabulary:

decimal a number such as **0.5** (five tenths) and **3.67** (three and sixty-seven hundredths). A decimal is sometimes called a decimal fraction.

numerical expression a combination of one or more numbers and operations

algebraic expression a combination of one or more variables, numbers, and operations

evaluate to substitute a given value for a variable

Dear Family,

During the next few weeks, our math class will be learning about decimals. You can expect to see homework that provides practice with multiplying and dividing decimals by **10, 100,** or **1,000.** Here is a sample you may want to keep handy to give help if needed.

Multiplying and Dividing by **10, 100,** *or* **1,000**

Multiplying and dividing decimals by **10, 100,** or **1,000** can be done without using pencil and paper.

Dividing a decimal by 10 moves the decimal point one place to the left. **26.3 ÷ 10 = 2.63**	Multiplying a decimal by 10 moves the decimal point one place to the right. **26.3 × 10 = 263**
Dividing a decimal by 100 moves the decimal point two places to the left. **8.26 ÷ 100 = 0.0826**	Multiplying a decimal by 100 moves the decimal point two places to the right. **8.26 × 100 = 826**
Dividing a decimal by 1,000 moves the decimal point three places to the left. **47.9 ÷ 1,000 = 0.0479**	Multiplying a decimal by 1,000 moves the decimal point three places to the right. **47.9 × 1,000 = 47,900**

During this unit, students will need to continue practicing multiplying and dividing decimal numbers.

Sincerely,

Name ______________________

Decimals: Place Value

STANDARD

Each place in our base-ten number system represents a value **10** times the value of the place to its right.

Similarly, each place represents a value $\frac{1}{10}$ the value of the place to its left.

You can extend a place-value chart to include place values less than **1**. A decimal point separates the ones and tenths places.

Thousands	Hundreds	Tens	Ones		Tenths	Hundredths	Thousandths	Ten-Thousandths
5	7	6	9	.	1	3	2	4

$$5{,}000 + 700 + 60 + 9 + \frac{1}{10} + \frac{3}{100} + \frac{2}{1{,}000} \quad \frac{4}{10{,}000}$$

Standard form : **5, 7 6 9 . 1 3 2 4**

Expanded form : 5,000 + 700 + 60 + 9 + 0.1 + 0.03 + 0.002 + 0.0004

Word form : five thousand seven hundred sixty-nine **and** one thousand, three hundred twenty-four ten-thousandths.

Write the word name for each number.

1. 0.1 ______________ 0.19 ______________

2. 0.0018 ______________ 2.3 ______________

3. 0.60 ______________ 0.082 ______________

4. 0.03 ______________ 0.0003 ______________

5. 7.01 ______________ 0.900 ______________

6. 1.304 ______________ 32.005 ______________

Write the standard form for each number.

7. thirty-nine thousandths ________ four and six tenths ________

8. eight and seven hundredths ________ twenty-three hundredths ________

9. twenty and three hundredths ________ six and eight ten-thousandths ________

10. two hundred three thousandths ________ two hundred and three thousandths ________

11. fourteen and five tenths ________ fifty-four and four hundredths ________

STANDARD

Write each number in expanded form.

12. 678.402 = ______

13. 99.008 = ______

14. 455.09 = ______

15. 3.83 = ______

16. 300.3 = ______

Write each number in standard form.

17. 70 + 8 + 0.01 ______ 9 + 0.4 + 0.0009 ______

18. 10 + 3 + 0.6 + 0.05 ______ 50 + 0.1 + 0.02 ______

19. 100 + 4 + 0.8 + 0.09 ______ 200 + 0.05 + 0.003 ______

20. 400 + 80 + 8 + 0.9 ______ 40 + 9 + 0.1 + 0.006 ______

21. 8 + 0.9 + 0.05 + 0.006 ______ 800 + 60 + 0.2 ______

22. 4 + 0.6 + 0.003 ______ 1,000 + 7 + 0.007 ______

Problem Solving
Reasoning

Is the number in the sentence exact or an estimate?

23. The odometer of an automobile reads **8,510.3** miles. ______

24. The smallest insects are the feather-winged beetles, which are less than **0.2** mm long.

______

25. A snail can move as fast as **0.05** km/h.

______

26. Electricity costs **$.035** per kilowatt hour. ______

Test Prep ★ Mixed Review

27 Melanie has 266 pennies in a jar. Together, she and her mother have 798 pennies. Which equation could be used to find the number of pennies her mother has?

A $p \div 266 = 798$

B $266p = 798$

C $266 + p = 798$

D $p - 266 = 798$

28 How is this number written in standard form? Two billion, eighty-four million, six hundred two thousand, forty-nine

F 284,602,049

G 2,846,200,049

H 2,840,602,049

J 2,084,602,049

Name ________________________

Comparing, Ordering, and Rounding Decimals

STANDARD

Decimals can be shown as points on a number line. This number line shows that **0.1 = 0.10**.

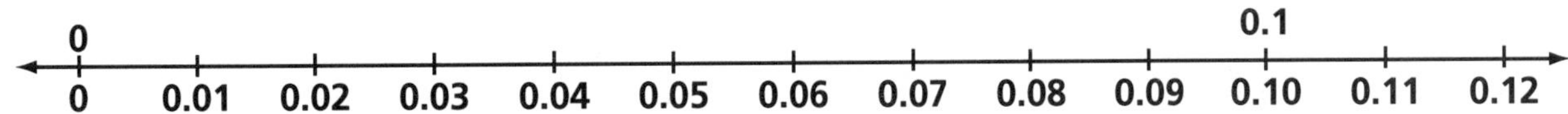

Numbers equivalent to **2**: **2.0 2.00 2.000**
3: **3.0 3.00 3.000**

Here are two ways to compare **0.72** and **0.076**.

0.72 (?) 0.076

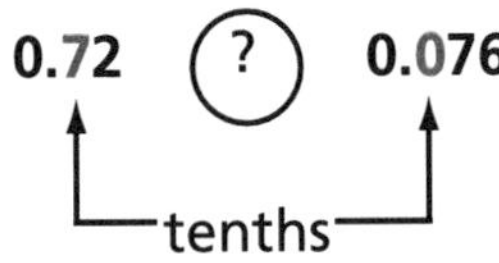

7 tenths > 0 tenths

0.72 (>) 0.076

0.720 (?) 0.076

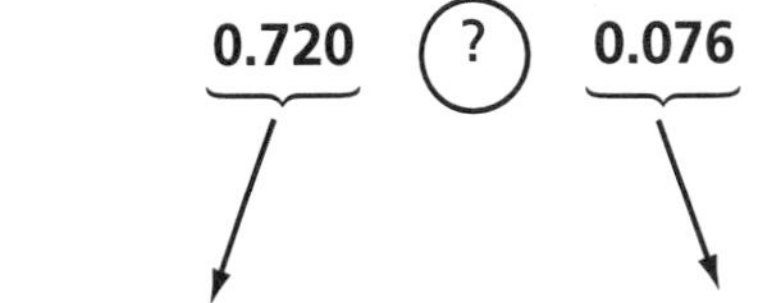

720 thousandths > 76 thousandths

0.720 (>) 0.076

Compare. Write <, >, or =.

1.	0.8	◯	0.35	0.536	◯	0.5604	0.4	◯	0.45
2.	0.901	◯	0.0915	0.666	◯	0.7	0.2	◯	0.02
3.	0.3	◯	0.300	1.04	◯	2.4	6.8	◯	67
4.	5.2	◯	5.5	0.65	◯	0.75	46.29	◯	45.29
5.	67.1	◯	67.01	0.6	◯	0.60	4.1101	◯	4.1
6.	7.29	◯	7.3	7.59	◯	75.9	4.814	◯	4.804
7.	2.667	◯	2.677	550.34	◯	55.34	439.80	◯	439.800

Write each group in order from least to greatest.

8. 0.5, 0.7, 0.1 ____________ 21.94, 22.49, 21.93 ____________ 30.67, 30.6, 30.7 ____________

9. 4.70, 4.07, 40.7 ____________ 6.559, 6.579, 6.569 ____________ 628.04, 628.40, 638.04 ____________

STANDARD

You can round decimals the same way you round whole numbers.

If the digit to the right of the place you are rounding to is equal to or **greater than 5**, round up.

Rounded to the nearest hundredth, **15.428** rounds up to **15.43**.

If the digit to the right of the place you are rounding to is **less than 5**, round down.

Rounded to the nearest whole number, **15.428** rounds down to **15**.

Round to the nearest whole number.

10. 15.8 → ______ 37.3 → ______ 94.5 → ______

11. 53.43 → ______ 62.29 → ______ 74.928 → ______

Round to the nearest tenth.

12. 8.456 → ______ 5.902 → ______ 89.48 → ______

13. 9.04 → ______ 0.15 → ______ 8.449 → ______

Round to the nearest hundredth.

14. 7.459 → ______ 99.555 → ______ 0.730 → ______

15. 3.457 → ______ 0.2951 → ______ 40.672 → ______

Problem Solving Reasoning Solve.

16. The Paynes bought gas that cost **$1.129** for each gallon. They spent **$12.00** on gas. Is that amount a rounded or an exact total?

____

Test Prep ★ Mixed Review

17 Mr. Assad has 25 boxes of canned vegetables to sell. These boxes contain a total of 600 cans of vegetables. Which equation could be used to find the number of cans in each box?

A $b \times 25 = 600$

B $b \div 25 = 600$

C $b + 25 = 600$

D $b - 25 = 600$

18 Jason biked 2.7 miles to his friend's home from his own home, then 5.4 miles to the video store, then 5.9 back to his own home. About how many miles did he bike?

F 12 miles

G 13 miles

H 14 miles

J 15 miles

Name ______________________

Adding and Subtracting Decimals

STANDARD

Add decimals the same way you add whole numbers.

Add **8.86 + 0.9 + 5.352**.

1. Estimate first. Be sure to line up the decimal points.

```
  8.86   →    9
  0.9    →    1
+ 5.352  →  + 5
             15
```

2. Add. Write the decimal point in the sum.

```
  2 1
  8.860
  0.900
+ 5.352
 15.112
```

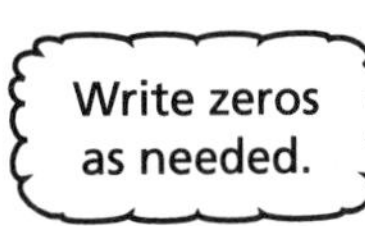

3. Compare the sum and your estimate.

15.112 is close to **15**. The sum is reasonable.

Subtract decimals the same way you subtract whole numbers.

Subtract **7.2 − 3.18**.

1. Estimate first. Be sure to line up the decimal points.

```
  7.2   →   7
− 3.18  → − 3
            4
```

2. Subtract. Write the decimal point in the difference.

```
    1 10
  7.2 0   (2 and 0 crossed out)
− 3.1 8
  4.0 2
```

Write zeros as needed.

3. Compare the difference and your estimate.

4.02 is close to **4**. The difference is reasonable.

Add.

1.

$5.34	4.752	0.538	0.389	0.56
+ $2.96	+ 2.396	+ 0.257	+ 0.257	+ 2.489

Subtract.

2.

8.6	25.6	3.74	$5.30	5.296
− 3.4	− 19.9	− 1.685	− 2.64	− 3.8

Rewrite in vertical form. Then add or subtract.

3. 3.54 + 0.63   9.784 − 2.659   24.6 − 18.8

4. 0.95 − 0.21   5.6 + 9.48   15.3 + 2.95

STANDARD

Add or subtract.

5. $\begin{array}{r} 69.356 \\ -\ 7.281 \\ \hline \end{array}$ $\begin{array}{r} 99.9 \\ +\ 0.99 \\ \hline \end{array}$ $\begin{array}{r} 8.001 \\ -\ 3.456 \\ \hline \end{array}$ $\begin{array}{r} 3.8 \\ +\ 2.09 \\ \hline \end{array}$ $\begin{array}{r} 7 \\ -\ 6.52 \\ \hline \end{array}$

6. $\begin{array}{r} 7.7 \\ +\ 0.77 \\ \hline \end{array}$ $\begin{array}{r} 4.96 \\ +\ 3.859 \\ \hline \end{array}$ $\begin{array}{r} 14.6 \\ -\ 3.826 \\ \hline \end{array}$ $\begin{array}{r} \$6.32 \\ -\ 1.78 \\ \hline \end{array}$ $\begin{array}{r} 7.236 \\ +\ 15.974 \\ \hline \end{array}$

Problem Solving
Reasoning

Decide whether you need an exact answer or an estimate to solve the problem. Then solve.

7. Jennifer has **$60**. She wants to buy a blouse for **$22.99** and a skirt for **$39.00**. Does she have enough money?

____

8. Manuel is writing a check for several purchases. He bought a belt for **$16.99**, a hat for **$19.50**, and a jacket for **$43.80**. What should the amount of his check be?

____

Quick Check

9. Write in standard form: forty and **44** thousandths

____

Round the decimal to the place indicated.

10. **90.076**; tenths place

____

11. **5.6998**; thousandths place

____

Find the sum or difference.

12. $\begin{array}{r} 16.34 \\ +\ 2.484 \\ \hline \end{array}$

13. $\begin{array}{r} 45.975 \\ -\ 1.231 \\ \hline \end{array}$

14. $\begin{array}{r} 0.0489 \\ -\ 0.017 \\ \hline \end{array}$

15. 25.02 + 9.631 + 15.9

____

16. 8.29 − 0.032

____

Work Space.

Name ______________________________

Multiplying Decimals by Whole Numbers

STANDARD

Multiply decimals the same way you multiply whole numbers.

Multiply **8 × 6.421**.

1. Estimate the product first.

6.421 → 6
× 8 → × 8
48

2. Then multiply.

6.421
× 8
51368

3. Count the number of digits in decimal places in the factors. That is the number of decimal places in the product. Place the decimal point in the product.

6.421 ← 3 decimal places
× 8
51.368 ← 3 decimal places

Use your estimate to check if your answer is reasonable.
51.368 is close to **48**, so the answer is reasonable.

Place the decimal point in each product. Estimate to check that the answer is reasonable.

1. 1 9 9 .6 × 8 = 1 5 9 6 8 | 1 9 .9 6 × 8 = 1 5 9 6 8 | 1 .9 9 6 × 8 = 1 5 9 6 8

2. 5 9 9 .8 × 4 = 2 3 9 9 2 | 5 9 .9 8 × 4 = 2 3 9 9 2 | 5 .9 9 8 × 4 = 2 3 9 9 2

3. 3 0 0 .4 × 6 = 1 8 0 2 4 | 3 0 .0 4 × 6 = 1 8 0 2 4 | 3 .0 0 4 × 6 = 1 8 0 2 4

4. 2 5 0 .2 × 4 = 1 0 0 0 8 | 2 5 .0 2 × 4 = 1 0 0 0 8 | 2 .5 0 2 × 4 = 1 0 0 0 8

Estimate first. Then find each product.

5. 7.8 × 2 | 3.2 × 4 | 7.5 × 5 | 0.14 × 6 | 25.7 × 3 | $9.13 × 4

6. 12.6 × 4 | 8.23 × 6 | $6.23 × 4 | 0.7 × 3 | 25.1 × 8 | $7.06 × 5

7. 0.072 × 4 | 1.279 × 6 | 399.9 × 2 | 12.79 × 6 | 3.769 × 2 | $80.37 × 4

8. 0.4 × 9 | 5.2 × 6 | 0.8 × 7 | $4.59 × 2 | 2.015 × 8 | 31.7 × 5

STANDARD

Multiply.

9.

306	0.91	286	\$9.23	\$6.85	\$3.07
× 0.2	× 64	× 4.3	× 51	× 36	× 17

10.

86.4	29.8	6.73	473	\$4.38	674
× 6.5	× 56	× 48	× 0.247	× 324	× 2.06

11.

\$4.72	0.523	398	0.647	404	271
× 218	× 412	× 13.6	× 382	× 11.1	× 0.564

Problem Solving Reasoning

Solve.

12. Kim bought **3** notebooks. Each notebook cost **\$4.89**. What was the total cost?

____

13. Lee bought **6** notebooks for **\$4.89** each.

What was the total cost? __________

14. What is the cost of **6** pens if each pen costs **\$0.39**? __________

15. What is the cost of a **12**-minute phone call if each minute costs **\$0.08**? __________

Test Prep ★ Mixed Review

16 Jamal bought 3.52 pounds of oranges, 3.89 pounds of apples, 3.54 pounds of pears, and 3.25 pounds of grapefruit. He bought the *least* amount of which fruit?

A apples

B grapefruit

C oranges

D pears

17 Ms. Huang knows that it takes her 18 hours to build a birdhouse. Which expression shows how many hours it will take her to build *n* birdhouses?

F $18 - n$ hours

G $18n$ hours

H $18 + n$ hours

J $18 \div n$ hours

Name ___________________________

Multiplying a Decimal by a Decimal

STANDARD

You can use what you know about whole numbers to multiply decimals.

Multiply **1.37** by **0.8**.

1. Multiply as you would with whole numbers.

$$\begin{array}{r} 1.37 \\ \times\ 0.8 \\ \hline 1096 \end{array}$$

2. Count the digits in decimal places in the factors.

$$\begin{array}{r} 1.37 \\ \times\ 0.8 \\ \hline 1096 \end{array}$$

2 and 1 → 3 decimal places

3. Write the decimal point in the product.

$$\begin{array}{r} 1.37 \\ \times\ 0.8 \\ \hline 1.096 \end{array}$$

← 3 decimal places

Place the decimal point in each product.

1.

$$\begin{array}{r} 81.9 \\ \times\ 0.03 \\ \hline 2457 \end{array} \qquad \begin{array}{r} 81.9 \\ \times\ 0.3 \\ \hline 2457 \end{array} \qquad \begin{array}{r} 8.19 \\ \times\ 0.3 \\ \hline 2457 \end{array} \qquad \begin{array}{r} 0.819 \\ \times\ 3 \\ \hline 2457 \end{array} \qquad \begin{array}{r} 819 \\ \times\ 0.03 \\ \hline 2457 \end{array}$$

Multiply.

2.

$$\begin{array}{r} 1.3 \\ \times\ 0.7 \\ \hline \end{array} \qquad \begin{array}{r} 8.1 \\ \times\ 0.2 \\ \hline \end{array} \qquad \begin{array}{r} 5.9 \\ \times\ 6.7 \\ \hline \end{array} \qquad \begin{array}{r} 5.21 \\ \times\ 0.8 \\ \hline \end{array} \qquad \begin{array}{r} 91.4 \\ \times\ 0.7 \\ \hline \end{array} \qquad \begin{array}{r} 64.9 \\ \times\ 0.9 \\ \hline \end{array}$$

3.

$$\begin{array}{r} 37.01 \\ \times\ 0.2 \\ \hline \end{array} \qquad \begin{array}{r} 40.31 \\ \times\ 0.4 \\ \hline \end{array} \qquad \begin{array}{r} 30.91 \\ \times\ 0.3 \\ \hline \end{array} \qquad \begin{array}{r} 8.1 \\ \times\ 10.04 \\ \hline \end{array} \qquad \begin{array}{r} 71.9 \\ \times\ 0.91 \\ \hline \end{array} \qquad \begin{array}{r} 2.56 \\ \times\ 1.8 \\ \hline \end{array}$$

4.

$$\begin{array}{r} 0.91 \\ \times\ 26.4 \\ \hline \end{array} \qquad \begin{array}{r} 24.5 \\ \times\ 0.92 \\ \hline \end{array} \qquad \begin{array}{r} 138.2 \\ \times\ 0.68 \\ \hline \end{array} \qquad \begin{array}{r} 14.63 \\ \times\ 2.14 \\ \hline \end{array} \qquad \begin{array}{r} 20.31 \\ \times\ 46.5 \\ \hline \end{array} \qquad \begin{array}{r} 386.5 \\ \times\ 33.4 \\ \hline \end{array}$$

5.

$$\begin{array}{r} 3.21 \\ \times\ 0.8 \\ \hline \end{array} \qquad \begin{array}{r} 4.7 \\ \times\ 12.5 \\ \hline \end{array} \qquad \begin{array}{r} 10.16 \\ \times\ 2.21 \\ \hline \end{array} \qquad \begin{array}{r} 249.9 \\ \times\ 0.52 \\ \hline \end{array} \qquad \begin{array}{r} 5.82 \\ \times\ 4.06 \\ \hline \end{array} \qquad \begin{array}{r} 73.27 \\ \times\ 1.2 \\ \hline \end{array}$$

STANDARD

Sometimes you need to write one or more zeros in the product before you can place the decimal point.

$$\begin{array}{r} 1.13 \\ \times\, 0.06 \\ \hline 678 \end{array} \quad \begin{array}{l} \leftarrow \text{2 decimal places} \\ \leftarrow \text{2 decimal places} \\ \end{array} \qquad \begin{array}{r} 1.13 \\ \times\, 0.06 \\ \hline 0.0678 \end{array}$$

Multiply.

6. $\begin{array}{r} 0.52 \\ \times\, 0.04 \\ \hline \end{array}$ $\begin{array}{r} 3.8 \\ \times\, 0.02 \\ \hline \end{array}$ $\begin{array}{r} 0.12 \\ \times\, 0.03 \\ \hline \end{array}$ $\begin{array}{r} 1.32 \\ \times\, 0.05 \\ \hline \end{array}$ $\begin{array}{r} 0.352 \\ \times\, 0.06 \\ \hline \end{array}$

7. $\begin{array}{r} 2.36 \\ \times\, 0.25 \\ \hline \end{array}$ $\begin{array}{r} 5.19 \\ \times\, 0.18 \\ \hline \end{array}$ $\begin{array}{r} 0.005 \\ \times\, 0.9 \\ \hline \end{array}$ $\begin{array}{r} 0.012 \\ \times\, 0.08 \\ \hline \end{array}$ $\begin{array}{r} 0.007 \\ \times\, 0.03 \\ \hline \end{array}$

Multiply. Then round each product to the nearest cent.

8. $\begin{array}{r} \$1.59 \\ \times\, 2.5 \\ \hline \end{array}$ $\begin{array}{r} \$2.63 \\ \times\, 8.6 \\ \hline \end{array}$ $\begin{array}{r} \$7.81 \\ \times\, 4.2 \\ \hline \end{array}$ $\begin{array}{r} \$5.73 \\ \times\, 0.73 \\ \hline \end{array}$ $\begin{array}{r} \$7.16 \\ \times\, 0.91 \\ \hline \end{array}$

Problem Solving
Reasoning

Solve. Round each answer to the nearest cent.

Grapes **$1.29** per pound	Apples **$.79** per pound	Cherries **$2.49** per pound	Pears **$.88** per pound

9. What is the cost of **1.36** pounds of apples? ________

10. What is the cost of **2.18** pounds of pears? ________

11. What is the cost of **1** pound of cherries and **1.25** pounds of grapes? ________

Test Prep ★ Mixed Review

12 Keshor is planning to spend between $4.25 and $4.75 each week on football cards. Which is the most reasonable estimate of how much he will spend in the next 8 weeks?

A $32 C $40

B $36 D $44

13 Nine students in Mr. Hargrove's class got these scores on a book report.

83, 76, 87, 78, 82, 92, 86, 88, 82

What was the median score for these students?

F 16 H 83

G 82 J 83.8

Name ______________________________

Problem Solving Strategy: Work Backward

STANDARD

Sometimes a problem can be solved by working backward.

When working backward, you can often use inverse operations.

Problem

Scott and Benito hiked on a marked trail that began and ended at a lodge. During the first hour, they hiked 2.3 miles. During the second hour, they hiked half of the remaining distance. During the third hour, they hiked 1.4 miles. During the fourth hour, they hiked the last 0.75 miles and returned to the lodge. How long was the entire trail?

1 Understand

As you reread, organize the information.

Miles Hiked	
1st hour	2.3
2nd hour	$\frac{1}{2}$ of miles left
3rd hour	1.4
4th hour	

- What do you need to find out?

____

2 Decide

Choose a method for solving.

Try the strategy Work Backward.

- The chart below shows how the number of miles left on the trail changes after each hour.

? → −2.3 → ÷_ → ___ → ___ → 0

3 Solve

Work backward using inverse operations.

0 → +0.75 → ___ → __ → ___ → ? __

4 Look back

Check your answer. Write the answer below.

Answer ____________________

- Why is it important to go back to the problem to check your answer?

____

STANDARD

Solve. Use the Work Backward strategy or any other strategy you have learned.

1. Gen took her week's allowance and went to the movies. She spent **$3.50** for her ticket. Then she spent half of the remaining money on popcorn. On the way out, she bought a fruit bar for **$1.25**. She had **$.75** left of her allowance. How much was her allowance?

Think: Which number will you use to start your computation?

____

Answer ______________________

2. Eva opened a no-fee checking account and made an initial deposit. During the first month she deposited an additional **$14.22** and wrote checks totaling **$15.36**. During the second month she deposited **$35** and wrote a check for **$13.98**. She then had **$65.57** in the account. How much was Eva's initial deposit?

Think: When you work backward, will you add or subtract deposits?

____

Answer ______________________

3. Alec has written down a secret number. If you divide it by **2**, then subtract **1.4**, and add **2.91**, the result is **22.51**. What is Alec's secret number?

____

4. Nicole is thinking of a secret number. If you add **15.2** to it, then subtract **2.95**, and divide by **2**, the result is **11.675**. What is Nicole's secret number?

____

5. Use the clues to find the number.

- To the nearest ten, the number rounds to **460**.
- The sum of the digits in the hundreds and tens places is **9**.
- The digit in the tenths place is half the digit in the ones place.
- The digit in the ones place is greater than **5** and less than **7**.

____

6. Use the clues to find the number.

- The sum of the digits is **13**.
- The digit in the thousandths place is **3** times the digit in the tens place.
- To the nearest ten, the number rounds to **30**.
- The digit in the tenths place is one more than the digit in the hundredths place.

____

7. On Tuesday, Ky jogged **1.5** miles more than on Monday. On Wednesday, she jogged **2.3** miles less than on Tuesday. If she jogged **4.9** miles on Wednesday, how many miles did she jog on Monday?

____

8. Jake brought some money to spend on his vacation. On the first day he spent **$4.80**. On the second day he spent half of the money he had left. On the third day, he spent **$1.85**. He then had **$1** left. How much money did Jake start with?

____

9. How many seconds are in one week?

____

10. Estimate how long a billion seconds is.

____

Name ____________________

Dividing Decimals by Whole Numbers

STANDARD

Divide decimals by following the same steps as when you divide whole numbers.

Divide **32.5** by **5**.

1. First divide as you would whole numbers.

```
    6 5
5) 32.5
 - 30
   25
 - 25
    0
```

2. Then, place the decimal point in the quotient directly above the decimal point in the dividend.

```
    6.5   ← 1 decimal place
5) 32.5   ← 1 decimal place
 - 30
   25
 - 25
    0
```

3. Check by multiplying.

$$\begin{array}{r} 6.5 \\ \times\ 5 \\ \hline 32.5 \end{array}$$

Divide and check.

1.	6) $.12	7) $34.37	6) $2.76	8) $10.40
2.	2) 13.4	7) 1.4	5) 0.105	4) 2.44
3.	6) 5.88	4) 7.36	3) 0.564	8) 7.592
4.	6) 0.6732	8) 68.328	9) 37.062	5) 543.20

STANDARD

Sometimes you have to write one or more zeros in the dividend in order to complete the division.

Example: $4\overline{)2.5}$

1. Divide the tenths.

$$\begin{array}{r} 0.6 \\ 4\overline{)2.5} \\ \underline{-2\,4} \\ 1 \end{array}$$

2. Write a 0 in the hundredths. Regroup and divide.

$$\begin{array}{r} 0.62 \\ 4\overline{)2.50} \\ \underline{-2\,4} \\ 10 \\ \underline{-8} \\ 2 \end{array}$$

3. Write another 0 in the thousandths. Regroup and divide.

$$\begin{array}{r} 0.625 \\ 4\overline{)2.500} \\ \underline{-2.4} \\ 10 \\ \underline{-8} \\ 20 \\ \underline{-20} \\ 0 \end{array}$$

Divide and check.

5. $5\overline{)2.6}$ $4\overline{)4.6}$ $6\overline{)5.7}$ $6\overline{)15}$

6. $4\overline{)7.3}$ $8\overline{)25}$ $5\overline{)0.75}$ $4\overline{)0.31}$

7. $5\overline{)8.1}$ $4\overline{)6.3}$ $5\overline{)0.74}$ $4\overline{)4.2}$

8. $5\overline{)4.18}$ $5\overline{)3.74}$ $4\overline{)53.4}$ $2\overline{)0.113}$

Name ______________________________

STANDARD

Divide decimals by **2**-digit divisors the same way you divide by **1**-digit divisors.

```
    0.535
18) 9.630   ← Write a zero in the dividend
  - 9 0
     63
   - 54
     90
   - 90
      0
```

Use multiplication to check the quotient.

```
  0.535
 ×   18
  4 280
+ 5 35
  9.630
```

Divide.

9. $40\overline{)53.6}$ $16\overline{)5.2}$ $32\overline{)6.80}$ $56\overline{)9.8}$

Problem Solving Reasoning **Solve.**

10. Ryan paid **$51.25** for **5** tickets to a skating show. How much was each ticket if each one cost the same amount?

______

11. Becky paid **$.78** for **6** pencils. Each pencil was the same price. How much did she pay for each pencil?

______

Quick Check

Find the product.

12. 7.41×5

13. 12.06×43

14. 0.115×27

15. 6.04×1.2

16. 3.9×0.8

17. 0.065×0.07

Find the quotient.

18. $5\overline{)75.02}$

19. $16\overline{)8.416}$

20. $25\overline{)0.0675}$

Work Space.

STANDARD

Name ____________________

Multiplying and Dividing by 10, 100, and 1,000

These examples show how you can multiply decimals by **10**, **100**, and **1,000**.

3.51 × 10 = 35.1	**0.63 × 10 = 6.3**
3.51 × 100 = 351	**0.63 × 100 = 63**
3.51 × 1,000 = 3,510	**0.63 × 1,000 = 630**

Notice the decimal point moves to the right.

Complete.

1. To multiply a decimal by **10**, move the decimal point ______ place(s) to the right.

2. To multiply a decimal by **100**, move the decimal point ______ place(s) to the right.

3. To multiply a decimal by **1,000**, move the decimal point ______ place(s) to the right.

Multiply.

4. 4.72 × 10   0.37 × 10   65.8 × 10   1.269 × 10   31.94 × 10

5. 3.486 × 100   1.82 × 100   0.714 × 100   63.7 × 100   0.9631 × 100

These examples show how you can divide decimals by **10**, **100**, and **1,000**.

53.6 ÷ 10 = 5.36	**78 ÷ 10 = 7.8**
53.6 ÷ 100 = 0.536	**78 ÷ 100 = 0.78**
53.6 ÷ 1,000 = 0.0536	**78 ÷ 1,000 = 0.078**

Notice the decimal point moves to the left.

Complete.

6. To divide a decimal by **10**, move the decimal point ______ place(s) to the left.

7. To divide a decimal by **100**, move the decimal point ______ place(s) to the left.

8. To divide a decimal by **1,000**, move the decimal point ______ place(s) to the left.

Divide.

9. 10)7.4   10)1.86   10)23.7   10)0.163

10. 100)28.3   100)31   100)6.29   100)0.56

Name ______________________

STANDARD

Complete each table.

11.

	× 10	× 100	× 1,000
0.347	3.47	34.7	347
4.56			
0.307			
89.47			
0.048			
0.604			
2.5			
0.03			
54.1			
0.7			

12.

	÷ 10	÷ 100	÷ 1,000
47.2			
58.34			
718.6			
3.029			
49			
130			
417			
200			
0.05			
26.3			

Problem Solving Reasoning

Complete each table.

13. 100 centimeters = 1 meter

cm	m
325	
26.5	
	4.75
	7.4
1.5	
	12.6

14. 1,000 meters = 1 kilometer

m	km
5,826	
741.9	
	1.6
	0.745
25.1	
	3

Test Prep ★ Mixed Review

15 At Rice Brook School, 375 students ride to school on 8 buses. About how many students are on each bus?

A 30

B 40

C 50

D 60

16 In 1996, there were 1,599,604 people in Santa Clara County. There were 213,277 people in Placer County. How many more people lived in Santa Clara County?

F 386,327

G 1,386,327

H 1,386,337

J 1,812,881

STANDARD

Name ______________________

Dividing by a Decimal

Look at this example of dividing whole numbers. Notice that if you multiply the divisor and the dividend by the same number, the quotient is not changed.

$2\overline{)8}$ = 4

Multiply the divisor and the dividend by 10.

$20\overline{)80}$ = 4

Multiply the divisor and the dividend by 100.

$200\overline{)800}$ = 4

Use this fact to divide decimals by decimals. Multiply the divisor and the dividend by the same number, so that the divisor is a whole number.

To divide **8.06** by **2.6**, multiply the divisor and the dividend by **10**.

$2.6\overline{)8.06} \rightarrow 26\overline{)80.6}$

3.1
−78
26
−26
0

To divide **2.61** by **0.003**, multiply the divisor and the dividend by **1,000**.

$0.003\overline{)2.61} \rightarrow 0.003\overline{)2.610}$

870
− 24
21
− 21
00

Divide. Draw arrows like the ones shown above to show the new position of each decimal point.

1. $0.7\overline{)4.34}$ $0.8\overline{)0.048}$ $0.9\overline{)0.0369}$ $0.3\overline{)17.7}$

2. $0.07\overline{)4.62}$ $0.08\overline{)0.272}$ $0.05\overline{)14.2}$ $0.04\overline{)0.192}$

3. $0.002\overline{)0.614}$ $0.009\overline{)2.16}$ $0.007\overline{)7.28}$ $0.005\overline{)0.515}$

Name ______________________________

STANDARD

Sometimes you need to find a quotient rounded to a certain place.

Divide **3.478** by **7.1** and round the quotient to the nearest hundredth.

1. Divide to the thousandth place, so you can round the quotient to the nearest hundredth.

```
      0.489
7.1) 3.4780
    - 2.84
       638
     - 568
       700
     - 639
        61
```

2. Round the quotient to the nearest hundredth.

0.489 ⟶ 0.49

Divide. If a quotient contains thousandths, round to the nearest hundredth.

4. 5.5) 1.29   0.6) 6.48   1.41) 4.591   7.3) 20.83

5. 3.2) 6.5   0.2) 416.8   0.65) 568.55   1.52) 4.16

6. 0.67) 3.643   0.9) 18.99   9.5) 0.8265   0.09) 34.283

7. 4.5) 63.49   0.54) 4.433   0.08) 7.221   0.07) 36.4

STANDARD

When you divide a whole number by a decimal, you follow the same steps as when you divide a decimal by a decimal.

To divide **117** by **0.09,** multiply the divisor and the dividend by **100**.

```
         1,300
0.09) 117.00
      - 9
        27
      - 27
        000
```

Divide **32** by **4.6**. Round the quotient to the nearest hundredth.

```
       6.956  →  6.96   rounded to the nearest hundreth
4.6) 32.0000
    - 276
       440
     - 414
       260
     - 230
        300
      - 276
         24
```

Divide. Round each quotient to the nearest hundredth, when necessary.

8. 0.32) 25 　　 0.35) 71 　　 0.036) 27 　　 0.41) 1,108

9. 0.76) 265 　　 0.38) 322 　　 8.5) 15,215 　　 1.2) 25,801

Problem Solving Reasoning **Solve.**

10. If a car travels **270** kilometers in **4.5** hours, what is its average rate of speed in kilometers per hour?

____

11. Roger won the **75**-meter race in **8.1** seconds. What was his speed in meters per second? Round the answer to the nearest hundredth.

____

Test Prep ★ Mixed Review

12 **Eva has a small dog that weighs 14.85 pounds. How is this number written in words?**

A fourteen and eighty-five hundredths

B fourteen and eighty-five tenths

C fourteen and eighty-five thousandths

D fourteen and eighty-five ten thousandths

13 **The Pasta Company uses boxes that are 5.85 inches tall. Which expression could you use to find how tall p boxes would be stacked together?**

F $5.85 \div p$

G $5.85 \cdot p$

H $5.85 + p$

J $5.85 - p$

Name ______________________________

Problem Solving Application: Is the Answer Reasonable?

STANDARD

Sometimes when you are solving a division problem, the answer has a remainder. You need to go back to the problem and decide how to use the remainder to write the answer.

- Sometimes you will write the remainder as a whole number. Then you need to decide whether to include the remainder in your answer, drop the remainder, or round your answer to the next whole number.
- Sometimes you need to write the quotient as a fraction.
- Sometimes you need to write the quotient as a decimal.

Tips to Remember:

1. Understand 2. Decide 3. Solve 4. Look back

- Try to remember a real-life situation like the one described in the problem. What do you remember that might help you find a solution?
- Ask yourself: Does the answer use the remainder correctly?

Solve.

1. The librarian has **329** extra books that she wants to divide equally among **3** classrooms. How many books should she give to each classroom?

Think: Do fractions or decimals make sense in this situation? Explain.

____

____

Answer ______________________________

2. Eight people share dinner at a restaurant. The total bill including tax and tip is **$98**. If they divide the bill evenly, what is each person's share?

Think: Do fractions or decimals make sense in this situation? Explain.

____

____

Answer ______________________________

3. How long will it take to drive **125** miles driving at an average speed of **50** miles per hour?

Think: How can you express the remainder?

____

____

Answer ______________________________

4. A van holds **15** passengers. How many vans are needed to transport **50** passengers?

Think: If **50** is not evenly divisible by **15**, what will you do about the vans?

____

Answer ______________________________

STANDARD

Solve.

5. Six students shared **9** mini pizzas. Each student ate the same amount. How many pizzas did each eat?

____

6. T-shirts are on sale. You can buy **3** for **$25**. How much will one T-shirt cost?

____

7. Paper plates come in packages of **8**. How many packages are needed to have **138** plates?

____

8. Each round table can seat up to **12** people. How many round tables are needed to seat **185** people?

____

9. Rogerio bought **75** blueberry muffins. How many dozen was that?

____

10. How many **33**-cent stamps can you buy for **$5.00**?

____

11. The batting average of a baseball player is calculated by dividing the number of "hits" by the number of "at bats." It is written as a decimal rounded to the nearest thousandth. In **1998** Larry Walker of the Colorado Rockies had **165** hits out of **454** at bats. What was his batting average?

____

12. In **1998,** Bernie Williams of the New York Yankees had **169** hits out of **499** at bats. His teammate Paul O'Neil had **191** hits out of **602** at bats. Which player had the higher batting average that year? How much higher was his average?

____

13. The buttons Pam wants to buy come in packages of **4**. She needs **10** buttons for a coat she is making. How many packages should she buy?

____

14. Four brothers and sisters are sharing the cost of a gift. They bought flowers for **$25.95** and a vase for **$5.85**. How much is each person's share?

____

Extend Your Thinking

15. Explain the method you used to solve problem **6**.

____

____

____

____

16. Go back to problem **8**. Did you round your answer to the nearest whole number? Why or why not?

____

____

____

Name ______________________________

Expressions, Equations, and Decimals

STANDARD

You have learned about expressions with whole numbers. You can write and evaluate expressions with decimals the same way you do with whole numbers.

Word Expression: one tenth more than six tenths

Numerical Expression: $1.25 + (2 \times 6.5)$

Algebraic Expression: $n \div 0.7$

Write each expression in words.

1. $6.13 - 0.9$ ______________________________
2. $n + 1.1$ ______________________________

Write a numerical or algebraic expression for each word expression.

3. Seven tenths less than the product of four and two ______________
4. Seventy-three hundredths added to the quotient of eight divided by some number ______________

Evaluate each expression. $n = 3.5$, $t = 0.25$

5. $n + 7.48$ ________ $t + 43.32$ ________ $t + 0.75$ ________ $n + t$ ________
6. $n - 0.48$ ________ $9.13 - t$ ________ $n - 0.95$ ________ $n - t$ ________
7. $n \cdot 6.75$ ________ $6.78t$ ________ $5(n + t)$ ________ nt ________
8. $\frac{n}{t}$ ________ $16.8 \div n$ ________ $t \div 0.05$ ________ $\frac{n + t}{5}$ ________
9. $23.8 \times (n - t)$ ________ $4.5n - 5.9$ ________ $(n + t) \div t$ ________ $\frac{5.5}{t} + 3.44$ ________
10. $n + t + n$ ________ $\frac{n - t}{t}$ ________ $(t \div t) + n$ ________ $\frac{n + t}{10}$ ________

STANDARD

You can use what you know about solving equations with whole numbers to solve equations with decimals. Use inverse operations.

These examples are solved for n.

$n - 5.2 = 8.1$ $n - 5.2 + 5.2 = 8.1 + 5.2$ $n = 8.1 + 5.2$ $n = 13.3$	$n + 17.5 = 23.8$ $n + 17.5 - 17.5 = 23.8 - 17.5$ $n = 23.8 - 17.5$ $n = 6.3$
$n \times 25.5 = 255$ $n \times 25.5 \div 25.5 = 255 \div 25.5$ $n = 255 \div 25.5$ $n = 10$	$n \div 15 = 12.3$ $n \div 15 \times 15 = 12.3 \times 15$ $n = 12.3 \times 15$ $n = 184.5$

Solve each equation.

11. $a + 2.04 = 9.1$ ____ $r - 5.5 = 7$ ____ $n \times 2.1 = 23.1$ ____

12. $h - 6.05 = 33.6$ ____ $\frac{c}{1.25} = 10$ ____ $q + 9.2 = 12.4$ ____

13. $x - 7.5 = 100$ ____ $z \div 0.14 = 2.8$ ____ $n \times 3 = 309.3$ ____

14. $b \div 0.04 = 18$ ____ $d \times 5 = 50.5$ ____ $w + 87.91 = 96.4$ ____

Quick Check

Find the product or quotient.

Work Space.

15. 7.562×10

16. $\$9.97 \times 100$

17. $100\overline{)\,4.432}$

18. $8\overline{)\,94}$

19. $1.2\overline{)\,4.233}$

20. $2.5\overline{)\,0.055}$

21. Solve the equation $\frac{k}{3.2} = 0.062$ ____

22. Evaluate the expression $\frac{1.2\,m}{0.5} + 0.922$ for $m = 0.35$ ____

Name ______________________________

Unit 2 Review

Write the standard form for each number.

1. two hundred six thousandths ________

2. 400 + 9 + 0.05 + 0.009 ________

Compare. Write >, <, or =.

3. 0.6 ◯ 0.28

4. 14.30 ◯ 14.300

5. 2.7 ◯ 11.0

Round 25.753 to the given place.

6. nearest whole number ______

7. nearest tenth ______

8. nearest hundredth ______

Write each group in order from greatest to least.

9. 50.9, 5.90, 59.0 ________________

10. 7.07, 7.70, 7.707 ________________

Add, subtract, multiply, or divide.

11. $0.217 + 3.916$

12. $4.2 - 2.85$

13. $15.05 + 29.6$

14. $104.99 − $92.50

15. $9.4 + 0.929$

16. 8.04×9

17. 23.6×0.52

18. $9\overline{)2.52}$

19. $12\overline{)408.84}$

20. $0.3\overline{)0.0279}$

Evaluate each expression when $a = 0.4$ and $b = 0.75$.

21. $b - a$ ________

22. $a + 17$ ________

23. $a \times b$ ________

24. $2.03 + (8 \div a)$ ________

Solve each equation.

25. $n \times 5 = 7.5$ ________

26. $h \div 0.3 = 10.1$ ________

27. $133.6 + p = 209.04$ ________

Solve.

28. To the nearest tenth, a number rounds to **1.5**. To the nearest whole number, it rounds to **1**. The digit in the hundredths place is twice as great as the digit in the tenths place. The number has no places greater than ones or less than hundredths.

For what number is this true? ________

29. Each banquet table in a large room can seat up to **16** people. What is the minimum number of tables that would be needed to seat **200** people? Explain.

____

____

Name ______________________________

Cumulative Review
★ Test Prep

1 **Tran buys 3 packages of raisins. Each package costs $2.29. How much change should he get from a $10 bill?**

A Eight $1 bills, 3 quarters, 1 nickel, and 1 penny

B Seven $1 bills, 2 quarters, 2 dimes, and 1 penny

C Four $1 bills, 2 dimes, and 3 pennies

D Three $1 bills, 2 dimes, and 3 pennies

E Three $1 bills, 1 dime, and 3 pennies

2 **Rhonda is planning a race that has three parts. The first part is 118.9 meters long. The second part is 152.68 meters long. The third part is 208.42 meters long. How long is the whole race?**

F 361.1 m　　H 480 m　　K NH

G 479.9 m　　J 4,800 m

3 **Miguel ran his part of a relay race in 12.8685 seconds. What is that decimal rounded to the nearest hundredth?**

A 12.86　　C 12.869　　E NH

B 12.868　　D 12.87

4 **Elizabeth bought 19.5 feet of ribbon. One foot of ribbon cost $0.36. How much did Elizabeth's ribbon cost?**

F $70.20　　H $7.20　　K NH

G $19.86　　J $7.02

5 **What do you need to do to each side of this equation to solve it?**

$$m - 2{,}436.876 = 234.90$$

A Add 2,436.876

B Add m

C Subtract 2,436.876

D Subtract m

6 **The Hilltop School is having a raffle. The school needs $3,166.25 to buy computers. Tickets cost $1.25. Which equation could you use to find how many tickets the school needs to sell?**

F $3{,}166.25 + t = 1.25$

G $3{,}166.25 \div t = 1.25$

H $3{,}166.25 - t = 1.25$

J $3{,}166.25 \times t = 1.25$

7 **The mass of 3 planets relative to Earth are shown in the table. List planets from least to greatest mass.**

Planet	Mass
Mercury	0.054
Venus	0.81
Earth	1.000
Mars	0.1

A Mercury, Venus, Earth, Mars

B Mars, Venus, Mercury, Earth

C Mars, Mercury, Venus, Earth

D Mercury, Mars, Venus, Earth

UNIT 3 • TABLE OF CONTENTS

Number Theory and Fraction Concepts

We will be using this vocabulary:

base (of an exponent) the number that is raised to a power

exponent a number that tells how many times a base number is to be used as a factor

prime number a counting number greater than **1** that has only two distinct factors, itself and **1**

greatest common factor (GCF) the greatest number that is a common factor of two or more given numbers

least common multiple (LCM) the least nonzero number that is a common multiple of each of two or more given numbers

Dear Family,

During the next few weeks, our math class will be learning about number theory. You can expect to see homework that provides practice with exponents. Here is a sample you may want to keep handy to give help if needed.

Exponents

An exponent tells how many times a base is used as a factor.

base → 2^6 ←exponent Read: Two to the sixth power.

$$2^6 = 2 \times 2 \times 2 \times 2 \times 2 \times 2 = 64$$

base → 5^4 ←exponent Read: Five to the fourth power.

$$5^4 = 5 \times 5 \times 5 \times 5 = 625$$

base → 10^2 ←exponent Read: Ten to the second power, or ten squared.

$$10^2 = 10 \times 10 = 100$$

base → 8^3 ←exponent Read: Eight to the third power, or eight cubed.

$$8^3 = 8 \times 8 \times 8 = 512$$

During this unit, students will need to continue to practice simplifying numerical and algebraic expressions that contain exponents.

Sincerely,

Name ___________________________________

Divisibility Rules

STANDARD

Knowing divisibility rules can help you find factors and common factors.

A number is divisible by **2** if the last digit is **0**, **2**, **4**, **6**, or **8**.

A number is divisible by **5** if the last digit is **0** or **5**.

A number is divisible by **10** if the last digit is **0**.

Numbers that are divisible by **2** are called **even** numbers.
Numbers that are not divisible by **2** are called **odd** numbers.

Place a ✓ by the numbers that are divisible by 2, 5, or 10.

1.

	2	5	10
56			
40			
85			
32			

	2	5	10
120			
128			
125			
150			

2. Circle the even numbers in the tables above.

A number is divisible by **3** if the sum of the digits is divisible by **3**.

A number is divisible by **9** if the sum of the digits is divisible by **9**.

51 → **5 + 1 = 6**   **6 ÷ 3 = 2**   Therefore, **51** is divisible by **3**.
846 → **8 + 4 + 6 = 18**   **18 ÷ 9 = 2**   Therefore, **846** is divisible by **9**.

Place a ✓ by the numbers that are divisible by 3 or 9.

3.

	3	9
57		
63		
111		
5,391		

	3	9
87		
81		
54,108		
31,479		

STANDARD

A number is divisible by **4** if the last **2** digits are divisible by **4**.

A number is divisible by **6** if it is divisible by both **2** and **3**.

Place a ✓ by the numbers that are divisible by 4, 2, 3, or 6.

4.

	4	2	3	6
116				
48				
123				
114				

	4	2	3	6
136				
24				
140				
138				

Place a ✓ by the numbers that are divisible by 2, 3, 4, 5, 6, 9, or 10.

5.

	2	3	4	5	6	9	10
30							
28							
91							
135							
153							
180							
132							

Problem Solving
Reasoning

Solve.

Write a rule for deciding whether or not a number is divisible by

6. 15 ______________________________

7. 18 ______________________________

Test Prep ★ Mixed Review

8 Jeanette bought 2 packs of invitations. Each pack had 24 cards. She used 32. Which equation could you use to find how many invitations (l) she had left?

A $(2 \cdot 24) - 32 = l$

B $2 \cdot 24 + 32 = l$

C $(2 \cdot 32) - 24 = l$

D $(2 \cdot 32) + 24 = l$

9 Which number is indicated on the number line?

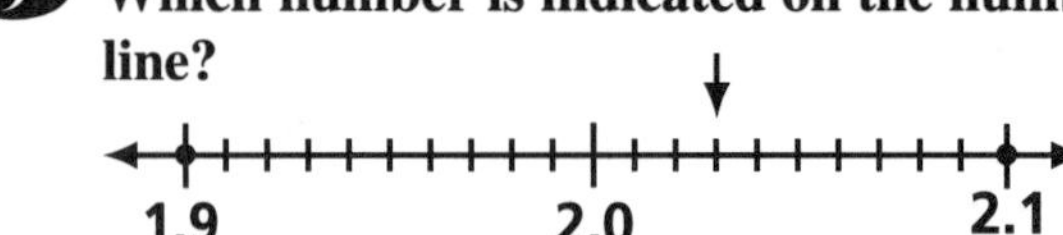

F 2.33

G 2.3

H 2.23

J 2.03

Name ___________________________

Factors and Prime Numbers

STANDARD

Factors are numbers that are multiplied to obtain a product. Every counting number (**1, 2, 3, . . .**) has at least one pair of **factors.**

A factor of a number is also a **divisor** of that number. For example, because **6** = **3** × **2** and **6** = **1** × **6**, **1**, **2**, **3**, and **6** are both factors and divisors of **6**.

Complete by writing each product using as many different *pairs* of factors as possible.

1.

1	2	3	4	5	6	7
1 × 1	1 × 2					

2.

8	9	10	11	12	13	14

3.

15	16	17	18	19	20	21

Some of the numbers given in exercises **1–3** can be written as the product of only one pair of factors, itself and **1**.

These numbers are **1, 2, 3, 5, 7, 11, 13, 17,** and **19**.

If a counting number greater than **1** has only one pair of factors, itself and **1**, then it is called a **prime number** or a **prime**.

A counting number that has factors other than itself and **1** is called a **composite number**.

The number **1** is neither prime nor composite.

Complete by writing each product using as many different pairs of factors as possible. Circle the primes.

4.

23	25	27	29	31	33	35

STANDARD

In Ancient Greece, a man named Eratosthenes (ehr uh TAHS thuh neez) invented a way to find all the prime numbers between **1** and **100**. This is his method. It is called the **Sieve of Eratosthenes.**

1. Cross out **1** because **1** is not prime.
2. Circle **2** because **2** is prime. Cross out all multiples of **2**.
3. Go to the next number that is not crossed out. Circle the **3**. Then cross out all multiples of **3**.
4. Repeat step **3** until all the numbers up to and including **100** are either circled or crossed out.

THE SIEVE OF ERATOSTHENES

1	2	3	4	5	6	7	8	9	10
11	12	13	14	15	16	17	18	19	20
21	22	23	24	25	26	27	28	29	30
31	32	33	34	35	36	37	38	39	40
41	42	43	44	45	46	47	48	49	50
51	52	53	54	55	56	57	58	59	60
61	62	63	64	65	66	67	68	69	70
71	72	73	74	75	76	77	78	79	80
81	82	83	84	85	86	87	88	89	90
91	92	93	94	95	96	97	98	99	100

Complete.

5. List all the primes less than **100**. ____________________

____

Problem Solving Reasoning

Write True or False. Give an example to prove your answer.

6. Only odd numbers are prime.

____

7. When you add two prime numbers, the sum is never prime.

____

8. Some numbers greater than **100** are prime. ____________________

9. When you multiply two prime numbers, the product is always composite.

____

10. One is a factor of every number.

____

11. Two is a factor of every number.

____

Test Prep ★ Mixed Review

12 **A game company is making up a new card game. For each game, the players need an equal number of cards with none left over. Which number of cards could be used so that 2, 3, or 4 people could play?**

A 26 **C** 42

B 36 **D** 54

13 **What is the inverse operation of multiplying by 25?**

F Multiplying by 4 **H** Multiplying by 25

G Dividing by 4 **J** Dividing by 25

Name ______________________________

Exponents

STANDARD

You can use an exponent to express multiplication when the same factor is repeated.

$2 \cdot 2 \cdot 2 \cdot 2$ can be written **2^4**.

This is read "two to the fourth **power**." In this example, **2** is the **base** and **4** is the **exponent** or power.

> Remember, the dot means multiplication.

Write in standard form.

1. 4^2 = $4 \cdot 4$ = 16 10^3 = ________ = ____

2. 6^3 = ________ = ____ 6^4 = ________ = ____

3. 9^2 = ________ = ____ 12^2 = ________ = ____

4. 3^3 = ________ = ____ 5^3 = ________ = ____

5. 7^2 = ________ = ____ 4^3 = ________ = ____

6. 3^4 = ________ = ____ 2^6 = ________ = ____

Write in exponent form.

7. $6 \cdot 6 \cdot 6$ = ____ $7 \cdot 7 \cdot 7 \cdot 7 \cdot 7 \cdot 7 \cdot 7$ = ____

8. $3 \cdot 3$ = ____ $9 \cdot 9 \cdot 9 \cdot 9$ = ____

9. $5 \cdot 5 \cdot 5 \cdot 5 \cdot 5 \cdot 5$ = ____ $4 \cdot 4 \cdot 4 \cdot 4 \cdot 4 \cdot 4 \cdot 4$ = ____

Simplify each expression.

10. $2^4 \cdot 3$ = ________ = ____ $3 \cdot 5^2$ = ________ = ____

11. $2^3 \cdot 3^2$ = ________ = ____ $2 \cdot 7^2$ = ________ = ____

12. $3^3 \cdot 5$ = ________ = ____ $5^2 \cdot 7$ = ________ = ____

13. $2^2 \times 3^2$ = ________ = ____ $2^5 \times 3$ = ________ = ____

Write True or False.

14. $3^2 = 6$ ____ $4^2 = 16$ ____ $9^2 = 18$ ____ $10^3 = 1{,}000$ ____

15. $5^3 = 15$ ____ $2^4 = 16$ ____ $4^4 = 166$ ____ $2^5 = 64$ ____

16. $2 \cdot 5^2 = 100$ ____ $3^2 \cdot 4 = 24$ ____ $2^2 \times 2^2 = 16$ ____ $3^3 \cdot 5^2 = 90$ ____

17. $3^2 \cdot 5^2 = 225$ ____ $2^2 \cdot 3^3 = 36$ ____ $5 \times 7^2 = 245$ ____ $2^2 \times 9^2 = 334$ ____

STANDARD

When expressions contain exponents, you can use the order of operations to simplify the expression.

Order of Operations	**Simplify $0.3 \times 6 + (8 - 5)^2$**
1. Simplify inside parentheses.	$0.3 \times 6 + (3)^2$
2. Simplify powers.	$0.3 \times 6 + 9$
3. Multiply and divide from left to right.	$1.8 + 9$
4. Add and subtract from left to right.	10.8

Simplify. Use the order of operations.

18. $50 \div 0.5^2$ ______ $6^2 - 9$ ______ $(4 + 5)^2$ ______ $(7 + 3)^2 \div 0.25$ ______

19. $6^2 - 2 \times 6$ ______ $0.2^3 + 8 \div 4$ ______ $7^2 - 4^2 \times 3$ ______ $9 - (4 - 1)^2$ ______

Insert parentheses to make each equation true.

20. $2 \times 3 + 6 = 18$ $20 \times 4.5 - 2 = 50$ $4 + 4^2 \div 5 = 4$ $2 \times 6^2 - 8 = 56$

21. $6 + 8 \div 2 = 10$ $12 + 10 \div 11 = 2$ $40 \div 4 \times 2 = 20$ $30 + 0.9 \div 3 = 10.3$

Problem Solving Reasoning **Compare. Write >, <, or =.**

22. $(9 \div 3)^2 + (15 - 13)^3$ ◯ $9 \div 3^2 + (15 - 13)^3$

23. $(7 + 3)^2 \div (3 + 2)^2$ ◯ $7^2 + 3^2 \div 3^2 + 2^2$

Quick Check

Is the number divisible by 2, 3, 4, 5, 6, 9, or 10? Write each of the numbers that apply.

24. 375 ______ **25.** 507 ______ **26.** 7,326 ______

List all the factors of the number.

27. 32 ______ **28.** 135 ______ **29.** 124 ______

Evaluate the expression. Use the order of operations.

30. 9^3 ______ **31.** $7 + 20^2$ ______ **32.** $3(12 - 8)^4$ ______

Work Space.

Name ______________________

Prime Factorization

STANDARD

Counting numbers that are greater than **1** and are not prime are called **composite numbers.** Renaming a composite number as a product of prime factors is called **prime factorization.**

You can use a **factor tree** to show the prime factorization of a number. A factor tree is complete when the bottom numbers are prime.

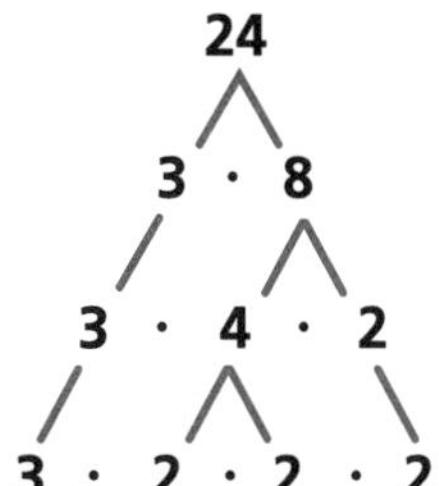

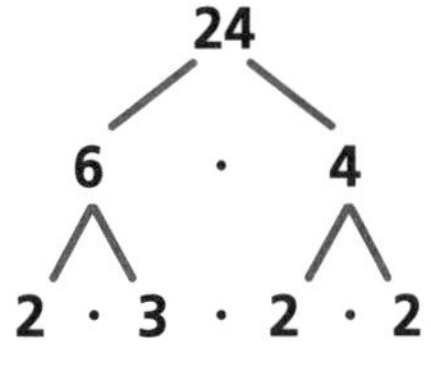

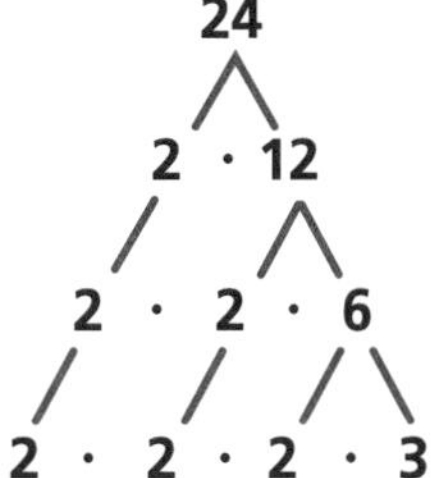

In each factor tree for 24, the bottom row contains the same prime factors in a different order. However, the prime factorization of a number should be written in order from least to greatest.

The **prime factorization** of **24** is **2 · 2 · 2 · 3** or **$2^3 \cdot 3$**.

Use exponents to write each prime factorization in order from least to greatest. Draw a factor tree to help you.

1. 35 ________ 54 ________ 81 ________

2. 100 ________ 48 ________ 34 ________

STANDARD

Write P for prime or C for composite. If a number is composite, then write it as a product of a pair of factors other than itself and 1.

3. 32 ______ 17 ______

4. 31 ______ 57 ______

5. 99 ______ 29 ______

6. 77 ______ 55 ______

7. 91 ______ 108 ______

8. 73 ______ 103 ______

Complete.

	Pair of Factors	Prime Factorization	Prime Factorization in Exponent Form	Prime Factor(s)
9. 18 =	______	______	______	______
10. 20 =	______	______	______	______
11. 25 =	______	______	______	______
12. 32 =	______	______	______	______
13. 36 =	______	______	______	______
14. 42 =	______	______	______	______
15. 75 =	______	______	______	______
16. 120 =	______	______	______	______

List all the factors of each number.

17. 10 ______ 18 ______

18. 30 ______ 37 ______

19. 42 ______ 51 ______

Test Prep ★ Mixed Review

20 What fraction is another name for $6\frac{2}{3}$?

A $\frac{18}{30}$ C $\frac{20}{3}$

B $\frac{9}{3}$ D $\frac{21}{3}$

21 What is the value of $5x^3$ when $x = 2$?

F 30 H 500

G 40 J 1,000

Name ______________________

Finding the Greatest Common Factor

STANDARD

The **common factors** of two or more numbers are all the factors that appear in the lists of factors for each number. The **greatest common factor (GCF)** is the greatest of these common factors.

Factors of **18**: 1, 2, 3, 6, **9**, **18**

Factors of **30**: 1, 2, 3, **5**, 6, **10**, **15**, **30**

The **common factors** of **18** and **30** are **1**, **2**, **3**, and **6**.

The **greatest common factor (GCF)** of **18** and **30** is **6**.

When **1** is the only common factor, the GCF is **1**.

Complete.

		All Factors	Common Factors	GCF
1.	7:	______		
	9:	______	______	______
2.	8:	______		
	12:	______	______	______
3.	21:	______		
	18:	______	______	______
4.	70:	______		
	36:	______	______	______
5.	42:	______		
	48:	______	______	______
6.	9:	______		
	18:	______	______	______
7.	12:	______		
	16:	______	______	______
8.	14:	______		
	18:	______	______	______

STANDARD

You can use prime factorization to find the **GCF** of two or more numbers.

Find the GCF of **60** and **24**.

1. Write the prime factorization of each number.
2. Circle the factors common to both groups.
3. Find the product of the least power of the common factors.

60 = ②·②·③·5
24 = ②·②· 2 ·③
GCF: $2^2 \cdot 3 = 12$

The **greatest common factor (GCF)** of **60** and **24** is **12**.

Use the method above to find the GCF.
Circle the factors common to both groups.

9. 5 = ______	**10.** 14 = ______	**11.** 25 = ______
20 = ______	18 = ______	30 = ______
GCF = ______	GCF = ______	GCF = ______

12. 12 = ______	**13.** 20 = ______	**14.** 15 = ______
18 = ______	24 = ______	18 = ______
24 = ______	32 = ______	36 = ______
GCF = ______	GCF = ______	GCF = ______

Problem Solving Reasoning **Solve.**

15. Vivian is making key chains with beads. She wants each key chain to have the same number of beads. She has **12** blue beads and **21** yellow beads. What is the greatest number of key chains she can make that are exactly the same?

____

Test Prep ★ Mixed Review

16 A high school band marches in a formation of rows and columns. Each row or column has more than one musician. All rows have the same number of musicians, and so do all columns. Which number of musicians can march at one time?

A 47 **C** 53
B 51 **D** 61

17 Sue bought 3 bags of dog food for $2.89 each. Which equation can be used to find the amount of change (c) she should get from $10?

F $(3 \cdot 2.89) + c = 10$

G $(3 \cdot 2.89) - c = 10$

H $c + 10 = 2.89 \div 3$

J $c - 10 = 2.89 \div 3$

Name ___________________________

Multiples and Least Common Multiple

STANDARD

The **common multiples** of two or more numbers are all the numbers that appear in both lists of multiples for each number. The **least common multiple (LCM)** is the least of these common multiples.

Find the **LCM** of **8** and **12**.

Multiples of **8**: **8, 16,** 24, **32, 40,** 48, **56, 64,** 72, . . .

Multiples of **12**: **12,** 24, **36,** 48, **60,** 72, **84,** . . .

The common multiples of **8** and **12** are **24, 48, 72,** . . .

The **least common multiple (LCM)** of **8** and **12** is **24**.

Complete.

		Multiples	Common Multiples	LCM
1.	4:	______		
	5:	______	______	______
2.	6:	______		
	10:	______	______	______
3.	10:	______		
	15:	______	______	______
4.	12:	______		
	9:	______	______	______
5.	6:	______		
	15:	______	______	______
6.	8:	______		
	10:	______	______	______
7.	18:	______		
	30:	______	______	______
8.	12:	______		
	20:	______	______	______

STANDARD

You can use prime factorization to find the **LCM** of two or more numbers.

Find the **LCM** of **12** and **16**.

1. Write the prime factorization of each number.
2. Circle the greatest power of each different prime factor.
3. Find the product of the greatest powers.

$12 = 2^2 \cdot 3$ (3 circled)
$16 = 2^4$ (2^4 circled)
LCM: $2^4 \cdot 3 = 48$

Use the method above to find the LCM.
Circle the greatest power of each different prime factor.

9. 10 = ________
8 = ________
LCM: ____________

10. 9 = ________
15 = ________
LCM: ____________

11. 4 = ________
5 = ________
LCM: ____________

12. 10 = ________
8 = ________
6 = ________
LCM: ____________

13. 18 = ________
15 = ________
12 = ________
LCM: ____________

14. 4 = ________
5 = ________
8 = ________
LCM: ____________

Problem Solving Reasoning Solve.

15. Mike can buy red push pins in packages of **24** and yellow push pins in packages of **36**. What is the least number of each color he must buy in order to have the same number of each color? How many packages of each is this?

____

Quick Check

Write the factorization of the number or write *prime*.

Work Space.

16. 24 ________ **17.** 31 ________ **18.** 225 ________

Write the greatest common factor of the two numbers.

19. 6, 8 ________ **20.** 24, 36 ________ **21.** 15, 16 ________

Write the least common multiple of the two numbers.

22. 6, 8 ________ **23.** 30, 45 ________ **24.** 4, 9 ________

Name ________________________

Problem Solving Strategy: Make a List

Some problems can be solved by making one or more organized lists.

Problem

I'm thinking of a number. It is less than 20. When you divide my number by 3, the remainder is 1. When you divide my number by 5, the remainder is 2. What is my number?

1 Understand

As you reread, ask yourself questions.

- How can you find numbers which when divided by **3** have a remainder of **1**?

  Add **1** to the multiples of **3**.

- How can you find numbers which when divided by **5** have a remainder of **2**? ________________

2 Decide

Choose a method for solving.

Try the Make a List strategy.

- First list numbers (less than **20)** which when divided by **3** have a remainder of **1**.

Multiples of 3	3	6	9	12	15	18
Multiples of 3 plus 1	4	7	10	___	___	___

- Then list numbers (less than **20**) which when divided by **5** have a remainder of **2**.

Multiples of 5	5	10	15
Multiples of 5 plus 2	___	___	___

3 Solve

Look for the number that is in both lists.

The only number in both lists is ______.

4 Look back

Check your answer. Write the answer below.

Answer ______

- Why was it helpful to list the numbers in order?

____

STANDARD

Solve. Use the Make a List strategy or any other strategy you have learned.

1. Steve is thinking of a number. It is less than **40**. When you divide it by **6**, the remainder is **5**. It is not a prime number. What is Steve's number?

Think: What numbers less than **40** are **5** more than a multiple of **6**?

____

Answer ______________________

2. Sandra is thinking of a number. It is less than **25**. When you divide it by **5**, the remainder is **1**. When you divide it by **7**, the remainder is **4**. What is Sandra's number?

Think: What numbers less than **25** are **4** more than a multiple of **7**?

____

Answer ______________________

3. Write the number that comes next in this sequence.

3.5, 4.7, 5.9, 7.1, ______

4. The sum of two numbers is **10**. Their difference is **0.6**. What are the two numbers?

____

5. What is the greatest possible **3**-digit number for which the sum of the digits is **10**?

____

6. What is the least possible **4**-digit number for which the sum of the digits is **5**?

____

7. List all **2**-digit numbers for which the sum of the digits is **6**.

____

8. List all **2**-digit numbers for which the sum of the digits is a prime number less than **7**.

____

9. What is the tenth number in the sequence?

1, 2, 4, 7, 11, . . .

____

10. What is the least number that is divisible by both **5** and **12**?

____

11. Kunio bought a pair of blue shorts, a pair of black shorts, a pair of gray shorts, and a pair of white shorts. He also bought a red shirt and a blue shirt. How many different outfits can he make?

____

12. A bakery has **3** choices of cake—white, chocolate, or marble—and **3** choices of frosting—butter cream, whipped cream, or fudge. How many cake and frosting combinations are there?

____

13. Each ticket costs **$4.50**. Tickets purchased in pairs cost **$7.50**. How much do **9** tickets cost?

____

14. One bag of potatoes is twice the weight of another bag of potatoes. If they weigh **45** lb together, what does each bag weigh?

____

Name ______________________

Writing Equivalent Fractions

STANDARD

Fractions can be used to name points on a number line.

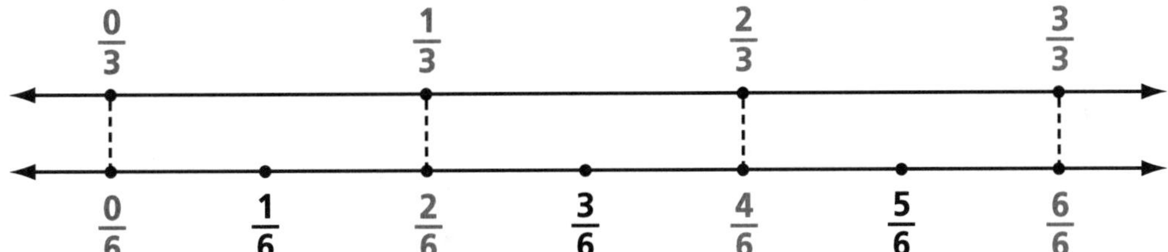

The two number lines above show these pairs of **equivalent fractions:**

$\frac{0}{3} = \frac{0}{6}$ $\frac{1}{3} = \frac{2}{6}$ $\frac{2}{3} = \frac{4}{6}$ $\frac{3}{3} = \frac{6}{6}$

Write the equivalent fractions shown by the number lines.

1.

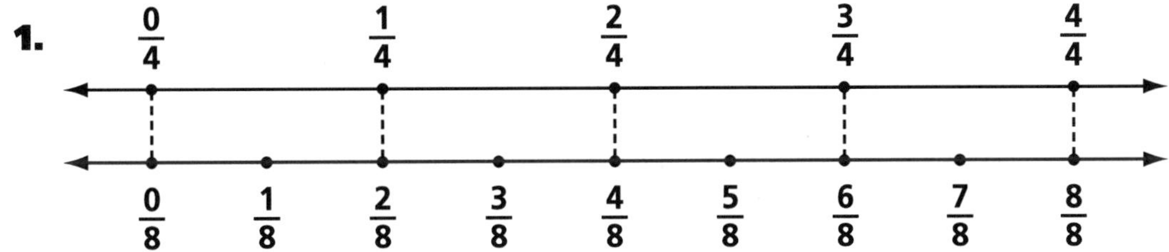

____

numerator → 1
denominator → 3

The **terms** of a fraction are the numerator and the denominator. When you multiply each term of a fraction by the same whole number greater than **1**, you get an equivalent fraction.

$\frac{1}{3} = \frac{1 \times 2}{3 \times 2} = \frac{2}{6}$ $\frac{1}{3} = \frac{1 \times 3}{3 \times 3} = \frac{3}{9}$ $\frac{1}{3} = \frac{1 \times 4}{3 \times 4} = \frac{4}{12}$ $\frac{1}{3} = \frac{1 \times 5}{3 \times 5} = \frac{5}{15}$

The fractions equivalent to $\frac{1}{3}$ are $\frac{1}{3}, \frac{2}{6}, \frac{3}{9}, \frac{4}{12}, \frac{5}{15}, \frac{6}{18}, \frac{7}{21}$, and so on.

Write 5 equivalent fractions.

2. $\frac{1}{2}$ ______________________ $\frac{4}{5}$ ______________________

3. $\frac{1}{4}$ ______________________ $\frac{2}{9}$ ______________________

4. $\frac{2}{3}$ ______________________ $\frac{7}{8}$ ______________________

5. $\frac{9}{10}$ ______________________ $\frac{3}{7}$ ______________________

STANDARD

You can also divide the numerator and the denominator of a fraction by the same whole number greater than **1** to get an equivalent fraction.

$\frac{24}{30} = \frac{24 \div 2}{30 \div 2} \rightarrow \frac{12}{15}$ $\frac{24}{30} = \frac{24 \div 3}{30 \div 3} \rightarrow \frac{8}{10}$ $\frac{24}{30} = \frac{24 \div 6}{30 \div 6} \rightarrow \frac{4}{5}$

The fractions $\frac{24}{30}$, $\frac{12}{15}$, $\frac{8}{10}$, and $\frac{4}{5}$ are equivalent.

Use division to write two equivalent fractions.

6. $\frac{14}{28}$ ____ $\frac{12}{18}$ ____ $\frac{36}{48}$ ____

7. $\frac{8}{16}$ ____ $\frac{12}{20}$ ____ $\frac{18}{42}$ ____

8. $\frac{15}{30}$ ____ $\frac{6}{12}$ ____ $\frac{27}{36}$ ____

9. $\frac{18}{27}$ ____ $\frac{16}{40}$ ____ $\frac{24}{60}$ ____

Write an equivalent fraction.

10. $\frac{6}{12} =$ ____ $\frac{9}{21} =$ ____ $\frac{6}{9} =$ ____ $\frac{12}{18} =$ ____

11. $\frac{7}{21} =$ ____ $\frac{8}{10} =$ ____ $\frac{3}{12} =$ ____ $\frac{15}{20} =$ ____

12. $\frac{4}{14} =$ ____ $\frac{10}{12} =$ ____ $\frac{6}{20} =$ ____ $\frac{16}{24} =$ ____

13. $\frac{18}{32} =$ ____ $\frac{5}{35} =$ ____ $\frac{10}{22} =$ ____ $\frac{8}{12} =$ ____

14. $\frac{10}{25} =$ ____ $\frac{16}{18} =$ ____ $\frac{8}{30} =$ ____ $\frac{2}{16} =$ ____

Test Prep ★ Mixed Review

15 Which expression is the prime factorization of 72?

A $36 \cdot 2$ C $12 \cdot 2 \cdot 3$

B $18 \cdot 2 \cdot 2$ D $2 \cdot 2 \cdot 2 \cdot 3 \cdot 3$

16 The population of California in 1997 was 31.88 million people. What is this number rounded to the nearest 0.1 million?

F 31 H 31.9

G 31.8 J 32

Name ____________________

Simplest Form

STANDARD

You can use division to write fractions less than **1** and fractions greater than **1** in **simplest form.**

A fraction is in simplest form when the only common factor of the numerator and denominator is **1**.

$$\frac{4}{6} = \frac{4 \div 2}{6 \div 2} \rightarrow \frac{2}{3}$$

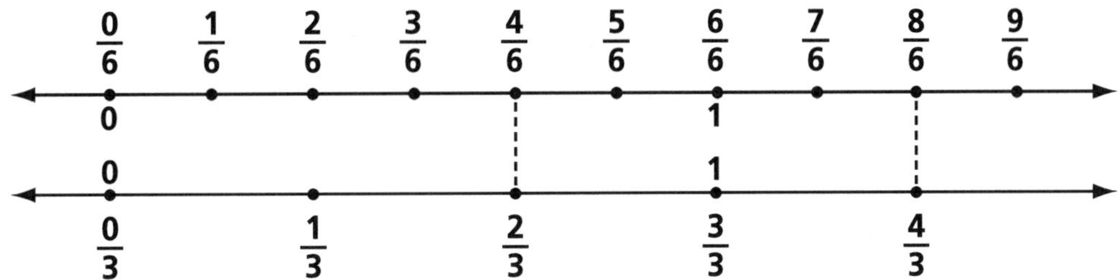

A fraction greater than **1** is in simplest form when it is written as a mixed number and the fraction part is less than **1** and in simplest form.

$$\frac{8}{6} = \frac{8 \div 2}{6 \div 2} \rightarrow \frac{4}{3}$$

$$\frac{4}{3} \rightarrow 3\overline{)\,4} \quad \text{quotient } 1,\ 4 - 3 = 1 \qquad \frac{4}{3} = 1\frac{1}{3}$$

Write the fraction in simplest form.

1. $\frac{6}{8}$ = ______ $\frac{8}{4}$ = ______ $\frac{8}{10}$ = ______ $\frac{10}{8}$ = ______
2. $\frac{9}{12}$ = ______ $\frac{12}{9}$ = ______ $\frac{5}{20}$ = ______ $\frac{2}{8}$ = ______
3. $\frac{6}{4}$ = ______ $\frac{12}{15}$ = ______ $\frac{16}{48}$ = ______ $\frac{21}{49}$ = ______
4. $\frac{13}{26}$ = ______ $\frac{6}{18}$ = ______ $\frac{25}{15}$ = ______ $\frac{8}{30}$ = ______

Write the missing numerator or denominator.

5. $\frac{1}{3} = \frac{4}{\ \ }$ $\frac{3}{4} = \frac{15}{\ \ }$ $\frac{3}{10} = \frac{15}{\ \ }$ $\frac{2}{5} = \frac{6}{\ \ }$
6. $\frac{8}{9} = \frac{\ \ }{18}$ $\frac{4}{3} = \frac{\ \ }{15}$ $\frac{7}{4} = \frac{35}{\ \ }$ $\frac{9}{2} = \frac{\ \ }{8}$
7. $\frac{8}{20} = \frac{2}{\ \ }$ $\frac{16}{28} = \frac{\ \ }{7}$ $\frac{9}{24} = \frac{\ \ }{8}$ $\frac{10}{32} = \frac{5}{\ \ }$

STANDARD

To write a fraction such as $\frac{20}{30}$ in simplest form, divide both the numerator and the denominator by their greatest common factor.

Factors of **20**: **1, 2, 4, 5, 10, 20**
Factors of **30**: **1, 2, 3, 5, 6, 10, 15, 30**
The GCF of **20** and **30** is **10**.

$$\frac{20 \div 10}{30 \div 10} = \frac{2}{3}$$

To write a mixed number such as $7\frac{4}{6}$ in simplest form, divide both the numerator and denominator of the fraction part by their greatest common factor.

$$\frac{4}{6} = \frac{4 \div 2}{6 \div 2} \text{ or } \frac{2}{3}$$

$$7\frac{4}{6} = 7\frac{2}{3}$$

Write in simplest form.

8. $\frac{10}{3} =$ ______ $\frac{9}{4} =$ ______ $\frac{12}{5} =$ ______ $\frac{16}{10} =$ ______

9. $\frac{9}{12} =$ ______ $\frac{20}{4} =$ ______ $\frac{8}{10} =$ ______ $\frac{11}{8} =$ ______

10. $\frac{20}{6} =$ ______ $\frac{25}{4} =$ ______ $\frac{22}{8} =$ ______ $\frac{0}{5} =$ ______

Problem Solving Reasoning Solve.

11. Dan is planning to buy enough pizza so that each of **18** people can have one-fourth of a pizza. How many pizzas should he buy if he can only buy whole pizzas?

Explain. ______________________________

Quick Check

Write three equivalent fractions for the given fraction.

12. $\frac{4}{5}$ ______ **13.** $\frac{3}{21}$ ______ **14.** $\frac{4}{12}$ ______

Write the fraction or mixed number in simplest form.

15. $\frac{12}{18}$ ______ **16.** $\frac{15}{35}$ ______ **17.** $\frac{24}{100}$ ______

18. $\frac{22}{4}$ ______ **19.** $\frac{44}{11}$ ______ **20.** $\frac{225}{200}$ ______

Work Space.

Name ________________________________

Comparing Fractions

STANDARD

You can use number lines to compare fractions.

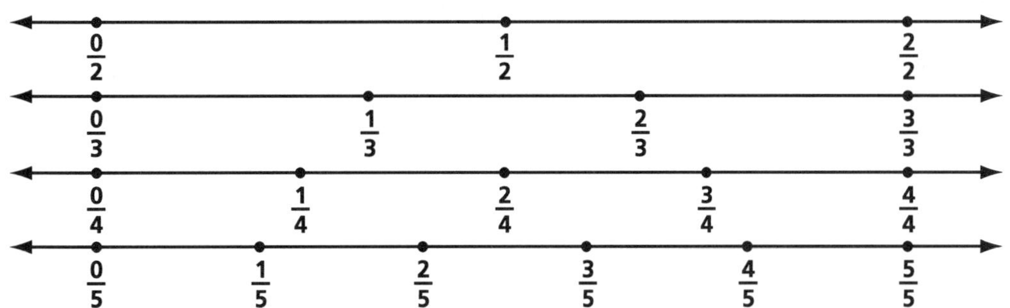

$\frac{2}{4} < \frac{3}{4}$ because $\frac{2}{4}$ is to the left of $\frac{3}{4}$.

$\frac{2}{3} > \frac{3}{5}$ because $\frac{2}{3}$ is to the right of $\frac{3}{5}$.

Use a number line to compare.

1. $\frac{3}{4}$ ◯ $\frac{3}{5}$ $\qquad$ $\frac{2}{3}$ ◯ $\frac{3}{4}$ $\qquad$ $\frac{3}{4}$ ◯ $\frac{4}{5}$ $\qquad$ $\frac{1}{3}$ ◯ $\frac{1}{4}$

2. $\frac{2}{4}$ ◯ $\frac{1}{2}$ $\qquad$ $\frac{3}{5}$ ◯ $\frac{1}{2}$ $\qquad$ $\frac{1}{4}$ ◯ $\frac{2}{4}$ $\qquad$ $\frac{3}{4}$ ◯ $\frac{2}{2}$

To compare fractions with different denominators you can write equivalent fractions with a common denominator. Use multiples to find a common denominator.

$\frac{5}{6} ? \frac{7}{9}$

$\frac{5}{6} = \frac{15}{18}$ $\qquad$ $\frac{7}{9} = \frac{14}{18}$

$\frac{5}{6} > \frac{7}{9}$

Multiples of **6**: **6, 12, 18, 24, 30, 36**

Multiples of **9**: **9, 18, 27, 36, 45**

The first common multiple is the LCM.

The LCM of the denominators is the **least common denominator (LCD).**

Compare. Write >, <, or =.

3. $\frac{3}{4}$ ◯ $\frac{7}{10}$

LCD = ________

$\frac{3}{4}$ → ________

$\frac{7}{10}$ → ________

4. $\frac{6}{5}$ ◯ $\frac{9}{7}$

LCD = ________

$\frac{6}{5}$ → ________

$\frac{9}{7}$ → ________

5. $\frac{5}{12}$ ◯ $\frac{3}{8}$

LCD = ________

$\frac{5}{12}$ → ________

$\frac{3}{8}$ → ________

6. $\frac{5}{4}$ ◯ $\frac{6}{5}$ $\qquad$ **7.** $\frac{5}{9}$ ◯ $\frac{2}{3}$ $\qquad$ **8.** $\frac{5}{12}$ ◯ $\frac{4}{9}$

STANDARD

You can use prime factorization to help you compare fractions.

Compare: $\frac{5}{9} \bigcirc \frac{7}{12}$

To compare fractions, you find the **LCD** of the denominators. You can find the **LCD** of the denominators by writing the prime factorizations of the denominators.

$9 = 3^2$
$12 = 2^2 \cdot 3$

The product of the greatest powers of the prime factors is the **LCD.**

LCD $= 2^2 \cdot 3^2$ or 36

Write equivalent fractions using the **LCD,** then compare.

$\frac{5}{9} = \frac{20}{36}$ and $\frac{7}{12} = \frac{21}{36}$

$\frac{5}{9} \bigcirc \frac{7}{12}$

Use the prime-factorization method to find the LCD of each pair of denominators. Then compare using >, <, or =.

9. $\frac{4}{9} \bigcirc \frac{7}{15}$

LCD = ______

$\frac{4}{9} \rightarrow$ ______

$\frac{7}{15} \rightarrow$ ______

10. $\frac{9}{8} \bigcirc \frac{11}{10}$

LCD = ______

$\frac{9}{8} \rightarrow$ ______

$\frac{11}{10} \rightarrow$ ______

11. $\frac{1}{3} \bigcirc \frac{4}{12}$

LCD = ______

$\frac{1}{3} \rightarrow$ ______

$\frac{4}{12} \rightarrow$ ______

12. $\frac{3}{10} \bigcirc \frac{4}{15}$

LCD = ______

$\frac{3}{10} \rightarrow$ ______

$\frac{4}{15} \rightarrow$ ______

13. $\frac{7}{5} \bigcirc \frac{11}{8}$

LCD = ______

$\frac{7}{5} \rightarrow$ ______

$\frac{11}{8} \rightarrow$ ______

14. $\frac{7}{12} \bigcirc \frac{9}{16}$

LCD = ______

$\frac{7}{12} \rightarrow$ ______

$\frac{9}{16} \rightarrow$ ______

Compare: Use >, <, or =.

15. $\frac{1}{2} \bigcirc \frac{4}{7}$

16. $\frac{6}{5} \bigcirc \frac{5}{4}$

17. $\frac{22}{25} \bigcirc \frac{7}{8}$

Test Prep ★ Mixed Review

18 What is the exact decimal equivalent of $\frac{1}{33}$?

A 0.3 **C** 0.03

B $0.\overline{3}$ **D** $0.\overline{03}$

19 What is the solution to the equation $y + 1{,}964 = 2{,}003$?

F 39 **H** 61

G 49 **J** 161

Name ________________________________

Fractions, Mixed Numbers, and Decimals

STANDARD

Fractions and mixed numbers can be written as decimals.

$\frac{7}{10} = 0.7$ $\quad 4\frac{19}{100} = 4.19$ $\quad \frac{13}{10} \rightarrow 1\frac{3}{10} = 1.3$

$\frac{1}{2} \rightarrow \frac{5}{10} = 0.5$ $\quad 1\frac{3}{4} \rightarrow 1\frac{75}{100} = 1.75$ $\quad \frac{4}{5} \rightarrow \frac{8}{10} = 0.8$

Decimals can be written as fractions or mixed numbers.

$0.3 = \frac{3}{10}$ $\quad 2.09 = 2\frac{9}{100}$ $\quad 5.231 = 5\frac{231}{1{,}000}$

Write each fraction or mixed number as a decimal.

1. $\frac{7}{10}$ ______ $\quad \frac{9}{10}$ ______ $\quad \frac{43}{100}$ ______ $\quad \frac{87}{100}$ ______

2. $\frac{3}{100}$ ______ $\quad \frac{439}{1{,}000}$ ______ $\quad \frac{351}{1{,}000}$ ______ $\quad \frac{17}{1{,}000}$ ______

3. $\frac{9}{1{,}000}$ ______ $\quad \frac{23}{1{,}000}$ ______ $\quad 1\frac{3}{10}$ ______ $\quad 4\frac{29}{100}$ ______

4. $8\frac{37}{1{,}000}$ ______ $\quad 2\frac{3}{1{,}000}$ ______ $\quad 5\frac{7}{100}$ ______ $\quad \frac{83}{10}$ ______

5. $\frac{1}{5}$ ______ $\quad \frac{9}{20}$ ______ $\quad \frac{4}{25}$ ______ $\quad \frac{8}{5}$ ______

Write each decimal as a fraction or mixed number in simplest form.

6. 0.1 ______ 0.3 ______ 0.6 ______ 0.8 ______

7. 0.75 ______ 0.45 ______ 0.80 ______ 0.06 ______

8. 1.5 ______ 2.3 ______ 1.4 ______ 2.6 ______

9. 4.25 ______ 2.75 ______ 1.48 ______ 2.96 ______

10. 1.004 ______ 8.2 ______ 0.013 ______ 3.73 ______

11. 3.05 ______ 0.107 ______ 6.04 ______ 9.029 ______

STANDARD

You can compare and order fractions, mixed numbers, and decimals on a number line.

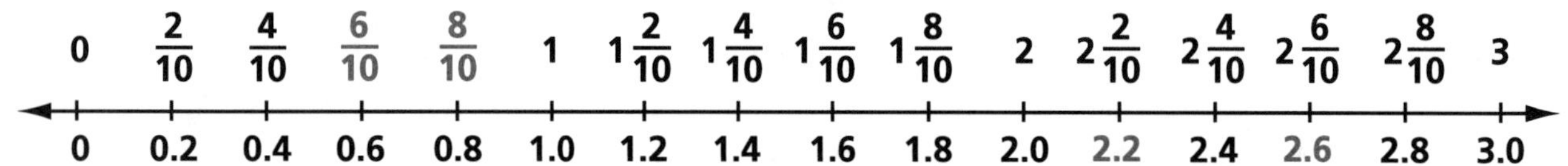

One way is to rewrite the fractions, mixed numbers, and decimals as fractions with the same denominator. Then compare using a number line.

Compare **0.8** (?) $\frac{3}{5}$.

$0.8 = \frac{8}{10}$ $\quad \frac{3}{5} = \frac{6}{10}$

Since $\frac{8}{10} > \frac{6}{10}$, $0.8 > \frac{3}{5}$.

Another way is to rewrite the fractions and mixed numbers as decimals. Then compare using a number line.

Write **2.6**, $2\frac{1}{5}$, and $\frac{11}{4}$ in order from least to greatest.

$2\frac{1}{5} = 2\frac{2}{10}$ or 2.2 $\qquad \frac{11}{4} = 2\frac{3}{4}$ or 2.75

2.2, 2.6, 2.75 → $2\frac{1}{5}$, 2.6, $\frac{11}{4}$

Compare. Write >, <, or =.

12. $\frac{9}{10}$ ◯ 0.13 $\qquad 3\frac{1}{5}$ ◯ 3.2 $\qquad \frac{3}{4}$ ◯ 0.8 $\qquad \frac{8}{20}$ ◯ 0.33

Rewrite as decimals or fractions. Then write them in order from least to greatest.

13. $\frac{9}{20}$, 0.42, $\frac{5}{4}$ ________ $\qquad \frac{3}{5}$, $\frac{3}{4}$, 0.7 ________

14. $1\frac{1}{4}$, 1.65, $\frac{3}{2}$ ________ $\qquad$ 1.3, 0.75, $\frac{7}{4}$ ________

Problem Solving Reasoning Solve.

15. List 3 decimals and 3 fractions between **0.1** and **0.2**. ________

Test Prep ★ Mixed Review

16 The size of a poster is 18 inches by 30 inches. How much can it be reduced and still have dimensions that are a whole number of inches?

A To $\frac{1}{2}$ size
B To $\frac{1}{4}$ size
C To $\frac{1}{6}$ size
D To $\frac{1}{12}$ size

17 Each jar of Brand A popcorn contains 10 oz of popcorn and the jar weighs 2 ounces. The contents of a carton of this popcorn weigh 288 ounces. Which equation can be used to find the number (n) of full popcorn jars in the carton?

F $288 \div n = 10 + 2$
G $288 \div n = 10 \cdot 2$
H $(10 \cdot 2) \cdot n = 288$
J $(10 + 2) \div n = 288$

Name ____________________

Terminating and Repeating Decimals

STANDARD

You can write a fraction as a decimal by dividing the numerator by the denominator.

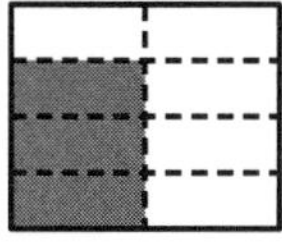

$\frac{3}{8} = 0.375$

$$\begin{array}{r} 0.375 \\ 8\overline{)3.000} \\ -2\,4 \\ \hline 6\,0 \\ -5\,6 \\ \hline 4\,0 \\ -4\,0 \\ \hline 0 \end{array}$$

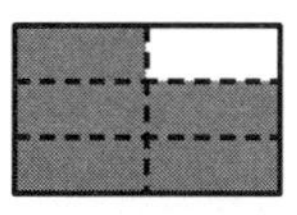

$\frac{5}{6} = 0.8333...$ or $0.8\overline{3}$

$$\begin{array}{r} 0.8333 \\ 6\overline{)5.0000} \\ -4\,8 \\ \hline 2\,0 \\ -1\,8 \\ \hline 2\,0 \\ -1\,8 \\ \hline 2\,0 \\ -1\,8 \\ \hline 2 \end{array}$$

The remainder in the division above is zero and the decimal quotient terminates or stops.

Decimals that terminate are called **terminating decimals.**

The digit **3** repeats in the quotient above. You write a bar over the digit or digits that repeat.

Decimals that have repeating digits are called **repeating decimals.**

Write the fraction as a decimal. Use a bar to show a repeating decimal.

1. $\frac{1}{5}$ ______

2. $\frac{5}{2}$ ______

3. $\frac{7}{10}$ ______

4. $\frac{2}{9}$ ______

5. $\frac{3}{4}$ ______

6. $\frac{9}{20}$ ______

7. $\frac{4}{3}$ ______

8. $\frac{1}{50}$ ______

9. $\frac{8}{3}$ ______

10. $\frac{4}{25}$ ______

11. $\frac{5}{11}$ ______

12. $\frac{1}{6}$ ______

STANDARD

Write the fraction as a decimal. Use a bar to show a repeating decimal.

13. $\frac{11}{16}$ ______ **14.** $\frac{8}{11}$ ______ **15.** $\frac{13}{9}$ ______

Problem Solving
Reasoning

Solve.

16. Write $\frac{1}{9}$, $\frac{2}{9}$, $\frac{3}{9}$, and $\frac{4}{9}$ as decimals. Using patterns, write $\frac{5}{9}$, $\frac{6}{9}$, $\frac{7}{9}$, and $\frac{8}{9}$ as decimals.

______

______

17. Write $\frac{1}{11}$, $\frac{2}{11}$, $\frac{3}{11}$, and $\frac{4}{11}$ as decimals. Using patterns, write $\frac{5}{11}$, $\frac{6}{11}$, $\frac{7}{11}$, and $\frac{8}{11}$ as decimals.

______

______

Quick Check

Write the least common denominator for the two fractions.

18. $\frac{7}{8}$ and $\frac{3}{4}$ ______ **19.** $\frac{2}{3}$ and $\frac{3}{5}$ ______ **20.** $\frac{5}{12}$ and $\frac{7}{15}$ ______

21. Rewrite the pair of fractions in item 20 using the least common denominator. ______

Write the equivalent decimal. Round to the nearest hundredth.

22. $\frac{27}{1,000}$ ______ **23.** $\frac{5}{8}$ ______ **24.** $\frac{3}{11}$ ______

Write as a fraction in simplest form.

25. 0.76 ______ **26.** 2.008 ______ **27.** 7.335 ______

Write as an exact decimal, using bar notation.

28. $\frac{5}{18}$ ______ **29.** $\frac{5}{27}$ ______ **30.** $\frac{8}{27}$ ______

Work Space.

Name ______________________________

Problem Solving Application: Use a Bar Graph

STANDARD

This vertical bar graph shows the heights of some buildings in the United States.

In this lesson, you will use bar graphs to compare, make estimates, and draw conclusions about data.

Tips to Remember:

1. Understand 2. Decide 3. Solve 4. Look back

- Ask yourself: Have I solved a problem like this one before? How did I solve it?
- Compare the labels on the graph with the words and numbers in the problem. Find the facts you need from the graph.
- When you can, make a prediction about the answer. Then compare your answer with your prediction.

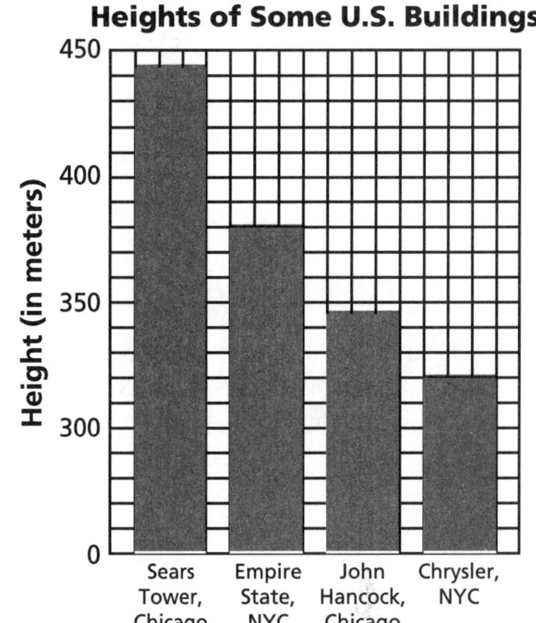

Solve. Use the graph above.

1. Can you conclude from the graph that the Empire State Building is about twice as tall as the Chrysler Building? Why or why not?

Think: Should you compare the heights of the bars or the numbers on the scale?

____

Answer ______________________________

2. To the nearest **10** meters, what is the difference in the height of the Sears Tower and the height of the Empire State Building?

Think: How many meters are represented by each vertical block?

____

Answer ______________________________

3. The World Trade Center in New York City is **410** meters tall. Is it the tallest building in the United States? Explain.

____

4. The Chrysler Building is about twice as tall as the Washington Monument in Washington, D.C. About how tall is the Washington Monument?

____

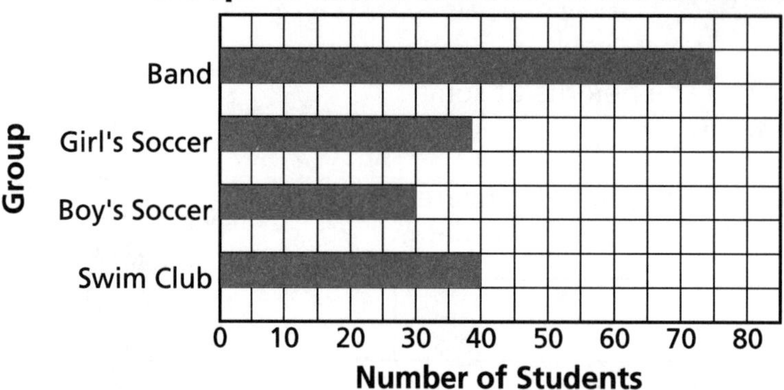

Solve. Use the graph above.

5. Do the Boy's Soccer and Girl's Soccer groups combined have more members than the Band?

______

6. Estimate the average membership for all the groups. (Round your answer to the nearest whole number.)

____

7. Which group has $\frac{3}{4}$ as many members as the Swim Club?

____

8. Which group has $1\frac{7}{8}$ times as many members as the Swim Club?

____

9. Which club has about $\frac{3}{4}$ as many members as Girl's Soccer?

____

10. Complete this statement using a fraction or mixed number.

The Band has ______ times as many members as Boy's Soccer.

Extend Your Thinking

11. Takiya looked at the graph and decided that there must be more girls than boys in the sixth level. Do you agree or disagree? Explain.

____

____

____

12. Mark looked at the graph and concluded that there are 184 students in the sixth level. Do you agree or disagree? Explain.

____

____

____

13. Explain how you found your answer to exercise **10**.

____

14. Explain how you found your answer to exercise **7**.

____

Name ______________________

Unit 3 Review

Write whether each number is divisible by 2, 3, 4, 5, 6, 9, or 10.

1. **117** divisible by: __________

2. **120** divisible by: __________

Simplify each expression.

3. $5^2 - 2 \times 3$ ______

4. $10(5 - 2)^2$ ______

Write P or C to indicate whether the number is prime or composite. If it is composite, write the prime factorization in exponent form.

5. 11 ________

6. 15 ________

7. 36 ________

Write the GCF and LCM of each pair of numbers.

8. 15 and 25 ________________

9. 6 and 18 ________________

Write two equivalent fractions for each.

10. $\frac{6}{9}$ ________

11. $\frac{14}{20}$ ________

Write each as a fraction or mixed number in simplest form.

12. 0.38 ________

13. $\frac{24}{14}$ ________

Compare. Write >, <, or =.

14. $\frac{4}{5}$ ◯ 0.6

15. 4.9 ◯ $3\frac{5}{8}$

16. 0.55 ◯ $\frac{55}{10}$

Write these numbers in order from least to greatest.

17. 0.5. , $\frac{3}{9}$, $\frac{1}{8}$, 0.45 ________________

18. 6.3, $\frac{44}{5}$, $\frac{10}{12}$, 3.45 ________________

Use graph at right to answer each question.

19. Which city has more than **3** times as much annual rainfall as Sacramento?

____

20. Fairbanks has a recorded average annual snowfall of about **67** in. About how many times greater is its snowfall than its rainfall?

____

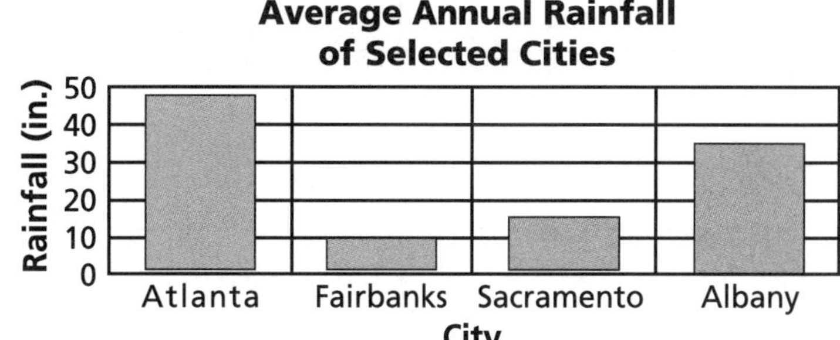

21. Mia, Joe, Sue, and Ty are standing in line. How many different ways can they stand in line if Ty is first in line? ______

Name ____________________

Cumulative Review
★ Test Prep

1 **The cost of 3.25 pounds of bananas is \$1.17. What is the cost for 1 pound?**

A \$.31 C \$.33 E \$.36

B \$.32 D \$.35

2 **Greg drives 16.9 miles to his workplace each day. His wife drives 34.2 miles to her workplace. How much farther does Greg's wife drive to her workplace each day?**

F 7.3 miles

G 8.3 miles

H 17.3 miles

J 18.3 miles

K N H

3 **The Brite-White Cleaning Company cleans the office of Client A every 9 days. It cleans the office of Client B every 6 days. The schedule for three weeks is shown below. After how many weekdays will both clients next need their offices cleaned?**

Mon	Tue	Wed	Thu	Fri
		Client B		
Client A			Client B	
				Client A Client B

A 9 days C 15 days

B 12 days D 18 days

4 **A theater seats a total of 750 people. There are 50 seats in each section. Which equation can be used to find the number (n) of sections in the theater?**

F $50 + n = 750$ H $750n = 50$

G $750 \div n = 50$ J $750 - n = 50$

5 **What number does the picture represent?**

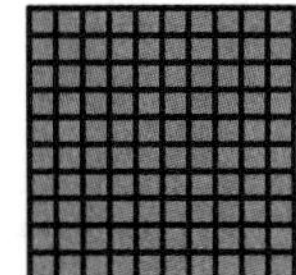
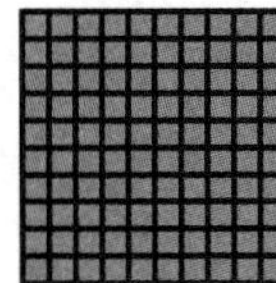
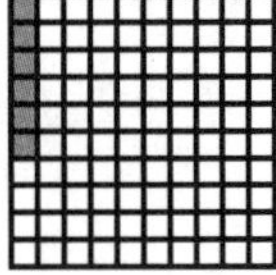

A 0.26 C 2.06

B 2.6 D 26

6 **Which number could represent the indicated point on the number line?**

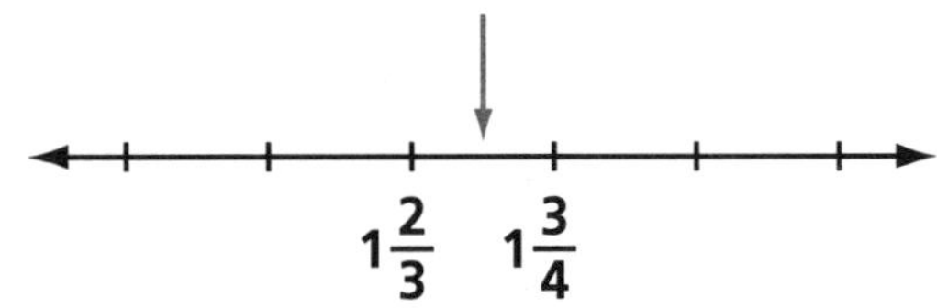

F $1\frac{13}{24}$ H $1\frac{17}{24}$

G $1\frac{3}{8}$ J $1\frac{19}{24}$

7 **Carmen has 4 routes she can take to go from home to school. Order the routes from shortest to longest.**

Route	Length
A	$1\frac{1}{4}$ mi
B	$1\frac{1}{2}$ mi
C	$1\frac{3}{8}$ mi
D	$1\frac{1}{8}$ mi

F Route A, Route B, Route C, Route D

G Route B, Route A, Route D, Route C

H Route D, Route A, Route C, Route B

J Route B, Route C, Route A, Route D

UNIT 4 • TABLE OF CONTENTS

Fractions

We will be using this vocabulary:

formula a general rule expressed using symbols

reciprocals two numbers whose product is **1**

mixed number a number that is made up of a fraction and a whole number

numerator of a fraction the number above the fraction bar

denominator of a fraction the number below the fraction bar

Dear Family,

During the next few weeks, our math class will be learning about fractions. You can expect to see homework that provides practice with multiplying fractions. Here is a sample you may want to keep handy to give help if needed.

Multiplying Fractions

One way to multiply fractions is to multiply the numerators and multiply the denominators, then use division to write the answer in simplest form.

$$\frac{2}{15} \times \frac{1}{7} \times \frac{5}{6} = \frac{2 \times 1 \times 5}{15 \times 7 \times 6} \rightarrow \frac{10}{630} \qquad \frac{10 \div 10}{630 \div 10} = \frac{1}{63}$$

Another way to multiply fractions is to simplify before multiplying. To simplify, divide any numerator and any denominator by a common factor.

$$\frac{\overset{1}{\cancel{2}}}{15} \times \frac{1}{7} \times \frac{5}{\underset{3}{\cancel{6}}}$$ Divide **2** and **6** by **2**.

Simplify as many times as you can.

$$\frac{\overset{1}{\cancel{2}}}{\underset{3}{\cancel{15}}} \times \frac{1}{7} \times \frac{\overset{1}{\cancel{5}}}{\underset{3}{\cancel{6}}}$$ Divide **5** and **15** by **5**.

Then multiply.

$$\frac{\overset{1}{\cancel{2}}}{\underset{3}{\cancel{15}}} \times \frac{1}{7} \times \frac{\overset{1}{\cancel{5}}}{\underset{3}{\cancel{6}}} = \frac{1}{63}$$

During this unit, students will need to continue to practice multiplying fractions.

Sincerely,

Name ________________________________

Adding and Subtracting with Like Denominators

STANDARD

To add or subtract fractions that have the same denominator:

1. Add or subtract the numerators to find the numerator of the answer.

2. Write the denominator of the fractions as the denominator of the answer.

3. Write the sum or difference in simplest form.

$\frac{1}{8} + \frac{3}{8} = \frac{4}{8}$ or $\frac{1}{2}$

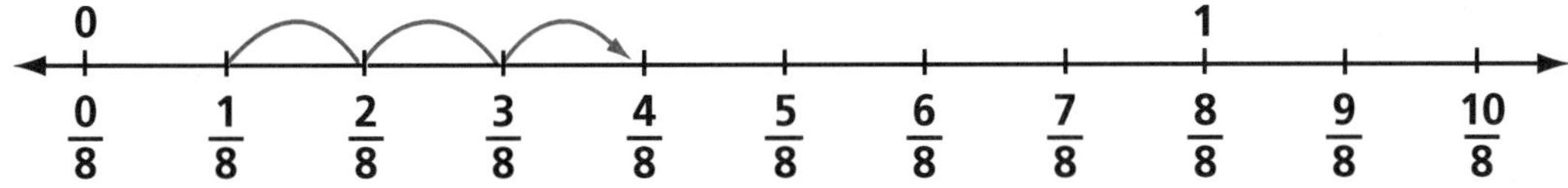

$\frac{7}{8} - \frac{3}{8} = \frac{4}{8}$ or $\frac{1}{2}$

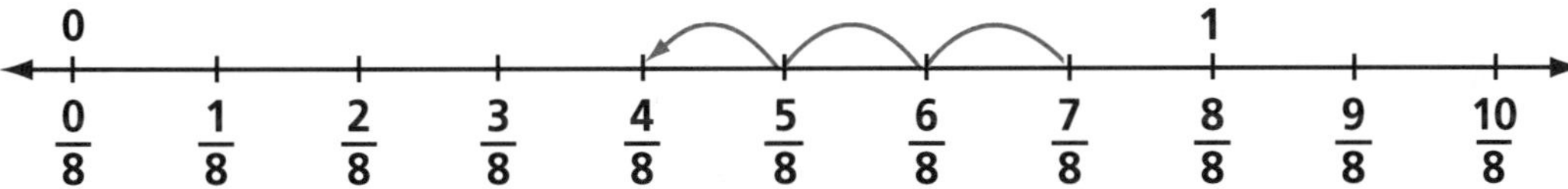

Write each sum or difference in simplest form.

1. $\frac{5}{7} - \frac{4}{7} =$ ________ $\frac{3}{10} + \frac{7}{10} =$ ________ $\frac{7}{12} - \frac{1}{12} =$ ________

2. $\frac{5}{6} + \frac{5}{6} =$ ________ $\frac{2}{15} + \frac{8}{15} =$ ________ $\frac{2}{5} + \frac{4}{5} =$ ________

3. $\frac{15}{20} - \frac{8}{20} =$ ________ $\frac{10}{11} + \frac{4}{11} =$ ________ $\frac{10}{11} - \frac{4}{11} =$ ________

4. $\frac{4}{9} + \frac{8}{9}$ $\frac{3}{5} + \frac{4}{5}$ $\frac{5}{6} - \frac{1}{6}$ $\frac{4}{9} - \frac{2}{9}$ $\frac{1}{3} - \frac{1}{3}$

5. $\frac{9}{10} - \frac{3}{10}$ $\frac{4}{7} + \frac{6}{7}$ $\frac{3}{8} - \frac{1}{8}$ $\frac{5}{12} + \frac{11}{12}$ $\frac{3}{4} - \frac{1}{4}$

STANDARD

To add or subtract mixed numbers with the same denominator:

1. Add or subtract the numerators of the fraction parts.

$$\begin{array}{r} 2\frac{7}{9} \\ +4\frac{8}{9} \\ \hline \frac{15}{9} \end{array}$$

2. Add or subtract the whole numbers.

$$\begin{array}{r} 2\frac{7}{9} \\ +4\frac{8}{9} \\ \hline 6\frac{15}{9} \end{array}$$

3. Simplify.

$$\begin{array}{r} 2\frac{7}{9} \\ +4\frac{8}{9} \\ \hline 6\frac{15}{9} \end{array} = 7\frac{6}{9} \text{ or } 7\frac{2}{3}$$

Write the sum or difference in simplest form.

6. $2\frac{4}{9} - 1\frac{1}{9}$ $\quad$ $4\frac{7}{8} + 1\frac{1}{8}$ $\quad$ $4\frac{5}{6} - \frac{1}{6}$ $\quad$ $6\frac{7}{10} - 2\frac{3}{10}$ $\quad$ $3\frac{1}{3} + 1\frac{2}{3}$

7. $6\frac{4}{5} + 3\frac{3}{5}$ $\quad$ $3\frac{7}{12} - 2\frac{1}{12}$ $\quad$ $3\frac{1}{2} - 1\frac{1}{2}$ $\quad$ $5\frac{2}{3} - 4$ $\quad$ $4\frac{1}{2} + 4\frac{1}{2}$

8. $4\frac{6}{7} - 1\frac{2}{7}$ $\quad$ $8\frac{3}{15} + 7\frac{7}{15}$ $\quad$ $5\frac{11}{14} - 2\frac{3}{14}$ $\quad$ $6\frac{3}{4} + \frac{3}{4}$ $\quad$ $7\frac{3}{8} - 5$

9. $6\frac{9}{10} + 2\frac{7}{10}$ $\quad$ $1\frac{7}{9} - 1\frac{4}{9}$ $\quad$ $4\frac{5}{6} - 1\frac{5}{6}$ $\quad$ $7\frac{2}{3} - 7$ $\quad$ $3\frac{5}{12} - 2$

10. $3\frac{3}{4} - 1\frac{1}{4}$ $\quad$ $2\frac{5}{8} + 4\frac{3}{8}$ $\quad$ $6\frac{1}{5} + 1\frac{2}{5}$ $\quad$ $9\frac{3}{16} - 5\frac{1}{16}$ $\quad$ $2\frac{8}{10} + 3\frac{5}{10}$

Name ________________________________

STANDARD

You may need to rename a mixed number before you subtract.

$7\frac{1}{9} - 2\frac{4}{9}$

1. Since $\frac{4}{9} > \frac{1}{9}$, rename $7\frac{1}{9}$

$7\frac{1}{9} = 6 + \frac{9}{9} + \frac{1}{9} = \quad 6\frac{10}{9}$

$-2\frac{4}{9} \qquad -2\frac{4}{9}$

2. Subtract and write the difference in simplest form.

$6\frac{10}{9}$

$-2\frac{4}{9}$

$4\frac{6}{9} = 4\frac{2}{3}$

Sometimes you may need to rename a whole number before you subtract.

$4 \rightarrow 3\frac{6}{6}$

$-1\frac{5}{6} \rightarrow -1\frac{5}{6}$

$2\frac{1}{6}$

Write the difference in simplest form.

11. $4\frac{3}{7} - 1\frac{5}{7}$ $\qquad 7\frac{1}{4} - 3\frac{3}{4}$ $\qquad 5\frac{1}{6} - 2\frac{5}{6}$ $\qquad 2\frac{5}{8} - \frac{7}{8}$ $\qquad 7\frac{4}{9} - 2\frac{4}{9}$

12. $6 - 1\frac{1}{2}$ $\qquad 5 - 2\frac{3}{4}$ $\qquad 7 - 1\frac{5}{8}$ $\qquad 8 - 3\frac{1}{5}$ $\qquad 6\frac{4}{15} - 4\frac{7}{15}$

Test Prep ★ Mixed Review

13 Mr. Somer's art class made clay pots. There are 28 students in the class. They used 78.4 pounds of clay altogether. Which equation could be used to find the average amount of clay each student used?

A $78.4 \div c = 28$ **C** $78.4 - c = 28$

B $78.4c = 28$ **D** $c \div 78.4 = 28$

14 Which list contains only composite numbers?

F 2, 3, 5, 7 **H** 4, 6, 8, 9

G 3, 4, 5, 6 **J** 4, 6, 7, 9

STANDARD

Name ______________________________

Adding Fractions with Unlike Denominators

When you add fractions with unlike denominators, it can help to think of a model of the fractions.

How much is shaded all together?

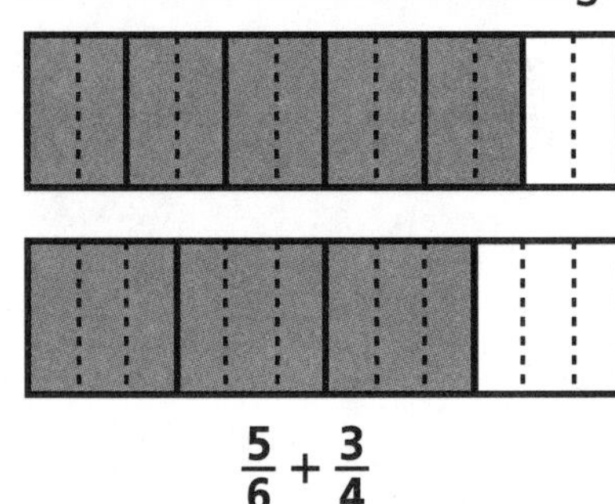

$\frac{5}{6} + \frac{3}{4}$

1. Estimate first.

$\frac{5}{6}$ rounds up to 1.

$\frac{3}{4}$ rounds up to 1.

$1 + 1 = 2$

So $\frac{5}{6} + \frac{3}{4}$ is about 2.

2. Write equivalent fractions. Then, add. Write the sum in simplest form.

$$\frac{5}{6} = \frac{10}{12}$$
$$+\frac{3}{4} = +\frac{9}{12}$$
$$\frac{19}{12} = 1\frac{7}{12}$$

Estimate. Then write the sum in simplest form.

1. $\frac{2}{5} + \frac{7}{10}$ ______ $\frac{5}{6} + \frac{4}{9}$ ______ $\frac{2}{3} + \frac{1}{4}$ ______

2. $\frac{1}{2} + \frac{7}{8}$ ______ $\frac{3}{8} + \frac{5}{6}$ ______ $\frac{3}{5} + \frac{1}{4}$ ______

3. $\frac{1}{2} + \frac{3}{10}$ ______ $\frac{3}{10} + \frac{3}{4}$ ______ $\frac{2}{3} + \frac{3}{5}$ ______

4. $\frac{2}{3} + \frac{5}{9}$ ______ $\frac{3}{10} + \frac{1}{6}$ ______ $\frac{1}{2} + \frac{4}{5}$ ______

5. $\frac{5}{12} + \frac{1}{4}$ ______ $\frac{2}{15} + \frac{1}{6}$ ______ $\frac{1}{6} + \frac{1}{12}$ ______

Name ______________________________

STANDARD

You can also estimate using mixed numbers.

Estimate: $4\frac{1}{6} + \frac{2}{9}$

$4\frac{1}{6}$ rounds down to **4**.

$\frac{2}{9}$ rounds down to **0**.

The sum is about **4**.

$$\begin{array}{r} 4\frac{1}{6} = 4\frac{3}{18} \\ +\ \frac{2}{9} = +\ \frac{4}{18} \\ \hline 4\frac{7}{18} \end{array}$$

Estimate: $3\frac{5}{6} + 5\frac{3}{4}$

$3\frac{5}{6}$ rounds up to **4**.

$5\frac{3}{4}$ rounds up to **6**.

The sum is about **10**.

$$\begin{array}{r} 3\frac{5}{6} = 3\frac{10}{12} \\ +\ 5\frac{3}{4} = +\ 5\frac{9}{12} \\ \hline 8\frac{19}{12} = 9\frac{7}{12} \end{array}$$

Estimate. Then write the sum in simplest form.

6. $4\frac{1}{10} + 2\frac{1}{2}$ ______ $6\frac{4}{5} + 2\frac{1}{6}$ ______ $6\frac{7}{8} + 2\frac{3}{4}$ ______

7. $4\frac{3}{4} + 2\frac{2}{5}$ ______ $2\frac{3}{4} + 1\frac{1}{6}$ ______ $12\frac{7}{8} + 6\frac{1}{3}$ ______

8. $9\frac{7}{8} + 4\frac{5}{6}$ ______ $8\frac{1}{10} + 5\frac{1}{4}$ ______ $15\frac{3}{4} + 12\frac{5}{8}$ ______

Problem Solving Reasoning Solve.

9. A cave is $5\frac{1}{2}$ miles west of a waterfall. A group of hikers is $2\frac{1}{4}$ miles east of the waterfall.
How far is the group of hikers from the cave? ______

Test Prep ★ Mixed Review

10 Lisa decorated a box with buttons. She used 6^3 buttons in all. How many buttons is that?

A 6

B 36

C 63

D 216

11 What is the least common multiple of 4, 5, and 6?

F 15

G 20

H 60

J 120

STANDARD

Name ______________________

Subtracting Fractions with Unlike Denominators

When you subtract fractions with unlike denominators think about fraction models. $\frac{5}{6} - \frac{1}{4}$

How much more is shaded red?

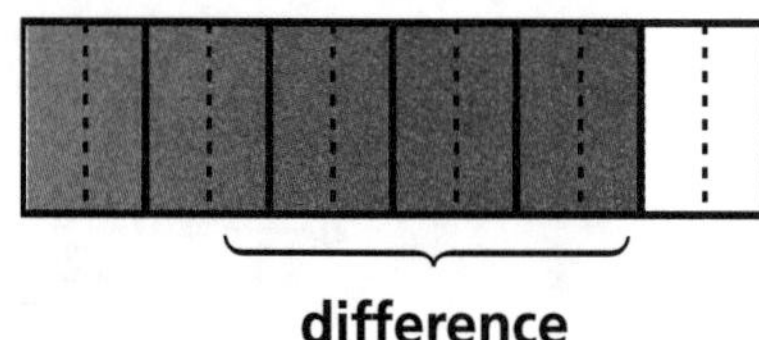

difference

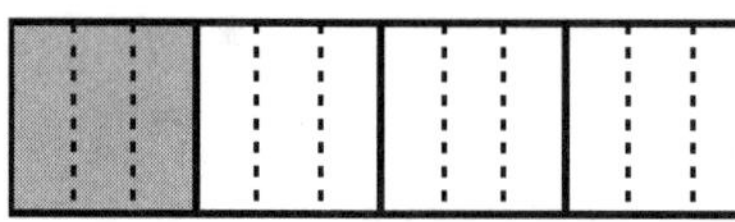

1. Estimate first.

$\frac{5}{6}$ is about **1** − **0**

$-\frac{1}{4}$ is about **0**

The difference is about **1**.

2. Write equivalent fractions. Then, subtract. Write the difference in simplest form.

$$\frac{5}{6} = \frac{10}{12}$$
$$-\frac{1}{4} = -\frac{3}{12}$$
$$\frac{7}{12}$$

Estimate. Then write the difference in simplest form.

1. $\frac{7}{10} - \frac{1}{5}$ $\quad$ $\frac{5}{6} - \frac{2}{9}$ $\quad$ $\frac{3}{4} - \frac{1}{3}$

2. $\frac{5}{8} - \frac{1}{2}$ $\quad$ $\frac{5}{6} - \frac{3}{8}$ $\quad$ $\frac{3}{4} - \frac{2}{5}$

3. $\frac{1}{2} - \frac{3}{10}$ $\quad$ $\frac{3}{4} - \frac{7}{10}$ $\quad$ $\frac{4}{5} - \frac{2}{3}$

4. $\frac{8}{9} - \frac{2}{3}$ $\quad$ $\frac{5}{6} - \frac{3}{10}$ $\quad$ $\frac{4}{5} - \frac{1}{2}$

5. $\frac{5}{12} - \frac{1}{4}$ $\quad$ $\frac{7}{15} - \frac{1}{6}$ $\quad$ $\frac{5}{6} - \frac{1}{12}$

Name ______________________________

STANDARD

You can estimate the difference of mixed numbers.

Estimate: $7\frac{5}{6} - 3\frac{4}{9}$

about $8 - 3\frac{1}{2}$

The difference is about $4\frac{1}{2}$.

Subtract.

$$\begin{array}{r} 7\frac{5}{6} = 7\frac{15}{18} \\ -3\frac{4}{9} = -3\frac{8}{18} \\ \hline 4\frac{7}{18} \end{array}$$

Estimate. Then write each difference in simplest form.

6. $4\frac{1}{2} - 2\frac{1}{3}$ $\qquad$ $6\frac{3}{5} - 2\frac{1}{4}$ $\qquad$ $6 - 2\frac{3}{4}$

7. $4\frac{3}{4} - 2\frac{2}{5}$ $\qquad$ $2 - 1\frac{1}{6}$ $\qquad$ $12\frac{7}{8} - 6\frac{1}{3}$

8. $9\frac{7}{8} - 4\frac{5}{6}$ $\qquad$ $8\frac{3}{8} - 5\frac{1}{6}$ $\qquad$ $15 - 12\frac{5}{8}$

9. $27\frac{5}{12} - 14\frac{1}{3}$ $\qquad$ $19 - 11\frac{3}{10}$ $\qquad$ $36\frac{1}{2} - 25\frac{3}{10}$

10. $6 - 4\frac{3}{5}$ $\qquad$ $8\frac{2}{3} - 5\frac{1}{4}$ $\qquad$ $15\frac{5}{9} - 9\frac{1}{3}$

11. $7\frac{6}{10} - 3\frac{1}{5}$ $\qquad$ $5 - 1\frac{1}{5}$ $\qquad$ $6\frac{10}{18} - 2\frac{2}{9}$

STANDARD

When subtracting mixed numbers whose fractions have unlike denominators, you may have to rename a mixed number in order to subtract.

Subtract: $8\frac{1}{6} - 3\frac{7}{9}$

1. Estimate.

$8\frac{1}{6}$ rounds down to **8**.

$3\frac{7}{9}$ rounds up to **4**.

The difference is about **4**.

common denominator of 6 and 9 is 18

2. Rename.

$$8\frac{1}{6} = 7 + 1 + \frac{1}{6}$$
$$= 7 + \frac{6}{6} + \frac{1}{6}$$
$$= 7 + \frac{7}{6}$$
$$= 7 + \frac{7 \times 3}{6 \times 3}$$
$$= 7\frac{21}{18}$$

3. Subtract. Simplify if you can.

$$\begin{array}{r} 7\frac{21}{18} \\ -3\frac{14}{18} \\ \hline 4\frac{7}{18} \end{array}$$

The difference $4\frac{7}{8}$ is close to the estimate. So the answer is reasonable.

Estimate. Then write the difference in simplest form.

12. $\begin{array}{r} 4\frac{1}{3} \\ -1\frac{1}{2} \\ \hline \end{array}$ $\begin{array}{r} 6\frac{1}{4} \\ -2\frac{2}{3} \\ \hline \end{array}$ $\begin{array}{r} 5\frac{7}{8} \\ -2\frac{1}{4} \\ \hline \end{array}$

13. $\begin{array}{r} 6\frac{1}{6} \\ -4\frac{3}{8} \\ \hline \end{array}$ $\begin{array}{r} 9\frac{3}{5} \\ -\frac{7}{8} \\ \hline \end{array}$ $\begin{array}{r} 4\frac{3}{10} \\ -1\frac{5}{6} \\ \hline \end{array}$

Quick Check

Write the sum or difference in simplest form.

Work Space.

14. $\frac{2}{9} + \frac{4}{9}$ ____

15. $\frac{3}{5} + \frac{4}{5}$ ____

16. $\frac{7}{12} - \frac{5}{12}$ ____

17. $9 - \frac{7}{8}$ ____

18. $\begin{array}{r} 10\frac{1}{6} \\ +4\frac{5}{6} \\ \hline \end{array}$

19. $\begin{array}{r} 3\frac{5}{8} \\ +4\frac{7}{8} \\ \hline \end{array}$

20. $\begin{array}{r} \frac{7}{8} \\ +\frac{3}{4} \\ \hline \end{array}$

21. $\begin{array}{r} 1\frac{1}{5} \\ +2\frac{2}{3} \\ \hline \end{array}$

22. $\begin{array}{r} 3\frac{5}{7} \\ -2\frac{1}{7} \\ \hline \end{array}$

23. $\begin{array}{r} 6\frac{5}{8} \\ -5\frac{7}{8} \\ \hline \end{array}$

24. $\begin{array}{r} \frac{11}{12} \\ -\frac{2}{3} \\ \hline \end{array}$

25. $\begin{array}{r} 4\frac{1}{3} \\ -2\frac{3}{4} \\ \hline \end{array}$

Name ______________________

Problem Solving Application: Use a Pictograph

STANDARD

A **pictograph** uses a symbol to represent a certain number. The key shows the number that each symbol represents.

The pictograph on this page shows the number of students who take part in the activities listed.

You will use pictographs to solve the problems in this lesson.

Tips to Remember:

1. Understand 2. Decide 3. Solve 4. Look back

- Read the problem carefully. Ask yourself questions about any part that does not make sense. Reread to find answers.
- When using a pictograph, remember to use the key.
- Think about the strategies you have already learned. Try using one of them to solve the problem.

STUDENTS TAKING PART IN SCHOOL ACTIVITIES	
Softball	3½ symbols
Basketball	2 symbols
Soccer	4½ symbols
Baseball	3½ symbols
Tennis	1½ symbols
Chorus	2 symbols
Chess	2½ symbols

KEY: Each (symbol) represents 10 students.

Solve. Use the pictograph above.

1. How many students take part in soccer?

Think: Only half of the last symbol is shown. What is $\frac{1}{2}$ of **10**?

____

Answer ______________________

2. Which activities have **35** students?

Think: How many symbols would be used to represent **35** students?

____

Answer ______________________

3. How many more students are taking part in basketball than tennis?

____

4. Suppose all the students in the chorus can take part in chess. How many students could take part in both?

____

5. Three-fourths of the chorus came to rehearsal. How many students did not show up?

____

6. All of the students in softball, basketball, soccer, baseball, and tennis went to a banquet. How many attended?

____

STANDARD

AVERAGE AMOUNT OF FOOD EATEN BY ONE PERSON IN ONE YEAR	
Meat	●●●●●●●●● and three-fourths of a ●
Fruit	●●●●●●●●●●
Vegetables	●●●●●●●●●●●●●● and part of a ●
Flour	●●●●●●● and three-fourths of a ●
KEY: Each ● represents 20 pounds.	

Solve. Use the pictograph above.

7. For which item is the average **180** pounds?

____

8. For which item is the average **270** pounds?

____

9. Three-fourths of the last symbol is shown for meat. What is the average for meat?

____

10. What is the difference between the average for meat and the average for vegetables?

____

11. The average for sugar is **90** pounds. How many symbols would be needed to represent that amount?

____

12. The average for milk and cream is **310** pounds. How many symbols would be needed to represent that amount?

____

13. On the average, how many pounds of fruits and vegetables combined does a person eat in a year?

____

14. If a person ate about the same amount of meat each month, estimate the amount eaten each month; each week.

____

Extend Your Thinking

15. Would it be correct to say on the average, for every **2** lb of fruit, **3** lb of vegetables are eaten? Explain.

____

16. Which item shows an average amount that is half as much as another item? Explain.

____

17. Go back to problem **11**. Suppose each symbol represents **25** pounds. How many symbols would be needed?

____

18. Do you think the average for flour is closer to **120** pounds or **140** pounds? Explain how you decided.

____

____

____

Name ____________________

Multiplying Fractions Using Area

STANDARD

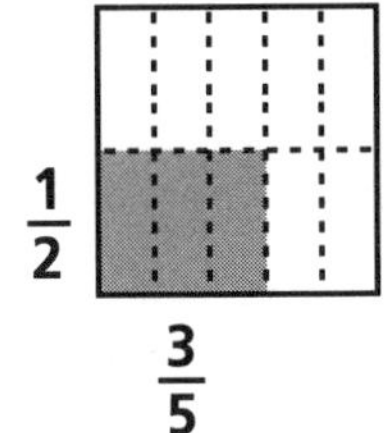

You can find the area of the shaded rectangle by counting or by multiplying.

Counting You can count **6** square units. So the area is **6** square units.

Multiplying The shaded rectangle is **3** squares long and **2** squares wide.

$$\mathbf{2 \times 3 = 6} \text{ square units}$$

You can also find the area of a shaded part of a unit square by counting or by multiplying.

$\frac{1}{2}$

$\frac{3}{5}$

Counting Each small rectangle is $\frac{1}{10}$ of the whole.

You can count **3** small rectangles that are shaded. So the area is $\frac{3}{10}$ of the square.

Multiplying The shaded rectangle is $\frac{3}{5}$ as long and $\frac{1}{2}$ as wide as the whole square.

$$\frac{1}{2} \times \frac{3}{5} = \frac{1 \times 3}{2 \times 5} \text{ or } \frac{3}{10}$$

Multiply. Use the picture to check your answer.

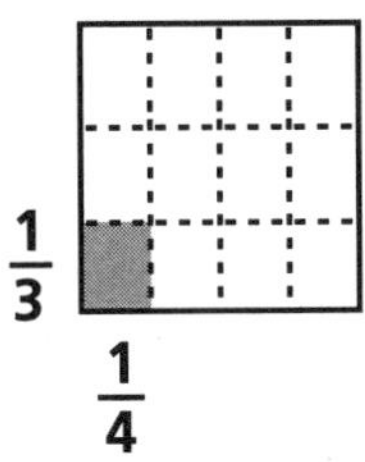

$\frac{1}{3}$ $\frac{1}{4}$

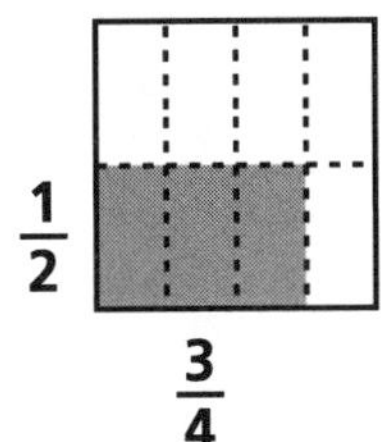

$\frac{1}{2}$ $\frac{3}{4}$

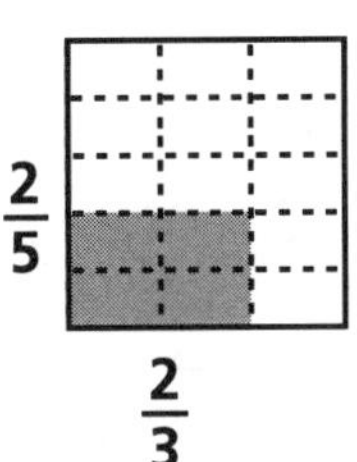

$\frac{2}{5}$ $\frac{2}{3}$

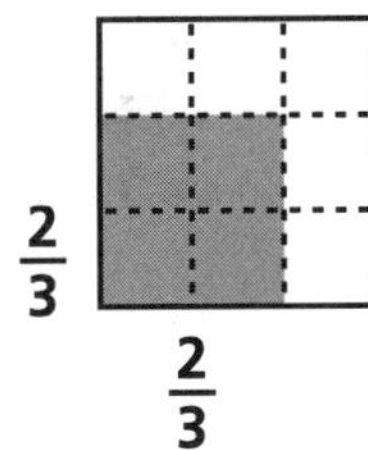

$\frac{2}{3}$ $\frac{2}{3}$

1. $\frac{1}{3} \times \frac{1}{4} =$ ______ $\frac{1}{2} \times \frac{3}{4} =$ ______ $\frac{2}{5} \times \frac{2}{3} =$ ______ $\frac{2}{3} \times \frac{2}{3} =$ ______

Shade a part of each picture to show the product. Multiply.

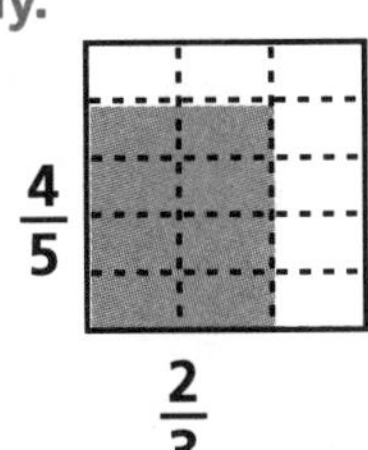

$\frac{4}{5}$ $\frac{2}{3}$

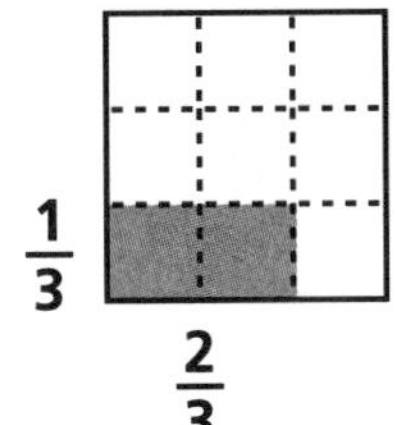

$\frac{1}{3}$ $\frac{2}{3}$

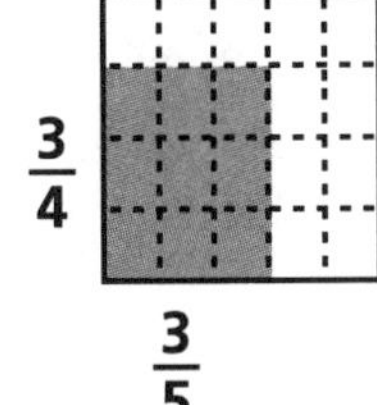

$\frac{3}{4}$ $\frac{3}{5}$

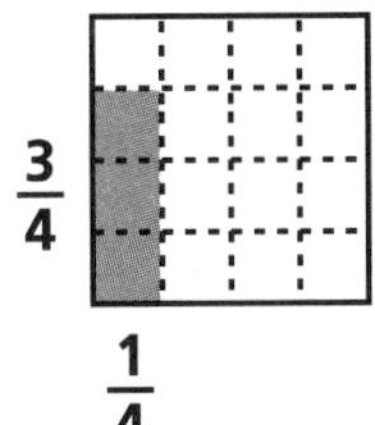

$\frac{3}{4}$ $\frac{1}{4}$

2. $\frac{4}{5} \times \frac{2}{3} =$ ______ $\frac{1}{3} \times \frac{2}{3} =$ ______ $\frac{3}{4} \times \frac{3}{5} =$ ______ $\frac{3}{4} \times \frac{1}{4} =$ ______

STANDARD

To multiply two fractions:

1. Multiply the numerators to find the numerator of the product.

2. Multiply the denominators to find the denominator of the product.

$\frac{1}{4} \times \frac{2}{5} \rightarrow 1 \times \frac{2}{4} \times 5 = \frac{2}{20}$

Multiply. Write the product in simplest form.

3. $\frac{1}{2} \times \frac{1}{5} =$ ______ $\frac{2}{3} \times \frac{4}{9} =$ ______ $\frac{1}{2} \times \frac{7}{5} =$ ______ $\frac{1}{3} \times \frac{5}{8} =$ ______

4. $\frac{2}{1} \times \frac{1}{5} =$ ______ $\frac{3}{4} \times \frac{1}{5} =$ ______ $\frac{4}{7} \times \frac{2}{3} =$ ______ $\frac{1}{2} \times \frac{3}{8} =$ ______

5. $\frac{1}{8} \times \frac{1}{7} =$ ______ $\frac{4}{9} \times \frac{1}{3} =$ ______ $\frac{3}{10} \times \frac{1}{2} =$ ______ $\frac{2}{5} \times \frac{3}{5} =$ ______

6. $\frac{3}{4} \times \frac{1}{7} =$ ______ $\frac{2}{3} \times \frac{7}{5} =$ ______ $\frac{4}{3} \times \frac{5}{9} =$ ______ $\frac{3}{2} \times \frac{3}{7} =$ ______

7. $\frac{1}{5} \times \frac{5}{7} =$ ______ $\frac{3}{8} \times \frac{8}{9} =$ ______ $\frac{2}{3} \times \frac{6}{10} =$ ______ $\frac{3}{4} \times \frac{4}{5} =$ ______

8. $\frac{3}{7} \times \frac{7}{12} =$ ______ $\frac{1}{2} \times \frac{4}{9} =$ ______ $\frac{5}{6} \times \frac{1}{5} =$ ______ $\frac{7}{9} \times \frac{3}{7} =$ ______

Problem Solving Reasoning

Solve.

9. When a fraction is multiplied by another fraction and both fractions are less than **1**, is the product greater than, less than, or equal to **1**? Explain.

____

10. Pat multiplied $\frac{1}{3}$ by another fraction. The product was $\frac{1}{8}$.

What was the fraction? ______

Test Prep ★ Mixed Review

11 Joanna made a quilt using 72 squares. Of these squares $\frac{1}{4}$ were green, $\frac{2}{9}$ were blue, $\frac{4}{9}$ were yellow, and $\frac{1}{12}$ were white. She used the least number of squares of which color?

A blue

B green

C white

D yellow

12 Yesterday, Steven practiced basketball for $1\frac{3}{4}$ hours. Today, he practiced for $2\frac{3}{8}$ hours. How long did he practice during the two days?

F 3 h

G $3\frac{1}{8}$ h

H $3\frac{1}{2}$ h

J $4\frac{1}{8}$ h

Name ______________________

Multiplying Fractions

STANDARD

Whenever you multiply fractions, write the product in simplest form.

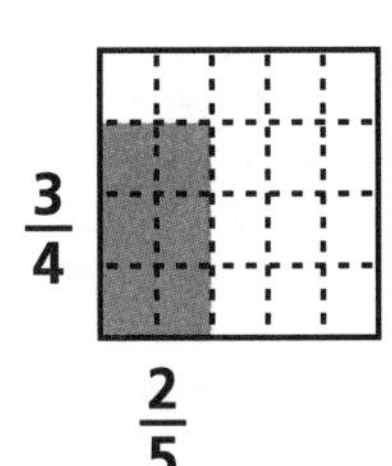

$\frac{3}{4} \times \frac{2}{5} = \frac{6}{20}$

$= \frac{3}{10}$

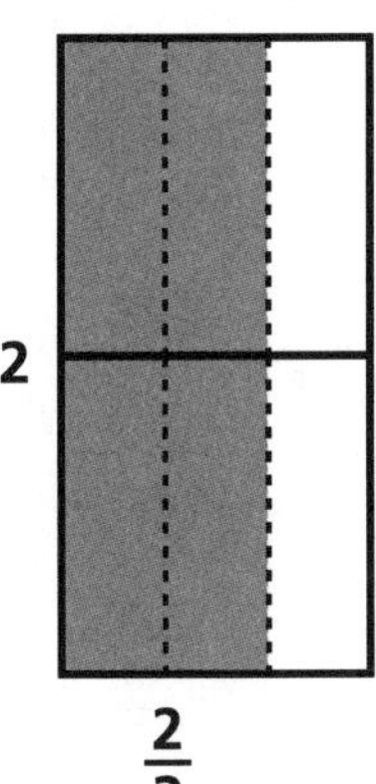

$2 \times \frac{2}{3}$

$\frac{2}{1} \times \frac{2}{3} = \frac{4}{3}$

$= 1\frac{1}{3}$

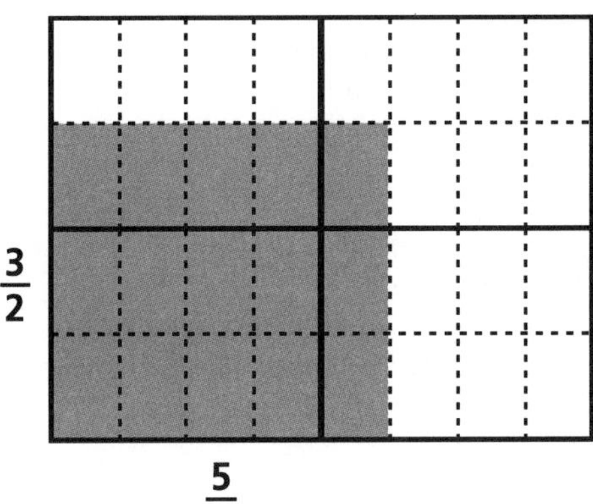

$\frac{3}{2} \times \frac{5}{4} = \frac{15}{8}$

$= 1\frac{7}{8}$

Multiply. Write the product in simplest form.

1. $\frac{1}{2} \times \frac{1}{3} =$ ______	$\frac{1}{2} \times \frac{5}{6} =$ ______	$\frac{1}{2} \times \frac{3}{4} =$ ______
2. $\frac{1}{3} \times \frac{2}{5} =$ ______	$\frac{3}{4} \times \frac{1}{3} =$ ______	$\frac{2}{3} \times \frac{3}{4} =$ ______
3. $\frac{3}{5} \times \frac{1}{4} =$ ______	$\frac{3}{8} \times \frac{1}{2} =$ ______	$\frac{3}{5} \times \frac{3}{4} =$ ______
4. $\frac{5}{8} \times \frac{3}{4} =$ ______	$2 \times \frac{2}{3} =$ ______	$2 \times \frac{1}{3} =$ ______
5. $5 \times \frac{3}{4} =$ ______	$7 \times \frac{1}{2} =$ ______	$6 \times \frac{1}{2} =$ ______
6. $\frac{3}{8} \times \frac{8}{3} =$ ______	$\frac{2}{5} \times \frac{4}{7} =$ ______	$\frac{3}{8} \times \frac{2}{2} =$ ______
7. $\frac{3}{4} \times 7 =$ ______	$\frac{3}{8} \times \frac{5}{3} =$ ______	$\frac{5}{6} \times \frac{3}{3} =$ ______
8. $\frac{4}{3} \times 5 =$ ______	$\frac{2}{7} \times \frac{3}{4} =$ ______	$5 \times \frac{1}{5} =$ ______

STANDARD

If a numerator and a denominator have a common factor, you can simplify before you multiply by dividing the numerator and denominator by the common factor.

$\frac{5}{6} \times \frac{2}{3}$

$\frac{5}{\cancel{6}_3} \times \frac{\cancel{2}^1}{3} = \frac{5}{9}$

Divide **2** and **6** by **2.**

$6 \times \frac{3}{4}$

$\frac{\cancel{6}^3}{1} \times \frac{3}{\cancel{4}_2} = \frac{9}{2}$

$= 4\frac{1}{2}$

Divide **6** and **4** by **2.**

$\frac{6}{8} \times \frac{8}{12}$

$\frac{\cancel{6}^1}{\cancel{8}_1} \times \frac{\cancel{8}^1}{\cancel{12}_2} = \frac{1}{2}$

Divide **6** and **12** by **4.**
Divide **8** and **8** by **8.**

Multiply. Write each product in simplest form.

9. $\frac{3}{4} \times \frac{1}{6} =$ ______ $\quad 6 \times \frac{1}{2} =$ ______ $\quad \frac{4}{5} \times \frac{5}{6} =$ ______

10. $\frac{1}{6} \times 3 =$ ______ $\quad 2 \times \frac{3}{8} =$ ______ $\quad \frac{3}{10} \times \frac{5}{8} =$ ______

11. $\frac{4}{5} \times \frac{2}{3} =$ ______ $\quad \frac{3}{8} \times 12 =$ ______ $\quad \frac{1}{2} \times \frac{1}{6} =$ ______

12. $\frac{3}{4} \times \frac{5}{8} =$ ______ $\quad \frac{1}{2} \times \frac{1}{4} =$ ______ $\quad \frac{3}{4} \times \frac{1}{3} =$ ______

13. $\frac{3}{4} \times \frac{2}{9} =$ ______ $\quad \frac{2}{3} \times \frac{2}{3} =$ ______ $\quad \frac{15}{6} \times \frac{3}{25} =$ ______

Problem Solving Reasoning

Solve.

14. Mandy's father has $\frac{1}{2}$ of a box of tiles to use in a mosaic picture. Of those tiles, $\frac{1}{4}$ will be used to make a border. What fraction of a whole box of tiles will be used for the border? ______

Test Prep ★ Mixed Review

15 **What do you need to do to each side of this equation to solve it?**

$$x - 34{,}608 = 85{,}209$$

A Add x

B Add 34,608

C Subtract 85,209

D Subtract 34,608

16 **Michaela is $4\frac{1}{3}$ feet tall. Her sister Catherine is $3\frac{1}{2}$ feet tall. How much taller is Michaela than Catherine?**

F $1\frac{5}{6}$ ft

G 1 ft

H $\frac{5}{6}$ ft

J $\frac{1}{6}$ ft

Name ______________________

Fraction of a Number

STANDARD

You can use compatible numbers to estimate a fraction of a whole number.

$\frac{1}{2}$ of **25**

Think of a number close to **25** that you can find $\frac{1}{2}$ of easily. Try **24**.

$\frac{1}{2}$ of **24** is **12**.

$\frac{1}{2}$ of **25** is about **12**.

$\frac{2}{3}$ of **31**

Think of a number close to **31** that you can find $\frac{2}{3}$ of easily. Try **30**.

$\frac{2}{3}$ of **30** is **20**.

$\frac{2}{3}$ of **31** is about **20**.

You can multiply to find a fraction of a whole number or of another fraction. Use your estimate to determine if your answer is reasonable.

Find $\frac{3}{8}$ of **70**.

Estimate: $\frac{3}{8}$ of **72** or **27**

$\frac{3}{8}$ of $70 = \frac{3}{8} \times \frac{70}{1}$

$= \frac{3}{\cancel{8}_4} \times \frac{\cancel{70}^{35}}{1}$

$= \frac{105}{4}$ or $26\frac{1}{4}$

Find $\frac{2}{3}$ of $\frac{6}{7}$.

Estimate: $\frac{2}{3}$ of **1** or $\frac{2}{3}$

$\frac{2}{3}$ of $\frac{6}{7} = \frac{2}{3} \times \frac{6}{7}$

$= \frac{2}{\cancel{3}_1} \times \frac{\cancel{6}^{2}}{7}$

$= \frac{4}{7}$

Estimate.

1. $\frac{1}{2}$ of **19** is about ______ $\frac{1}{4}$ of **22** is about ______

2. $\frac{2}{3}$ of **34** is about ______ $\frac{3}{4}$ of **37** is about ______

Estimate first. Then solve.

3. $\frac{3}{4}$ of $28 =$ ______ $\frac{2}{3}$ of $18 =$ ______ $\frac{5}{4}$ of $20 =$ ______

4. $\frac{2}{3}$ of $\frac{1}{2} =$ ______ $\frac{4}{5}$ of $\frac{2}{3} =$ ______ $\frac{1}{2}$ of $\frac{1}{10} =$ ______

STANDARD

Estimate first. Then solve.

5. $\frac{4}{9}$ of 15 ______ $\frac{7}{10}$ of 30 ______ $\frac{3}{8}$ of 28 ______ $\frac{1}{7}$ of 16 ______

6. $\frac{8}{9}$ of 120 ______ $\frac{1}{5}$ of $\frac{5}{7}$ ______ $\frac{8}{11}$ of 44 ______ $\frac{1}{2}$ of 19 ______

7. $\frac{2}{3}$ of 31 ______ $\frac{3}{8}$ of $\frac{1}{2}$ ______ $\frac{1}{4}$ of 35 ______ $\frac{5}{7}$ of 28 ______

8. $\frac{1}{16}$ of 20 ______ $\frac{2}{3}$ of $\frac{1}{7}$ ______ $\frac{2}{5}$ of $\frac{1}{3}$ ______ $\frac{3}{4}$ of 16 ______

Problem Solving Reasoning Solve.

9. A baker made **100** dozen cookies. She sold $\frac{3}{5}$ of them before noon.

   How many dozen were sold before noon? ______________

10. One recipe required $\frac{3}{4}$ cup of flour. The baker doubled the recipe.

    How much flour was used? ______________

11. Left-over baked items are sold the next day at $\frac{2}{5}$ off the regular price.

    How much will cookies cost if they are left-over and their regular price is $20?

    ____

Quick Check

Shade each rectangle to show the product. Write the product.

Work Space.

12. 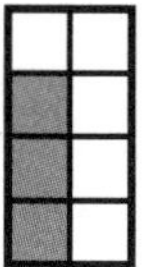

$\frac{3}{4} \times \frac{1}{2}$ ______

13. 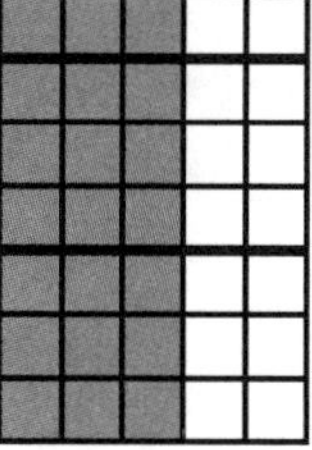

$2\frac{1}{3} \times \frac{3}{5}$ ______

Find the product.

14. $\frac{1}{3} \times \frac{1}{6}$ ______ 15. $\frac{1}{5} \times \frac{1}{7}$ ______ 16. $\frac{2}{3} \times \frac{4}{5}$ ______

17. $\frac{5}{8} \times \frac{3}{5}$ ______ 18. $\frac{3}{4}$ of 12 ______ 19. $\frac{2}{5}$ of 22 ______

Name ________________________________

Multiplying Mixed Numbers

STANDARD

To estimate the product of two mixed numbers, you can round each mixed number to its nearest whole number.

Estimate $1\frac{1}{6} \times 2\frac{2}{3} \Rightarrow 1 \times 3 = 3$ The product of $1\frac{1}{6} \times 2\frac{2}{3}$ is close to **3**.

To multiply a mixed number by a mixed number, first change both mixed numbers to fractions. Then multiply and simplify.

Multiply $1\frac{1}{6} \times 2\frac{2}{3} = \frac{7}{6} \times \frac{8}{3}$

$= \frac{7}{\not{6}_3} \times \frac{\not{8}^4}{3}$

$= \frac{28}{9}$ or $3\frac{1}{9}$

$1\frac{1}{6} = \frac{1 \times 6 + 1}{6}$ or $\frac{7}{6}$

$2\frac{2}{3} = \frac{2 \times 3 + 2}{3}$ or $\frac{8}{3}$

You can multiply mixed numbers to solve distance problems. You know that at a speed of **50** miles per hour (m.p.h.), you can go **50** miles in **1** hour, **100** miles in **2** hours, and **150** miles in **3** hours. This can be written as the formula $d = r \times t$.

Distance Formula

distance = rate of speed × time

or

$d = r \times t$

Suppose you swim for $1\frac{1}{4}$ hour at an average speed of $3\frac{1}{3}$ miles per hour. How far do you travel?

$d = r \times t$ Use the distance formula.

$= 3\frac{1}{3} \times 1\frac{1}{4}$ Substitute for r and t.

$= \frac{10}{3} \times \frac{5}{4}$ Write each number as a fraction.

$= \frac{\not{10}^5}{3} \times \frac{5}{\not{4}_2}$ Multiply.

$= \frac{25}{6}$ or $4\frac{1}{6}$ **miles**

Estimate. Then multiply and write each product in simplest form. Use your estimate to decide if your answer is reasonable.

1. $1\frac{2}{3} \times 2\frac{1}{2} =$ ______ $3\frac{1}{2} \times 1\frac{3}{4} =$ ______ $1\frac{1}{2} \times 1\frac{1}{3} =$ ______

2. $2\frac{2}{5} \times 1\frac{2}{3} =$ ______ $4\frac{3}{4} \times 3\frac{1}{5} =$ ______ $3\frac{2}{3} \times 1\frac{1}{3} =$ ______

3. $3 \times 5\frac{1}{2} =$ ______ $5\frac{1}{2} \times 4\frac{3}{4} =$ ______ $2\frac{4}{5} \times 3 =$ ______

STANDARD

Estimate. Then multiply and write each product in simplest form. Use your estimate to decide if your answer is reasonable.

4. $2\frac{1}{4} \times 3\frac{1}{2} =$ ______ $2\frac{1}{5} \times 3 =$ ______ $5\frac{3}{4} \times 2\frac{1}{2} =$ ______

5. $4\frac{2}{3} \times 2\frac{3}{4} =$ ______ $3\frac{1}{4} \times 6 =$ ______ $3\frac{1}{6} \times 2\frac{2}{3} =$ ______

6. $4\frac{1}{2} \times 2\frac{5}{6} =$ ______ $1\frac{1}{2} \times 4\frac{2}{3} =$ ______ $3\frac{2}{3} \times 4\frac{1}{3} =$ ______

7. $6 \times 6\frac{1}{4} =$ ______ $1\frac{3}{5} \times 2\frac{1}{2} =$ ______ $5\frac{3}{8} \times 4\frac{1}{5} =$ ______

Problem Solving Reasoning

Use the distance formula to solve each problem.

8. A space satellite traveling at **18,000** m.p.h. circles Earth in $1\frac{2}{5}$ hours. How long is its orbit? ______

9. Shana swam for **45** minutes at a speed of $3\frac{3}{5}$ m.p.h. How far did she swim?

______

10. A giant tortoise moves at a rate of **15** feet per minute. How far does it travel in **20** seconds? (Hint: Write **20** s as minutes.)

______

11. A spacecraft needs to travel at least **18,000** m.p.h. to escape Earth's gravity. At this speed, how far will it travel in **15** minutes?

______

12. Emil drove for $3\frac{3}{4}$ hours at a speed of **50** m.p.h. How far did he drive?

______

13. A cheetah can run for **5** minutes at a speed of **30** m.p.h. How far can it run at this speed?

______

Test Prep ★ Mixed Review

14 Patrick is buying cheese at the store. The cheese costs $2.98 a pound. Which expression shows how much *n* pounds of cheese will cost?

A $2.98 + n$ C $2.98n$

B $2.98 - n$ D $2.98 \div n$

15 Ms. Parker had 600 sheets of construction paper. Her class used $\frac{5}{8}$ of the paper. How many sheets of paper did the class use?

F 375 H 75

G 120 J 58

Name ______________________

Reciprocals

STANDARD

Two numbers are **reciprocals** of each other when their product is **1**.

$\frac{2}{3}$ and $1\frac{1}{2}$ are reciprocals, because $1\frac{1}{2} = \frac{3}{2}$ and $\frac{2}{3} \times \frac{3}{2} = \frac{6}{6}$ or **1**.

$1\frac{3}{4}$ and $\frac{4}{7}$ are reciprocals, because $1\frac{3}{4} = \frac{7}{4}$ and $\frac{7}{4} \times \frac{4}{7} = \frac{28}{28}$ or **1**.

The number **0** has no reciprocal.

Write the reciprocal of the number.

1. $\frac{2}{3}$ _____ 7 _____ $\frac{4}{9}$ _____ $\frac{1}{3}$ _____ $\frac{8}{5}$ _____ 4 _____

2. $4\frac{1}{2}$ _____ $2\frac{4}{5}$ _____ 1 _____ 10 _____ $7\frac{2}{9}$ _____ $\frac{1}{8}$ _____

3. 5 _____ $\frac{3}{4}$ _____ $2\frac{1}{2}$ _____ $\frac{7}{3}$ _____ $\frac{1}{2}$ _____ $4\frac{3}{8}$ _____

4. $11\frac{1}{3}$ _____ $6\frac{1}{8}$ _____ $\frac{5}{7}$ _____ $\frac{10}{9}$ _____ 2 _____ 100 _____

Complete. Write your answer in simplest form.

5. $\frac{2}{3} \times$ _____ $= 1$ _____ $\times \frac{4}{7} = 1$ $\frac{2}{5} \times \frac{5}{2} =$ _____

6. $4\frac{2}{3} \times$ _____ $= 1$ _____ $\times 3\frac{1}{7} = 1$ $\frac{3}{5} \times$ _____ $= 1$

7. _____ $\times 5 = 1$ _____ $\times \frac{1}{7} = 1$ _____ $\times \frac{5}{2} = 1$

8. _____ $\times \frac{6}{8} = 1$ _____ $\times \frac{4}{7} = 1$ $\frac{1}{10} \times$ _____ $= 1$

9. $\frac{5}{13} \times$ _____ $= 1$ _____ $\times 1\frac{5}{13} = 1$ _____ $\times 10\frac{1}{5} = 1$

10. _____ $\times 4 = 1$ $\frac{3}{4} \times$ _____ $= 1$ $\frac{3}{7} \times \frac{7}{3} =$ _____

11. $3\frac{3}{5} \times$ _____ $= 1$ _____ $\times 2\frac{1}{3} = 1$ _____ $\times \frac{1}{5} = 1$

12. _____ $\times 4\frac{2}{3} = 1$ $\frac{7}{8} \times$ _____ $= 1$ $\frac{5}{9} \times$ _____ $= 1$

STANDARD

Problem Solving Reasoning Solve.

13. What is the product of $\frac{3}{5}$ and the reciprocal of $\frac{1}{15}$?

____

14. What is the product of $\frac{7}{22}$ and the reciprocal of $\frac{3}{11}$?

____

15. Nancy is 2 times as old as her cousin. What fraction describes how old her cousin is compared to Nancy?

____

16. If Frank traveled 3 times faster than he planned to travel on a trip, what fraction describes the time the trip took?

____

17. Monroe spent $\frac{2}{3}$ of his money. What fraction of his money was not spent? ______________

18. Elizabeth ran a race twice as fast as Julie. What fraction describes how fast Elizabeth ran the race compared to Julie?

____

19. If a fraction is between **0** and **1,** what can you say about the reciprocal of the fraction?

____

20. If a number is greater than **1,** what can you say about the reciprocal of the number?

____

21. Does every whole number have a reciprocal? Explain.

____

____

Test Prep ★ Mixed Review

22 **Luisa's cat weighs 10.937 pounds. What is that number rounded to the nearest tenth?**

A 10 **C** 10.93

B 10.9 **D** 10.94

23 **What is the greatest common factor of 60, 75, and 90?**

F 30 **H** 3

G 15 **J** 1

Name ________________________________

Dividing by a Fraction

STANDARD

You can use models to find the quotient $\frac{5}{2} \div \frac{3}{4}$, or the number of $\frac{3}{4}$'s in $\frac{5}{2}$.

Represent $\frac{5}{2}$ as its equivalent fraction in fourths.

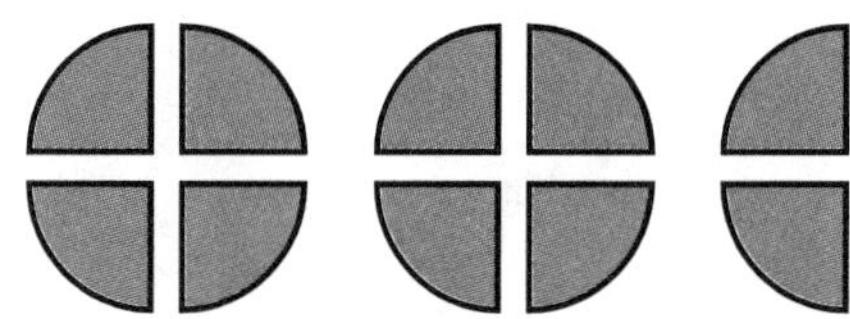

$\frac{5}{2} = \frac{10}{4}$

Circle the number of $\frac{3}{4}$'s in $\frac{10}{4}$.

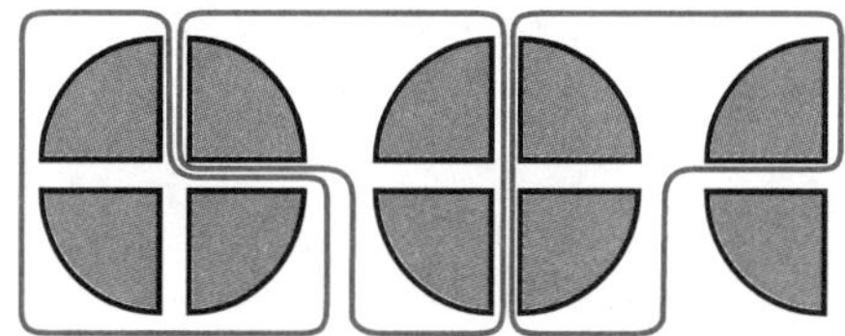

$3\frac{1}{3}$ sets of $\frac{3}{4}$ $\qquad \frac{5}{2} \div \frac{3}{4} = 3\frac{1}{3}$

To find $\frac{5}{2} \div \frac{3}{4}$, you could also multiply $\frac{5}{2}$ by the reciprocal of $\frac{3}{4}$.

$\frac{5}{\cancel{2}_1} \times \frac{\cancel{4}^2}{3} \rightarrow \frac{10}{3} = 3\frac{1}{3}$

Complete.

1. $\frac{7}{2} \div \frac{1}{2} =$ ______

   $\frac{7}{2} \times \frac{2}{1} =$ ______

2. $\frac{9}{2} \div \frac{1}{2} =$ ______

   $\frac{9}{2} \times \frac{2}{1} =$ ______

3. $\frac{4}{2} \div \frac{1}{2} =$ ______

   $\frac{4}{2} \times \frac{2}{1} =$ ______

4. $\frac{8}{2} \div \frac{1}{2} =$ ______

   $\frac{8}{2} \times \frac{2}{1} =$ ______

5. $\frac{4}{3} \div \frac{2}{3} =$ ______

   $\frac{4}{3} \times \frac{3}{2} =$ ______

6. $\frac{8}{3} \div \frac{2}{3} =$ ______

   $\frac{8}{3} \times \frac{3}{2} =$ ______

7. $\frac{2}{3} \div \frac{2}{3} =$ ______

   $\frac{2}{3} \times \frac{3}{2} =$ ______

8. $\frac{6}{3} \div \frac{2}{3} =$ ______

   $\frac{6}{3} \times \frac{3}{2} =$ ______

9. $\frac{6}{4} \div \frac{3}{4} =$ ______

   $\frac{6}{4} \times \frac{4}{3} =$ ______

10. $\frac{15}{4} \div \frac{3}{4} =$ ______

    $\frac{15}{4} \times \frac{4}{3} =$ ______

11. $\frac{4}{12} \div \frac{2}{3} =$ ______

    $\frac{4}{12} \times \frac{3}{2} =$ ______

12. $\frac{6}{12} \div \frac{3}{4} =$ ______

    $\frac{6}{12} \times \frac{4}{3} =$ ______

13. $\frac{1}{2} \div \frac{1}{4} =$ ______

    $\frac{1}{2} \times \frac{4}{1} =$ ______

14. $\frac{7}{8} \div \frac{7}{10} =$ ______

    $\frac{7}{8} \times \frac{10}{7} =$ ______

15. $\frac{12}{30} \div \frac{4}{15} =$ ______

    $\frac{12}{30} \times \frac{15}{4} =$ ______

STANDARD

Divide. Write each quotient in simplest form.

16. $\frac{5}{6} \div \frac{5}{9} =$ ______ $\frac{3}{4} \div \frac{5}{2} =$ ______ $\frac{4}{5} \div \frac{4}{3} =$ ______

17. $\frac{3}{8} \div \frac{3}{4} =$ ______ $\frac{5}{8} \div \frac{1}{8} =$ ______ $\frac{4}{7} \div \frac{2}{7} =$ ______

18. $\frac{5}{8} \div \frac{3}{4} =$ ______ $\frac{2}{5} \div \frac{4}{5} =$ ______ $\frac{5}{4} \div \frac{1}{2} =$ ______

19. $\frac{7}{8} \div \frac{3}{4} =$ ______ $\frac{7}{9} \div \frac{2}{3} =$ ______ $\frac{4}{7} \div \frac{1}{2} =$ ______

Problem Solving Reasoning Solve.

20. If the length of one of Rick's steps is $2\frac{1}{3}$ ft, how many steps will he take in a distance of 220 ft? ______________

Quick Check

Write the mixed number as a fraction.

21. $2\frac{2}{3}$ **22.** $4\frac{3}{5}$

Write the reciprocal in simplest form.

23. $\frac{2}{3}$ **24.** $3\frac{1}{6}$

Find the product.

25. $3\frac{3}{4} \times \frac{4}{5}$ **26.** $1\frac{5}{8} \times 4\frac{4}{7}$ **27.** $2\frac{1}{2} \times 3\frac{5}{9}$

Find the quotient.

28. $3\frac{1}{3} \div \frac{5}{6}$ **29.** $3\frac{3}{10} \div \frac{3}{5}$ **30.** $4\frac{1}{2} \div \frac{3}{4}$

Work Space.

Name ______________________________

Dividing Fractions and Whole Numbers

STANDARD

To divide a fraction by a whole number, multiply the fraction by the reciprocal of the whole number.

$$\frac{6}{7} \div 3 = \frac{6}{7} \div \frac{3}{1}$$
$$= \frac{6}{7} \times \frac{1}{3}$$
$$= \frac{\overset{2}{\cancel{6}}}{7} \times \frac{1}{\underset{1}{\cancel{3}}}$$
$$= \frac{2}{7}$$

To divide a whole number by a fraction, multiply the whole number by the reciprocal of the fraction.

$$5 \div \frac{3}{4} = \frac{5}{1} \div \frac{3}{4}$$
$$= \frac{5}{1} \times \frac{4}{3}$$
$$= \frac{20}{3}$$
$$= 6\frac{2}{3}$$

Divide. Write each quotient in simplest form.

1. $\frac{4}{9} \div 6 =$ ______ $\frac{3}{5} \div 4 =$ ______ $\frac{3}{4} \div 5 =$ ______

2. $\frac{5}{8} \div 5 =$ ______ $\frac{9}{10} \div 4 =$ ______ $\frac{1}{6} \div 3 =$ ______

3. $\frac{9}{4} \div 6 =$ ______ $\frac{5}{3} \div 4 =$ ______ $\frac{4}{3} \div 5 =$ ______

4. $\frac{8}{5} \div 5 =$ ______ $\frac{10}{9} \div 4 =$ ______ $\frac{7}{4} \div 3 =$ ______

5. $8 \div \frac{2}{3} =$ ______ $10 \div \frac{4}{5} =$ ______ $9 \div \frac{2}{3} =$ ______

6. $5 \div \frac{3}{2} =$ ______ $8 \div \frac{5}{4} =$ ______ $6 \div \frac{3}{2} =$ ______

7. $\frac{1}{2} \div \frac{2}{3} =$ ______ $\frac{4}{9} \div \frac{1}{3} =$ ______ $\frac{3}{2} \div \frac{3}{4} =$ ______

8. $\frac{1}{8} \div \frac{9}{5} =$ ______ $\frac{1}{5} \div \frac{5}{4} =$ ______ $3 \div \frac{2}{3} =$ ______

STANDARD

Divide. Write each quotient in simplest form.

9. $\frac{3}{10} \div \frac{1}{5} =$ ______ $5 \div \frac{5}{3} =$ ______ $6 \div \frac{3}{8} =$ ______

10. $\frac{5}{8} \div 2 =$ ______ $\frac{3}{8} \div 5 =$ ______ $\frac{1}{4} \div \frac{7}{8} =$ ______

11. $\frac{3}{10} \div \frac{3}{4} =$ ______ $\frac{1}{2} \div \frac{7}{2} =$ ______ $\frac{3}{4} \div \frac{3}{4} =$ ______

12. $9 \div \frac{3}{5} =$ ______ $\frac{7}{12} \div 7 =$ ______ $\frac{1}{3} \div \frac{5}{9} =$ ______

Problem Solving
Reasoning

Solve.

13. Ryan has $3\frac{1}{2}$ feet of licorice to share equally with **5** friends and himself. How many feet will each person receive?

______

14. Kim has $\frac{3}{4}$ of a pound of grapes. If she eats the same amount each day for **5** days, how much does she eat each day?

______

15. Each bead on Maria's necklace is $\frac{1}{8}$ inch long. All the beads together measure $\frac{3}{4}$ inch. How many beads are a part of her necklace?

______

16. When a mixed number is divided by a whole number, is the quotient greater than, less than, or equal to the mixed number?

______

Test Prep ★ Mixed Review

17 A relay team ran a race. Each team member ran $\frac{1}{4}$ of the distance. The whole race was $\frac{8}{9}$ mile. How far did each team member run?

A $1\frac{5}{36}$ mi

B $\frac{8}{9}$ mi

C $\frac{9}{32}$ mi

D $\frac{2}{9}$ mi

18 What is the prime factorization of 66?

F 6×11

G 2×33

H $2 \times 3 \times 11$

J 1×66

Name ________________________________

Dividing Mixed Numbers

STANDARD

To divide mixed numbers, write each mixed number as a fraction. Then divide and simplify. Use estimation to check the reasonableness of your answer.

$$2\frac{4}{5} \div 1\frac{1}{6}$$

Estimate: $3 \div 1 = 3$

Divide: $2\frac{4}{5} \div 1\frac{1}{6} = \frac{14}{5} \div \frac{7}{6}$

$= \frac{\cancel{14}^{2}}{5} \times \frac{6}{\cancel{7}_{1}}$

$= \frac{12}{5}$ or $2\frac{2}{5}$

The quotient $2\frac{2}{5}$ is close to the estimate **3**. So the answer is reasonable.

Divide. Write the quotient in simplest form.
Use estimation to check the reasonableness of your answer.

1. $3\frac{1}{2} \div 1\frac{3}{4} =$ ______	$9 \div 2\frac{2}{3} =$ ______	$10\frac{3}{4} \div 2 =$ ______
2. $5\frac{1}{4} \div 3 =$ ______	$3\frac{1}{2} \div 2 =$ ______	$11\frac{1}{2} \div 2\frac{7}{8} =$ ______
3. $4\frac{1}{4} \div 3\frac{1}{8} =$ ______	$3\frac{3}{4} \div 5 =$ ______	$6\frac{1}{3} \div 2 =$ ______
4. $8 \div 1\frac{1}{5} =$ ______	$2\frac{1}{2} \div 2\frac{1}{2} =$ ______	$12\frac{3}{8} \div 2\frac{3}{4} =$ ______
5. $5\frac{3}{5} \div 4\frac{2}{3} =$ ______	$2\frac{7}{8} \div 3\frac{1}{4} =$ ______	$9 \div 2\frac{5}{8} =$ ______
6. $7\frac{1}{2} \div 2\frac{1}{2} =$ ______	$1\frac{1}{4} \div 2\frac{1}{2} =$ ______	$4\frac{1}{2} \div 1\frac{1}{3} =$ ______
7. $7 \div 3\frac{1}{2} =$ ______	$7 \div 2\frac{1}{3} =$ ______	$4\frac{1}{6} \div 5 =$ ______
8. $2\frac{3}{4} \div 5\frac{2}{3} =$ ______	$4\frac{7}{8} \div 6\frac{1}{4} =$ ______	$4\frac{3}{8} \div 4 =$ ______
9. $10\frac{1}{2} \div 2\frac{1}{4} =$ ______	$6\frac{2}{3} \div 5\frac{1}{3} =$ ______	$6\frac{3}{4} \div 3\frac{1}{2} =$ ______

STANDARD

Divide. Write each quotient in simplest form.

10. $\frac{3}{5} \div \frac{5}{6} =$ ______ $\frac{7}{6} \div \frac{3}{4} =$ ______ $\frac{3}{4} \div \frac{5}{2} =$ ______

11. $\frac{1}{3} \div \frac{1}{5} =$ ______ $\frac{4}{5} \div \frac{10}{3} =$ ______ $\frac{9}{2} \div \frac{8}{3} =$ ______

12. $1\frac{2}{3} \div 2\frac{1}{3} =$ ______ $6\frac{7}{8} \div 1\frac{3}{4} =$ ______ $8 \div 3\frac{1}{4} =$ ______

13. $4\frac{2}{5} \div 3 =$ ______ $6 \div 1\frac{2}{3} =$ ______ $3\frac{1}{2} \div 2\frac{1}{4} =$ ______

14. $10\frac{1}{2} \div 1\frac{3}{4} =$ ______ $2\frac{2}{3} \div 1\frac{3}{4} =$ ______ $1\frac{1}{3} \div 4 =$ ______

15. $9\frac{1}{3} \div 2\frac{3}{4} =$ ______ $4\frac{2}{5} \div 3\frac{3}{4} =$ ______ $8 \div 6\frac{1}{4} =$ ______

Problem Solving
Reasoning

Solve.

16. A box contains **10** ounces of cereal. If one serving is $1\frac{1}{4}$ ounces, how many servings are in the box? ________

17. A can contains **3** servings of soup. If one serving is $6\frac{1}{4}$ ounces, how many ounces are in a can? ________

18. Ten melons weigh $17\frac{1}{2}$ pounds. What is the average weight of each melon?

____

19. Margaret had $5\frac{3}{4}$ cups of flour. She used one–half of it to make bread. How much flour did she use? ________

Test Prep ★ Mixed Review

20 Will has $31.92. He wants to buy as many posters as he can. Each poster costs $7.98. How many posters can he buy?

A 3

B 4

C 5

D 6

21 Which answer shows *equivalent* fractions?

F $\frac{2}{12}, \frac{3}{18}, \frac{1}{6}$

G $\frac{1}{4}, \frac{1}{2}, \frac{1}{3}$

H $\frac{2}{4}, \frac{3}{6}, \frac{3}{5}$

J $\frac{2}{3}, \frac{3}{2}, \frac{1}{3}$

Name ______________________________

Problem Solving Strategy: Draw a Diagram

STANDARD

Sometimes you can draw a picture to help you solve a problem. Or, the picture itself may be the solution to the problem.

Problem

On dot paper, draw 6 different triangles that each have an area of 2 square units.

In this lesson, you will draw pictures to solve problems. Some of the problems may have more than one solution.

1 Understand

As you reread, ask yourself questions.

- What does the problem ask you to do?

  Draw **6** different triangles that each have an area of

  ______ square units.

- Any triangle can be thought of as half of a parallelogram. If the area of a parallelogram is **4** square units, what is the area of the triangle?

  ____

2 Decide

Choose a method for solving.

Try the strategy Draw a Picture.

- Complete the parallelograms below.

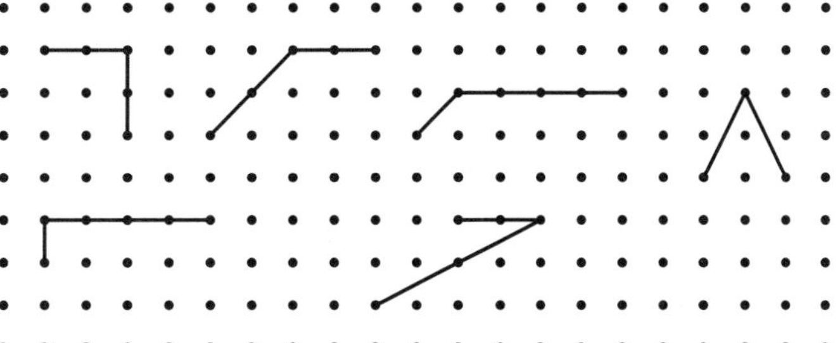

- Does each parallelogram have an area of **4** square units? ______

3 Solve

Shade half of each parallelogram to make a triangle.

- Be sure each triangle is different.

4 Look back

Check your answer.

- What is the area of each triangle? ____________________

- There are other solutions to this problem. Draw another triangle that has an area of **2** square units.

STANDARD

Solve. Use the Draw a Diagram strategy or any other strategy you have learned.

1. Draw two triangles that each have an area of **3** square units.

Think: How many half units equal one whole unit?

____

2. Draw two triangles that each have an area of $2\frac{1}{2}$ square units.

Think: The area of a triangle is half the area of what polygon?

____

3. Marcia has some nickels and pennies. She has **22** coins in all and the total value of the coins is **$.94**. How many of each coin does she have?

____

4. Sean has some quarters and dimes. He has **14** coins in all and the total value of the coins is **$2.75**. How many of each coin does he have?

____

5. How many oatmeal squares **2** inches by **3** inches can you cut from a pan that is **8** inches by **12** inches?

____

6. How many oatmeal squares $1\frac{1}{2}$ inches square can you cut from a pan that is **9** inches square?

____

7. Make a list of all **3**-digit numbers for which each digit is a multiple of **3** and no two digits are the same.

____

8. Make a list of all **2**-digit numbers for which each digit is a prime number.

____

____

9. Samantha is thinking of a number. If you add **2.3** to it and then multiply the sum by **1.9**, the result is **12.35**. What is Samantha's number?

____

10. Jamie is thinking of a number. If you subtract **3.5** from it and then divide the difference by **5**, the result is **1.142**. What is Jamie's number?

____

11. Tom wants to fence a field. It goes **40** m due west, then **25** m due south, then **8** m due east, then **10** m due north, then **32** m due east, and then back to the starting point. How much fencing does he need?

____

12. A kitchen is rectangular. Its length is **2** ft more than its width and its area is **120** ft. What are the length and width of the kitchen?

____

Name ______________________

Guided Practice: 1,4
Independent Practice: 2–3, 5–18

Solving Equations with Fractions

STANDARD

You can use inverse operations to solve equations that contain fractions.

1. The inverse of subtracting $\frac{3}{4}$ is adding $\frac{3}{4}$. $n - \frac{3}{4} = \frac{2}{4}$
2. Add $\frac{3}{4}$ to both sides of the equation. $n - \frac{3}{4} + \frac{3}{4} = \frac{2}{4} + \frac{3}{4}$
3. Simplify. $n = \frac{5}{4}$ or $1\frac{1}{4}$

1. The inverse of adding $\frac{3}{4}$ is subtracting $\frac{3}{4}$. $n + \frac{3}{4} = \frac{11}{12}$
2. Subtract $\frac{3}{4}$ from both sides of the equation. $n + \frac{3}{4} - \frac{3}{4} = \frac{11}{12} - \frac{3}{4}$
3. Rewrite fractions with a common denominator if necessary. $n = \frac{11}{12} - \frac{9}{12}$
4. Subtract and simplify. $n = \frac{2}{12}$ or $\frac{1}{6}$

1. The inverse of multiplying by $\frac{3}{4}$ is dividing by $\frac{3}{4}$. $n \times \frac{3}{4} = \frac{6}{20}$
2. Divide both sides of the equation by $\frac{3}{4}$. $n \times \frac{3}{4} \div \frac{3}{4} = \frac{6}{20} \div \frac{3}{4}$
3. Multiply by the reciprocal. $n \times \frac{3}{4} \times \frac{4}{3} = \frac{6}{20} \times \frac{4}{3}$
4. Simplify. $n = \frac{\cancelto{2}{6}}{\cancelto{5}{20}} \times \frac{\cancelto{1}{4}}{\cancelto{1}{3}}$ or $\frac{2}{5}$

1. The inverse of dividing by $\frac{3}{4}$ is multiplying by $\frac{3}{4}$. $n \div \frac{3}{4} = \frac{20}{24}$
2. First divide n by $\frac{3}{4}$. So, multiply by the reciprocal. $\left(n \times \frac{4}{3}\right) \times \frac{3}{4} = \frac{20}{24} \times \frac{3}{4}$
3. Multiply. $n \times \frac{\cancelto{1}{4}}{\cancelto{1}{3}} \times \frac{\cancelto{1}{3}}{\cancelto{1}{4}} = \frac{\cancelto{5}{20}}{\cancelto{8}{24}} \times \frac{\cancelto{1}{3}}{\cancelto{1}{4}}$
4. Simplify. $n = \frac{5}{8}$

Solve.

1. $n - \frac{3}{8} = \frac{2}{8}$ $n =$ ______ $n + \frac{1}{2} = 2\frac{1}{2}$ $n =$ ______ $n - \frac{3}{7} = \frac{1}{7}$ $n =$ ______

2. $n + \frac{1}{3} = \frac{4}{5}$ $n =$ ______ $n - \frac{7}{10} = \frac{2}{6}$ $n =$ ______ $n + \frac{2}{3} = \frac{11}{12}$ $n =$ ______

3. $n - \frac{3}{8} = \frac{2}{8}$ $n =$ ______ $n + \frac{1}{2} = \frac{7}{10}$ $n =$ ______ $n + \frac{5}{6} = \frac{7}{8}$ $n =$ ______

STANDARD

Solve.

4. $n \times \frac{3}{10} = \frac{2}{3}$ $n =$ ______

$n \times \frac{1}{2} = \frac{1}{2}$ $n =$ ______

$n \div \frac{2}{9} = \frac{1}{5}$ $n =$ ______

5. $n \div \frac{1}{15} = \frac{3}{5}$ $n =$ ______

$n + \frac{7}{8} = 3\frac{1}{4}$ $n =$ ______

$n \times \frac{5}{6} = \frac{1}{3}$ $n =$ ______

6. $n - 6\frac{1}{4} = 3\frac{5}{8}$ $n =$ ______

$n \div \frac{3}{10} = 12$ $n =$ ______

$n \times \frac{3}{6} = 1\frac{1}{8}$ $n =$ ______

Problem Solving Reasoning

Use the distance formula $d = r \times t$ to write an equation. Then solve.

7. In baseball a fastball can travel at a speed of **140** ft per s. How long does it take a pitch thrown at this speed to reach the batter who is **$60\frac{1}{2}$** ft away?

Equation ______________

Solution ______________

8. A penguin swims at an average speed of **15** m.p.h. At this speed, how long would it take a penguin to travel **9** miles to a favorite feeding spot?

Equation ______________

Solution ______________

Quick Check

Write the quotient.

9. $2\frac{1}{4} \div 5$ ______ **10.** $\frac{2}{3} \div 6$ ______ **11.** $1\frac{2}{3} \div \frac{1}{5}$ ______

12. $3\frac{3}{8} \div \frac{3}{5}$ ______ **13.** $1\frac{1}{2} \div 1\frac{3}{4}$ ______ **14.** $4\frac{4}{5} \div 1\frac{2}{3}$ ______

Solve the equation.

15. $k + 2\frac{1}{2} = 5\frac{1}{4}$ ______ **16.** $\frac{9}{10} = \frac{s}{45}$ ______

17. $7\frac{2}{3} = k - 2\frac{3}{4}$ ______ **18.** $t \times 4\frac{1}{5} = 1\frac{3}{4}$ ______

Work Space.

Name ______________________

Write each sum, difference, product, or quotient in simplest form.

1. $2\frac{1}{10} - \frac{1}{2}$ ______

2. $\frac{1}{6} + \frac{4}{9}$ ______

3. $5\frac{3}{4} + \frac{1}{3}$ ______

4. $14\frac{1}{8} - 7\frac{2}{3}$ ______

5. $\frac{2}{5} \times \frac{5}{9}$ ______

6. $\frac{7}{12} \div \frac{1}{4}$ ______

7. $1\frac{1}{3} \div 6$ ______

8. $7 \times 1\frac{7}{12}$ ______

Solve. Write your answer in simplest form.

9. $\frac{3}{4}$ of 32 = ______

10. $\frac{5}{8}$ of $1\frac{1}{2}$ = ______

11. $\frac{1}{16}$ of 40 = ______

Solve for n. Write your answer in simplest form.

12. $n + \frac{5}{8} = 2$ $n =$ ______

13. $n \times \frac{3}{8} = \frac{1}{8}$ $n =$ ______

14. $n \div \frac{2}{9} = 18$ $n =$ ______

15. $n - \frac{1}{4} = \frac{3}{4}$ $n =$ ______

16. $n \times 1\frac{1}{3} = 3$ $n =$ ______

17. $n \div \frac{7}{10} = \frac{2}{3}$ $n =$ ______

18. $n - \frac{5}{6} = \frac{9}{24}$ $n =$ ______

19. $n + \frac{4}{5} = 3\frac{1}{2}$ $n =$ ______

Solve.

20. Suppose a pictograph was made to display the data in the table. One symbol on the pictograph would represent how many hours of studying? Explain.

____

____

Hours Studied Last Week	
Jason	12
Su	6
Reg	18
Marie	9

21. Without overlapping, what is the maximum number of **2** × **4** rectangles that can be drawn on a **6** × **10** grid? ______

Name ______________________________

1

Sunny Days, By Month	
May	☼ ☼ ◖
June	☼ ☼ ☼
July	☼ ☼ ☼ ◖
August	☼ ☼ ☼ ◖
September	☼ ☼ ◖
Key: ☼ = 6 days	

How many more sunny days were there in July than in May?

A 1 **C** 3

B 2 **D** 6

2 **What do you need to do to each side of this equation to solve it?**

$$\frac{2}{3}n = \frac{8}{9}$$

F Multiply by n.

G Multiply by $\frac{3}{2}$.

H Multiply by $\frac{2}{3}$.

J Multiply by $\frac{9}{8}$.

3 **Martin has read $\frac{2}{5}$ of a book. He needs to read $\frac{3}{4}$ of it for school tomorrow. Which equation could be used to find how much more he needs to read?**

A $\frac{2}{5} + p = \frac{3}{4}$ **C** $\frac{3}{4}p = \frac{2}{5}$

B $p - \frac{3}{4} = \frac{2}{5}$ **D** $\frac{2}{5}p = \frac{3}{4}$

4 **Which number is divisible by *both* 5 and 9?**

F 18 **H** 40 **K** NH

G 25 **J** 45

5 **Jessica has $2\frac{3}{4}$ cups of sesame seeds. She needs $\frac{1}{4}$ cup for each batch of cookies she makes. How many batches can she make?**

A 1 **C** 8 **E** NH

B 6 **D** 11

6 **Stan's foot is $10\frac{3}{8}$ inches long. How is that number written as a decimal?**

F 10.3 **H** 10.38 **K** NH

G 10.375 **J** 10.385

7 **How much closer to Centerville is Easton than West Lake?**

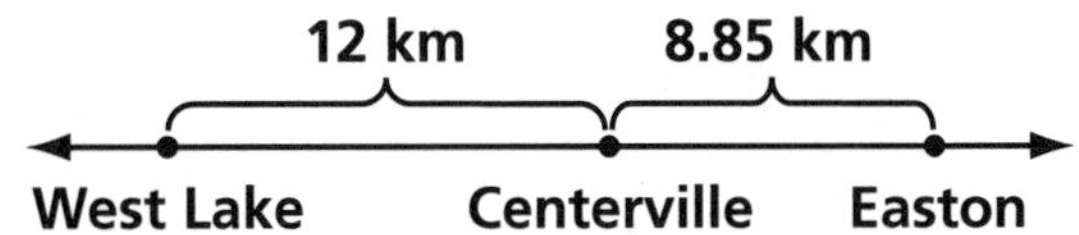

A 3.15 km **C** 4.15 km

B 3.85 km **D** 4.85 km

8 **What is the prime factorization of 60?**

F $3 \times 4 \times 5$

G $2 \times 2 \times 3 \times 5$

H $2 \times 5 \times 6$

J $2 \times 3 \times 10$

UNIT 5 • TABLE OF CONTENTS

Measurement

We will be using this vocabulary:

meter (m) a basic unit of length in the metric system

liter (L) a unit of capacity in the metric system

Celsius temperature scale (°C) the temperature scale in the metric system in which the freezing temperature of water is **0°C** and its boiling temperature is **100°C**

Fahrenheit temperature scale (°F) the temperature scale that is used in the United States in which the freezing temperature of water is **32°F** and its boiling temperature is **212°F**

Dear Family,

During the next few weeks, our math class will be learning about measurement. You can expect to see homework that provides practice with determining elapsed time. Here is a sample you may want to keep handy to give help if needed.

Elapsed Time

The amount of time that passes between the start and end of an event is the elapsed time.

Example: A movie begins at **1:15 P.M.** and ends at **3:30 P.M.** To determine how much time elapsed from the beginning of the movie to the end, subtract.

3:30	→	3 h 30 min
− 1:15	→	− 1 h 15 min
		2 h 15 min

Some elapsed time problems require renaming **1** hour as **60** minutes.

Example: A student begins studying at **7:15 P.M.** and stops at **9:05 P.M.** To determine how much time the student spent studying, subtract.

				8 h 65 min (renamed)
9:05	→	9 h 05 min	→	~~9~~ h ~~05~~ min
− 7:15	→	− 7 h 15 min	→	− 7 h 15 min
		1 h 50 min		1 h 50 min

During this unit, students will need to continue to practice finding elapsed time and using other forms of measurement.

Sincerely,

Name ______________________

Metric Units of Length

STANDARD

The basic unit for measuring length in the metric system is the **meter**.

Look at the chart. Notice how the prefix of each unit of measure tells you how that unit of length is related to the meter. The **dekameter** and the **decimeter** are used less often than the other units.

Units of Measure

1 **kilo**meter (km)	= 1,000 meters
1 **hecto**meter (hm)	= 100 meters
1 **deka**meter (da)	= 10 meters
1 **deci**meter (dm)	= 0.1 meter
1 **centi**meter (cm)	= 0.01 meter
1 **milli**meter (mm)	= 0.001 meter

A compact disc is about **1 millimeter** thick.
A penny is about **2 centimeters** wide.
A doorknob is about **1 meter** above the floor.
The distance from New York to San Francisco is about **4,720 kilometers.**

To change from one unit of measure to another in the metric system, multiply or divide by a power of 10. Study the chart at the right.

Divide	Multiply
To change from a lesser unit to a greater unit	To change from a greater unit to a lesser unit

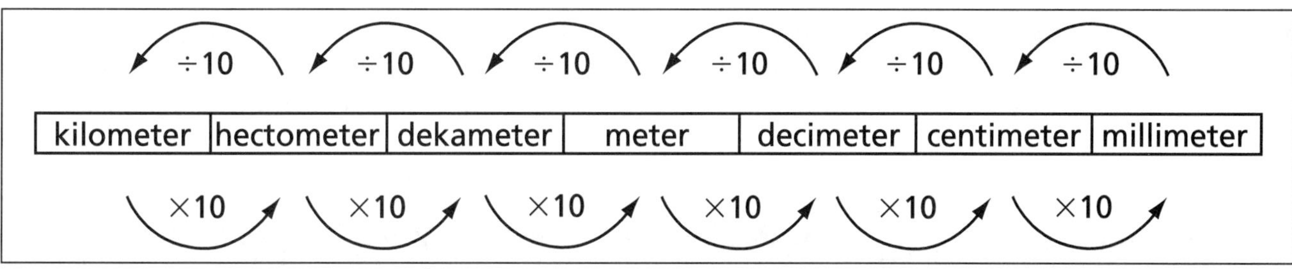

What metric unit of length would you use to measure each item?

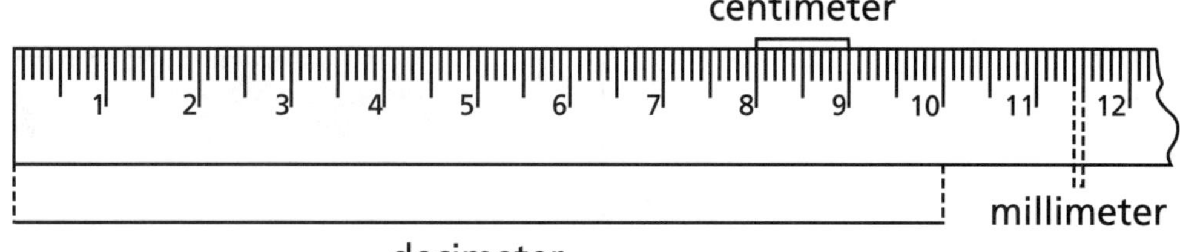

1. the width of a paper clip ______ the length of a baseball bat ______
2. the thickness of a rubber band ______ the width of this book ______
3. the length of your classroom ______ the distance to a city ______

Circle the greater length.

4. **10** cm or **96** mm **72** mm or **7** cm **3** m or **302** cm
5. **4** m or **380** cm **946** mm or **1** m **200** m or **215** cm

STANDARD

Complete the table. Each row should contain equivalent measures.

	Kilometer	Meter	Decimeter	Centimeter	Millimeter
6.	8				
7.		7			
8.			4,000		
9.					1,600,000
10.				3,200	

Find the equivalent measure.

11. 2 m = __________ cm   300 cm = __________ m   6 dm = __________ mm

12. 400 cm = __________ mm   2,000 mm = __________ m   40 cm = __________ dm

13. 300 cm = __________ dm   20 dm = __________ m   2,000 mm = __________ cm

14. 70 mm = __________ m   4 m = __________ da   500 m = __________ hm

15. 5,000 m = __________ km   47 km = __________ m   500 cm = __________ km

Problem Solving
Reasoning

Solve.

16. One race in the Summer Olympic Games is **5,000** meters long. How many kilometers is that? __________

17. In 1968, Bob Beamon set an Olympic long-jump record. He jumped **890.21** cm. How many meters is that, to the nearest meter? __________

Test Prep ★ Mixed Review

18 **Michelle ran a race in 17.4 seconds. Lorna ran the same distance in 1.64 fewer seconds. How long did Lorna run?**

A 19.04 s

B 15.86 s

C 15.76 s

D 15.7 s

19 **This table shows the results of a contest to see who could grow the heaviest squash.**

Owner	Weight of Squash
Latoya	13.5 lb
Mandy	14.8 lb
Robert	12.2 lb
Jonathan	13.2 lb

Which list shows the owners in order from heaviest to lightest squash?

F Latoya, Mandy, Robert, Jonathan

G Mandy, Latoya, Jonathan, Robert

H Jonathan, Robert, Mandy, Latoya

J Robert, Jonathan, Latoya, Mandy

Name ______________________

Metric Units of Capacity and Mass

STANDARD

The basic unit of capacity in the metric system is the **liter (L)**. Science experiments and European recipes both use the metric system of capacity. Liquid products are often labeled in metric units.

Units of Capacity	
1 liter (L)	= **1,000** milliliters (mL)
1 milliliter	= **0.001** liter
1 half liter	= **500** milliliters

Estimate the capacity of the container in milliliters.

1. mug ______ soda can ______

2. soup bowl ______ small water bottle ______

3. water glass ______ small milk carton ______

Estimate the capacity of the container in liters.

4. milk carton ______ laundry detergent bottle ______

5. flower vase ______ small wastebasket ______

Circle the best estimate of the capacity of each item.

6. spoon	**5** L	**500** mL	**5** mL
7. swimming pool	**75** mL	**750** L	**75,000** L
8. aquarium	**25** mL	**25** L	**250** mL
9. can of soup	**3** mL	**300** mL	**300** L

Write the equivalent measure.

10. **3** L = ________ mL **2,000** mL = ________ L

11. **250** mL = ________ L **1.3** L = ________ mL

12. **0.4** L = ________ mL **2,400** mL = ________ L

13. a half liter = ________ mL **0.05** L = ________ mL

Circle the greater capacity.

14. **5.0** mL or **0.05** L	**3.4** L or **250** mL	**2.15** L or **15** mL
15. **0.100** L or **1,000** mL	**12** L or **1,200** mL	**3.500** mL or **35** mL
16. **7.5** L or **7,500** L	**400** mL or **4** L	**3.66** L or **6,000.3** mL
17. **900** mL or **0.19** L	**900** L or **999** mL	**1,000** mL or **10** L

STANDARD

The basic unit of **mass** in the metric system is the **gram (g)**. A new pencil has a mass of about **5** grams. The mass of a smaller object, such as a vitamin pill, is measured in **milligrams (mg)**.

Units of Mass
1 metric ton = **1,000** kilograms (kg)
1 kilogram = **1,000** grams (g)
1 gram = **1,000** milligrams (mg)

Estimate the mass of each item in grams.

18. pencil ______ small notebook ______ pencil eraser ______

19. chalkboard eraser ______ ballpoint pen ______ clothespin ______

Circle the best estimate of the mass of each item.

20.	paper clip	**1** g	**1** mg	**1** kg
21.	dictionary	**2** kg	**2** g	**2** mg
22.	sandwich	**250** mg	**250** g	**250** kg
23.	scissors	**5.2** g	**52** g	**520** g
24.	key	**130** g	**1.3** g	**13** g
25.	fried egg	**50** mg	**50** g	**50** kg

Write the equivalent measure.

26. **3** kg = ______ g

15.2 g = ______ mg

27. **10,000** kg = ______ metric tons

683 g = ______ kg

28. **8.26** kg = ______ g

5.7 mg = ______ g

29. **0.097** kg = ______ g or ______ mg

3,256 mg = ______ g or ______ kg

Problem Solving
Reasoning

Solve.

30. If one new pencil has a mass of **5** g, how many new pencils would be needed to have a mass of **1** kg? ______

31. If 1 pill contains **8** mg of medicine, how many pills could be made from **2** g of medicine? ______

Test Prep ★ Mixed Review

32 **Mrs. Horn had a 25-pound bag of flour. Her daughter used some of the flour. Now Mrs. Horn has 23.66 pounds of flour. Which equation could be used to find how much flour (f) her daughter used?**

A $23.66 + f = 25$

B $23.66f = 25$

C $25 \div f = 23.66$

D $f - 23.66 = 25$

33 **What is the prime factorization of 72?**

F $2 \times 2 \times 2 \times 9$

G $2 \times 2 \times 2 \times 3 \times 3$

H $2 \times 4 \times 3 \times 3$

J 8×9

Name ________________________________

Temperature: The Celsius Scale

STANDARD

A thermometer measures temperature. A unit of measure for temperature is called the **degree** (°). The thermometer pictured here shows temperature in **degrees Celsius** (°C). The boiling point of water in degrees Celsius is **100°C**. The freezing point of water is **0°C**. Study the thermometer at the right and read the temperatures shown.

Temperatures below freezing are sometimes written with a raised minus sign. You read ⁻**20**° as "**20** degrees below **0**."

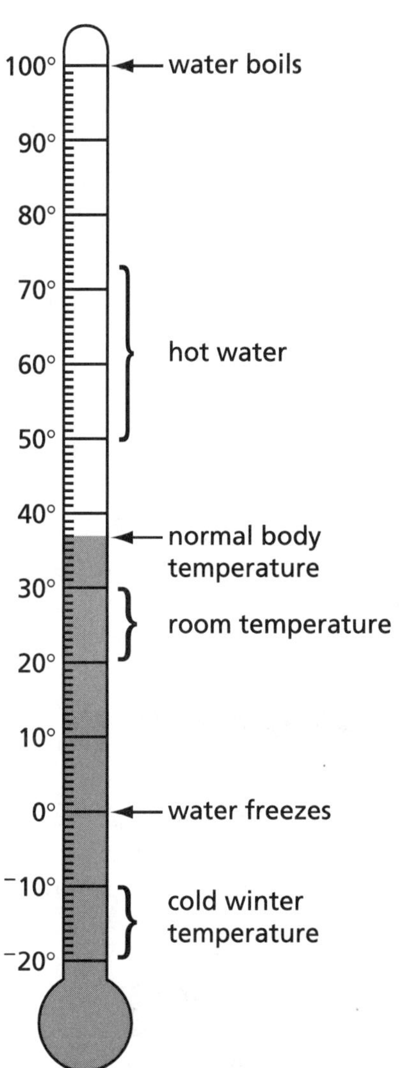

Complete.

1. Normal body temperature is ______ °C.

2. If the temperature of your classroom were **15°C,** would you be cold? Write *Yes* or *No.* ______

3. When water turns to ice, you know that the temperature of the water has reached ______°C.

4. What is the difference in degrees between the freezing and boiling points of water on the Celsius scale? ______

Complete each table. Use the thermometer to help you.

	Temperature	Change	New Temperature
5.	5°C	rise of 2°C	
6.	5°C	fall of 8°C	
7.	0°C		36°C
8.		fall of 15°C	21°C

	Temperature	Change	New Temperature
9.	7°C		⁻7°C
10.	24°C		21°C
11.	⁻8°C	fall of 2°C	
12.	⁻8°C	rise of 2°C	

Write *True* or *False* for each statement.

13. The difference between ⁻**10°C** and **10°C** is the same as the difference between **5°C** and ⁻**5°C.** ______

14. On a hot summer day, the temperature would be below **15°C.** ______

15. The temperature of a warm bath will be **20°C** or warmer. ______

STANDARD

The Science Club made a line graph of the average monthly temperature for eight months.

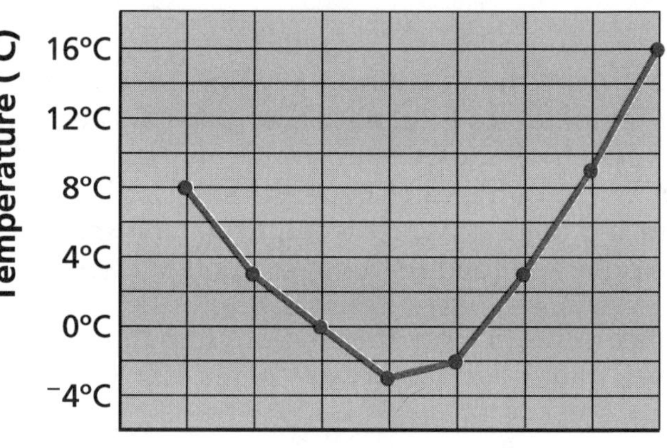

Complete each statement.

16. The average temperature in November was about _______ °C.

17. a. Which month was the coldest? ___________________

b. What was the average temperature for that month? _______

18. What was the increase in average temperature from April to May? _______ degrees.

19. Between which two consecutive months was the average change the greatest? ________________________

Problem Solving
Reasoning

Solve.

20. Find the daily high temperatures of your city or town for a week by using a newspaper, radio, or TV weather broadcast. Graph those temperatures on a separate sheet of graph paper.

Quick Check

Write the equivalent units of length, mass, or capacity.

Work Space.

21. 200 mm = _______ cm

22. 1.75 m = _______ cm

23. 755 mL = _______ L

24. 36 mg = _______ g

The thermometer shows the same scale as the one on p. 135. Use it to solve.

25. What temperature is shown on the thermometer? _______

26. At what temperature on this thermometer will water freeze? _______

Name ______________________________

Problem Solving Strategy: Use a Simpler Problem

STANDARD

Sometimes you can solve a problem by looking at simpler similar problems and finding a pattern.

Problem

How many squares are on a checkerboard?

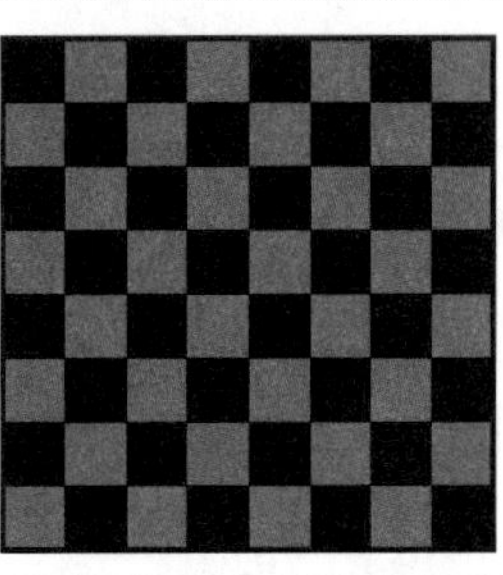

1 Understand As you reread, ask yourself questions.

- What are the different-size squares that are on the board?

1 × 1, 2 × 2, ______________________

2 Decide Choose a method for solving.

Try the strategy
Use a Simpler Problem.

- Make a chart to record the number of squares on a **1 × 1** board, a **2 × 2** board, and so on.

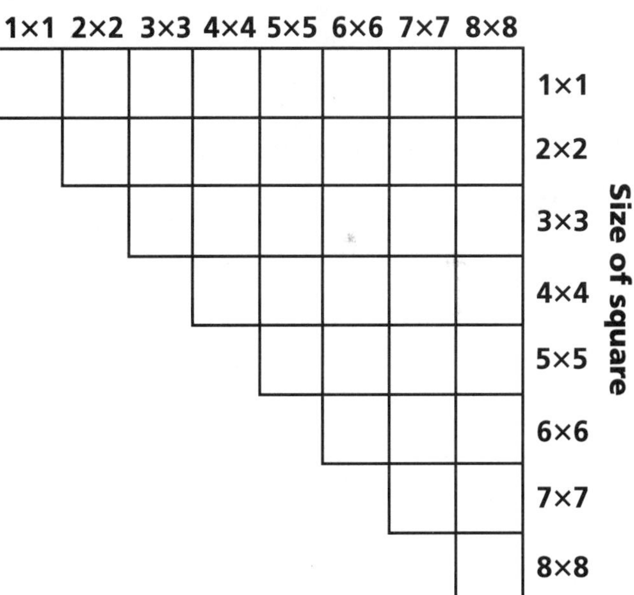

3 Solve Fill in the chart.

- Fill in the columns in the chart for the **1 × 1** board, the **2 × 2** board, the **3 × 3** board, and the **4 × 4** board.
- Look for a pattern that can help you complete the chart.
- Add the numbers in the last column. What is the total? ______

4 Look back Answer __________

- What kind of numbers are in the chart? ____________

STANDARD

Solve. Use the Use a Simpler Problem strategy or any other strategy you have learned.

Use this sequence of figures for problems 1 and 2.

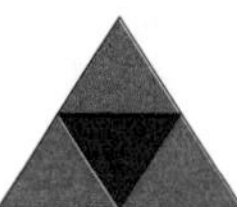

Figure 1 Figure 2 Figure 3

1. If the pattern continues, how many ▲'s will there be in Figure **6**? ______

2. If the pattern continues, how many 's will there be in Figure **6**? ______

Use this sequence of figures for problems 3 and 4.

Figure 1 Figure 2 Figure 3

3. If the pattern continues, how many 's will there be in Figure **6**? ______

4. 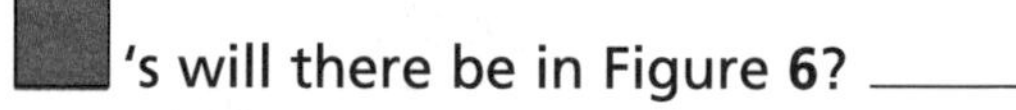
If the pattern continues, how many ■'s will there be in Figure **6**? ______

5. The organizers of a celebration plan to release **100** balloons. They have purchased a **100**-yard spool of string. They plan to cut the string into **100** **1**-yard pieces. How many cuts will they have to make?

______

6. Julian sold raffle tickets to earn money for a school play. The tickets were numbered in order. The first ticket he sold was numbered **389**. The last ticket was numbered **521**. How many tickets did Julian sell?

______

7. Write the next number in this sequence.

3.25, 6.5, 13, 26, ______

8. The sum of two numbers is **3**. Their product is **2.09**. What are the numbers?

______

9. The sum of a number and one-half of the number is 5.7. What is the number?

______

10. Ten students will work in pairs for a social studies project. How many ways can the 10 students be paired?

______

Name ______________________

Times Zones and Elapsed Time

STANDARD

All over the world, time is regulated by a single system called **Standard Time**. According to this system, the world is divided into regions called time zones. Within each time zone, a single time is used. In the continental United States, not including Alaska and Hawaii, there are four time zones. From east to west, they are the Eastern, Central, Mountain, and Pacific Standard Time.

The chart shows how the time changes as you travel from one zone to another. Look at the first row of the chart. It shows what time it is in each of the other zones when it is **1:00** in the Pacific Standard Time zone.

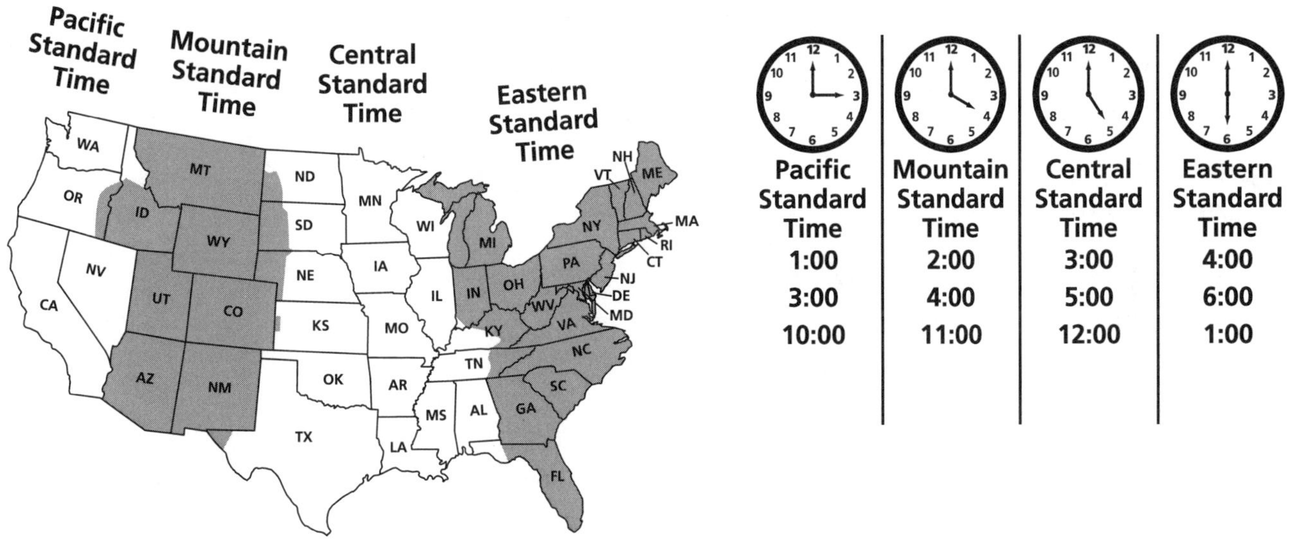

Pacific Standard Time	Mountain Standard Time	Central Standard Time	Eastern Standard Time
1:00	2:00	3:00	4:00
3:00	4:00	5:00	6:00
10:00	11:00	12:00	1:00

When it is **2:00** P.M. in Chicago, IL (Central Standard Time), what time is it in each city? Use A.M. and P.M.

1. Buffalo, NY ________ Atlanta, GA ________ Denver, CO ________

2. Dallas, TX ________ Baltimore, MD ________ Los Angeles, CA ________

3. Phoenix, AZ ________ Portland, OR ________ St. Louis, MO ________

Complete.

4. If it is **2:30** P.M. in the Eastern Standard Time zone, in the Pacific Standard Time zone it is ________

5. Joe lives in the Eastern Standard Time zone. At **9:00** P.M. he calls his aunt who lives in Montana. At his aunt's house the time is ________

6. If you travel across the country from the East to the Pacific Coast, do you gain or lose time? ________ If you travel from the West to the Atlantic Coast, you ________ time.

STANDARD

You can add, subtract, multiply, and divide with elapsed times.

The morning session in Sally's school lasts **2** h **45** min. The afternoon session lasts **2** h **15** min. What is the total number of hours and minutes of the two sessions?

```
  2 h 45 min
+ 2 h 15 min
  4 h 60 min = 5 h 0 min or 5 h
```

It took Juan **3** min **10** s to do an exercise routine. Carlos did it in **1** min **55** s. How much longer did it take Juan?

```
  2        70
  3̸ min 1̸0̸ s
− 1 min 55 s
  1 min 15 s
```

First rename **3** min **10** s as **2** min **70** s.

To assemble **1** automobile part takes **4** minutes and **13** seconds. How much time will it take to assemble **10** parts?

```
   4 min 13 s
        × 10
  40 min 130 s = 42 min 10 s
```

If Trina can assemble **8** parts in **33** minutes and **20** seconds, what is her average assembly time for **1** part?

```
    4 min 10 s
8)33 min 2̸0̸ s
 − 32min
     1 m̶i̶n̶ 80 s
         − 80 s
             0
```

Rename **1** min **20** s as **80** s.

Solve. Add, subtract, multiply, or divide.

7. 2 h 30 min + 6 h 15 min   1 h 45 min + 3 h 20 min   4 h 20 min − 2 h 40 min   2 h 15 min − 1 h 55 min

8. 14 min 6 s × 12   2 h 20 min × 10   8 h 5 min × 6   20 min 20 s × 15

9. 3)10 h 30 min   5)30 h 50 min   6)6 days 12 h   8)2 days 8 min

Problem Solving Reasoning Solve.

10. In 1952, Emil Zatopek of Czechoslovakia won the Olympic **5,000** meter run in **14** min **6** s. What was his average time per **1,000** meters? Give your answer to the nearest second. ________

Test Prep ★ Mixed Review

11 Renee ran a 6.2 kilometer road race. How many meters is 6.2 kilometers?

A 6.2   **C** 620

B 62   **D** 6,200

12 Jenna made punch for a school party. She used 2 liters of sparkling water, 1.5 liters of orange juice, and 1.75 liters of pineapple juice. How much punch did she make?

F 5.25 L   **H** 3.75 L

G 4.25 L   **J** 3.5 L

Name ______________________________

Customary Units of Length

STANDARD

The chart shows the relationship between units of length in the **Customary System.**

Units of Length	
12 inches (in.)	= 1 foot (ft)
3 feet	= 1 yard (yd)
36 inches	= 1 yard
5,280 feet	= 1 mile (mi)
1,760 yards	= 1 mile

Write the unit of length you would use to measure each of the following. If you cannot use a unit of length, write an X in the blank.

1. The length of a rug ______________

2. The weight of a dozen oranges ______________

3. The distance from Canada to Mexico ______________

4. The length of a pencil ______________

Circle the greater length.

5.	11 in. or 1 ft	1 ft 6 in. or 16 in.	3 ft or 38 in.
6.	7 ft or 2 yd	1 ft 9 in. or 2 ft	4 ft 2 in. or 54 in.
7.	$3\frac{1}{2}$ ft or 1 yd	29 in. or 2 ft	6 yards or 17 ft
8.	8,000 ft or 1 mi	10,000 ft or 2 mi	6,000 yards or 3 mi
9.	110 in. or 3 yd	3,510 ft or 2 mi	10,000 ft or 3 mi

Write the equivalent measure.

10.	6 ft = ______ in.	72 in. = ______ yd	$\frac{1}{2}$ mi = ______ yd
11.	$\frac{1}{2}$ ft = ______ in.	18 ft = ______ yd	6 in. = ______ ft
12.	$1\frac{1}{4}$ ft = ______ in.	2 mi = ________ ft	6 in. = ______ yd
13.	0.5 yd = ________ ft	$\frac{2}{3}$ yd = ______ ft	$1\frac{1}{3}$ yd = ______ in.
14.	5,280 yd = ______ mi	60 in. = ______ ft	2,640 ft = ________ mi
15.	36 in. = ______ ft	18 in. = ______ ft	$\frac{1}{12}$ yd = ______ in.
16.	$\frac{1}{10}$ mi = ______ ft	176 yd = ______ mi	10 yd = ______ in.

STANDARD

0 1 2 3 4
inches

The length of the line segment measured to the

nearest inch (") is **2** in. nearest $\frac{1}{2}$ inch is $1\frac{1}{2}$".

nearest $\frac{1}{4}$ inch is $1\frac{3}{4}$". nearest $\frac{1}{8}$ inch is $1\frac{5}{8}$".

Measure line segment *AB* as indicated.

A *B*

17. nearest inch ________ nearest half-inch ________

18. nearest quarter-inch ________ nearest eighth-inch ________

Draw a segment for each length.

19. $3\frac{1}{2}$"

20. $4\frac{1}{4}$"

Problem Solving Reasoning **Solve.**

21. If **2** curtains require fabric that is **7** yards long, how many curtains can be made from $17\frac{1}{2}$ yards of fabric? ______

22. One necktie uses a **30** in. length of fabric. How many feet of fabric are needed to make **6** neckties? ______

Quick Check

Find the elapsed time.

23. From **9:15** A.M. to **12:33** P.M. ________

24. From **2:34** P.M. to **4:08** P.M. ________

25. From **6** P.M. in New York to **10:30** P.M. in Seattle (**3** time zones west of New York) ________

Write the equivalent measure.

26. 20 ft = ________ yd

27. 79 in. = ________ ft

28. $\frac{1}{2}$ mi = ________ ft

Work Space.

Name ______________________________

Customary Units of Capacity and Weight

STANDARD

You can measure the amount of liquid a container can hold by using units such as the **cup** and the **quart.**

Have you heard of the liquid unit called **fluid ounce (fl oz)?** Many of the bottled liquids that you can buy are measured in fluid ounces. There are **8** fluid ounces in a cup, **16** fluid ounces in a **pint, 32** fluid ounces in a **quart,** and **128** fluid ounces in a **gallon.**

Units of Capacity

8 fluid ounces (fl oz) = **1** cup (c)
2 cups = **1** pint (pt)
16 fluid ounces = **1** pint
2 pints = **1** quart (qt)
4 quarts = **1** gallon (gal)

Write the equivalent measure.

1.	2 c = ______ pt	32 fl oz = ______ c	1 qt = ______ pt
2.	1 c = ______ fl oz	3 gal = ______ qt	1 pt = ______ fl oz
3.	$\frac{1}{2}$ gal = ______ qt	$\frac{1}{2}$ gal = ______ pt	$\frac{1}{4}$ gal = ______ c
4.	3 qt = ______ pt	1 pt = ______ qt	1 qt = ______ gal
5.	16 fl oz = ______ c	16 fl oz = ______ qt	16 fl oz = ______ gal
6.	$\frac{1}{4}$ pt = ______ fl oz	$\frac{1}{4}$ pt = ______ c	1 gal = ______ fl oz
7.	7 gal = ______ qt	8 qt = ______ gal	20 pt = ______ qt

Compare. Write <, >, or =.

8.	12 fl oz ◯ 1 c	64 fl oz ◯ 2 qt	3 gal ◯ 22 pt
9.	1 gal ◯ 8 pt	5 qt ◯ 2 gal	6c ◯ 44 fl oz
10.	12 pt ◯ 3 gal	$\frac{1}{2}$ c ◯ 3 fl oz	$\frac{1}{4}$ qt ◯ 1 c
11.	$\frac{1}{2}$ qt ◯ 18 fl oz	3 qt ◯ 7 pt	$\frac{1}{2}$ pt ◯ 1 c
12.	$\frac{1}{8}$ gal ◯ 2 pt	$\frac{1}{2}$ gal ◯ 8 pt	0.5 c ◯ 16 fl oz
13.	0.25 gal ◯ 1 qt	0.75 gal ◯ 7 pt	24 qt ◯ 4 gal
14.	100 qt ◯ 25 gal	100 fl oz ◯ 10 c	160 fl oz ◯ 10 pt

STANDARD

The basic unit of weight in the Customary System is the **pound.**

- Four sticks of margarine weigh 1 pound.
- A car weighs about $1\frac{1}{2}$ tons.

Units of Weight
16 ounces (oz) = 1 pound (lb)
2,000 pounds = 1 ton

Complete.

15. 9 tons = ________ lb 3 lb = ________ oz 96 oz = ________ lb

16. $\frac{1}{2}$ lb = ________ oz $3\frac{3}{4}$ lb = ________ oz 0.5 ton = ________ lb

17. 0.5 ton = ________ oz 160 oz = ________ lb 10,000 lb = ________ tons

18. 4 oz = ________ lb 0.75 lb = ________ oz $\frac{3}{4}$ ton = ________ lb

Compare. $<$, $>$, or $=$.

19. 32 oz ◯ 0.5 lb 96 oz ◯ 20 lb 0.5 ton ◯ 10,000 lb

20. 80 oz ◯ 6 lb 3 lb ◯ 50 oz 1,750 lb ◯ $\frac{3}{4}$ ton

21. 320 oz ◯ 10 lb 3,000 lb ◯ 1.5 tons 61 oz ◯ 4 lb

22. 82 oz ◯ 5 lb 0.75 ton ◯ 1,700 lb $1\frac{1}{4}$ tons ◯ 2,800 lb

Problem Solving
Reasoning

Solve.

23. How many pounds of nails will be needed to fill one hundred boxes with 8 oz of nails in each? ________

24. How many pint bottles can be filled from 16 gal 3 qt of water? ________

25. Mrs. Ross's car used an average of 8 gal 3 qt of gasoline per week. How many gallons did the car use in 4 weeks?

____

26. A class is mailing 10 gift packages weighing 2 lb 10 oz each. What is the total weight of the packages?

____

Test Prep ★ Mixed Review

27 What do you need to do to each side of this equation to solve it?

$x + 4\frac{7}{8} = 9\frac{3}{5}$

A Add x **C** Subtract x

B Add $4\frac{7}{8}$ **D** Subtract $4\frac{7}{8}$

28 This table shows how far John jogged after school during one week.

Day	Mon	Tues	Wed	Thurs	Fri
Distance	$2\frac{1}{2}$ mi	$2\frac{2}{3}$ mi	$1\frac{5}{8}$ mi	$1\frac{7}{8}$ mi	$2\frac{5}{8}$ mi

Which list shows the days he ran in order from greatest to least distance?

F Monday, Tuesday, Wednesday, Thursday, Friday
G Tuesday, Friday, Monday, Thursday, Wednesday
H Wednesday, Thursday, Monday, Friday, Tuesday
J Monday, Wednesday, Friday, Thursday, Tuesday

Name ______________________

Line Graphs and Fahrenheit Temperature

STANDARD

The line graph shows the average monthly high temperature in the city where Melanie lives. Study the graph and use it to answer the questions below.

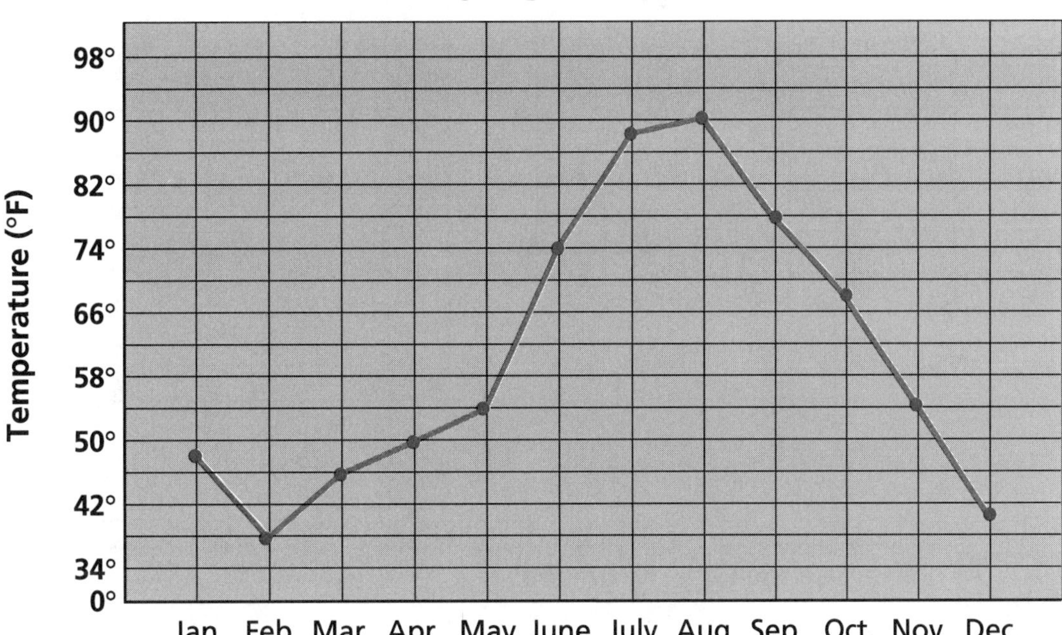

1. Look at the scale on the vertical axis. How many degrees does each interval represent?

____

2. What is the range of temperatures shown in the graph? ______________

3. True or false? The average high temperature was higher in January than in August.

____

4. What was the average high temperature in July? ______________

5. What was the average high temperature in January? ______________

6. Between which two consecutive months did the monthly high temperature change the most? ______________

7. Between which two consecutive months did the monthly high temperature change the least? ______________

8. How would the graph between August and December change if the number of degrees that each interval on the *y*-axis represents was divided by **2**? Explain.

____

____

STANDARD

For a project on weather, Julian recorded the greatest temperature each day for one week. The chart shows the data he collected. Use the data to complete the line graph. Remember to title the graph. Be sure to choose a scale that will allow you to show all the temperatures accurately.

Monday	78°
Tuesday	83°
Wednesday	85°
Thursday	80°
Friday	74°
Saturday	71°
Sunday	75°

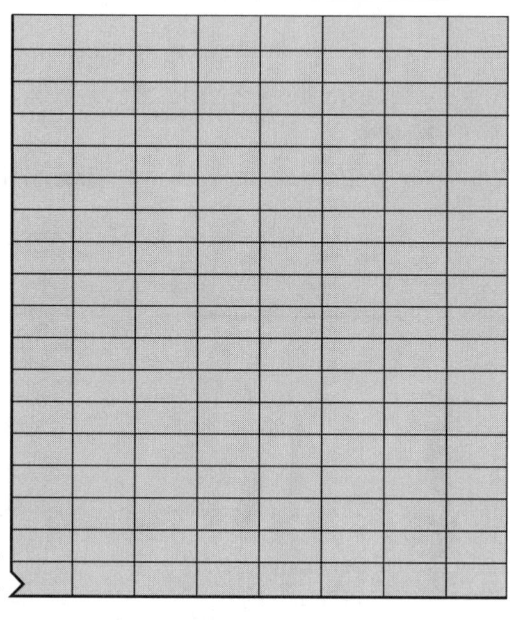

Problem Solving
Reasoning

Solve. Use the data shown above.

9. What was the average temperature recorded? ____________

10. What was the range of temperatures? ____________

11. How would the graph change if you increased the number of degrees represented by each interval along the *y*-axis? ____________

12. Describe how the temperatures changed during the week, according to the graph you made. ____________

Quick Check

Write the equivalent weight or capacity.

13. 36 oz = _____ lb **14.** 75 pt = _____ gal **15.** 50 fl oz = _____ c

Work Space.

Solve.

16. Suppose you are plotting the following temperatures on a line graph: **5°F, 25°F, 17°F, 45°F, 32°F.** If the graph will be drawn on 10-by-10 grid, what interval will you use on the *y*-axis?

____

Name ________________________________

Problem Solving Application: Choose the Operation

STANDARD

In this lesson you will solve problems about metric and customary measurements. You will need to decide whether to add, subtract, multiply, or divide. To solve some of the problems you may need to use more than one operation.

Tips to Remember:

1. Understand 2. Decide 3. Solve 4. Look back

- Try to remember a real-life situation like the one described in the problem. What do you remember that might help you find a solution?
- Find the action in the problem. Is there more than one action? Which operation shows the action best: addition, subtraction, multiplication, or division?
- Predict the answer. Then solve the problem. Compare your answer with your prediction.

Solve.

1. Walter is **1.29** meters tall. His sister is **8** centimeters taller. How tall is Walter's sister?

Think: How many centimeters is **1.29** meters?

____

Answer ________________________

2. Mary Lou is **6** feet **2** inches tall. Her brother is **10** inches shorter. How tall is Mary Lou's brother?

Think: How many inches are in a foot?

____

Answer ________________________

3. Rachel wants to buy a train of letters that spells the name of her sister Gloria. The engine and caboose cost **$4.95** each. Each letter costs **$2.95**. How much will the train cost?

____

4. Matthew has a **60**-foot length of cord that he plans to cut into **24** pieces of equal size. How long will each piece be?

____

5. A holiday roll of wrapping paper costs **$8.50**. A roll of plain wrapping paper costs $\frac{2}{5}$ less. How much does the plain wrapping paper cost?

____

6. A jumbo roll of ribbon is $\frac{2}{3}$ longer than the regular roll. The jumbo roll of ribbon is **55** ft. How long is the regular roll?

____

STANDARD

Solve.

7. When Peter was sick, he had a temperature of **38.5°** Celsius. A normal temperature is **37°** Celsius. How many degrees above normal was his temperature?

____

8. When Diego was born, he weighed **7** pounds **15** ounces. While he was in the hospital, he lost **2** ounces and then gained **4** ounces. What was his weight after the loss and gain?

____

9. In a two-day snowstorm, the total snowfall was **1** foot **4** inches. If **10** inches fell the first day, how much fell the second day?

____

10. When a truck driver left on a trip, the odometer read **1,356.7** miles. When the driver returned, it read **1,529.1** miles. How many miles were traveled?

____

11. For an experiment, the science class weighed **6** identical metal bars. The total weight was **46.8** kilograms. How much did each bar weigh?

____

12. The state of New Mexico has an area of **121,598** square miles. There is an average of **13.86** people per square mile. What is the population of New Mexico to the nearest whole number?

____

Extend Your Thinking

13. Use the information from problem **12** and the pictures below to estimate the area of the state of Mississippi.

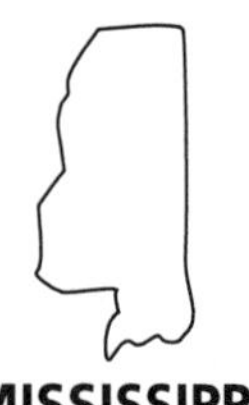

____

14. Explain the method you used to make your estimate in problem **13**. Then look up the actual area of Mississippi and compare your estimate with the actual area.

____

____

____

____

15. One train averages **48** mph. Another train averages **56** mph. How many more miles will the faster train cover in **8** hours?

____

16. A town received **6** ft **8** in. of rain last year. This year it received **10** in. less rain. How much rain did it receive this year?

____

Name ______________________________

Unit 5 Review

Measure segment *CD* to each unit of measure.

C ——————————————— *D*

1. nearest half-inch _____

2. nearest centimeter _____

Complete.

3. 1,000 mm = _____ cm

4. 2.4 km = _________ cm

5. 12 ft = _____ yd

Compare. Write <, >, or =.

6. 1 min 10 s ◯ 75 s

7. 45 min ◯ $\frac{3}{4}$ h

8. 4 h 30 min ◯ 200 min

Circle the greater measure.

9. 5 c or 2 pt

10. 13 oz or 1 lb

11. 2.7 kg or 350 g

Circle the temperature that is most likely.

12. Water freezes. 100°C or 0°C

13. Water boils. 100°F or 212°F

Solve.

14.
3 ft 4 in.
+ 4 ft 9 in.

15.
1 wk 5 days 12 h
× 4

16.
3 lb 10 oz
− 15 oz

Solve.

17. On another piece of paper, make a line graph of the data in the table.

Distance Terry Traveled	
Time	**Miles**
9:15 A.M.	1
9:30 A.M.	2
9:45 A.M.	3
10:00 A.M.	3
10:15 A.M.	3.5

18. Did Terry stop between 9:15 A.M. and 10:15 A.M.? Explain.

____

____

____

19. If Ian can travel 4 miles in $\frac{3}{4}$ hour, how far can he travel in 6 hours?

____

Name ____________________

Cumulative Review
★ Test Prep

1 **Binhan made multi-grain bread. He used $1\frac{1}{2}$ cups of wheat flour, $1\frac{3}{4}$ cups of rye flour, and $\frac{2}{3}$ cup of cornmeal. How much flour and cornmeal did he use in all?**

A $3\frac{6}{9}$ c **C** $4\frac{11}{12}$ c **E** N H

B $3\frac{11}{12}$ c **D** 5 c

2 **Louisa is making a banner. She tapes 15 sheets of paper together. Each sheet is $8\frac{1}{2}$ inches long. How long is the banner?**

F $12\frac{1}{2}$ **H** $127\frac{1}{2}$ in. **K** N H

G 120 in. **J** $128\frac{1}{2}$ in.

3 **Maria collects buttons. She has 2,156 buttons. She knows that $\frac{2}{7}$ of her buttons are green. How many buttons are green?**

A 38 **C** 308 **E** N H

B 76 **D** 616

4 **What is the value of $5x^3$ when $x = 4$?**

F 60 **H** 120 **K** 320

G 80 **J** 240

5 **Tommy practiced guitar for $\frac{1}{2}$ hour, piano for 45 minutes, and flute for 45 minutes. How long did he practice in all?**

A 1 h **C** $1\frac{1}{2}$ h **E** N H

B 1 h 15 min **D** 1 h 45 min

6 **Linda bought 3 quarts of milk. How many cups is that?**

F 12 **H** 3

G 6 **J** 1.5

Use the graph for exercises 7–8.

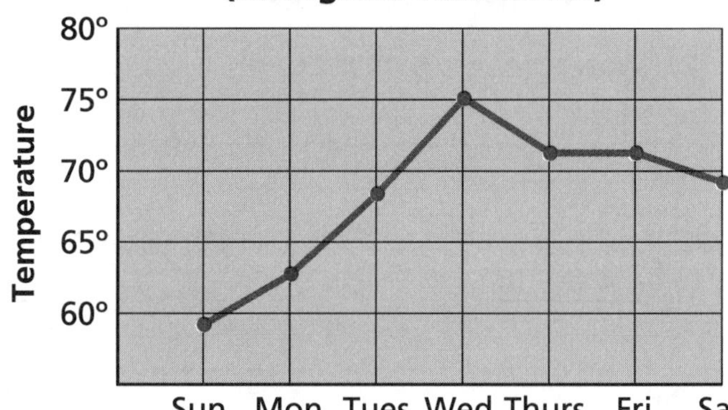

7 **Between which two days did the high temperature change the most?**

A Sunday and Monday

B Monday and Tuesday

C Tuesday and Wednesday

D Wednesday and Thursday

8 **About how much warmer was Saturday than the previous Sunday?**

F 5°F **H** 15°F

G 10°F **J** 20°F

UNIT 6 • TABLE OF CONTENTS

Ratios, Proportion, and Percents

We will be using this vocabulary:

rate a comparison of two quantities by division

ratio a comparison between two quantities in the same unit

proportion a statement that two ratios are equal

scale drawing a picture drawn in such a way that a given length in the picture represents a given length in the actual object

Dear Family,

During the next few weeks, our math class will be learning about ratios, proportions, and percent. You can expect to see homework that provides practice with finding discounts. Here is a sample you may want to keep handy to give help if needed.

Discounts

To find a discount, first change the percent to a decimal by moving the decimal point two places to the left and erasing the percent sign. Then multiply and subtract.

Example: A baseball glove that regularly costs **$60** is marked **20%** off. What is the sale price of the glove?

1. Change **20%** to a decimal. **20% = 0.20**

2. Multiply **$60** by **0.20**

$$\begin{array}{r} \$60 \\ \times\ 0.20 \\ \hline \$12.00 \end{array}$$

3. Subtract.

$$\begin{array}{r} \$60.00 \\ -\ 12.00 \\ \hline \$48.00 \end{array}$$

The sale price of the glove is **$48.**

During this unit, students will need to continue practicing working with percents, ratios, and proportions.

Sincerely,

Writing Ratios

A **ratio** is a comparison of two numbers. The two numbers being compared are called the **terms** of the ratio.

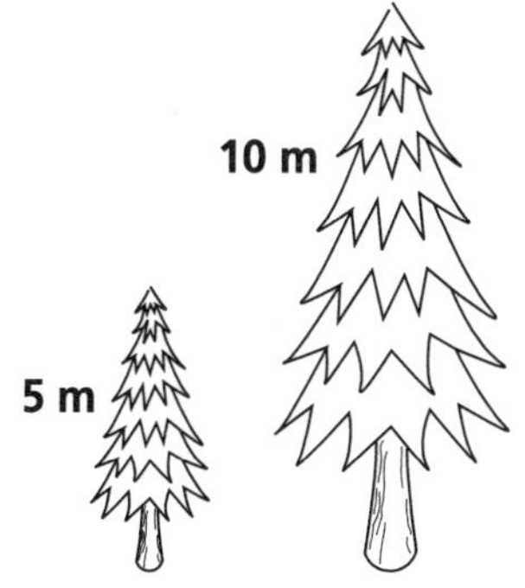

- The ratio of the height of the smaller tree to the height of the larger tree is $\frac{5}{10}$. This ratio is read "five to ten."

  The smaller tree is $\frac{1}{2}$ as tall as the larger tree because $\frac{5}{10} = \frac{1}{2}$.

- The ratio of the height of the larger tree to that of the smaller tree is $\frac{10}{5}$. This ratio is read "ten to five."

  The larger tree is **2** times as tall as the smaller tree because $\frac{10}{5} = 2$.

There are three ways to write a ratio: **10 to 5** $\quad \frac{10}{5} \quad$ **10 : 5**

The order in which you compare two numbers of a ratio is important.

○□□○○

The ratio of squares to circles is $\frac{2}{3}$.

But, the ratio of circles to squares is $\frac{3}{2}$.

Write the ratio three ways.

1. **1** m to **4** m ____________ **4** m to **1** m ____________

2. **3** min to **25** min ____________ **1¢** to **5¢** ____________

3. **8** cats to **5** dogs ____________ **6** chairs to **1** table ____________

4. **9** kg to **3** kg ____________ **8¢** to **40¢** ____________

Write the ratio as a fraction.

5. **5** lions to **6** leopards ______ **20** rosebuds to **13** thorns ______

6. **12** violins to **5** cornets ______ **4** taxis to **9** buses ______

7. Jane's **40¢** to Betty's **27¢** ______ **10** buses to **3** taxis ______

8. **9** books to **3** magazines ______ **9** cars to **36** trucks ______

STANDARD

The four ratios $\frac{18}{24}$, $\frac{6}{8}$, $\frac{9}{12}$, and $\frac{3}{4}$ represent the same relationship.

The ratio $\frac{3}{4}$ is in simplest form. You can simplify ratios just as you simplify fractions.

You can use a ratio to compare two measurements.

45 s to **1** min

To simplify a ratio of measurements, you must first express both measurements in the same unit. Since **1** min = **60** s, write the ratio as **45** s to **60** s. Then simplify.

$$\frac{45}{60} = \frac{3}{4}$$

Simplify the ratio.

9. 18 to 81 → ______ 56 to 32 → ______

10. 25 to 150 → ______ 21 to 24 → ______

11. 24 to 84 → ______ 120 to 75 → ______

Simplify the ratio.

12. 9 months to 2 years ______ 50 s to 2 s ______ 15 s to 2 min ______

13. 20 days to 4 weeks ______ 1 quarter to 1 dollar ______ 8 wk to 1 yr ______

Problem Solving
Reasoning

Solve.

14. A stamp collection has **40** U.S. stamps and **15** foreign stamps. What is the ratio of U.S. stamps to the total number of stamps?

______

15. Suppose cherry is your favorite flavor. Would you rather buy a bag of candy in which the ratio of cherry to lemon flavor is **2** to **3** or **3** to **2**?

______

Test Prep ★ Mixed Review

16 What is the value $n^3 + 27$ for $n = 4$?

A 31 **C** 43

B 39 **D** 91

17 The 28 students in Ms. Hill's class are planning a party. The food and decorations will cost $140. Which equation could be used to find each student's share of the cost, m?

F $28 + m = 140$ **H** $m \div 28 = 140$

G $m - 28 = 140$ **J** $28m = 140$

Name ______________________________

Rates and Unit Rates

STANDARD

A **rate** is a special type of ratio that compares quantities that are in different units, such as yards and seconds. For example, a runner runs at a rate of **80** yards in **10** seconds.

You can write a rate in the following ways:

$\frac{\textbf{80 yards}}{\textbf{10 seconds}}$ **80** yards: **10** seconds **80** yards per **10** seconds

Rates are usually written as a quantity **1**, called a **unit rate.** To find a unit rate, find an equal ratio with a denominator of **1**.

$\frac{\textbf{80 yards}}{\textbf{10 seconds}} = \frac{\textbf{8 yards}}{\textbf{1 second}}$

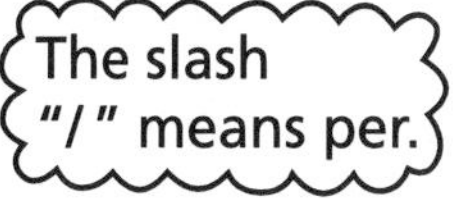

A runner runs at a unit rate of **8** yards per second, or **8** yd/s.

Other examples of rates are:

$8.25/h **70** heartbeats/min **98¢**/L **88** km/h

Write a rate that describes the situation.

1. a dozen eggs for **$1.19** __________ **5** for a quarter __________

2. **5** tickets for **$25** __________ **60** words per min __________

3. **120** miles per **6** gallons __________ **2** apples for **$1.00** __________

4. **10** for **50¢** __________ **90** miles in **2** hours __________

5. **45** yards in **3** passes __________ **360** bars in **3** boxes __________

Find the unit rate.

6. **200** m in **20** s __________ **$30** for **5** shirts __________

7. **$1.00** per **4** g __________ **16** km per **2** hr __________

8. **$32** for **4** __________ **48** baseball bats in **6** boxes __________

9. **250** miles per **10** gallons __________ **$10** for **2** __________

10. **$1.56** a dozen __________ **600** people per **15** square miles __________

11. **12** lessons for **$144** __________ **24** pictures for **$12.00** __________

12. **$25.30** for **23** gallons __________ **90** sheets for **15** students __________

13. **25** feet in **5** seconds __________ **675** trees for **5** acres __________

14. **96** pounds in **12** bags __________ **1,680** pages in **7** books __________

STANDARD

The **unit price** is the cost per unit. In the example below, the unit price is the cost per ounce of ketchup. To find the unit price, divide the price by the number of ounces.

12-oz bottle of ketchup for **$1.29**:

price → quantity → $\frac{\$1.29}{12 \text{ oz}} = \$.1075$ or **10.75¢** per **oz**

↑ unit price

16-oz bottle of ketchup for **$1.85**:

$\frac{\$1.85}{16 \text{ oz}} = \$.1175$ or **11.75¢** per **oz**

↑ unit price

The ketchup in the **12**-oz bottle is the better buy.

For each item, find the unit price in cents per ounce to two decimal places. Circle the item that is the better buy.

15.

______ ______

16.

$1.67
TOMATOES
2 lb

______ ______

17.

$4.15
CRACKERS
14 oz

______ ______

Problem Solving Reasoning **Solve.**

18. Instant photo film costs **$12.50** for **10** pictures. What is the unit price?

______

19. At one store, the price of film is **3** rolls for **$15.39**. At another, the same film is **5** rolls for **$24.99**. Which is the better buy?

______

Test Prep ★ Mixed Review

20 **What do you need to do to each side of this equation to solve it?**

$$\frac{4}{9} \times q = \frac{3}{5}$$

A Multiply by $\frac{4}{9}$

B Multiply by $\frac{9}{4}$

C Multiply by $\frac{3}{5}$

D Divide by $\frac{5}{3}$

21 **Oliver measured crickets for a science experiment. The table shows the length of the crickets.**

Cricket A	Cricket B	Cricket C	Cricket D
2.68 cm	2.64 cm	3.68 cm	2.86 cm

Which list shows the crickets in order from shortest to longest?

F Cricket A, Cricket B, Cricket C, Cricket D

G Cricket C, Cricket D, Cricket A, Cricket B

H Cricket B, Cricket A, Cricket D, Cricket C

J Cricket B, Cricket D, Cricket A, Cricket C

Name ______________________

Equal Ratios

STANDARD

Carl reads **2** books every **3** weeks. At that rate, how many books will he read in **12** weeks?

You need to find a ratio equal to $\frac{2}{3}$ with **12** as the second term. Because **3 × 4 = 12,** multiply **2 × 4** to get the first term of the ratio.

books → $\frac{2}{3} = \frac{n}{12}$ ← books
weeks → ← weeks

$\frac{2}{3} = \frac{2 \times 4}{3 \times 4} = \frac{8}{12}$

So $n = 8$

Carl will read **8** books in **12** weeks.

When one term of a ratio is multiplied by a given number, multiply the other term by the same number to get an equal ratio.

Find the missing term.

1. $\frac{2}{3} = \frac{n}{6}$ $n =$ ______ $\frac{5}{6} = \frac{x}{36}$ $x =$ ______ $\frac{3}{8} = \frac{y}{24}$ $y =$ ______ $\frac{5}{7} = \frac{a}{42}$ $a =$ ______ $\frac{8}{9} = \frac{b}{63}$ $b =$ ______

Use equal ratios to find the value of *n*.

2. **9** pencils per **7** pupils = ***n*** pencils per **63** pupils ______

3. **5** points per **2** games = ***n*** points per **16** games ______

4. **10** tickets per child = ***n*** tickets per **5** children ______

5. **52** kilometers per hour = ***n*** kilometers per **3** hours ______

6. **20** people in **4** cars = ***n*** people in **8** cars ______

7. **40** hours in **4** weeks = **10** hours in ***n*** weeks ______

8. **4** pounds for **16** people = ***n*** pounds for **48** people ______

9. **9** bars of soap for **3** dollars = **27** bars of soap for ***n*** dollars ______

10. **60** miles per hour = ***n*** miles per **4** hours ______

Are the ratios equal? Write Yes or No.

11. $\frac{3}{1}, \frac{9}{3}$ ______ 3 : 5, 7 : 12 ______ 2 to 5, 6 to 15 ______

12. $\frac{2}{5}, \frac{8}{25}$ ______ $\frac{18}{63}, \frac{2}{7}$ ______ 15 : 25, 3 : 5 ______

13. $\frac{24}{48}, \frac{1}{2}$ ______ 3 to 1, 9 to 3 ______ 12 : 32, 3 : 8 ______

14. 4 to 5, 16 to 25 ______ 1 : 4, 7 : 28 ______ $\frac{5}{9}, \frac{15}{18}$ ______

STANDARD

Find the missing term.

15. $\frac{4}{16} = \frac{k}{12}$ $k =$ ______ $\frac{2}{10} = \frac{p}{15}$ $p =$ ______ $\frac{6}{8} = \frac{9}{x}$ $x =$ ______ $\frac{12}{27} = \frac{n}{18}$ $n =$ ______

Problem Solving
Reasoning

Solve.

16. Two quarts of lemonade serve **5** people. At that rate, how much lemonade would serve **30** people? ______

17. Bill can type **9** words in **30** seconds. At that rate, how much time would be needed to type **45** words? ______

18. Three rolls of tape cost **80¢**. At that rate, how much would **6** rolls cost? ______

19. In a **7**-day week, Karen practices her violin **14** hours. At this rate, how many hours will she practice her violin in **28** days? ______

20. Jim traveled a distance of **90** miles in **2** hours. Bob traveled a distance of **150** miles in **3** hours. Who traveled at a faster average speed? ______

Quick Check

Write the ratio in three ways.

21. 3 feet out of every **5** feet ______

22. 7 students out of every **10** ______

23. 7 cars for every **3** vans ______

24. 5 computers for every class ______

Find the missing term.

25. $\frac{3}{4} = \frac{n}{32}$ ______

26. $\frac{21}{35} = \frac{3}{s}$ ______

27. $\frac{56}{25} = \frac{n}{100}$ ______

Write the unit rate.

28. 524 mi in **8** h ______

29. 6 muffins for **$4.47** ______

30. 740 mi on **25** gal ______

Work Space.

Name ____________________

STANDARD

In Lesson 3 you learned how to find equal ratios. An equation showing the equality of two ratios, such as $\frac{3}{7} = \frac{9}{21}$, is called a **proportion.** Proportions have an important property that you can use to solve problems: The cross products in a proportion are equal.

If $\frac{a}{b} = \frac{c}{d}$ then $\boldsymbol{a \cdot d = b \cdot c}$.

$\frac{3}{7} \bowtie \frac{9}{21}$

$3 \cdot 21 \qquad 7 \cdot 9$

cross products

The example below shows why this is true.

Original proportion

$$\frac{3}{7} = \frac{9}{21}$$

Write each ratio as a product of a fraction and a whole number.

$$3 \cdot \frac{1}{7} = 9 \cdot \frac{1}{21}$$

Use inverse operations. Multiply both sides by **7 · 21**.

$$3 \cdot \frac{1}{7} \cdot (7 \cdot 21) = 9 \cdot \frac{1}{21} \cdot (7 \cdot 21)$$

$$3 \cdot \left(\frac{1}{7} \cdot 7\right) \cdot 21 = 9 \cdot \left(\frac{1}{21} \cdot 21\right) \cdot 7$$

The multiplicative inverse property gives you the cross products.

$$3 \cdot 1 \cdot 21 = 9 \cdot 1 \cdot 7$$

$$3 \cdot 21 = 9 \cdot 7$$

Cross products: $\boldsymbol{a \cdot d = b \cdot c}$

$$63 = 63$$

You can use the cross-product property to find the missing term in a proportion.

At the rate of **60¢** a dozen, what is the cost of **8** apples?

To solve this equation, first establish the proportion.

$$\frac{60}{12} \bowtie \frac{n}{8}$$

Then solve the related multipication equation.

$$60 \times 8 = 12 \times n$$
$$480 = 12 \times n$$
$$n = 40$$

Therefore, **8** apples cost **40¢.**

Find the missing term.

1. $\frac{n}{9} = \frac{12}{4}$ ________ $\frac{5}{6} = \frac{15}{n}$ ________ $\frac{2}{6} = \frac{25}{n}$ ________ $\frac{9}{n} = \frac{3}{7}$ ________

2. $\frac{n}{7} = \frac{21}{49}$ ________ $\frac{10}{12} = \frac{n}{72}$ ________ $\frac{n}{25} = \frac{72}{9}$ ________ $\frac{8}{n} = \frac{12}{60}$ ________

STANDARD

Sometimes the missing term in a proportion may not be a whole number. Study the following examples.

$\frac{n}{8} = \frac{3}{5}$	$\frac{7.5}{6} = \frac{n}{2}$	$\frac{n}{6} = \frac{8}{15}$
$n \times 5 = 8 \times 3$	$7.5 \times 2 = 6 \times n$	$n \times 15 = 6 \times 8$
$n \times 5 = 24$	$15 = 6 \times n$	$n \times 15 = 48$
$n = 4\frac{4}{5}$	$2.5 = n$	$n = 3\frac{1}{5}$

Solve.

3. $\frac{n}{3} = \frac{5}{9}$ ______ $\frac{7}{n} = \frac{4}{6}$ ______ $\frac{4}{8} = \frac{2}{n}$ ______ $\frac{10}{4} = \frac{n}{0.6}$ ______

4. $\frac{n}{6} = \frac{15}{45}$ ______ $\frac{2}{10} = \frac{n}{35}$ ______ $\frac{15}{7} = \frac{n}{105}$ ______ $\frac{12}{13} = \frac{n}{130}$ ______

5. $\frac{6}{n} = \frac{4}{3}$ ______ $\frac{9}{n} = \frac{7}{4}$ ______ $\frac{8}{n} = \frac{5}{6}$ ______ $\frac{21}{6} = \frac{3.5}{n}$ ______

6. $\frac{n}{8} = \frac{6}{5}$ ______ $\frac{3}{3} = \frac{n}{3}$ ______ $\frac{n}{8} = \frac{3}{4}$ ______ $\frac{n}{10} = \frac{40}{1.6}$ ______

7. $\frac{5}{16} = \frac{n}{11}$ ______ $\frac{17}{23} = \frac{n}{15}$ ______ $\frac{8}{5} = \frac{6}{n}$ ______ $\frac{4.9}{n} = \frac{28}{8}$ ______

8. $\frac{13}{38} = \frac{24}{n}$ ______ $\frac{9}{100} = \frac{n}{50}$ ______ $\frac{n}{100} = \frac{5}{6}$ ______ $\frac{8}{2.5} = \frac{n}{18}$ ______

9. $\frac{15}{24} = \frac{19}{n}$ ______ $\frac{n}{18} = \frac{21}{12}$ ______ $\frac{16}{3.5} = \frac{n}{21}$ ______ $\frac{3}{4} = \frac{1.5}{n}$ ______

Name ______________________

Use cross products to tell whether the ratios form a proportion. Write Yes or No.

10. $\frac{18}{25}, \frac{7}{10}$ ______ $\frac{5}{8}, \frac{15}{24}$ ______ $\frac{4}{2}, \frac{2}{1}$ ______ $\frac{3}{5}, \frac{12}{2}$ ______

11. $\frac{3}{8}, \frac{12}{32}$ ______ $\frac{3}{4}, \frac{5}{6}$ ______ $\frac{20}{30}, \frac{4}{6}$ ______ $\frac{2}{9}, \frac{12}{6}$ ______

12. $\frac{4}{7}, \frac{7}{12}$ ______ $\frac{3}{7}, \frac{9}{28}$ ______ $\frac{5}{9}, \frac{15}{27}$ ______ $\frac{3}{5}, \frac{5}{8}$ ______

Problem Solving Reasoning Solve.

13. Fruit cocktail is on sale at **3** cans for a dollar. What is the cost of **12** cans?

______

14. Jamie buys **2** disks for **$19**. What does he pay for **6** disks, excluding tax? ______

15. If erasers are priced at **3** for **99¢**, what is the cost of **6** erasers? ______

16. Gum costs **55¢** for a pack of **5** sticks. How many sticks of gum can you buy for **$2.20**?

______

17. A **$1.95** loaf of bread has **20** slices. What is the cost of bread for **30** regular sandwiches? ______

18. At Discount Dora's you can buy **2** pairs of socks for **$5.80**. What is the cost of **12** pairs of socks? ______

Solve. Check that your answer makes sense.

19. Baseballs cost **$14.69** for **3** balls. How much do **100** balls cost? ______

20. Leila reads **40** pages per hour. How long does it take her to finish a **228**-page book? ______

21. Some orange paint is made by mixing **4** mL red paint and **15** mL yellow paint. How much red should be mixed with **100** mL of yellow to get the same color orange?

______

22. A company can buy packages of **500** sheets of computer paper for **$4.68**. At that rate, how much paper can be bought for **$2,000**? ______

Test Prep ★ Mixed Review

23 In Hollowell Park, there are 35 tulip plants for every 21 iris plants. What is the ratio of tulip plants to iris plants in simplest form?

A 35 : 21 **C** 3 : 5

B 5 : 3 **D** 7 : 3

24 The largest box of Supra-White Detergent weighs 43.4 ounces. The smallest box weighs 25.25 ounces. How much more does the largest box weigh?

F 18.15 oz **H** 25.25 oz

G 18.25 oz **J** 43.4 oz

STANDARD

Name ____________________

Scale Drawings

Three scale drawings are shown at the right.

This drawing of a leaf is actual size: **1** inch on the drawing represents **1** inch on the leaf. The scale is **1** inch to **1** inch.

In the drawing, the length of the leaf measures about **2** in. The real leaf is also about **2** in. long.

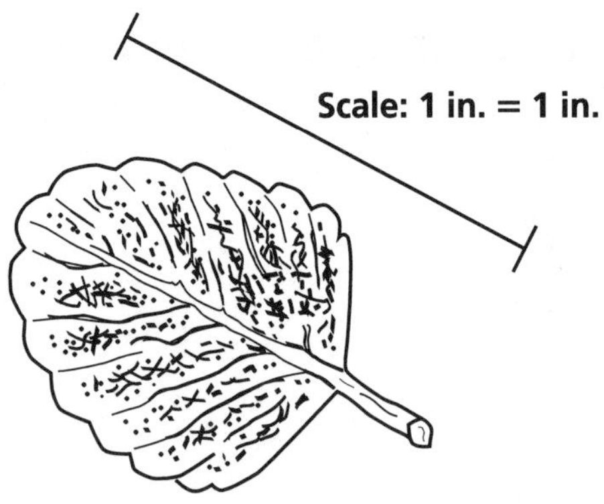

This drawing of a map is smaller than actual size: **1** inch on the drawing represents **10** miles on the land. The scale is **1** inch to **10** miles.

In the map, the distance from Springfield to Salem measures about **1.5** in. The real distance is about **15** mi.

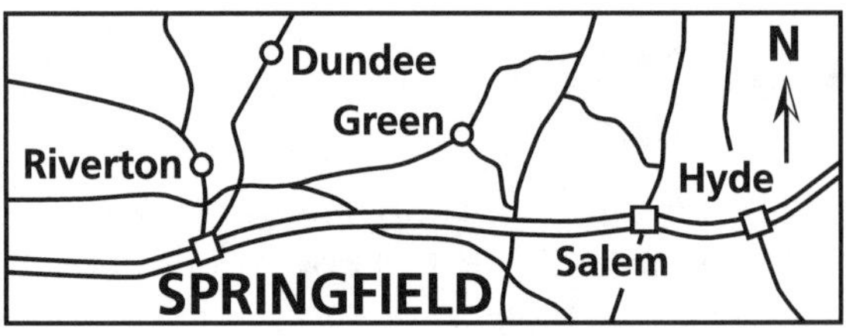

Scale: 1 in. = 10 mi

This drawing of a butterfly is larger than actual size: **1** inch on the drawing represents $\frac{9}{16}$ inch on the butterfly. The scale is **1** inch to $\frac{9}{16}$ inch. The drawing measures about **2** in. across. The real butterfly is about $\frac{18}{16}$ or $1\frac{1}{8}$ in. across.

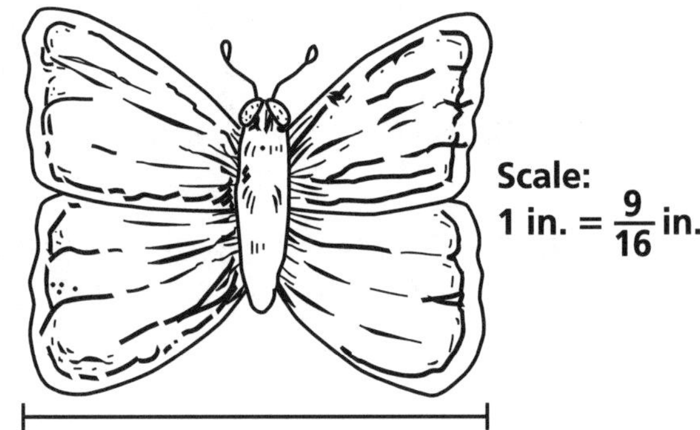

Scale: 1 in. = $\frac{9}{16}$ in.

Complete.

If **1** in. on a map represents **200** mi, then

1. ______ represents **400** mi. ______ represents **50** mi.

2. $1\frac{1}{2}$ in. represents ______ mi. ______ represents **250** mi.

If **1** in. on a map represents **30** ft, then

3. ______ represents **15** ft. **2** in. represents ______ ft.

4. $1\frac{1}{2}$ in. represents ______ ft. ______ represents $7\frac{1}{2}$ ft.

Complete the table.

5.	**Scale Length**	$\frac{1}{4}$ in.	1 in.	$\frac{1}{2}$ in.	2 in.		$1\frac{1}{2}$ in.		$3\frac{1}{4}$ in.	
6.	**Actual Length**	1 ft	4 ft			$\frac{1}{2}$ ft		11 ft		12 ft

Name ______________________________

STANDARD

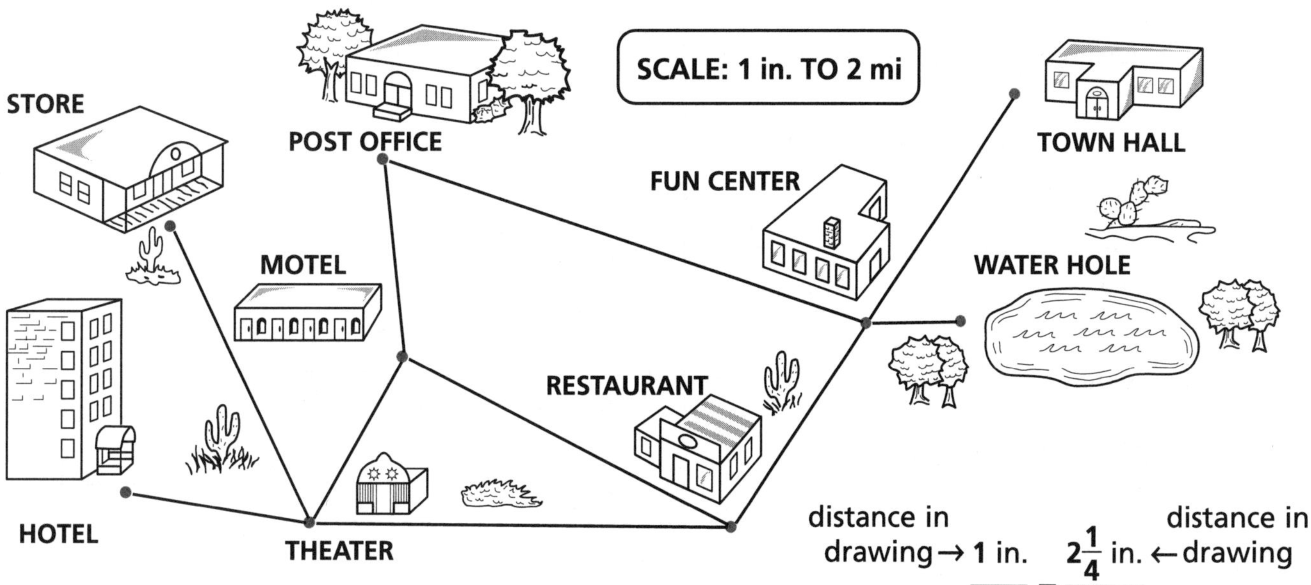

STORE

POST OFFICE

SCALE: 1 in. TO 2 mi

TOWN HALL

FUN CENTER

MOTEL

WATER HOLE

RESTAURANT

HOTEL

THEATER

You can write a proportion using the scale of a scale drawing to find actual distances.

To find the actual distance from the Theater to the Restaurant, measure the distance using the road on the scale drawing. The theater is $2\frac{1}{4}$ inches from the restaurant. Then write and solve the proportion.

distance in drawing → 1 in. / actual distance → 2 mi = $2\frac{1}{4}$ in. ← distance in drawing / n ← actual distance

$$\frac{1 \text{ in.}}{2 \text{ mi}} = \frac{2\frac{1}{4} \text{ in.}}{n}$$

$$1 \times n = 2 \times 2\frac{1}{4}$$

$$n = \overset{1}{\cancel{2}} \times \frac{9}{\underset{2}{\cancel{4}}}$$

$$n = 4\frac{1}{2}$$

Measure the distance along the roads to the nearest $\frac{1}{4}$ inch. Use a proportion to find the actual distance.

	Map Distance	Actual Distance
7. Fun Center to Store		
8. Water Hole to Motel		
9. Hotel to Post Office		
10. Post Office to Town Hall		
11. Motel to Store		
12. Hotel to Town Hall		
13. Water Hole to Town Hall		
14. Restaurant to Post Office		

STANDARD

Richard decided to make a scale drawing of his neighborhood. The scale he used was 1 cm to 1 km. Label the place on the map and draw the connecting road.

15. His friend Jim's house is **1** km east of Richard's house.

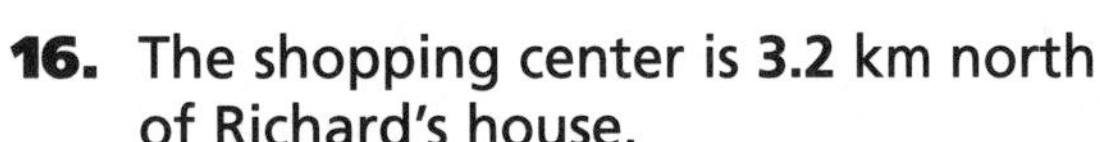

16. The shopping center is **3.2** km north of Richard's house.

17. To get to school from home, he goes **1.2** km west and then **2.6** km south.

18. The baseball field is **3.2** km east of the school in the same road.

19. His grandmother lives **4.5** km east of the shopping center.

20. His uncle lives **1.2** km west of the school.

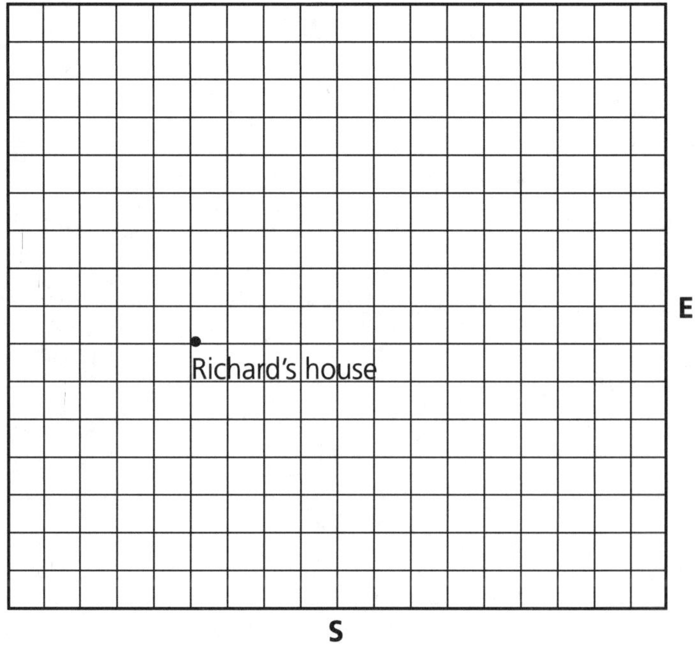

Problem Solving Reasoning Solve.

21. A map is drawn using a scale in which **1** in. represents **15** miles. What distance will be represented by **12** in. on the map? ______

22. The distance between two towns is **460** km. What length on a map will represent this distance, if the map scale is **10** km = **2** cm? ______

Quick Check

Is the proportion *True* or *False*?

23. $\frac{42}{56} = \frac{15}{20}$ ______

24. $\frac{15}{33} = \frac{25}{55}$ ______

Solve the proportion.

25. $\frac{45}{25} = \frac{h}{4}$ ______

26. $\frac{9}{24} = \frac{k}{36}$ ______

27. $\frac{10}{56} = \frac{25}{x}$ ______

An O-gauge model train has a scale of 1 inch = 4 feet. Find the missing length.

28. Engine length: **30** ft

Model length: ______

29. Height of boxcar: **15** ft

Model height: ______

30. Model gondola length: $5\frac{1}{2}$ in.; actual length: ______

Work Space.

Name ______________________________

Problem Solving Application: Too Much or Not Enough Information

STANDARD

Some problems give more facts than you need to solve the problem. Some problems do not give enough facts. In this lesson, you will read a problem and decide whether there are missing or unnecessary facts.

Tips to Remember:

1. Understand 2. Decide 3. Solve 4. Look back

- Read each problem more than once. Circle the important words and numbers. Cross out the words and numbers that you don't need.
- Think about each fact in the problem. Ask yourself: Is this an extra fact? Or do I need it to find a solution?
- Predict the answer. Then solve the problem. Compare your answer with your prediction.

Cross out the extra information. Then solve the problem. If information is missing, name the fact or facts needed on the answer lines.

1. The ratio of the cost of a small order of fries to the cost of a jumbo order of fries is **2:5**. A jumbo order contains an average of **47** fries. What is the cost of a small order of fries?

Think: How many terms must you know in order to solve a proportion?

____

____

Answer ______________________________

____

2. Alexander bought **3** cheeseburgers for a total of **$6.75**, **3** salads for a total of **$6.90**, and **3** shakes for a total of **$2.97**. How many cheeseburgers could he buy for **$15.75**?

Think: What proportion could you use to solve this problem?

____

____

Answer ______________________________

____

3. Allison's car uses **1** gallon of gasoline for every **32** miles she drives. She drives **35** miles to and from work each day. How far can Allison drive on **15** gallons of gas?

____

____

4. There are **327** students attending the Middleton Middle School. The sixth level has **89** boys. How many girls are in the sixth level?

____

____

STANDARD

Cross out the extra information. Then solve the problem. If information is missing, name the fact or facts that you need.

5. Jorge wrapped 6 packages. The wrapping weighed almost as much as the packages. The wrapping weighed $1\frac{1}{2}$ ounces. What was the ratio of the weight of the packages to the weight of the wrapping?

____

____

6. A medium order of rice costs **$1.25** and weighs **3** ounces. The large size weighs **6** ounces. The large size costs **$.38** per ounce. What is the unit price in cents per ounce for the medium order of rice?

____

____

7. Suppose an order of beans has **160** milligrams of sodium. An order of chips has **169** more milligrams of sodium than the beans. A full meal has 315 milligrams of sodium more than the chips. How many milligrams of sodium do the chips have?

____

8. A lunch included a sandwich, fruit salad, and frozen yogurt. The yogurt had **320** calories. The sandwich had **711** calories. The meal had half the calories needed for a day. How many calories are needed for a day?

____

____

9. A restaurant can seat **205** people. Five tables seat one person, **40** tables seat two people, and **30** tables seat three or four people. How many tables are there in all?

____

10. Louisa can buy a fish sandwich and a juice for **$6.95**. The daily special is **2** roll-ups and a juice. Which is the better buy?

____

Extend Your Thinking

11. One half of the students at Jefferson Middle School bring their lunch to school. How many students bring their lunch?

____

____

12. Six members of the Smith family traveled **4** days on their vacation. They averaged **450** miles per day. How many miles did they drive in the **4** days?

____

13. Choose a problem in which a fact is missing. Make up data for the fact and then solve the problem.

New Data for Problem ______

____

____

14. Go back to problem **7**. Write another question that can be answered using the information in the problem. Write the answer to your question.

____

____

Name ____________________

Percents

The large square is divided into **100** small squares, and **25** of these have been shaded. We can say that $\frac{25}{100}$ or **0.25** of the large square is shaded. Another way to write the same number is **25%**, read "twenty-five percent." The symbol % represents the word **percent,** which means "per hundred." Each small square is $\frac{1}{100}$ of the large square; that is, it represents **0.01**, or **1%**, of the large square.

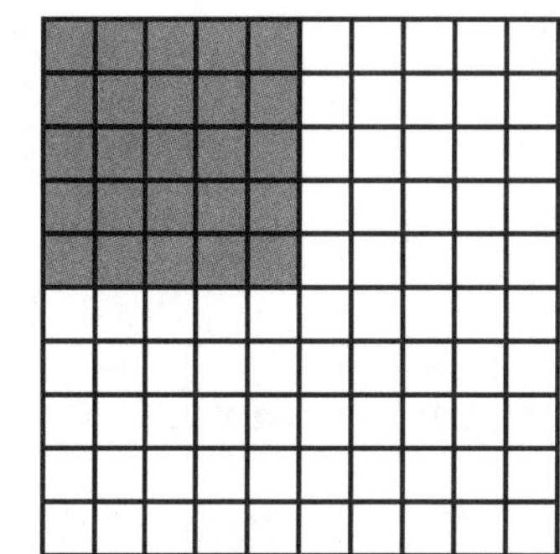

Use the squares to complete.

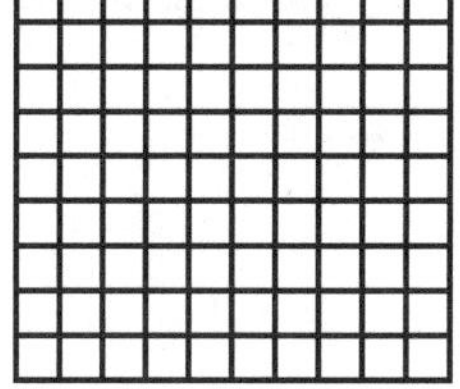

1. Shade **55%** of the large square.

2. How many small squares did you shade? ______

3. What percent of the large square is not shaded? ______

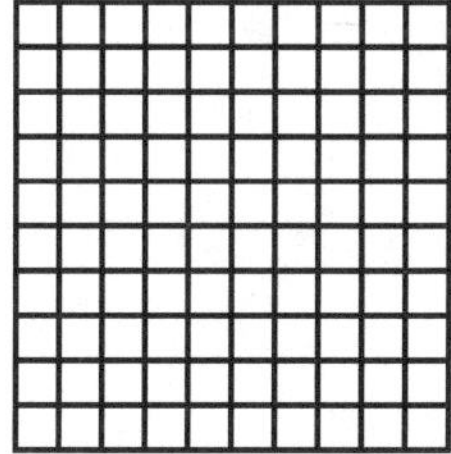

4. Shade **29%** of the large square.

5. How many small squares did you shade? ______

6. What percent of the large square is not shaded? ______

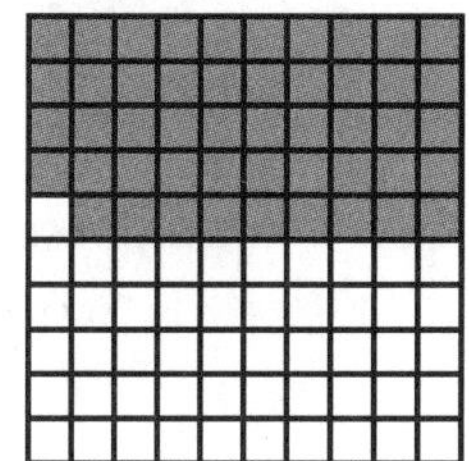

7. How many small squares of the large square are shaded? ______

8. What percent of the large square is shaded? ______

9. How many small squares are not shaded? ______

10. What percent of the large square is not shaded? ______

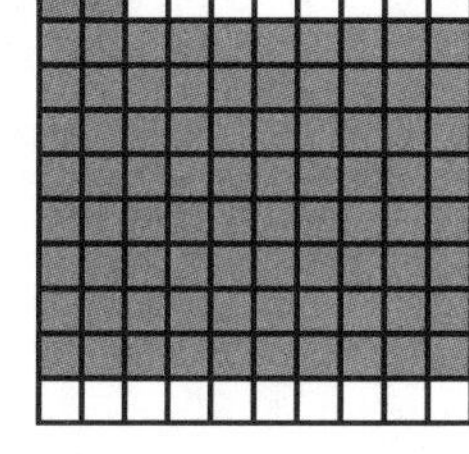

11. How many small squares are shaded? ______

12. What percent of the large square is shaded? ______

13. What percent is not shaded? ______

STANDARD

Sometimes you need to use percents that are greater than **100%**. For example, you might say that attendance at a game increased **150%** from the last game. The shading of large squares at the right shows **150** hundredths or **150%**.

Write the percent shown.

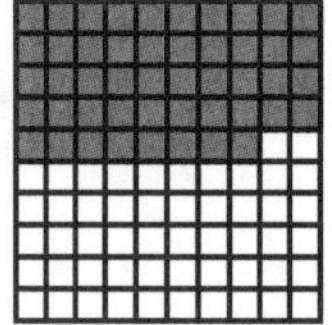

14. ______

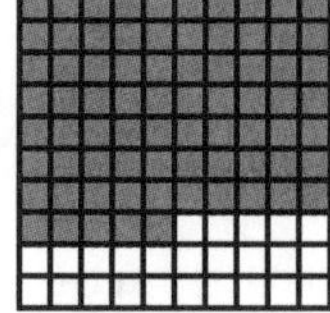

15. ______

Decide whether the statement is possible. Write P for *possible* or N for *not possible*. If the statement is not possible, explain why.

16. Sale on shoes: **100%** off.

____

The extra police force decreased crime **300%**.

____

17. Sales increased **175%**.

____

The team won **105%** of their games.

____

18. The shirt is **130%** cotton.

____

We guarantee your profit will be increased **200%**.

____

Problem Solving
Reasoning

Solve.

19. **Thirty** percent of Mrs. Smith's class pack their lunch. What percent of students in Mrs. Smith's class do not pack their lunch?

______

20. Jane's allowance is **2.5** times as much as Jerry's. What percent of Jerry's allowance is Jane's allowance?

______

Test Prep ★ Mixed Review

21 An oil-change shop uses 9 quarts of oil for every 2 cars that are serviced. How many quarts of oil are needed to service 36 cars?

A 8

B 18

C 162

D 648

22 Which three numbers are equivalent?

F $\frac{3}{2}$, 3.2, $3\frac{1}{2}$

G $\frac{3}{2}$, 1.5, $1\frac{1}{2}$

H $\frac{3}{2}$, 3.2, $1\frac{1}{2}$

J $\frac{3}{2}$, 2.3, $2\frac{1}{2}$

Name ______________________________

Fractions, Decimals, and Percents

STANDARD

Here are three ways to represent the shaded region.

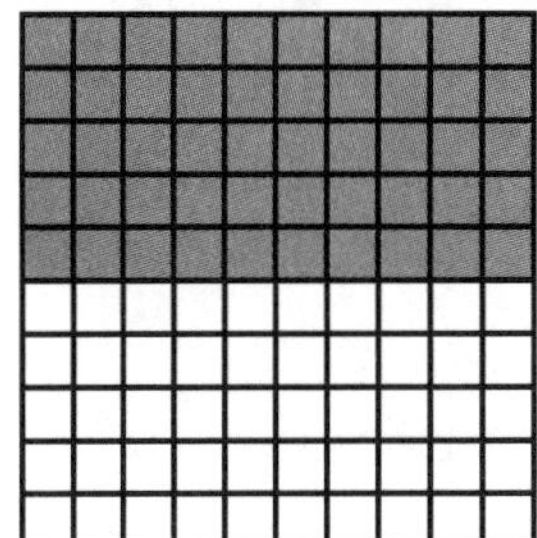

Fraction		Decimal		Percent
$\frac{50}{100}$	=	0.50	=	50%
fifty hundredths		fifty hundredths		fifty percent

Write an equivalent decimal and percent.

1. $\frac{79}{100}$ = ______ = ______ $\frac{5}{100}$ = ______ = ______ $\frac{27}{100}$ = ______ = ______

2. $\frac{75}{100}$ = ______ = ______ $\frac{9}{100}$ = ______ = ______ $\frac{80}{100}$ = ______ = ______

3. $\frac{4}{100}$ = ______ = ______ $\frac{50}{100}$ = ______ = ______ $\frac{85}{100}$ = ______ = ______

4. $\frac{150}{100}$ = ______ = ______ $\frac{190}{100}$ = ______ = ______ $\frac{200}{100}$ = ______ = ______

Write an equivalent percent.

5. 0.37 = ______   0.69 = ______   0.40 = ______   0.21 = ______

6. 0.80 = ______   0.55 = ______   0.99 = ______   0.44 = ______

7. 0.75 = ______   0.77 = ______   0.25 = ______   0.49 = ______

8. 1.37 = ______   2.75 = ______   4.15 = ______   3.29 = ______

9. To change a decimal to a percent, multiply it by ______ and write a % sign.

Write an equivalent decimal in hundredths.

10. 23% = ______   67% = ______   79% = ______   1% = ______

11. 17% = ______   9% = ______   10% = ______   87% = ______

12. 145% = ______   210% = ______   325% = ______   417% = ______

13. To change a percent to a decimal, delete the % sign and divide the number by ______.

Write an equivalent fractions in hundredths and in simplest form.

14. 75% = ______ = ______   20% = ______ = ______   4% = ______ = ______

15. 70% = ______ = ______   10% = ______ = ______   48% = ______ = ______

16. 5% = ______ = ______   50% = ______ = ______   80% = ______ = ______

STANDARD

You can rewrite a fraction as a percent by dividing.

$\frac{1}{4} \rightarrow 1 \div 4 \rightarrow 4\overline{)1.00}$ = 0.25

$$\begin{array}{r} 0.25 \\ 4\overline{)1.00} \\ -8 \\ \hline 20 \\ -20 \\ \hline 0 \end{array}$$

$\frac{1}{4} = 0.25$ or 25%

$\frac{1}{8} \rightarrow 1 \div 8 \rightarrow 8\overline{)1.00}$

$$\begin{array}{r} 0.12\frac{1}{2} \\ 8\overline{)1.00} \\ -8 \\ \hline 20 \\ -16 \\ \hline 4 \end{array}$$

Sometimes you need to write the remainder as a fraction and use a mixed number as a percent.

$\frac{1}{8} = 0.12\frac{1}{2}$ or $12\frac{1}{2}\%$

Rename the fraction as a percent. Do your work on another piece of paper.

17. $\frac{1}{2}$ = ______ $\frac{3}{7}$ = ______ $\frac{1}{9}$ = ______ $\frac{2}{5}$ = ______

18. $\frac{9}{10}$ = ______ $\frac{11}{20}$ = ______ $\frac{1}{12}$ = ______ $\frac{7}{25}$ = ______

19. $\frac{3}{50}$ = ______ $\frac{3}{8}$ = ______ $\frac{5}{9}$ = ______ $\frac{1}{15}$ = ______

20. $\frac{1}{7}$ = ______ $\frac{5}{16}$ = ______ $\frac{3}{8}$ = ______ $\frac{2}{100}$ = ______

Complete the table.

21.	**Fraction**				$\frac{2}{3}$	$\frac{1}{6}$	$\frac{5}{8}$				$\frac{5}{6}$
22.	**Decimal**	0.50	0.75							0.25	
23.	**Percent**			60%				$87\frac{1}{2}\%$	80%		

Problem Solving Reasoning

Solve.

24. Four-fifths of all sixth graders at the Middle School participate in sports. What percent of sixth graders participate in sports?

______

25. Mr. Morelos saves **0.15** of his earnings. What percent of his earnings does Mr. Morelos save?

______

Test Prep ★ Mixed Review

26 The Lopez family drove for 5 hours at a rate of 65 miles per hour. How far did they drive?

A 325 mi **C** 70 mi

B 305 mi **D** 65 mi

27 Andrew measured the length of his teacher's desk and found it was 60 inches. How many feet is 60 inches?

F 720 ft **H** 12 ft

G 60 ft **J** 5 ft

Name ____________________

Percent of a Number

STANDARD

In a survey of **130** students, **20%** had portable stereos. How many students had portable stereos?

Another way of stating this problem is:

What is **20%** of **130?**

Here are three ways to solve the problem:

Multiply by an equivalent fraction.

$20\% = \frac{1}{5}$ $\frac{1}{5} \times 130 = 26$

Multiply by an equivalent decimal.

$20\% = 0.2$

$$\begin{array}{r} 130 \\ \times\ 0.2 \\ \hline 26.0 \end{array}$$

Solve a proportion.

$\frac{20}{100} = \frac{n}{130}$ ← students with stereos / ← students in survey

$100n = 20 \times 130$

$n = 26$

So, **26** students had portable stereos.

Solve using the equivalent fraction method.

1. 20% of 50 ______ $66\frac{2}{3}$% of 75 ______ 25% of 40 ______

2. 80% of 50 ______ $16\frac{2}{3}$% of 36 ______ 25% of 78 ______

Solve using the equivalent decimal method.

3. 40% of 82 ______ 12.5% of 184 ______ 45% of 30 ______

4. 11% of 60 ______ 17% of 40 ______ 5.25% of 400 ______

Solve using a proportion.

5. $12\frac{1}{2}$% of 56 ______ $33\frac{1}{3}$% of 114 ______ 75% of 72 ______

6. 35% of 164 ______ $6\frac{1}{2}$% of 32 ______ 58% of 20 ______

STANDARD

Problem Solving Reasoning **Solve.**

7. If **4%** of the students are absent from a class of **25** students, how many students are absent? ________

8. In a survey of **120** students, it was found that **85%** ride a bus to school. How many students ride a bus? ________

9. A **10**-speed bicycle is on sale for **80%** of the regular price. The regular price is **$255**. What is the sale price? ________

10. The price of a certain lightweight touring bicycle is **$395** plus **5%** sales tax. What is the total cost? ________

11. A sporting goods store reduced all prices **10%** for a sale. What is the sale price of a **$37** rod and reel? ________

12. A fisherman caught **25%** more fish in the month of August than he caught in the month of July. How many total fish did he catch in August if he caught **28** in July? ________

Quick Check

Write the fraction or decimal as a percent. Round to the nearest whole percent, if necessary.

Work Space.

13. $\frac{6}{25}$ ________ **14.** 0.755 ________

15. $\frac{11}{12}$ ________ **16.** $3\frac{3}{5}$ ________

Write the percent as a fraction or mixed number.

17. 905% ________ **18.** 4.04% ________

Write the percent as a decimal.

19. 3.1% ________ **20.** 40.25% ________

Solve.

21. 15% of 88 ________ **22.** 8.6% of 250 ________

Name ____________________

Discounts and Simple Interest

STANDARD

A **discount** is an amount of decrease from a regular price.
A discounted price is often called a **sale price.**

Find the discount and the sale price for the television.

Sale 40% off

Regular Price $250

Discount = regular price × discount rate

= **$250 × 40%**

= **$250 × 0.4**

= **$100**

Sale Price = regular price − discount

= **$250 − $100**

= **$150**

Complete the table.

	Regular Price	Discount Rate	Discount	Sale Price
1.	$6	20%	$6 × 0.20 =	$6 − =
2.	$25	30%		
3.	$20	35%		
4.	$80	10%		
5.	$4	40%		
6.	$65	15%		
7.	$198	50%		
8.	$1,250	25%		
9.	$120	45%		
10.	$90	55%		
11.	$160	$12\frac{1}{2}$%		
12.	$144	$33\frac{1}{3}$%		
13.	$220	60%		
14.	$80	15%		

STANDARD

A person or bank who lends money usually collects **interest** on the loan. When you deposit money in a bank savings account, you earn interest.

- The amount of money borrowed or deposited is called the **principal.**
- The interest **rate** is the percent of the principal you pay or earn for a period of time.
- The **time** is number of years the principal is loaned for or saved.

To calculate simple interest on a loan of **$600** at **12%** for **2** years, use this formula.

Interest (*I*) = principal (*p*) × rate (*r*) × time (*t*)

Interest = **$600 × 12% × 2**

= **$600 × 0.12 × 2**

= **$144**

The simple interest on **$600** at **12%** over a period of two years is **$144.**

Complete.

	Principal	Rate	Time	Interest
15.	$340	12%	1 yr	= $340 × 0.12 × 1
16.	$485	11%	3 yr	
17.	$517	14%	2 yr	
18.	$800	8%	$\frac{3}{4}$ yr	

Problem Solving
Reasoning

Solve.

19. A radio with a regular price of **$120** is on sale at **25%** off. What is the sale price? Bonnie said, "**75%** of **$120** is **$90.**" Clyde said, "**25%** of **$120** is **$30** and **$120** – **$30** = **$90.**" Why do both Bonnie and Clyde's methods work? ____________________

____

20. Bank A offers a savings plan at **8%** interest computed and added to the principal every $\frac{1}{4}$ year. Bank B offers **8%** simple interest per year. How much more would you earn on a **$1,000** deposit in one year at Bank A? ____________________

____

Test Prep ★ Mixed Review

21 What do you need to do to both sides of this equation to solve it?

$a - 1{,}986 = 789$

A Add *a*
C Subtract *a*
B Add 1,986
D Subtract 1,986

22 What is the least common multiple of 5, 6, and 9?

F 30
H 90
G 54
J 270

Name ______________________

STANDARD

In a singing group there are **30** girls and **20** boys. The ratio **30:20** is a part-to-part ratio. The ratio of the number of girls to the number of students is a part-to-whole ratio and is written **30:50.** What percent of the group are girls?

$$\frac{30}{30 + 20} = \frac{30}{50} = \frac{60}{100} = 60\%$$

The percent of the group that are girls is **60%.** A percent is always a part-to-whole ratio.

What percent of the objects are red? First write the part-to-whole ratio, then the percent.

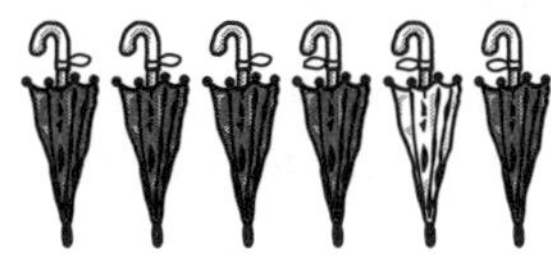

1. ______ ______ ______ ______ ______ ______

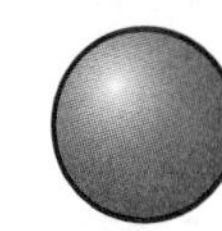

2. ______ ______ ______ ______ ______ ______

Express the situation as both a part-to-whole ratio and a percent. Divide to write a fraction as a percent if the denominator is not a factor of 100.

3. **15** games won out of **20** games played ______________

4. **2** successes out of **10** tries ______________

5. **6** red marbles out of **36** marbles ______________

6. **5** girls out of **15** children ______________

7. **11** baskets made, **9** missed ______________

8. **6** students out of **24** students ______________

9. **5** rainy days out of **25** days ______________

10. **10** sunny days out of **15** sunny days ______________

11. **16** questions correct, **4** wrong ______________

12. **1** purple shirt, **2** green shirts ______________

STANDARD

Sometimes you need to find what percent a fraction or mixed number is of another.

What percent of $13\frac{1}{3}$ is $1\frac{2}{3}$?

1. Write as a part-to-whole ratio. $\dfrac{1\frac{2}{3}}{13\frac{1}{3}}$ ← part ← whole

2. Divide. $1\frac{2}{3} \div 13\frac{1}{3}$ → $\frac{5}{3} \div \frac{40}{3} = \frac{1}{8}$ or **0.125**

3. Rewrite the quotient as a percent. **0.125** = **12.5%**

Complete.

13. 27 is what percent of 9? ________

14. 0.8 is what percent of 1.2? ________

15. 1.2 is what percent of 0.8? ________

16. 44 is what percent of 99? ________

17. 50 is what percent of 90? ________

18. 86 is what percent of 50? ________

19. 2 is what percent of $3\frac{1}{3}$? ________

20. $\frac{5}{6}$ is what percent of $3\frac{1}{3}$? ________

21. $1\frac{3}{8}$ is what percent of $2\frac{1}{2}$? ________

Problem Solving
Reasoning

Solve.

22. On a test, Lorraine scored **9** out of **11** multiple-choice questions correct, **4** out of **6** True-or-False questions correct, and **5** out of **7** fill-in-the blank questions correct. What percent of all the questions did she score correct? ________________

23. On Saturday Emma made a basket in **36** out of **80** attempts with a basketball. On Sunday, she made a basket in **11** out of **20** attempts. What percent of the baskets did she make on the weekend? ________________

Quick Check

Find the amount of the discount or interest.

24. 25% off of a price of **$15.29** ________

25. 30% off a price of **$244** ________

26. 8% interest for 1 year on **$550** ________

27. 4% interest for 6 months on **$1,220** ________

Find the percent. Round to the nearest whole percent.

28. 16 out of 30 ________

29. 39 out of 52 ________

30. 19 out of 40 ________

Work Space.

Name ___________________________

Finding the Number When a Percent Is Known

STANDARD

When a percent of the number is known, you can solve a proportion to find the number.

75% of Arlene's CDs are swing music. She has **15** swing music CDs. How many CDs does she have altogether?

Another way of stating this problem is:

75% of what number is **15?**

$$\begin{array}{r} \text{part} \rightarrow \\ \text{whole} \rightarrow \end{array} \frac{75}{100} = \frac{15}{n} \begin{array}{l} \leftarrow \text{part} \\ \leftarrow \text{whole} \end{array}$$

$$75 \times n = 100 \times 15$$

$$n = 20$$

Arlene has **20** CDs altogether.

Solve by using a proportion.

1. 25% of what number is **8**?

2. 20% of what number is **16**?

3. 60% of what number is **24**?

4. 5% of what number is **200**?

5. 175% of what number is **49**?

6. 30% of what number is **42**?

7. 50% of what number is **90**?

8. 15% of what number is **84**?

9. 40% of what number is **20**?

10. $16\frac{2}{3}$% of what number is **45**?

11. $37\frac{1}{2}$% of what number is **33**?

12. 75% of what number is **96**?

STANDARD

Solve by using a proportion.

13. What is 25% of 72?

14. 18% of what number is 9?

15. 12 is what percent of 20?

16. 72% of what number is 45?

17. 4 is what percent of 32?

18. What is 40% of 60?

19. 25 is what percent of 10?

20. What is $87\frac{1}{2}$% of 96?

21. $83\frac{1}{3}$% of what number is 45?

Problem Solving Reasoning Solve.

22. Tajma bought a CD on sale for 75% of the regular price. She paid $8.88. What was the regular price?

______

23. Eighteen of Maura's 45 CDs are country music. What percent are country music and what percent are not?

______

24. Arlene has 72 CDs. 25% of her CDs are jazz recordings. How many is that?

______

25. Bonnie had 42 CDs. She purchased $33\frac{1}{3}$% more CDs. How many CDs does Bonnie have now?

______

Test Prep ★ Mixed Review

26 Jenna made a poster for a class project. She painted $\frac{2}{5}$ of the poster green. What percent of the poster was green?

A 20%

B 25%

C 40%

D 60%

27 Sean had $5.76 in coins. Some coins fell out of his pocket. Now he has $3.98. Which equation could be used to find how much money (m) he lost?

F $5.76 - m = 3.98$

G $m - 3.98 = 5.76$

H $3.98m = 5.76$

J $5.76m = 3.98$

Name ______________________________

Problem Solving Strategy: Draw a Graph

STANDARD

Sometimes you can draw a graph to solve a problem.

Problem

The Johnson family wanted to make a display of their household expenses so they could see how they were spending their money. What could their display look like?

Food	**$12,000**
Housing	**$15,000**
Recreation	**$ 6,000**
Savings	**$ 3,000**
Clothing	**$ 9,000**
Miscellaneous	**$ 3,000**

1 Understand **As you reread, ask yourself questions.**

- What does the problem ask you to do?

____

2 Decide **Choose a method for solving.**

Try the strategy Draw a Graph.

- The data show how their expenses were divided up, so use a circle graph.
- Each of the numbers in the chart is a multiple of **$3,000**. If each section of the graph represents **$3,000**, how many sections would the graph have? ______

3 Solve **Draw the graph.**

- Use the table to complete the graph.

Johnson Family Expenses

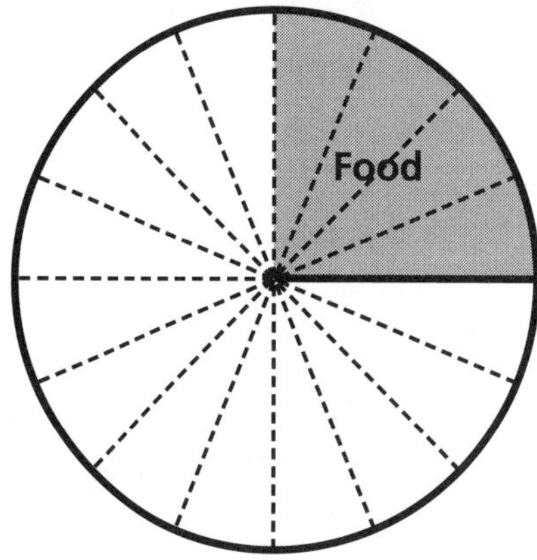

4 Look back **Check your graph.**

- Can you visually compare the amounts?

____

STANDARD

Use the Draw a Graph strategy or any other strategy you have learned.

1. The town board made a graph to present the town's budget for a year. What could their graph look like?

Think: Why is a circle graph appropriate for this data?

Middlefield's Budget for a Year	
Education	$1,000,000
Highways	$750,000
Health	$500,000
Library Expenses	$500,000
Miscellaneous	$250,000

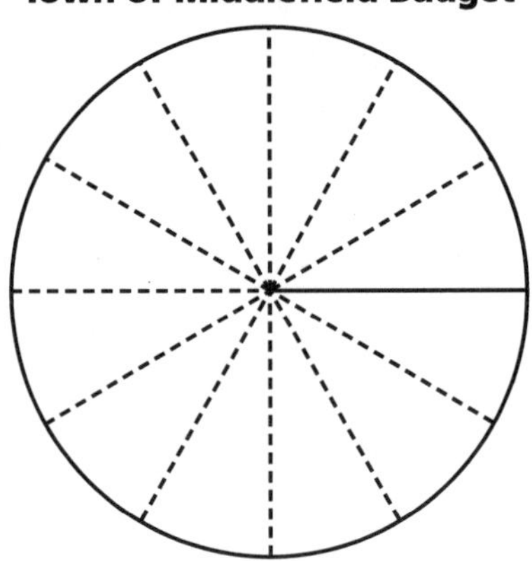

2. Bettina made a pictograph of the seating capacity of selected stadiums in the American Baseball League. She rounded the numbers to the nearest ten thousand. What did her graph look like?

Think: How many seats could one symbol represent?

Stadium	Seating Capacity
Anaheim Stadium	64,593
Yankee Stadium	57,545
Tiger Stadium	52,416
Fenway Park	33,871
Cominsky Park	44,431

3. George made a graph to show the lengths of selected suspension bridges in the United States. What could his graph look like?

Think: What type of graph is appropriate for this data?

Bridges	Length (in feet)
Golden Gate, CA	4,200
Mackinac, MI	3,800
Tacoma Narrows, WA	2,800
Verrazano-Narrows, NY	4,260
Benjamin Franklin, PA	1,750

4. Juanita made a circle graph of the Drama Club members for her school. She divided the circle into **8** sections. How many students did each section represent?

Grade	3	4	5	6
Members	5	10	10	15

5. Chion made a graph to show the average high temperature for his town over **5** days. What could his graph look like?

Mon	Tues	Wed	Thur	Fri
36° F	39° F	45° F	35° F	40° F

Name ___________________________

Estimating with Percents

STANDARD

One way to decide if a percent such as **40%** is closer to $\frac{3}{8}$ or $\frac{1}{2}$ is to write the fractions as percents, then compare.

$\frac{3}{8}$ = **37.5%** $\frac{1}{2}$ = **50%**

Since **40%** is closer to **37.5%** than to **50%**,

40% is closer to $\frac{3}{8}$ than to $\frac{1}{2}$.

You can estimate to check your computations with percents.

1. Exact Answer **11% × 480 = ___?___**

   0.11 × 480 = 52.8

   So, **11%** of **480** is **52.8**.

2. Estimate **11% of 480 = ___?___**

   11% is near **10%** or $\frac{1}{10}$

   10% or $\frac{1}{10}$ of **480** is **48**.

   52.8 is a little more than the estimate of **48**, so the exact answer is reasonable.

Circle the fraction that is closer to the percent.

1. 76%	$\frac{1}{2}$ $\frac{3}{4}$	89%	$\frac{9}{10}$ $\frac{8}{10}$	67%	$\frac{1}{2}$ $\frac{3}{4}$
2. 61%	$\frac{1}{2}$ $\frac{2}{3}$	33%	$\frac{1}{3}$ $\frac{3}{10}$	40%	$\frac{1}{3}$ $\frac{1}{2}$
3. 21%	$\frac{1}{4}$ $\frac{1}{5}$	72%	$\frac{3}{4}$ $\frac{2}{3}$	55%	$\frac{2}{3}$ $\frac{1}{2}$
4. 27%	$\frac{1}{3}$ $\frac{1}{4}$	42%	$\frac{2}{5}$ $\frac{3}{5}$	78%	$\frac{3}{4}$ $\frac{4}{5}$

First compute the exact product. Then estimate to check that your answer is reasonable.

		Exact Product	Estimate
5.	21% of 270		
6.	61% of 600		
7.	33% of 72		
8.	89% of 200		
9.	42% of 45		
10.	76% of 320		
11.	72% of 300		
12.	27% of 96		

STANDARD

Tell whether the estimate is an overestimate or an underestimate.

13. 18% of 38 ≈ 10 ____ 12% of 135 ≈ 10 ____ 99% of 799 ≈ 799 ____

14. 16% of 129 ≈ 30 ____ 55% of 800 ≈ 400 ____ 25% of 415 ≈ 100 ____

Problem Solving Reasoning Solve.

15. A sale of **75%** off is advertised. About what would be the sale price of a computer with a regular price of **$1,299?**

____

16. Storage disks are on sale at store A for **80%** off the regular price of **$10.50** and **75%** off the regular price of **$7.99** at store B. Estimate and explain which is the better buy.

____

____

17. Sales tax is **8%**. Estimate the amount of sales tax on a **$25.55** purchase. ____

18. Find the cost for each meal and estimate a tip of **15%**.

The Restaurant	
Salad	$1.95
Steak	$14.95
Milk	$1.25
Cherries Jubilee	$3.50
Tip:	____

The Restaurant	
Soup	$2.25
Chicken	$10.95
Milk	$1.25
Bananas Supreme	$3.75
Tip:	____

Quick Check

Write the number.

19. 21 is 15% of what number? ____

20. 72 is 120% of what number? ____

21. 91 is 7% of what number? ____

Estimate.

22. 23% of 58 ____ **23.** 35% of 157 ____ **24.** 83% of 92 ____

Work Space.

Name ______________________

Unit 6 Review

Write each ratio or rate three ways in simplest form.

1. 7 books to 3 shelves ________ **2.** 6 bats to 4 balls ________

Find each missing term.

3. $\frac{3}{4} = \frac{n}{20}$ ______ **4.** $\frac{2}{5} = \frac{x}{15}$ ______ **5.** $\frac{7}{8} = \frac{y}{32}$ ______ **6.** $\frac{9}{5} = \frac{r}{35}$ ______ **7.** $\frac{7}{1} = \frac{a}{6}$ ______

8. 12 people in 3 lines = n people in 9 lines $n =$ ______

Solve.

9. If 12 pencils cost **$1.44**, what is the cost of 4 pencils? ______

10. If a car travels 50 miles in 1 hour, how far will it travel in 90 minutes? ______

Complete.

11. If 1 inch on a map represents 200 miles, then 1.5 inches represent ______ miles.

12. If 2 feet on a model represent $\frac{1}{4}$ inch, then ______ feet represent 1 inch.

Rename each fraction as a percent and each percent as a fraction in simplest form.

13. $\frac{5}{6}$ ______ **14.** $\frac{3}{8}$ ______ **15.** 80% ______ **16.** 65% ______

Rename each decimal as a percent and each percent as a decimal.

17. 28% ______ **18.** 50% ______ **19.** 0.39 ______ **20.** 0.625 ______

Solve.

21. 7 is what percent of $3\frac{1}{2}$? ______ **22.** 16 is 20% of what number? ______

23. Use the information in the table to make a graph.

Class Election	
Candidate	**Number of Votes**
A	8
B	20
C	4

Class Election

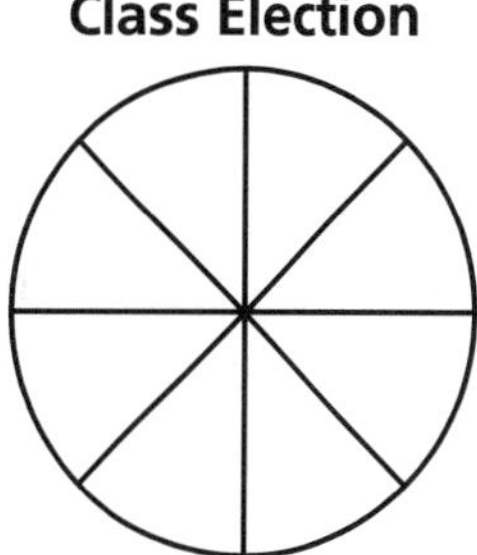

24. What percent of the students did not vote for Candidate B? ______

Name ______________________________

Cumulative Review
★ Test Prep

1 **A clerk at the Downtown Deli is making a super-long sandwich for a party. Each of the 54 guests will get 3 inches of sandwich. How long should the sandwich be?**

A 162 ft **C** 13 ft 6 in. **E** NH

B 136 in. **D** 13 ft

2 **Alison needs a piece of wood $3\frac{3}{4}$ feet long for her art project. She has a board that is 5 feet long. How much does she need to cut off?**

F $2\frac{1}{4}$ ft **H** 1 ft **K** NH

G $1\frac{1}{4}$ ft **J** $\frac{3}{4}$ ft

3 **Joel is making place cards for a dinner. He uses $\frac{1}{3}$ sheet of paper for each card. He has $5\frac{2}{3}$ sheets of paper. How many cards can he make?**

A $1\frac{8}{9}$ **C** $15\frac{2}{3}$ **E** NH

B 7 **D** 17

4 **Eduardo bought a sweater that was on sale for 80% of its regular price. He paid $24 for the sweater. What was the regular price of the sweater?**

F $19.20 **H** $30 **K** NH

G $24 **J** $32

5 **A length of 1 foot is 0.3048 m. What is this number rounded to the nearest 0.01 m?**

A 0.30 **C** 0.305 **E** NH

B 0.304 **D** 0.31

6

School Play Attendance	
Day	Number of People
Wednesday	345
Thursday	332
Friday	402
Saturday	402
Sunday	353

Which statement about the table is *true*?

F A different number of people came to the play each night.

G The most people came to the play on Sunday.

H More people came to the play on Wednesday than on Thursday.

J The same number of people came to the play on Thursday and Friday.

7 **Use your inch ruler and this drawing to help you answer this question.**

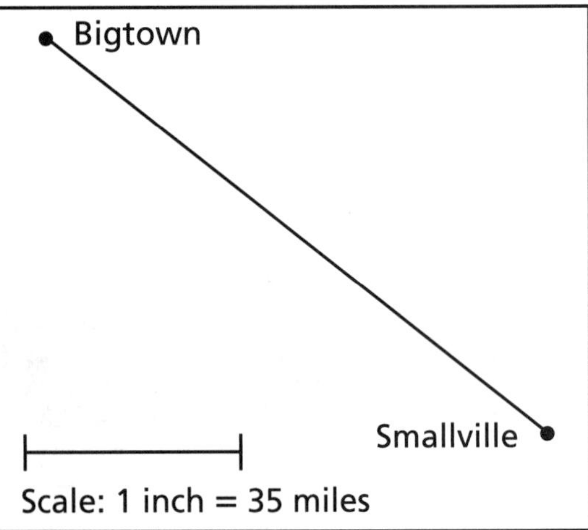

What is the actual distance from Bigtown to Smallville?

A 3 miles **C** 105 miles

B 35 miles **D** 140 miles

UNIT 7 • TABLE OF CONTENTS

Geometry of Plane Figures

We will be using this vocabulary:

quadrilateral a polygon with four sides

angle a figure formed by two rays that have a common endpoint

ray a part of a line with one endpoint

congruent figures figures that have exactly the same size and shape

Dear Family,

During the next few weeks, our math class will be learning about the geometry of plane figures. You can expect to see homework that provides practice with classifying polygons. Here is a sample you may want to keep handy to give help if needed.

Classifying Polygons

Polygons are simple closed plane figures formed by joining three or more segments. Examples of polygons include:

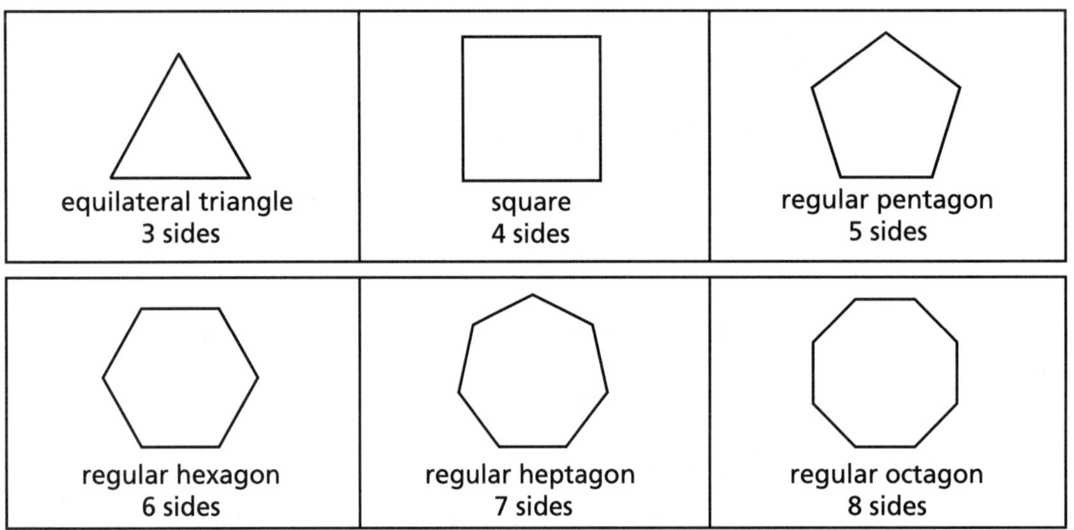

These polygons are **regular** polygons because all of the sides of each polygon have the same length and all of the angles have the same measure.

Explore your home with your child and try to find examples of regular polygons as well as other polygons such as rectangles and parallelograms.

During this unit, students will need to continue practicing identifying figures as well as determining congruence and symmetry.

Sincerely,

Name ______________________________

Plane Figures

STANDARD

A **point** is a location in space. **Space** is the set of all points. A **plane** is a set of points that forms a flat surface extending in all directions without limit.

Here are some figures that are contained in a plane:

Segment

The **endpoints** of this segment are ***A*** and ***B***.

A B

segment ***AB*** or $\overline{AB}$ segment ***BA*** or $\overline{BA}$

Ray

A ray has one endpoint and extends without end in one direction.

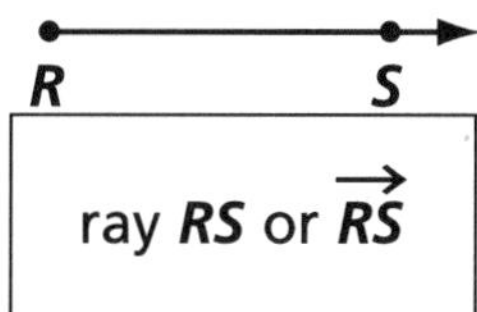

ray ***RS*** or $\overrightarrow{RS}$

Line

The arrowheads show that a line extends without end in two directions.

C D

line ***CD*** or $\overleftrightarrow{CD}$ line ***DC*** or $\overleftrightarrow{DC}$

Two rays that share a common endpoint form an **angle.** The common endpoint is the **vertex** of the angle. The two rays are the **sides** of the angle.

The symbol ∠ represents an angle. In naming an angle, write the letter that names the vertex in the middle. The angle at the right is ∠***QXR*** or ∠***RXQ.***

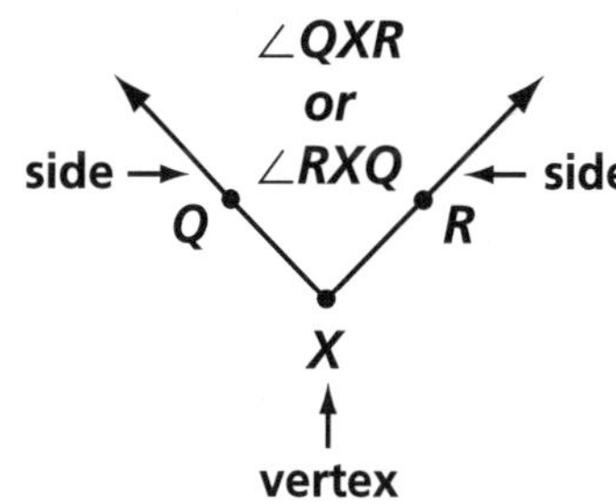

Sometimes you can name an angle using only the vertex. The angle at the right can also be called ∠***X***.

Write the name for the figure in two ways.

1. B A

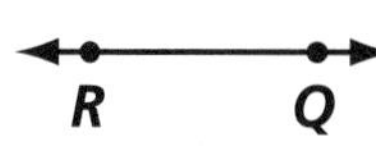

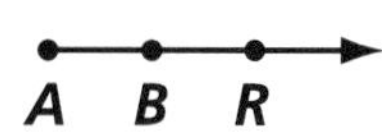

_______________ _______________ _______________ _______________

Write the name for the angle in three ways.

2.

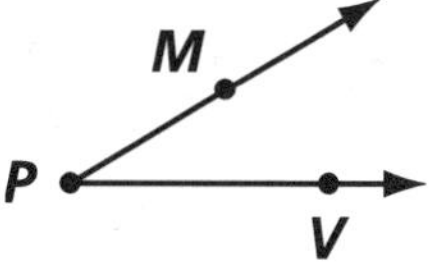

C G J

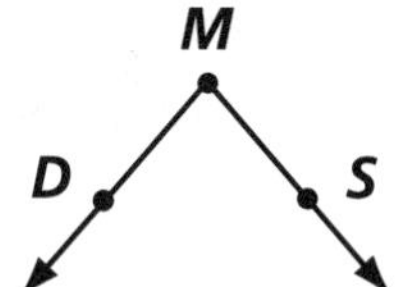

_______________ _______________ _______________ _______________

STANDARD

Two lines in the same plane that never intersect are **parallel** (∥) lines.

A B C D

$\overleftrightarrow{AB}$ is parallel to $\overleftrightarrow{CD}$

$\overleftrightarrow{AB} \parallel \overleftrightarrow{CD}$

Two lines in the same plane that intersect to form square corners or right angles are **perpendicular** (⊥) lines.

W Y Z X

$\overleftrightarrow{WX}$ is perpendicular to $\overleftrightarrow{YZ}$

$\overleftrightarrow{WX} \perp \overleftrightarrow{YZ}$

Draw the figures.

3. Draw $\overleftrightarrow{AB} \perp \overleftrightarrow{BC}$

Draw $\overleftrightarrow{GH} \parallel \overleftrightarrow{IJ}$

Draw $\overleftrightarrow{ST}$ and $\overleftrightarrow{WX}$ intersecting at point *Y*.

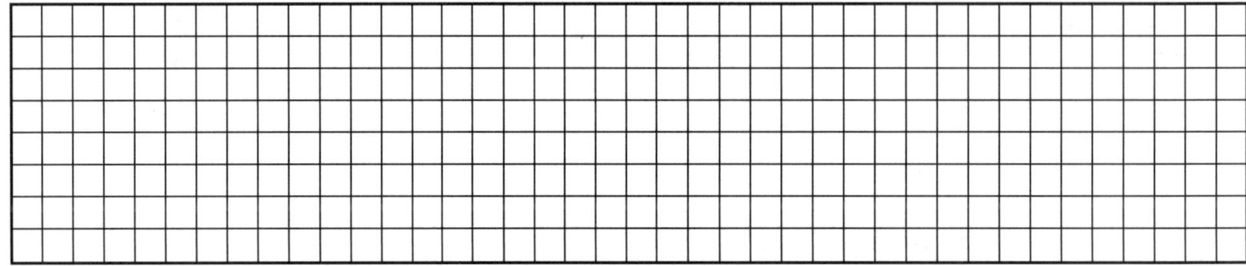

Problem Solving
Reasoning

Solve.

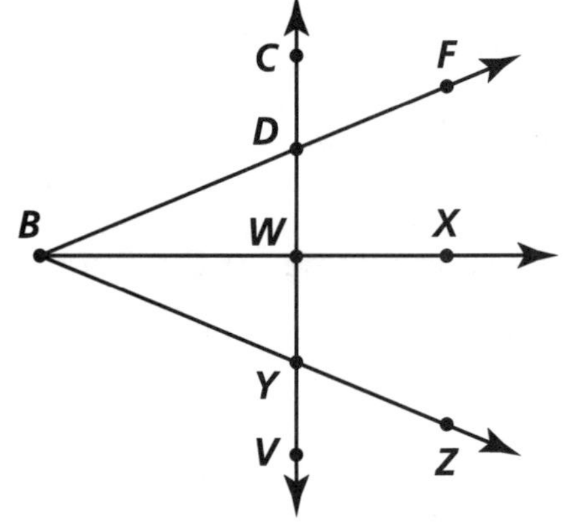

4. How many right angles are formed at the intersection of two perpendicular lines? ______

5. How many different angles are a part of this figure?

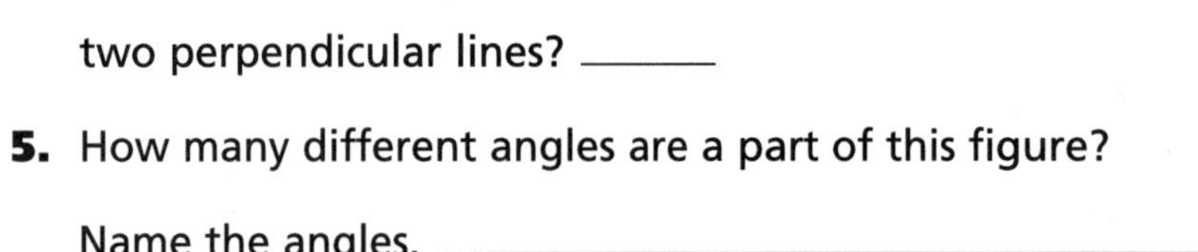

Name the angles. ______________________

____

____

6. How many lines are in the figure? ______________________

7. Name ten rays in the figure. ______________________

____

Test Prep ★ Mixed Review

8 **What should you do to both sides of this equation to solve it?**

$$t \div 456 = 654$$

A Multiply by *t*

B Divide by *t*

C Multiply by 456

D Divide by 456

9 **Rachel has 64 pennies and 32 nickels. What is the ratio of pennies to nickels in simplest form?**

F 64:32

G 32:64

H 1:2

J 2:1

Name ____________________

Measuring Angles

STANDARD

You can measure an angle using an instrument called a **protractor.** To measure $\angle BAC$:

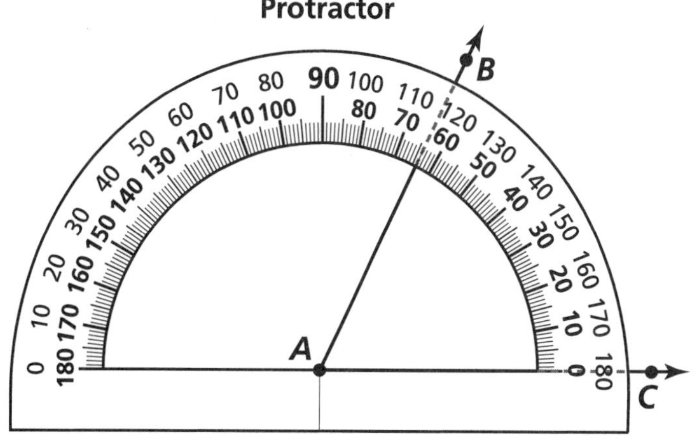

1 Place the center of the protractor at *A,* the vertex of the angle.

2 Place the zero mark on $\overrightarrow{AC}$, one side of the angle.

3 Read the measure of the angle where $\overrightarrow{AB}$, the other side of the angle, crosses the protractor. The measure of $\angle BAC$ is **64°**. You can classify angles by their measure.

Right angle → measures exactly **90°**
Acute angle → measures less than **90°**
Obtuse angle → measures greater than **90°**, but less than **180°**

Use a protractor to measure the angle. Then write the measure and classify the angle.

1.

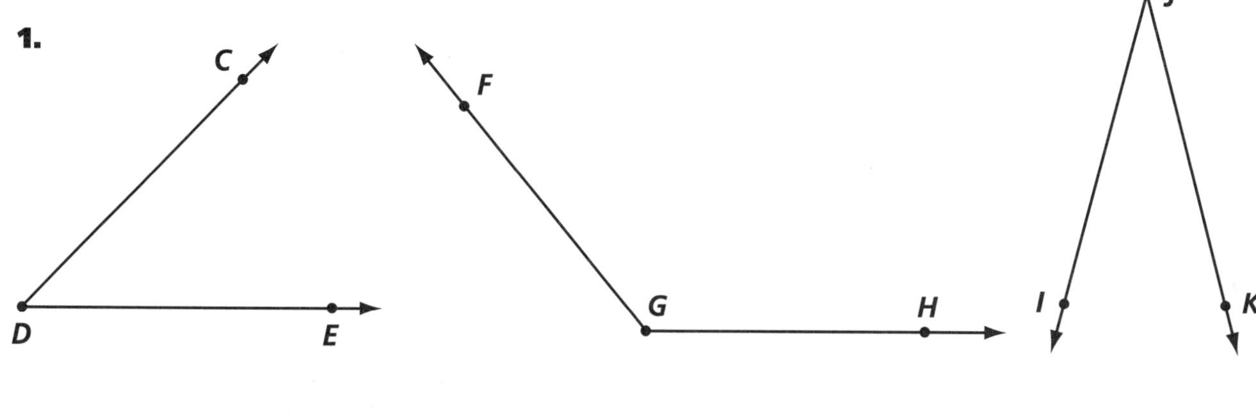

____________ ____________ ____________

2.

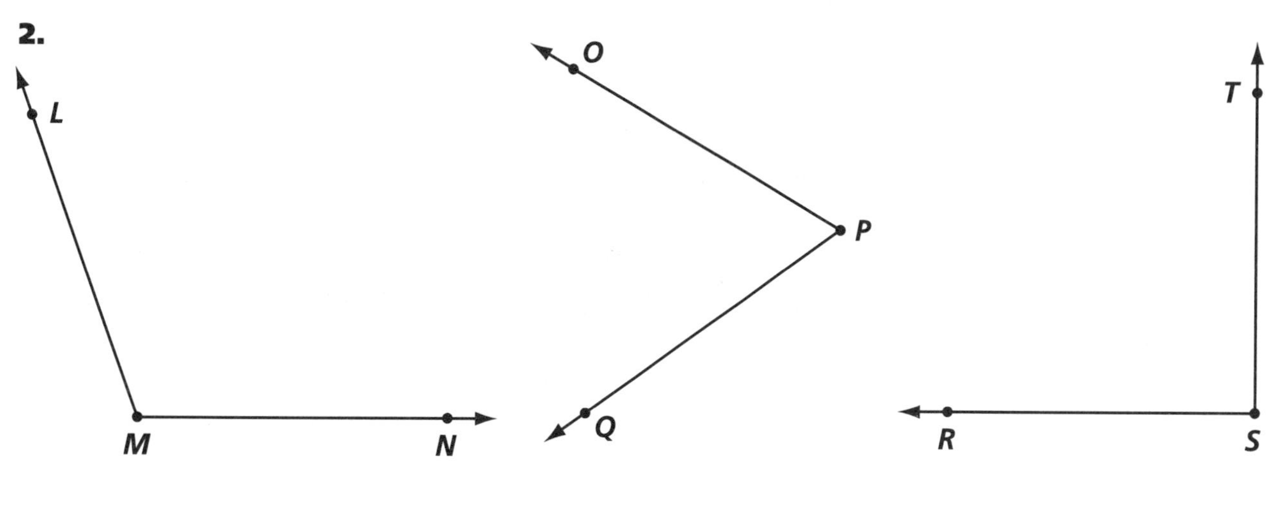

____________ ____________ ____________

STANDARD

Use a protractor to measure the angle. Then write the measure and classify the angle.

3.

4.

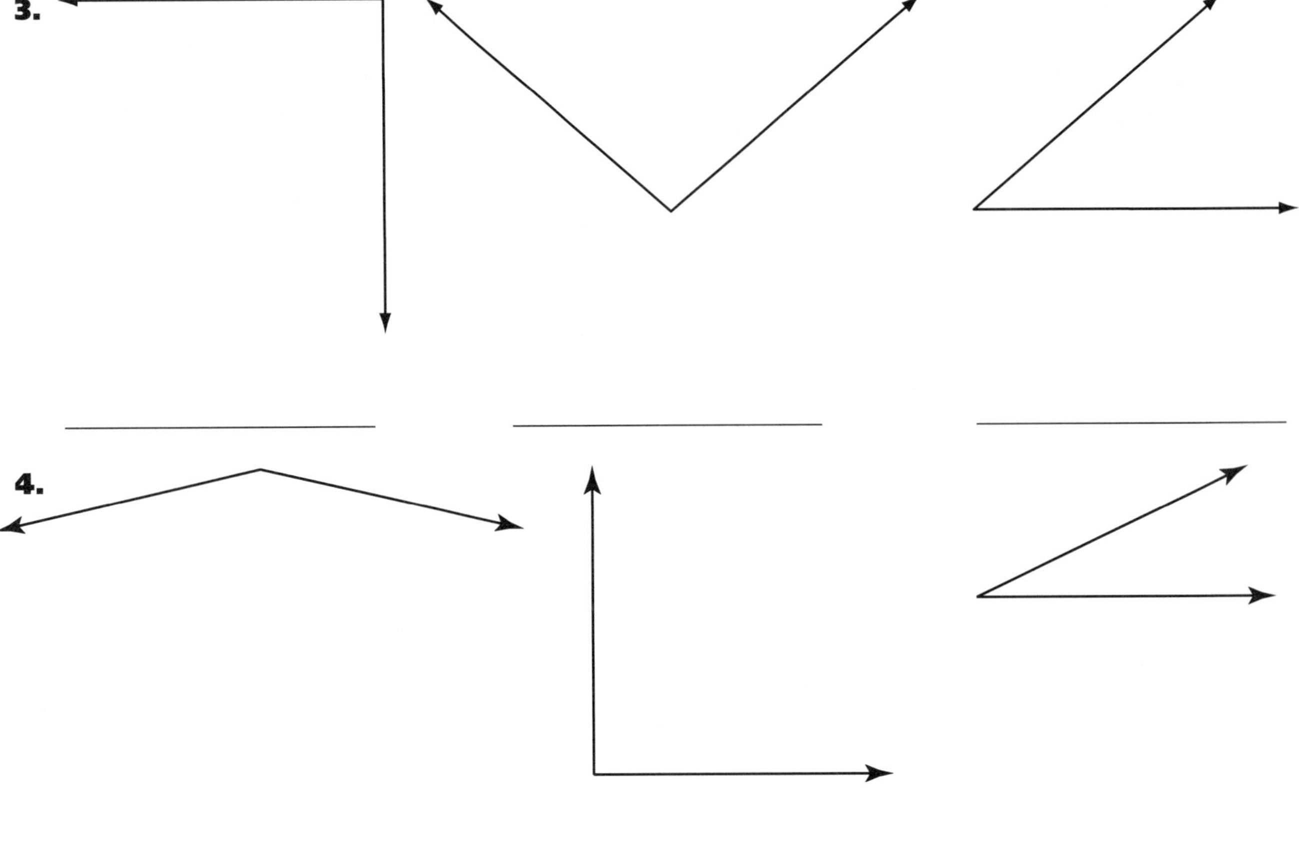

Problem Solving
Reasoning

Solve.

5. The sum of the measures of the angles in any triangle is **180°**. What is the greatest number of right angles a triangle could have? ______

6. The sum of the measures of the four angles in a quadrilateral is **360°**. What is the greatest number of obtuse angles a quadrilateral could have? ______

Test Prep ★ Mixed Review

7. Arthur needs 3 packages of craft sticks to make 5 models. This proportion shows how many packages he needs to make 15 models.

$$\frac{x}{15} = \frac{3}{5}$$

What is the value of x?

A 3
B 9
C 15
D 45

8. Sara used $\frac{4}{25}$ of a package of plaster for an art project. What percent of the package did she use?

F 16%
G 25%
H 84%
J 100%

Name ______________________________

Pairs of Angles

STANDARD

If the measures of two angles are equal, the angles are said to be **congruent**.
Since $\angle ABC = \angle DEF$, $\angle ABC$ is congruent to $\angle DEF$, or $\angle ABC \cong \angle DEF$.

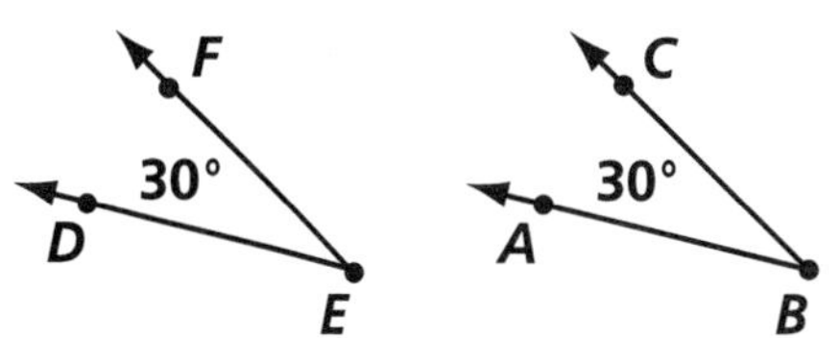

The angles on opposite sides of the intersection of two lines are called **vertical angles.** Vertical angles are always congruent.
Since $\angle PSR$ and $\angle QST$ are vertical angles, $\angle PSR \cong \angle QST$ and $\angle PSR = \angle QST$.
Since $\angle PSQ$ and $\angle RST$ are vertical angles, $\angle PSQ \cong \angle RST$ and $\angle PSQ = \angle RST$.

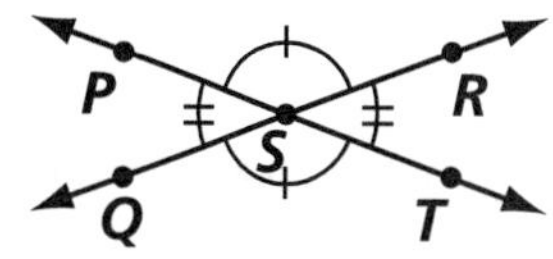

Curves with tics show congruent angles.

If the sum of the measures of two angles is **180°**, the angles are **supplementary**. $\angle MXL$ is supplementary to $\angle LXP$, because $\angle MXL + \angle LXP = 180°$.

If the sum of the measures of two angles is **90°**, the angles are **complementary**. $\angle BQK$ is complementary to $\angle KQS$, because $\angle BQK + \angle KQS = 90°$.

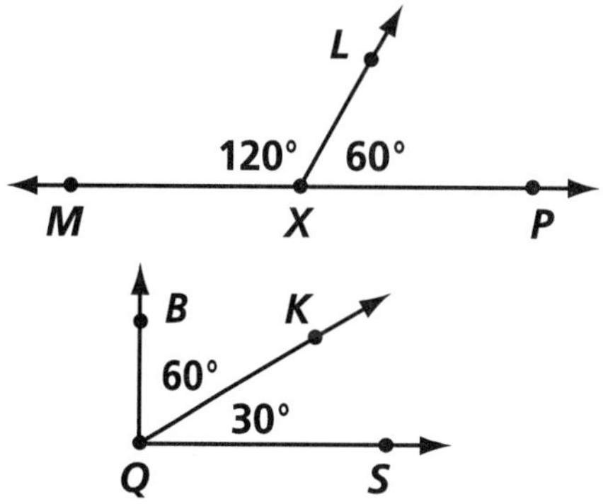

Name and write the measures of each pair of vertical angles. Use a protractor.

1. ______ ≅ ______

______ ≅ ______

$\angle DEF =$ ______

$\angle FEG =$ ______

$\angle HEG =$ ______

$\angle HED =$ ______

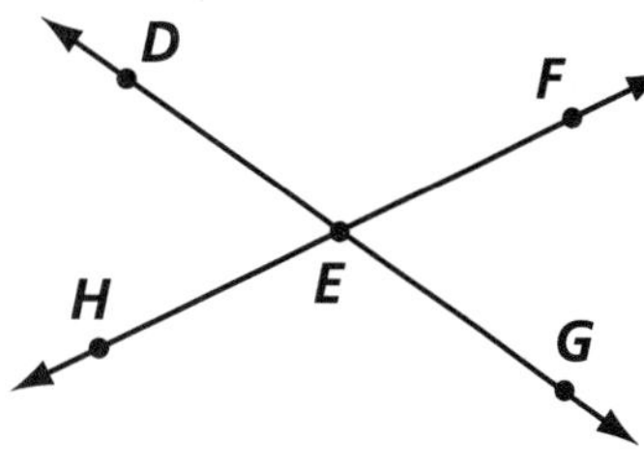

2. ______ ≅ ______

______ ≅ ______

$\angle MOZ =$ ______

$\angle ZOW =$ ______

$\angle LOW =$ ______

$\angle LOM =$ ______

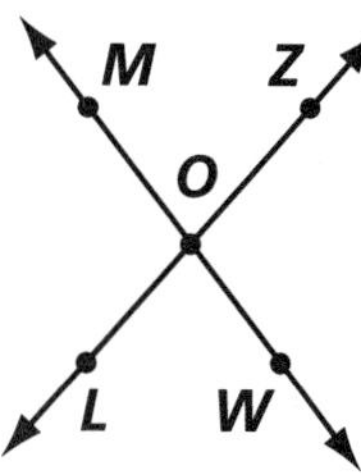

3. In exercise 1, what relationship is there between $\angle DEF$ and $\angle HED$? $\angle HEG$ and $\angle DEH$?

____

____

STANDARD

Complete.

Measure of given angle	Measure of complement	Measure of supplement	Measure of given angle	Measure of complement	Measure of supplement
4. 45°	_____	_____	**5.** 65°	_____	_____
6. 32°	_____	_____	**7.** 20°	_____	_____
8. 18°	_____	_____	**9.** 89°	_____	_____

Use the intersecting lines to answer the questions.

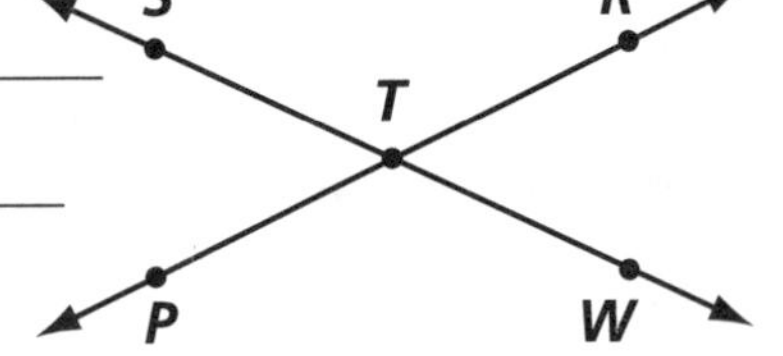

10. Which two angles are supplements to $\angle STP$? _____________

11. The measure of $\angle STP$ is $50°$. What is the measure of $\angle STR$? _____
$\angle RTW$? _____ $\angle PTW$? _____

Problem Solving Reasoning

$\angle BOA = n°$. Use $n°$ to write the measure of each angle.

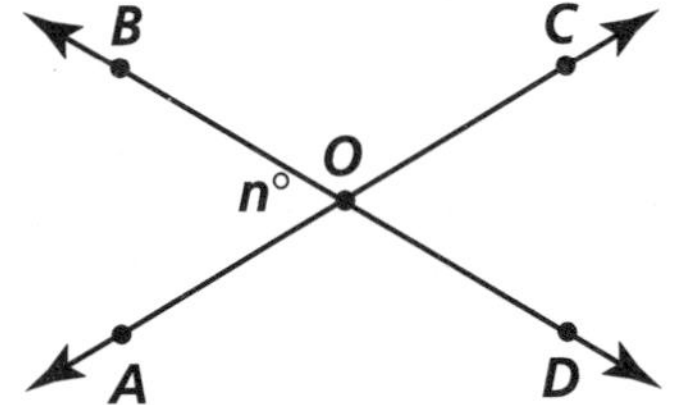

12. $\angle BOC =$ _____

$\angle DOC =$ _____

$\angle AOD =$ _____

$\angle AOB + \angle BOC =$ _____

Quick Check

Solve.

Work Space.

13. Three points *A*, *B*, and *C* are on one line. Point *B* is between the other two points. Name the longest segment in two ways. _____

14. $\overline{PA}$, $\overline{PQ}$, and $\overline{PB}$ are all in one plane. $\overline{PA} \perp \overline{PQ}$ and $\overline{PB} \perp \overline{PQ}$.

How are $\overline{PA}$ and $\overline{PB}$ related? _____________

Use the diagram at the right for exercises 15–18.

B
A D C

15. Name the two acute angles of the largest triangle. _____

16. Name an obtuse angle that has its vertex at *D*. _____

17. Name a complement of $\angle ABD$. _____

18. Name a supplement of $\angle ADB$. _____

Name ______________________________

Circles and Central Angles

STANDARD

You can use a compass to mark many points that are the same distance from a point. The set of all these points is called a **circle**.

A circle is named by its center.

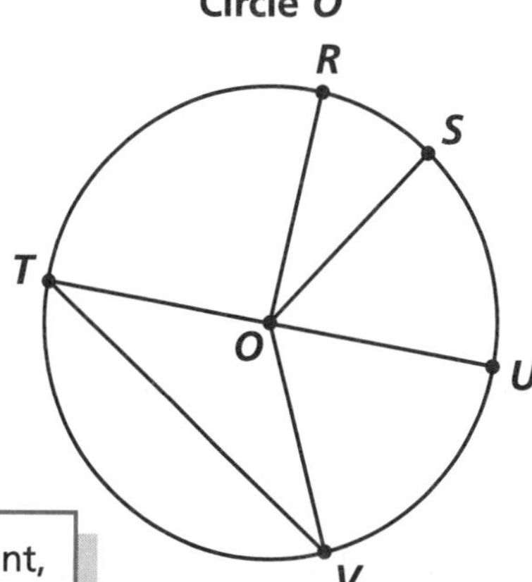

A line segment connecting the center of a circle to any point on the circle is a **radius** (plural, **radii**). A line segment connecting any two points on a circle is a **chord.** A chord passing through the center of a circle is a **diameter.** The measure of a diameter is twice the measure of a radius.

Center: point ***O***

Radii: $\overline{OT}, \overline{OR}, \overline{OS}, \overline{OU}, \overline{OV}$

Chords: $\overline{TU}, \overline{TV}$

Diameter: $\overline{TU}$

$\overline{TU}$ names the segment, ***TU*** is the length of the segment.

Measure the radius or diameter of circle *O* to the nearest $\frac{1}{8}$ inch.

1. *OT* = ______ *TU* = ______ *OR* = ______ *OV* = ______

Identify these parts of circle *R*.

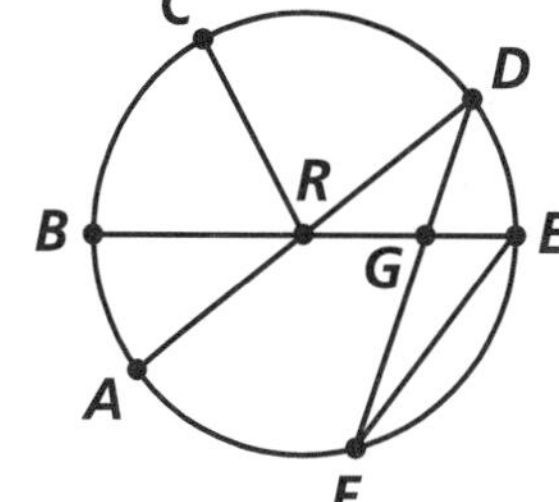

2. center ______________________

3. radii ______________________

4. chords ______________________

5. diameters ______________________

6. On a piece of paper, draw a circle with a radius of **4** cm. Use a centimeter ruler and a compass. ______________________

7. On a piece of paper, draw a circle with a diameter of **6** cm. Use a centimeter ruler and a compass. ______________________

Write A if the statement is always true.
Write S if the statement is sometimes true.
Write N if the statement is never true.

8. Two radii of a circle are congruent. ______

9. A diameter is a chord. ______

10. A chord is a diameter. ______

11. A diameter is twice as long as a radius. ______

STANDARD

A **central angle** is any angle whose vertex is the center of the circle.

$\angle SOR$ is a central angle of circle O. The common endpoint of $\overline{OR}$ and $\overline{OS}$ is the center of the circle, O.

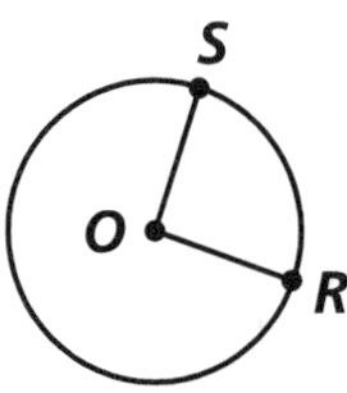

Complete for circle C.

12. Draw diameter $\overline{AB}$.

13. Draw the following radii: $\overline{CD}$, $\overline{CE}$, $\overline{CF}$, and $\overline{CG}$.

14. Draw a chord $\overline{HI}$ that is not a diameter.

15. Draw central angle $\angle JCK$.

16. Draw another central angle $\angle LCM$.

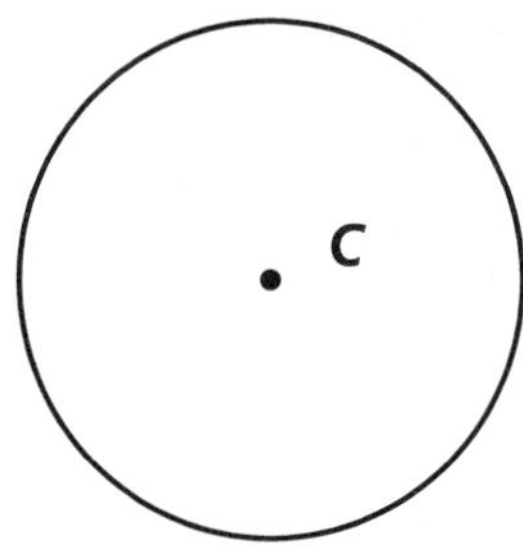

Problem Solving
Reasoning

Solve.

17. How many radii does a circle have? ______

18. How many diameters? ______

19. Use your centimeter ruler.

Measure a radius of circle K. ______

Measure a diameter of circle K. ______

20. Write a general rule about how to find the measure of a diameter, if you know the measure of a radius. ______

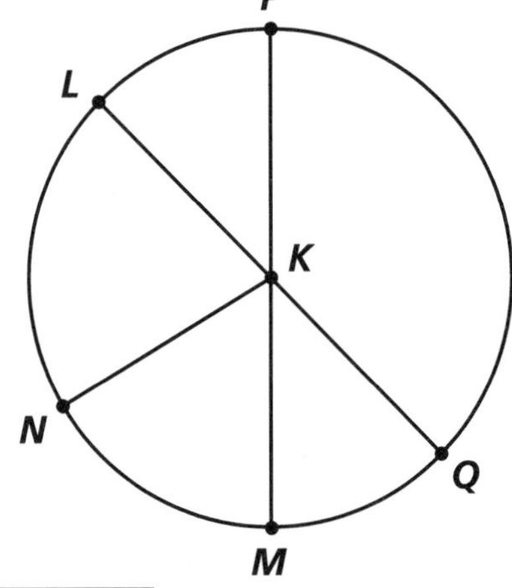

Test Prep ★ Mixed Review

21 Mike's Market is having a sale on peaches. The peaches cost $0.89 for 2 pounds. How much do 8 pounds cost?

A $7.12

B $6.12

C $3.56

D $.89

22 What is the greatest common factor of 27 and 81?

F 1

G 3

H 9

J 27

Name ____________________________________

Congruence and Constructions

STANDARD

A **polygon** is a simple closed plane figure that is formed by three or more line segments. Two polygons that have exactly the same size and shape are **congruent.**

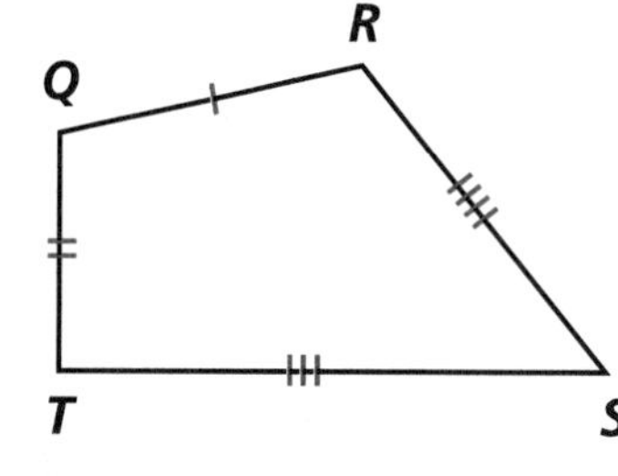

Congruent polygons have corresponding congruent sides and corresponding congruent angles. Congruent sides are the same length. Congruent angles have the same measure. The names of congruent polygons are written so the corresponding vertices are in the same order.

Tic marks are used to show that two or more sides are congruent.

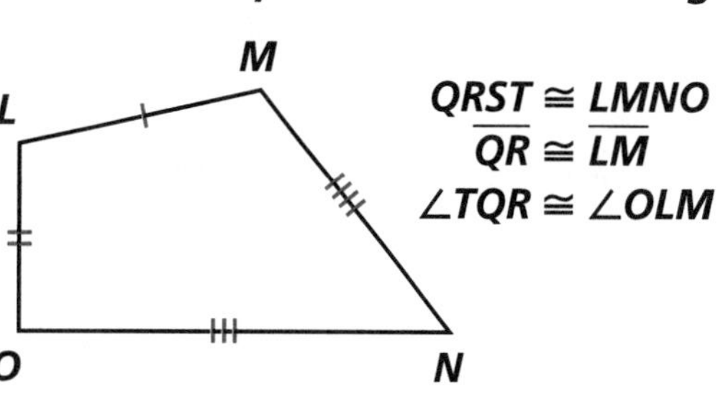

$QRST \cong LMNO$
$\overline{QR} \cong \overline{LM}$
$\angle TQR \cong \angle OLM$

Here is how to draw a **50°** angle:

1 Draw one side.

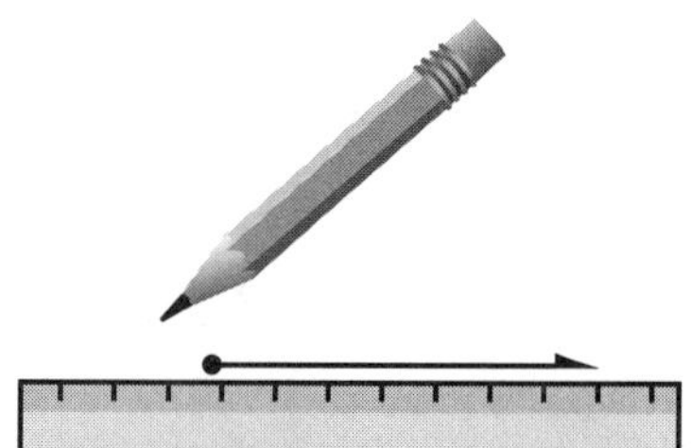

2 Place the protractor as you would for measuring and make a mark at **50°**.

3 Draw the other side.

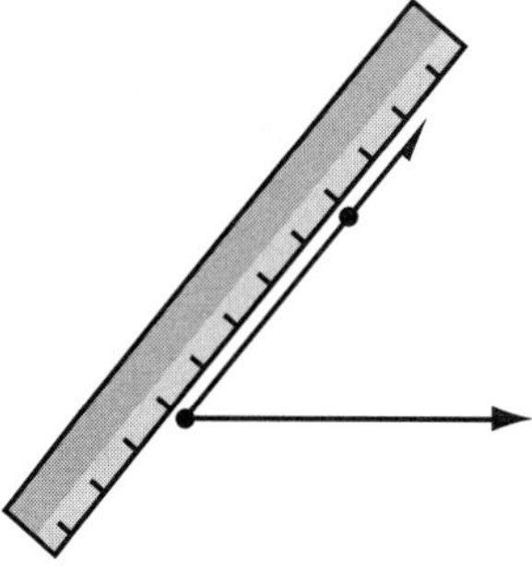

Complete the list of congruent sides and angles for *QRST* and *LMNO* shown above. Then use a protractor to measure the angles and a ruler to measure the sides.

1. $\overline{QR} \cong \overline{LM}$; Length of each: ______

$\overline{RS} \cong$ ______; Length of each: ______

$\overline{ST} \cong$ ______; Length of each: ______

$\overline{QT} \cong$ ______; Length of each: ______

2. $\angle TQR \cong \angle OLM$; Measure of each: ______

$\angle QRS \cong$ ______; Measure of each: ______

$\angle RST \cong$ ______; Measure of each: ______

$\angle STQ \cong$ ______; Measure of each: ______

Draw angles having these measures.

3. 30°

4. 120°

5. 45°

STANDARD

You can construct congruent line segments using a compass and straightedge.

Construct a line segment congruent to $\overline{AB}$.

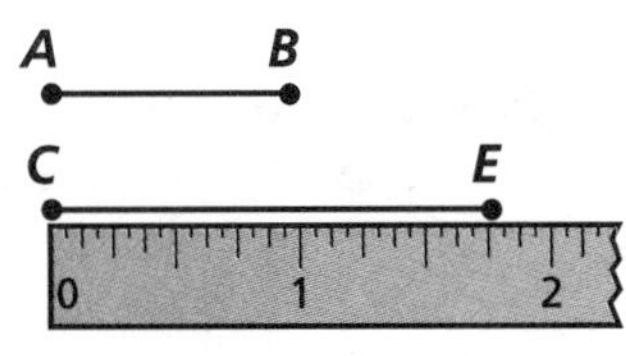

1 Use the straightedge to draw $\overline{CE}$, longer than $\overline{AB}$.

2 Measure the distance from *A* to *B* with the compass.

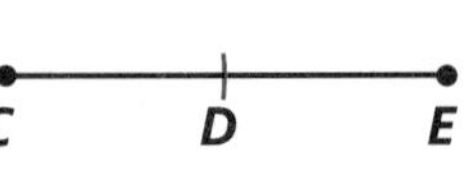

3 Keep the same setting on the compass. Place the compass point on *C*. Draw an arc on $\overline{CE}$. Label the point where the arc crosses the line *D*. $\overline{AB} \cong \overline{CD}$

On a piece of paper, construct a segment congruent to the given segment.

9.

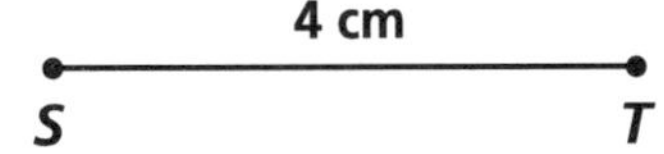

2 cm

G H

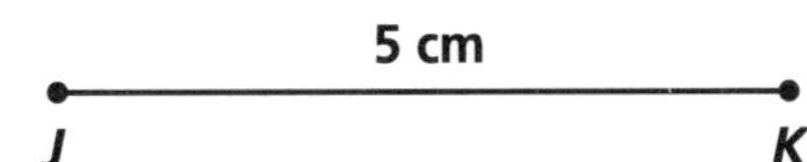

Problem Solving Reasoning Solve.

10. Name the pairs of congruent triangles in the diagram at the right.

____

11. Triangle *PQR* has **3** congruent sides and **3** congruent angles. How could you divide it into **2** congruent triangles?

____

____

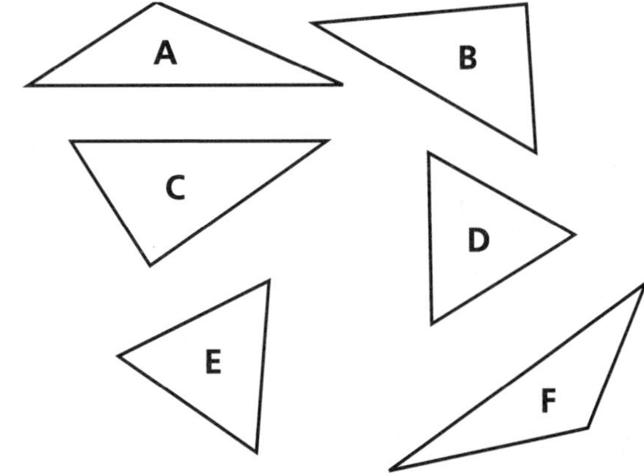

Test Prep ★ Mixed Review

12 **Neal bought some new shirts. He spent $51.80. The shirts cost $12.95 each. Which equation could you use to find how many shirts he bought?**

A $12.95 + n = 51.80$

B $51.80 \div n = 12.95$

C $51.80n = 12.95$

D $12.95 \div n = 51.80$

13 **The Sweater Shack is having a sale. All sweaters cost 60% of their normal price. Mia bought a sweater on sale for $24. What is the normal price of the sweater?**

F $14.40

G $24

H $40

J $144

Name ______________________________

Triangles

STANDARD

Figure ***ABC*** at the right is a polygon. It is called a **triangle**, because it has **3** angles. Triangle ***ABC*** can be written as $\triangle ABC$. Each of the points ***A***, ***B***, and ***C*** is a **vertex** (plural **vertices**) of the triangle.

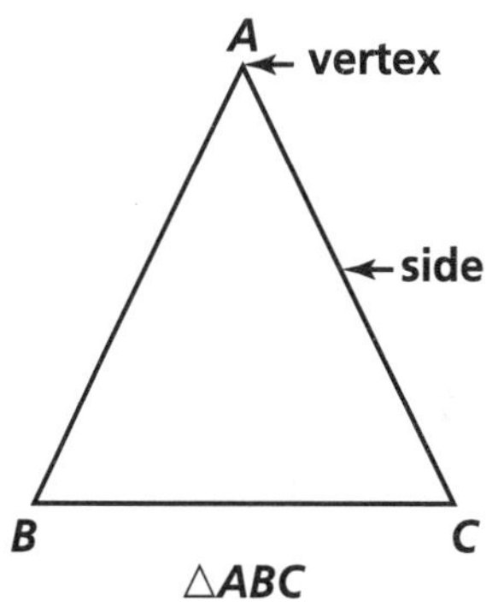

$\triangle ABC$ is made up of three sides and three vertices.

sides: $\overline{AB}$, $\overline{BC}$, $\overline{CA}$

vertices: ***A***, ***B***, ***C***

You can construct a triangle using a compass and a straightedge.

Construct an equilateral triangle with sides equal to $\overline{PQ}$.

1 Construct $\overline{GH}$ congruent to $\overline{PQ}$.

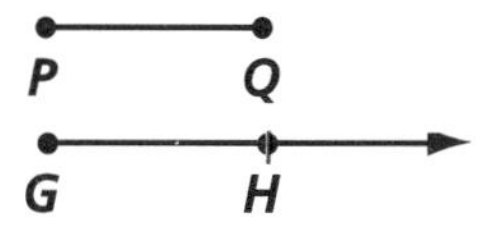

2 Keep the same setting on the compass. Put the point of the compass at ***G*** and make a large arc.

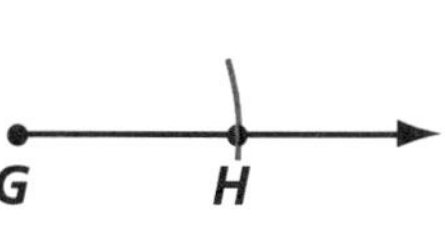

3 Keep the same setting on the compass. Put the point of the compass at ***H*** and make an arc that intersects the previous arc.

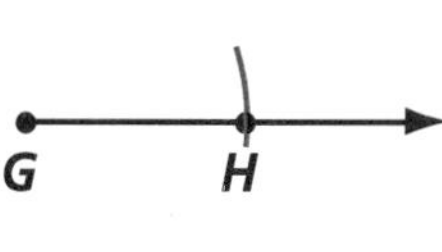

4 Connect the intersection of the arcs with the endpoints of $\overline{GH}$.

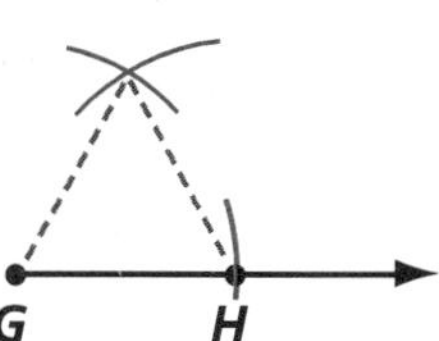

On a piece of paper, construct an equilateral triangle with sides whose lengths are equal to the length given.

1.    

R ________ *T*   *A* ________ *S*   *B* ________ *K*

2. Measure each angle of the triangles you drew in exercise **1**. What did you observe?

____

3. On a piece of paper, use the segments in exercise **1** for the two congruent sides and construct three isosceles triangles. Use any different length for the third side.

____

STANDARD

A triangle can be classified by its greatest angle measure.

Acute triangle: The greatest angle is an acute angle.
Right triangle: The greatest angle is a right angle.
Obtuse triangle: The greatest angle is an obtuse angle.

A triangle can also be classified by the number of congruent sides it has.

Equilateral triangle: 3 congruent sides
Isosceles triangle: at least **2** congruent sides
Scalene triangle: no congruent sides

Measure each angle and write the measure.
Circle the greatest angle measure, then classify the triangle according to its angle measures.

4.

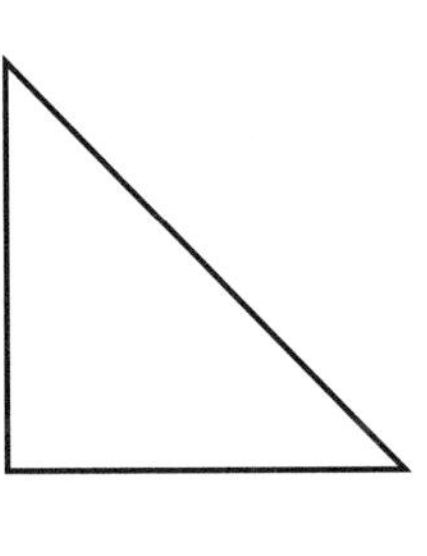

______

______

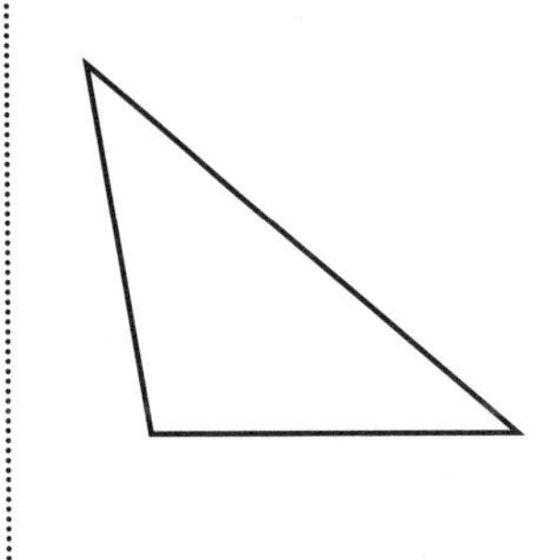

______

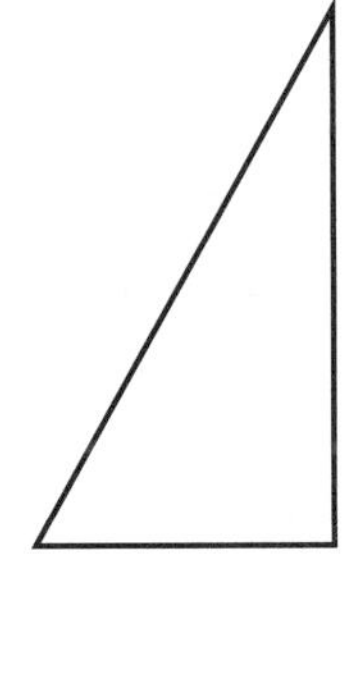

______

5. How many triangles in exercise 4 are

equilateral? ______ isosceles? ______ scalene? ______

Quick Check

Use the diagram below for excercises 6–9. Write whether the statement is *True* or *False*.

Work Space.

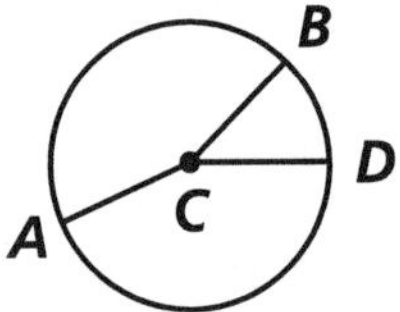

6. All central angles are acute. ______

7. $\overline{AB}$ is a diameter of the circle. ______

8. $\overline{AC} \cong \overline{CD}$. ______

9. All diameters of the circle are congruent. ______

10. Draw an acute isoceles triangle.

Name ______________________________________

Quadrilaterals and Angle Sums

STANDARD

Every polygon with **4** line segments joined to make **4** angles is called a **quadrilateral.** *Quadri* means "four." *Lateral* means "side." Here are some examples of quadrilaterals.

a polygon with **4** sides and **4** angles

parallelogram

a quadrilateral with **2** pairs of congruent parallel sides

rectangle

a parallelogram with **4** right angles

square

a rectangle with **4** congruent sides

rhombus

a parallelogram with **4** congruent sides

trapezoid

a quadrilateral with **1** pair of parallel sides

Draw the quadrilateral. Use tics to show congruent sides and arrows to show parallel sides.

1. square *ABCD*

2. rectangle *EFGH*

3. parallelogram *JKLM*

4. rhombus *PQRS*

5. a rhombus that is not a square

6. a quadrilateral that is not a parallelogram

7. a rectangle that is not a rhombus

8. a parallelogram with at least **1** right angle

9. a quadrilateral with **1** pair of parallel sides

10. a quadrilateral that is not a parallelogram or a trapezoid

STANDARD

You can use these properties to solve problems.

The sum of the measures of the three angles of any triangle is **180°**.

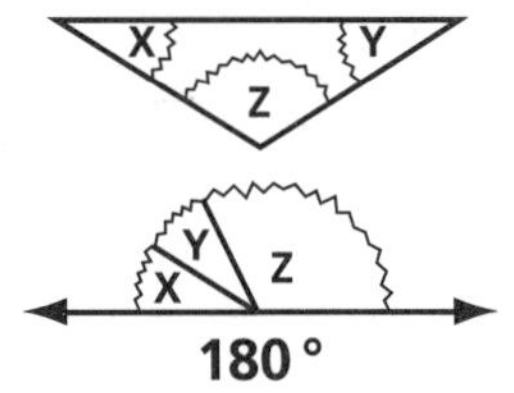

The sum of the measures of the fourangles of any quadrilateral is **360°**.

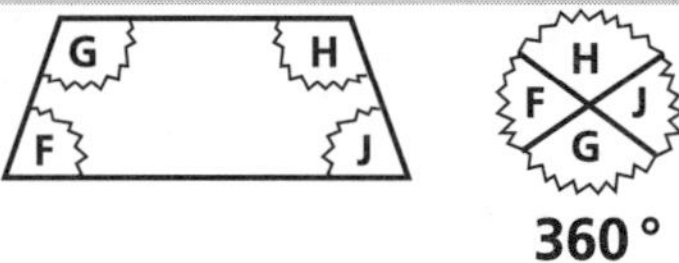

H F J G

360 °

Find the measure of the fourth angle of trapezoid ***MNOP.***

60° + 120° + 50° + n = 360°

230° + n = 360°

n = 360° − 230° or 130°

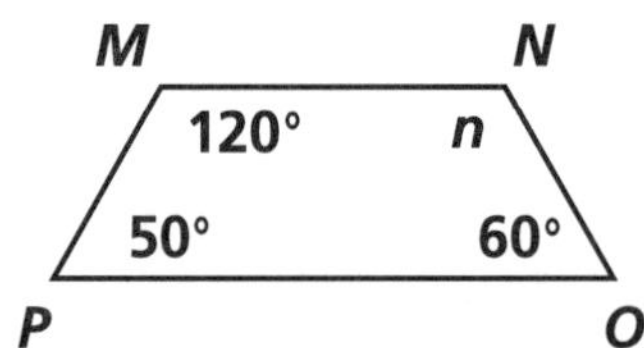

Find the measure of the missing angle.

11.

n = ______

12.

n = ______

13.

n = ______

Problem Solving Reasoning **Solve.**

14. On a piece of paper, draw three large parallelograms. Measure and label each of the angles. Look for a pattern. How are opposite angles in a parallelogram related?

____

15. One angle in a parallelogram is 36°. What are the measures of the other angles?

____

Test Prep ★ Mixed Review

16 **Which four numbers are prime numbers?**

A 5, 7, 11, 13

B 5, 7, 9, 11

C 5, 9, 13, 17

D 9, 10, 12, 14

17 **A scientist had 24.863 milligrams of a chemical. What is this number rounded to the nearest hundredth?**

F 24.86

G 24.87

H 24.9

J 25

Name ______________________________

Problem Solving Strategy: Make a Table

STANDARD

In this lesson, you will learn to make a table to help you solve a problem.

Problem

The sum of the measures of angles of a triangle is 180°. Find a formula that you can use to find the sum of the angles of any polygon.

1 Understand

As you reread, ask yourself questions.

- What facts do you know?

  The sum of the measures of the angles of a triangle is **180°**.

- What do you need to find?

  ____

2 Decide

Try the strategy Make a Table.

Name of polygon →	Triangle	Quadrilateral	Pentagon	Hexagon
Number of sides →	3	4	5	6
Number of triangles →	1			
Sum of measures of angles →	180°			

3 Solve

Complete the table.

A **diagonal** is a segment that connects two vertices of a polygon but is not a side.

How many triangles are formed from the diagonals drawn from one vertex in a quadrilateral, pentagon, and hexagon? Fill in the missing information in the third row of the table.

- What is the relationship between the number of sides of the polygon and the number of triangles formed?

  ____

- By what number should you multiply the number of triangles in a polygon to find the total number of degrees in the polygon? ______

Complete the bottom row of the table.

4 Look back

State the formula that you can use to find the sum of the angles of any polygon. Use *n* to represent the number of sides of the polygon. __________

STANDARD

Solve. Use the Make a Table strategy or any other strategy you have learned.

1. In a regular polygon, all the angles have the same measure. Find a formula that you can use to find the number of degrees in each angle of a regular polygon.

Think: Does a regular polygon have the same number of sides as angles?

______

Answer ______

______

2. Find a formula for the total number of diagonals that can be drawn from one vertex of a polygon.

Think: How many diagonals would a triangle have? a rectangle?

______

Answer ______

______

3. Find the total number of diagonals from all vertices in an octagon.

______

4. At the amusement park, **1** ticket costs **$.75**, **5** tickets cost **$3.75**, and **10** tickets cost **$7.50**. How much do **25** tickets cost?

______

5. Each week Teisha saves **$3** more than the previous week. She starts out with **$25** in savings. How much will she have at the end of **4** weeks?

______

6. There are **32** ounces in a quart. A punch bowl holds **4** quarts of punch. There are $1\frac{3}{4}$ quarts of punch left in the bowl. How many ounces of punch were served?

______

7. Triangle ***ABC*** is a right triangle. Find a formula that tells the relationship between the measure of angle ***A*** and angle ***B***.

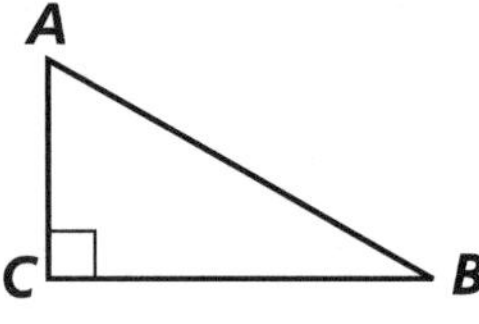

______

8. Brian had **$100**. He bought **4** gifts. He paid **$50** for the first gift. He paid half that for the second gift. The third gift cost half the price of the second gift, and the fourth gift was half the price of the third gift. How much money does he have left?

______

9. The price of each ticket to the lecture is **$5**. The price of **2** tickets is **$10** and so on. Make a table to show the price of up to **6** tickets. Then write a formula to show the relationship between the price ***p*** and the number of tickets ***t***.

______

10. Mona has a **50**-foot length of string. She plans to cut it into **25** equal sized pieces. Write a formula to show the relationship between the number of cuts ***c*** and the number of pieces ***p***.

______

Name ____________________

Similar Figures

STANDARD

Figures that have the same shape but are not necessarily the same size are **similar** figures. The symbol ~ means "is similar to." In the figures at the right, $\triangle SRP \sim \triangle NLM$ because their shapes are the same, but their sizes are different.

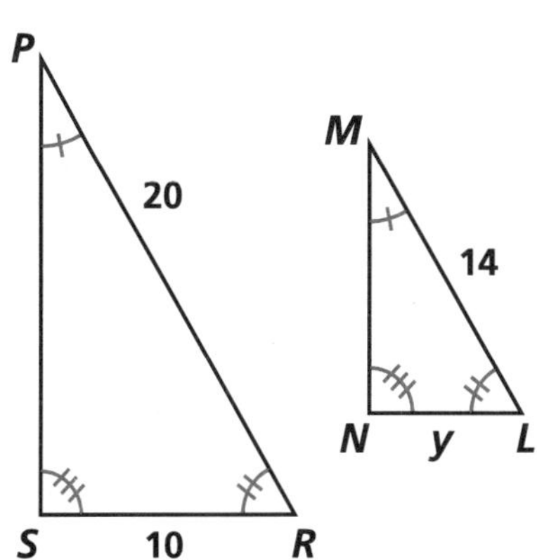

When figures are similar, the lengths of their corresponding sides are proportional.

Use a proportion to find the length of $\overline{NL}$.

1. Write a proportion. $\frac{SR}{NL} = \frac{PR}{ML}$

2. Substitute. $\frac{10}{y} = \frac{20}{14}$

3. Solve. $y \times 20 = 10 \times 14$

$y \times 20 = 140$

$y = 7$

So the length of $\overline{NL}$ is **7**.

Corresponding Sides		
$\overline{PS}$ and $\overline{MN}$	$\overline{PR}$ and $\overline{ML}$	$\overline{SR}$ and $\overline{NL}$
Corresponding Angles		
$\angle P$ and $\angle M$	$\angle R$ and $\angle L$	$\angle S$ and $\angle N$

When figures are similar, their corresponding angles are equal. Since $\triangle SRP \sim \triangle NLM$, $\angle S = \angle N$, $\angle R = \angle L$, and $\angle P = \angle M$.

Write whether the two figures appear to be congruent, similar, or neither.

1. 

______

2. 

______

3. 

______

The figures are similar. Use a proportion to find each missing length.

4. 10, y; 25, 10

$y =$ ______

5. 15, a, b, c; 21, 7, 7, 21

$a =$ ______, $b =$ ______, $c =$ ______

6.

3, x, y, z

$x =$ ______, $y =$ ______, $z =$ ______

7.

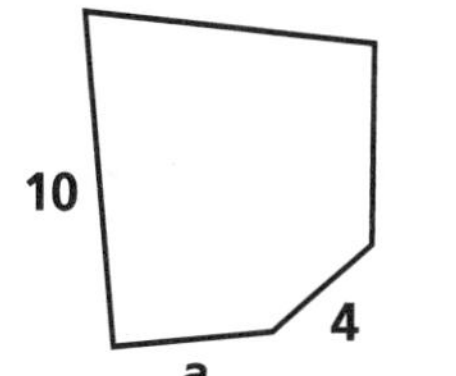

4, 2, b

$a =$ ______, $b =$ ______

STANDARD

The figures are similar. Find the measure of each missing angle.

8.

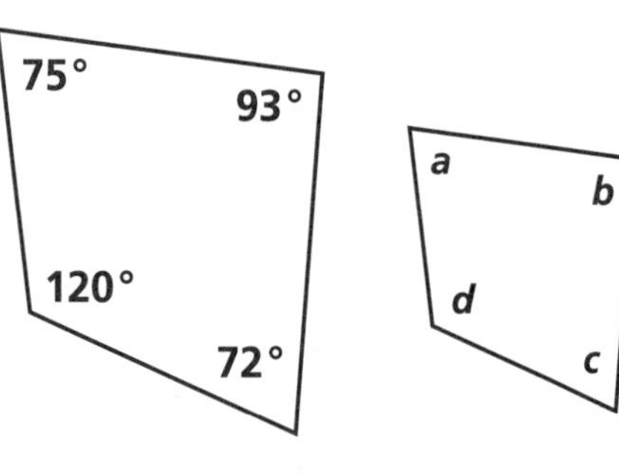

$a =$ ______, $b =$ ______, $c =$ ______, $d =$ ______

9.

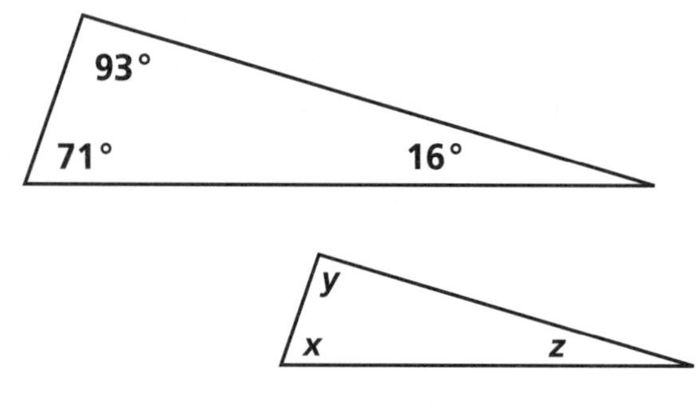

$x =$ ______, $y =$ ______, $z =$ ______

Problem Solving
Reasoning

A ratio that compares two similar figures is called a **scale factor**. For a triangle whose sides are one-half the length of the sides of a similar triangle, the scale factor is $\frac{1}{2}$. For a square whose sides are three times longer than the sides of another square, the scale factor is 3. Complete the table.

	Figure	Sides	Scale Factor	Sides of Similar Figure
10.	trapezoid	8, 16, 5, 7	$\frac{1}{2}$	
11.	parallelogram	2.8, 5.7	5	
12.	rectangle	145, 330	$\frac{1}{10}$	

Test Prep ★ Mixed Review

13 The table shows the biggest sunflowers shown at a summer carnival.

Farm	Size of Sunflower
Sunnydale	$4\frac{1}{8}$ in.
Brookside	$5\frac{1}{8}$ in.
Rock Point	$5\frac{3}{5}$ in.
Black Mesa	$5\frac{3}{8}$ in.

Which shows the farms in order from *smallest* to *largest* sunflower shown?

A Rock Point, Black Mesa, Brookside, Sunnydale

B Sunnydale, Brookside, Rock Point, Black Mesa

C Sunnydale, Brookside, Black Mesa, Rock Point

D Sunnydale, Rock Point, Brookside, Black Mesa

14 Carlos bought 3.5 yards of fabric to make costumes for the school play. The fabric cost $3.88 a yard. How much did all the fabric cost?

F $1.36

G $13.58

H $135.80

J $1,358

Name ____________________

Classifying Polygons

STANDARD

Polygons are classified by the number of sides they have. A triangle has **3** sides and a quadrilateral has **4**.

Pentagons, hexagons, and **octagons** are three other types of polygons.

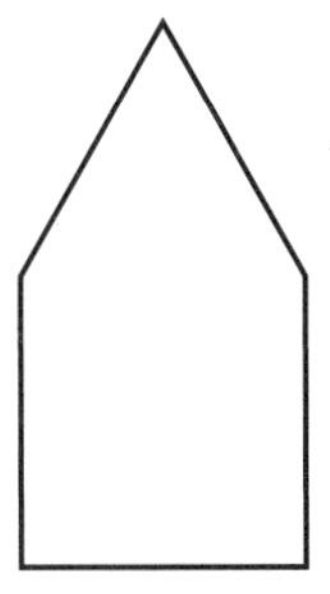

Pentagon A

penta means five

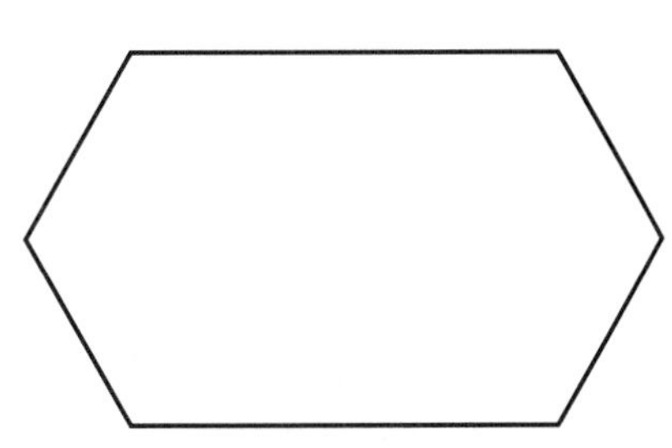

Hexagon B

hexa means six

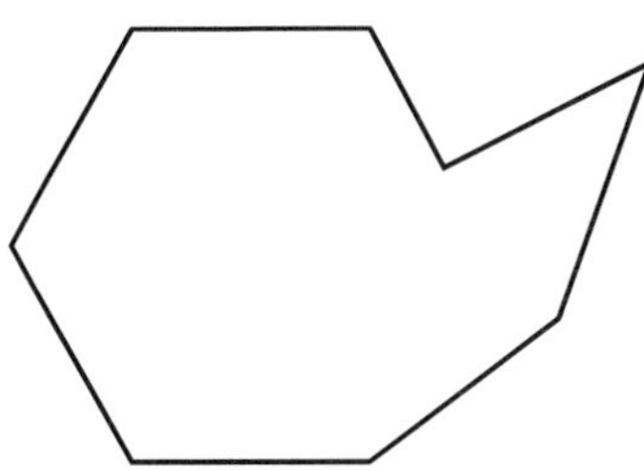

Octagon C

octa means eight

Regular polygons are polygons that have all sides congruent and all angles congruent.

Regular Polygons

Triangle

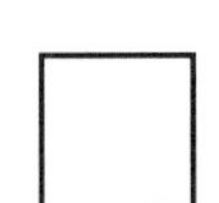

Quadrilateral

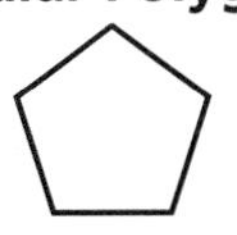

Pentagon

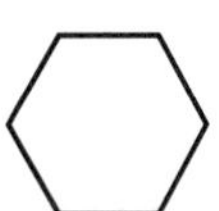

Hexagon

Octagon

Use a centimeter ruler or a protractor to answer.

1. Measure the sides of Pentagon A. Are they all congruent? ________
2. Measure the angles of the same pentagon. Are they all congruent? ________
3. Is Pentagon A regular? Why or why not? ____________________
   ____
4. Measure the sides of Hexagon B. Are they all congruent? ________
5. Measure the angles of the same hexagon. Are they all congruent? ________
6. Is Hexagon B regular? Why or why not? ____________________
   ____
7. A rectangle has four **90°** angles. Is a rectangle always a regular quadrilateral? ________
8. A rhombus has four congruent sides. Is a rhombus always a regular quadrilateral? ________
9. Which quadrilateral is always a regular quadrilateral? ________

STANDARD

Use a protractor to measure the angles of each regular polygon on page 205. Then complete the chart.

	Name of Regular Polygon	Measure of One Angle	Sum of the Measures of All Angles
10.	Triangle		
11.	Quadrilateral		
12.	Pentagon		
13.	Hexagon		
14.	Octagon		

15. Look for a pattern in the last column. A **heptagon** is a seven-sided polygon. Use your pattern to predict the sum of the angle measures of a heptagon. ______

16. What do you think is the measure of each angle of a regular heptagon? Justify your reasoning. ______

Problem Solving Reasoning

Solve.

17. Jerome knows that the total distance around his house is **120** feet. His house is in the shape of a regular quadrilateral. What are the dimensions of his house?

______

18. Paula has been told that the product of the length and width of her house is **900** square feet. Her house is in the shape of a rectangle. Name three possible dimensions of her house.

______

______

Quick Check

Solve.

Work Space.

19. Two angles of a quadrilateral have measures **80°** and **40°**. The other two angles are congruent. What is the measure of each of these two angles? ______

Suppose $\triangle ABC \sim \triangle PQR$ and $\angle A = 40°$, $\angle B = 70°$, $AB = 4.6$ cm and $BC = 3$ cm. In $\triangle PQR$, $PQ = 3.6$ cm. Write the other measures.

20. $\angle C$ ______ **21.** $\overline{AC}$ ______ **22.** $\angle P$ ______

23. $\overline{PR}$ ______ **24.** $\overline{QR}$ ______

25. The sum of the angles of a regular hexagon is **720°**. What is the measure of each angle? ______

Name ___________________________

Problem Solving Application: Use a Diagram

STANDARD

Sometimes it is helpful to use a diagram to solve problems.

In this lesson, you will draw a geometric figure to help you solve problems involving angles, triangles, and quadrilaterals.

Tips to Remember:

1. Understand 2. Decide 3. Solve 4. Look back

- Ask yourself: Have I solved a problem like this before? How did I solve it?
- Picture the situation described in the problem. Draw a picture to show what is happening.
- Think about strategies you have already learned. Try using one of them to solve the problem.

Solve.

1. Two angles of a triangle measure **54°** and **23°**. What type of triangle is it? Explain your answer.

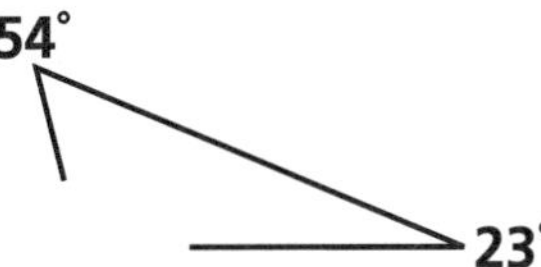

Think: How do you find the measure of the third angle of the triangle? What is its measure?

____

____

Answer ___________________________

____

2. Two lines intersect to form vertical angles. The measure of one angle is **145°**. What are the measures of the other three angles?

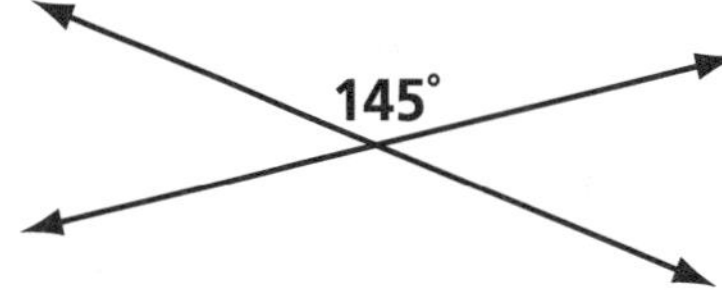

Think: What do you know about vertical angles?

____

____

Answer ___________________________

____

3. An equilateral triangle has a perimeter of **15** ft. What is the measure of each side and each angle?

____

4. Two angles of a triangle have the same measure. The third angle measures **30°**. What is the measure of each angle?

____

STANDARD

Solve.

5. Two angles of a triangle measure **102°** and **39°**. What is the measure of the third angle of the triangle?

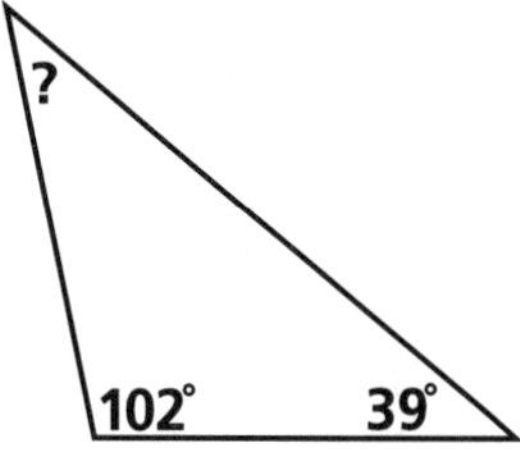

6. Two angles of a triangle measure **42°** and **48°**. What type of triangle is it?

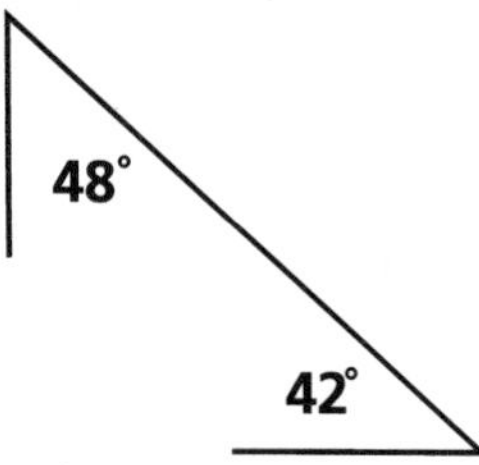

7. A triangle is an isosceles right triangle. What is the measure of the congruent angles of the triangle?

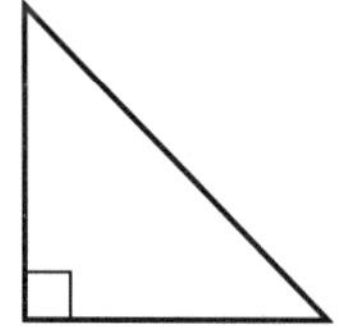

8. Three angles of a quadrilateral measure **57°**, **123°**, and **49°**. What is the measure of the fourth angle of the quadrilateral?

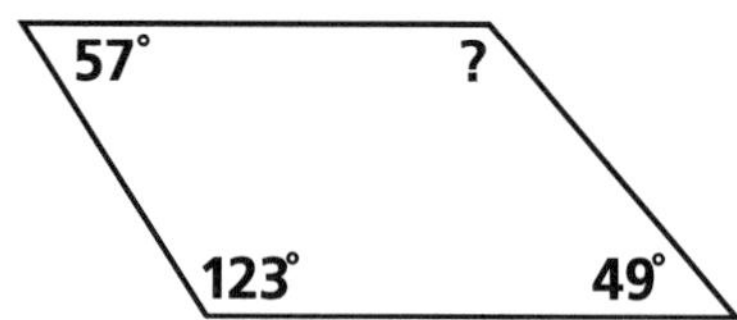

9. An exterior angle of a triangle is supplementary to the interior angle next to it. If one exterior angle is **70°**, what type of triangle is it?

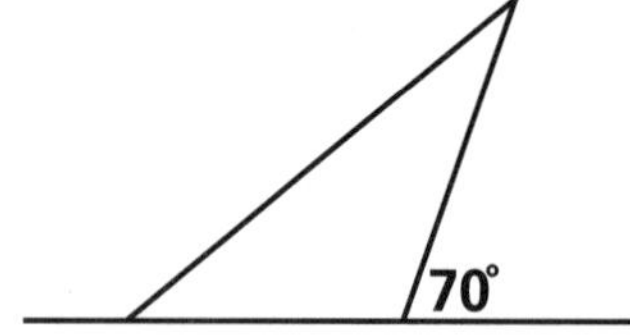

10. A **20**-foot tall flagpole casts a shadow of **4** feet. What will be the length of a shadow of a **5**-foot tall student standing next to the flagpole?

Extend Your Thinking

11. Look back at problem **5**. What type of triangle is it? Explain your answer.

12. Look back at problem **9**. What is the sum of the measures of the two interior angles opposite the exterior angle?

Name ______________________

Unit 7 Review

Draw and label a figure to illustrate the description.

1. ray *XY*

2. line segment *RS*

3. line *PQ*

4. $\triangle XYZ$

5. radius $\overline{OY}$

6. right angle *ABC*

7. $\overleftrightarrow{AB} \perp \overleftrightarrow{FG}$

8. $\overleftrightarrow{CD} \parallel \overleftrightarrow{JK}$

9. $\overleftrightarrow{TR}$ intersecting $\overleftrightarrow{MN}$ at *G*

Give the name of each figure.

10. 
____

11. 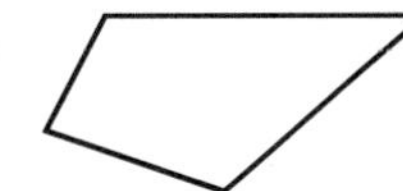
____

12. 
____

13. 
____

14. 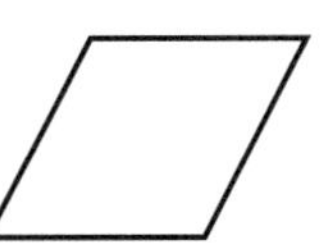
____

15. 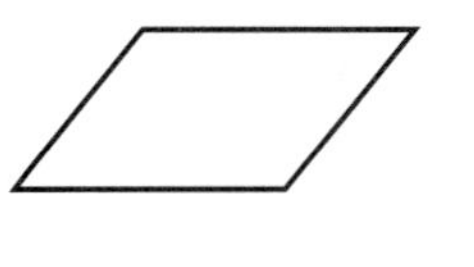
____

Measure, then classify the angle.

16. 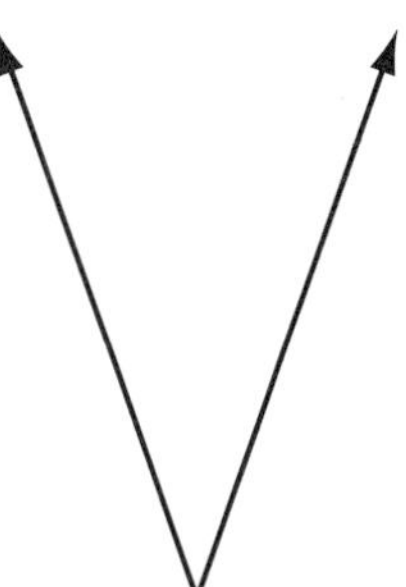
__________, __________

17. 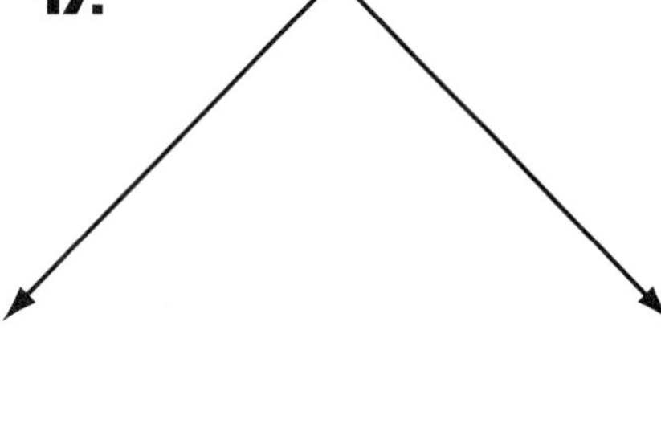
__________, __________

18. 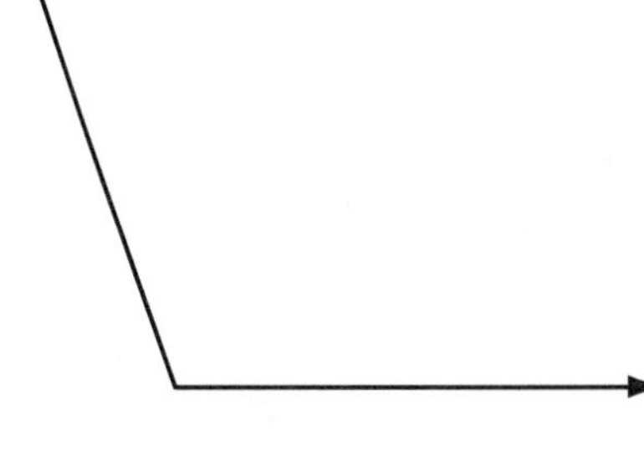
__________, __________

***ABCD* ~ *QRST.* Use these figures to answer problems 19–22.**

19. Find the length of $\overline{AB}$. ________

20. Find the measure of ∠*ABC*. ________

21. ∠*QTS* measures 135°. Find the measure of ∠*DCB*. ________

22. What is the measure of the complement of ∠*TSR*? ________

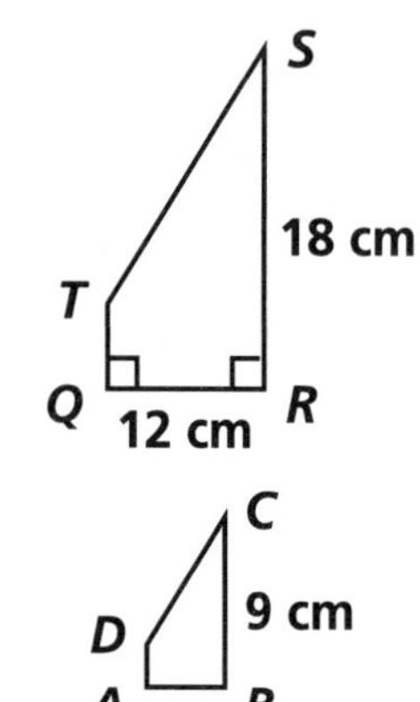

23. Draw a 35° angle.

24. Construct a segment congruent to $\overline{MX}$.

25. Construct an obtuse isosceles triangle. Label the obtuse angle *ABC*.

△*SQR* is isosceles. Find the measure of each angle.

26. ∠*SRQ* = ________

27. ∠*SQR* = ________

28. ∠*RSU* = ________

29. ∠*UST* = ________

30. ∠*QST* = ________

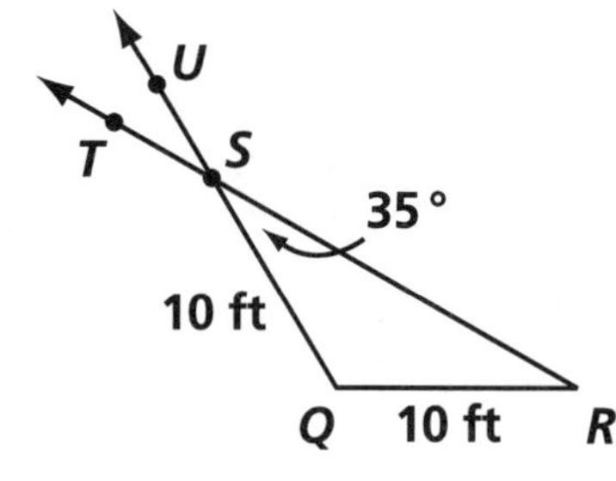

Solve.

31. One diameter divides a circle into 2 equal parts. What is the greatest number of equal parts 8 diameters can divide a circle into? ________

Name ______________________________

Cumulative Review
★ Test Prep

1 **Which picture shows perpendicular segments?**

A

C

B

D

2 **$\angle A$ and $\angle B$ are complements. The measure of $\angle A$ is 43°. What is the measure of $\angle B$?**

F 137° **H** 47°

G 90° **J** 43°

3 **Use this picture to answer the question.**

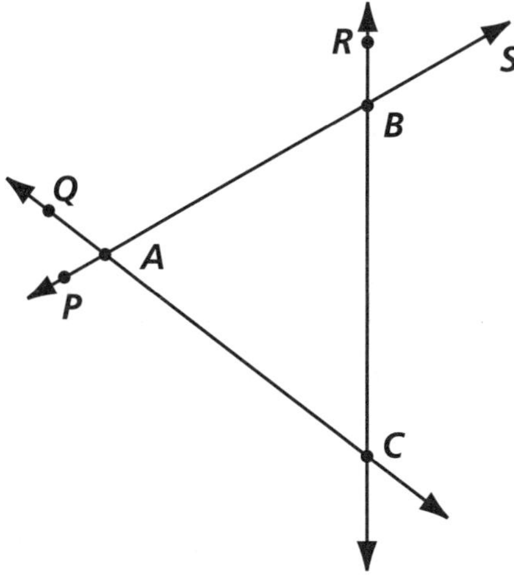

Which two angles are vertical angles?

A $\angle PAQ$ and $\angle QAB$

B $\angle PAQ$ and $\angle BAC$

C $\angle PAQ$ and $\angle ABR$

D $\angle PAQ$ and $\angle RBS$

4 **Which answer shows a regular hexagon?**

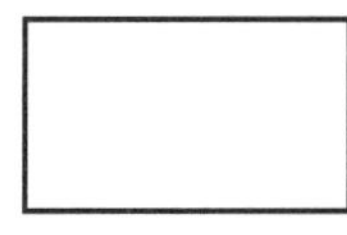

F

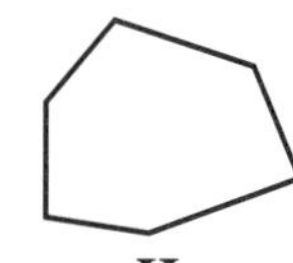

H

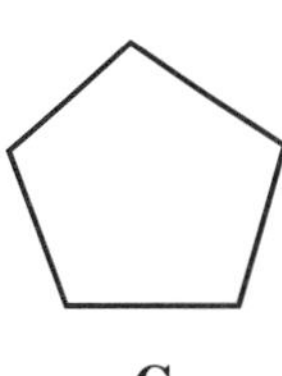

G

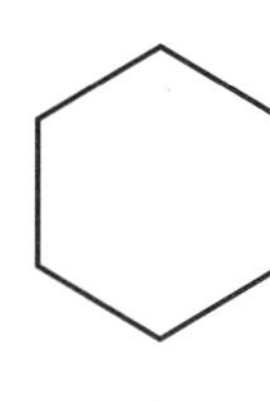

J

5 **Which figure below is similar to this figure?**

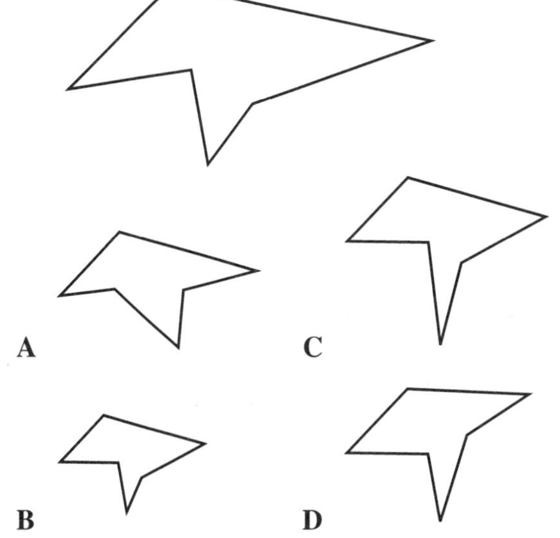

6 **Which of these figures are congruent?**

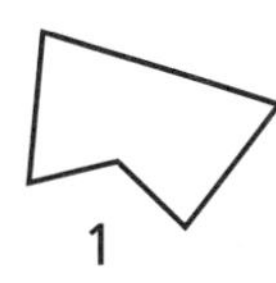

1

2

3

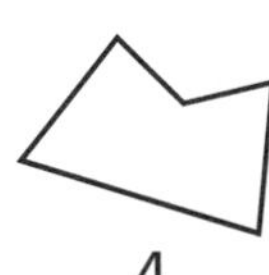

4

5

F 1 and 2 **H** 1 and 4

G 1 and 3 **J** 2 and 5

7 Use this figure.

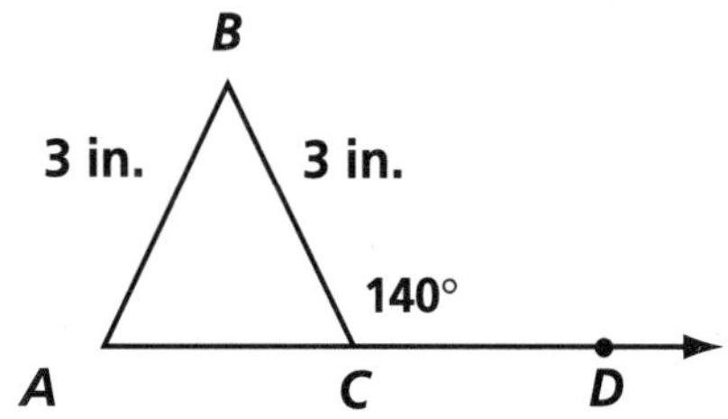

What is the measure of $\angle A$?

A 30° **C** 50°

B 40° **D** 60°

8 Use this figure.

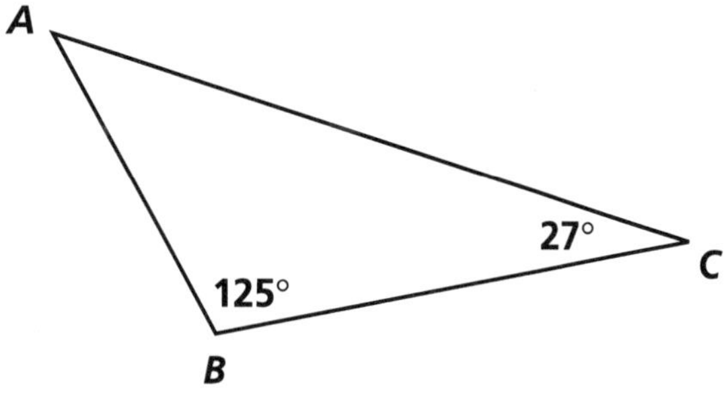

What is the measure of $\angle BAC$?

F 180° **H** 62°

G 152° **J** 28°

9 Use your ruler and the figure to answer the question.

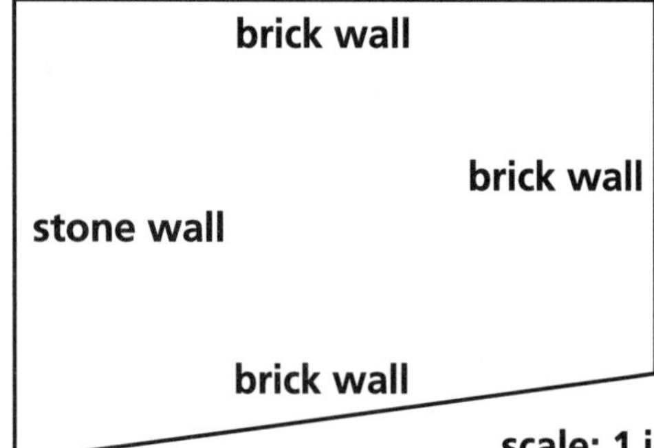

This drawing shows the plan for a walled garden. How long will the stone wall be?

A $1\frac{3}{4}$ inches **C** $3\frac{1}{2}$ feet

B $1\frac{3}{4}$ feet **D** 7 feet

10 Which three fractions are equivalent to $\frac{3}{5}$?

F $\frac{3}{5}, \frac{4}{6}, \frac{5}{7}$

G $\frac{6}{10}, \frac{9}{15}, \frac{12}{20}$

H $\frac{6}{10}, \frac{9}{10}, \frac{5}{3}$

J $\frac{9}{15}, \frac{12}{20}, \frac{15}{20}$

K Not here

11 Wilson had 28 sheets of stickers. He gave $\frac{1}{4}$ of the sheets to his sister. How many sheets did he give to his sister?

A 4 **C** 14 **E** NH

B 7 **D** 28

12 Use your protractor. What is the measure of this angle?

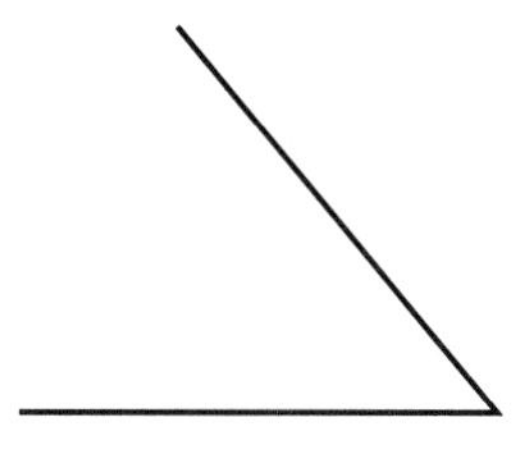

F 40° **H** 70° **K** NH

G 50° **J** 130°

13 What is the prime factorization of 108?

A $2^2 \times 3^2$

B $2^3 \times 3^2$

C $2 \times 6 \times 9$

D 3×6^2

E NH

UNIT 8 • TABLE OF CONTENTS

Using Formulas in Geometry

We will be using this vocabulary:

area a measure in square units of a region or surface

formula a general rule expressed using symbols

perimeter the sum of the measures of the sides of a polygon

circumference the distance around a circle

volume a measure in cubic units of the capacity of a three-dimensional or space figure

Dear Family,

During the next few weeks, our math class will be using formulas in geometry. You can expect to see homework that provides practice with determining the area and perimeter of a polygon. Here is a sample you may want to keep handy if needed.

Area and Perimeter of a Rectangle

Area is a measure in square units of a region or surface. To find the area of a rectangle, use the formula $A = l \times w$ where l = **length** and w = **width**.

Example: Find the area of rectangle **C**.

7 ft

14 ft C 14 ft

7 ft

Write the formula.	$A = l \times w$
Substitute for l and w.	$A = (14) \times (7)$
Multiply. Label the answer.	$A = 98$ ft^2

Perimeter is a measure of the distance around a figure. To find the perimeter of a rectangle, use the formula $P = 2(l + w)$.

Example: Find the perimeter of rectangle **C** shown above.

$P = 2(l + w)$	Write the formula.
$P = 2(14 + 7)$	Substitute for l and w.
$P = 2(21)$	Work inside ( ) first.
$P = 42$ ft	Multiply. Label the answer.

During this unit, students will need to continue to practice finding the area and perimeter of various figures.

Sincerely,

Name ___________________________

Perimeter and Area

STANDARD

The **perimeter** (*P*) of a figure is the distance around it. The **area** (*A*) of a figure is the amount of surface it covers.

A **complex figure** is made up of more than one shape.

Find the perimeter (*P*) of this complex figure.

Perimeter of a rectangle: $P = 2(l + w)$

Find any missing measures.
The measure *m* is missing. You can see that
$2 + m + 2 = 7$. So, $m = 7 - 2 - 2$, or 3.

2. Find the sum of the lengths of its sides.
$P = 2 + 3 + 3 + 1 + 2 + 4 + 7 + 6$
= 28 units

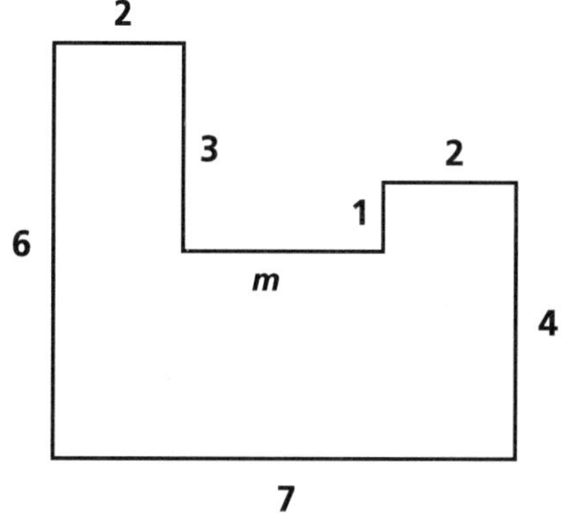

Find the area (*A*) of the complex figure.

1. Divide the figure into simple shapes.
2. Determine any missing measures. The length of Rectangle **C** is **7**. The width is **6 − 3** or **4 − 1**.
3. Find the area of each shape. Since the figure was divided into rectangles, use $A = lw$.

   Area of rectangle **B = 3 × 2,** or **6,** units^2
   Area of rectangle **C = 3 × 7,** or **21,** units^2
   Area of rectangle **D = 1 × 2,** or **2,** units^2

4. Find the sum of the areas.

   $A = 6 + 21 + 2$
   = 29 units^2

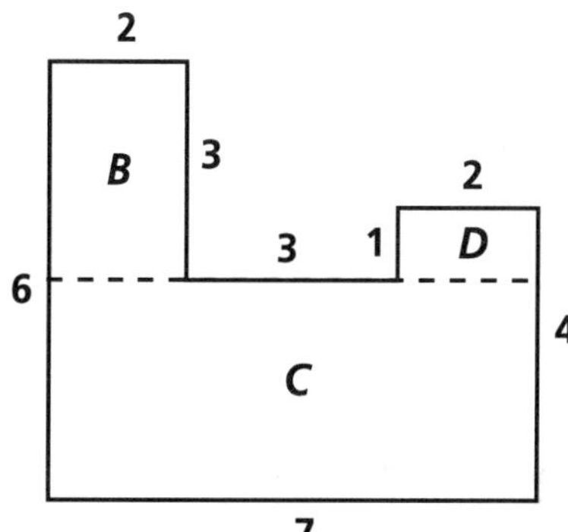

Find the perimeter and area.

1. Perimeter ___________________________

Area ___________________________

____

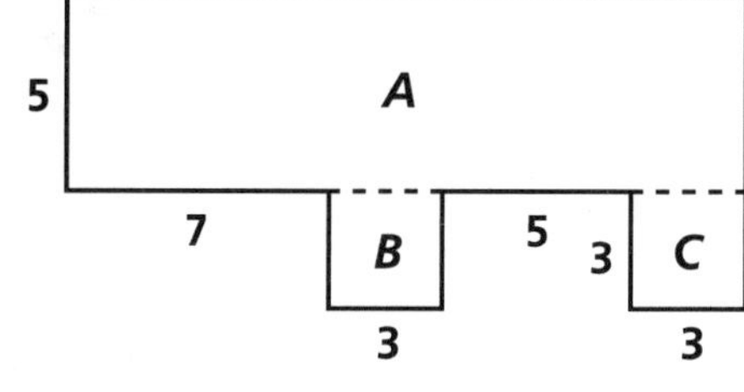

STANDARD

Find the perimeter and area of each figure.

2.

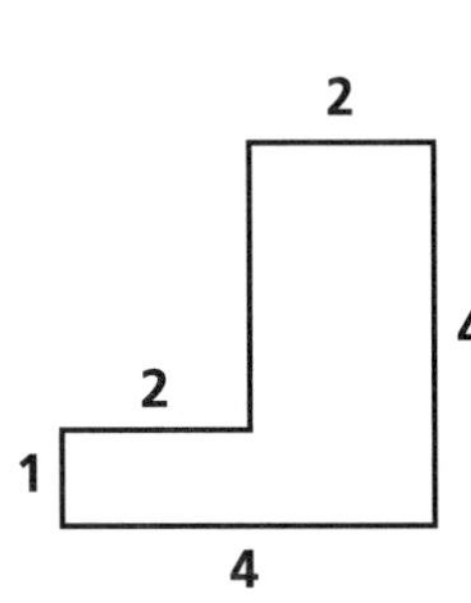

$P =$ ________

$A =$ ________

3.

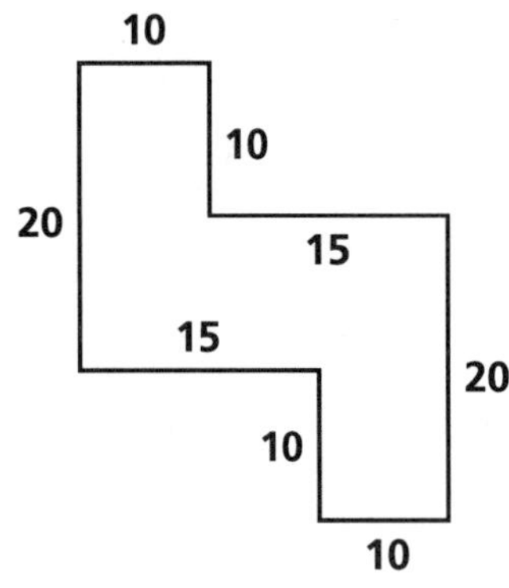

$P =$ ________

$A =$ ________

4.

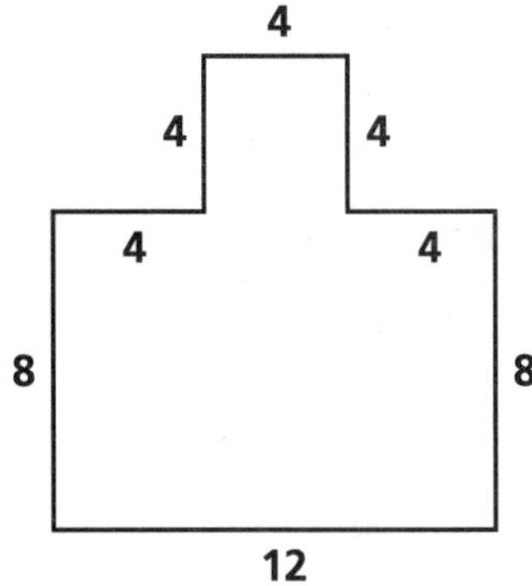

$P =$ ________

$A =$ ________

5.

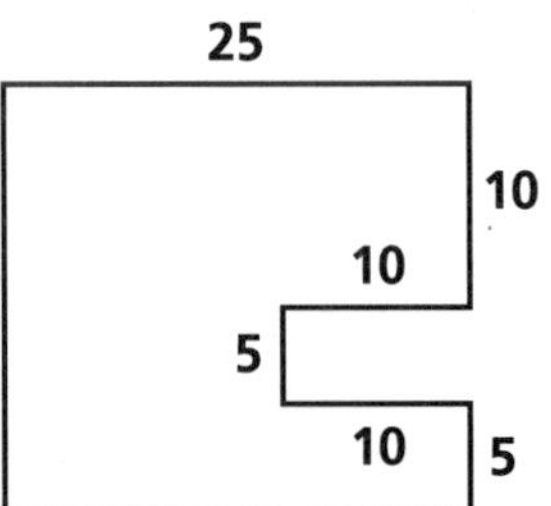

$P =$ ________

$A =$ ________

6.

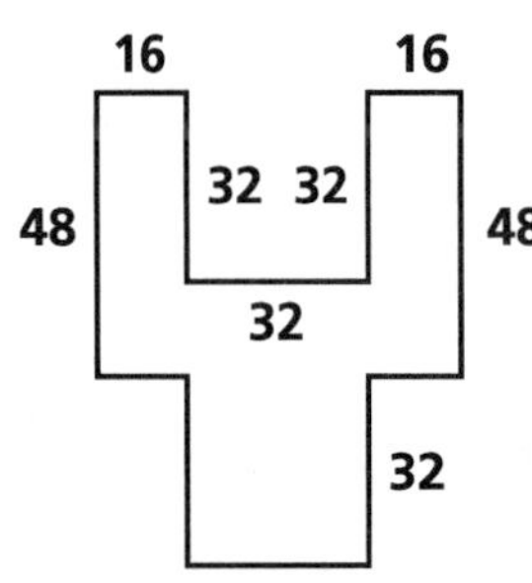

$P =$ ________

$A =$ ________

7.

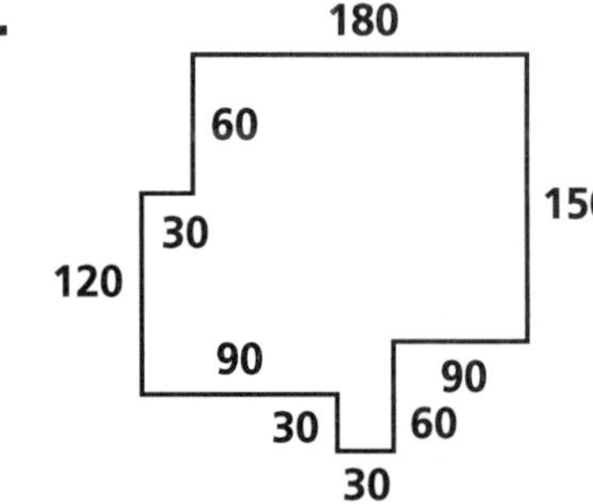

$P =$ ________

$A =$ ________

Problem Solving Reasoning Solve.

8. A lawn is rectangular and measures **120** feet by **90** feet. One bag of fertilizer covers **4,000** ft². How many bags of fertilizer must be purchased? Explain.

____

____

____

Test Prep ★ Mixed Review

9 What do you need to do to each side of this equation to solve it?

$n - \frac{5}{8} = \frac{2}{3}$

A Add $\frac{5}{8}$ **C** Add $\frac{2}{3}$

B Subtract $\frac{5}{8}$ **D** Subtract $\frac{2}{3}$

10 Lindsey is planning a party. She will have 3 tables for every 14 guests. Which answer shows three ways to write the ratio of tables to guests?

F 14 : 3, 14 to 3, $\frac{14}{3}$ **H** 3 : 14, 3 to 14, $\frac{3}{14}$

G 4 : 13, 4 to 13, $\frac{4}{13}$ **J** 3 : 14, 3 to 14, $\frac{14}{3}$

Name ______________________

Areas of Triangles and Parallelograms

Look at the figures below. The length of the rectangle and the **base** of the triangle are the same. The width of the rectangle and the **height** of the triangle are the same.

The area of the triangle is $\frac{1}{2}$ the area of the rectangle.

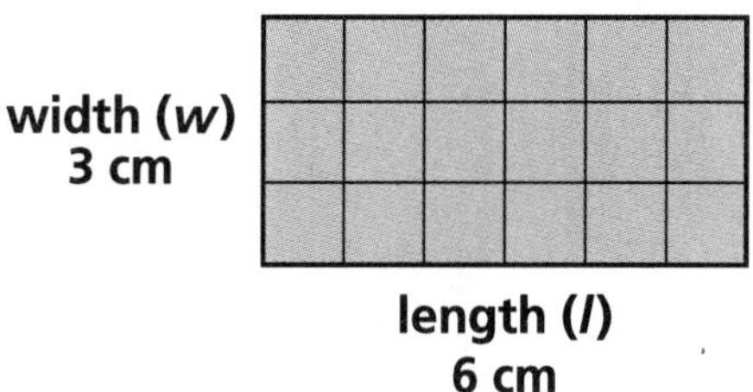

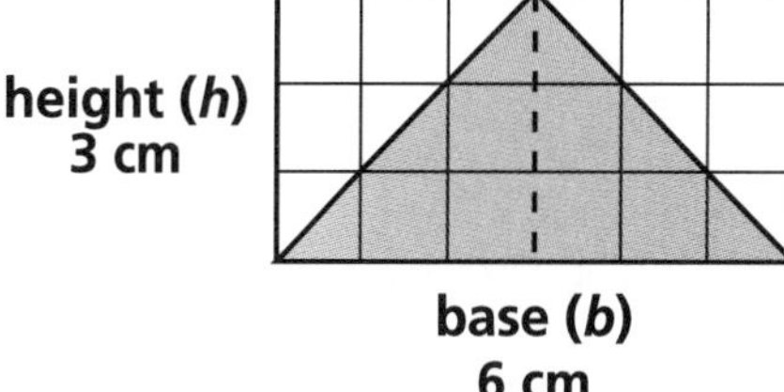

Area (A) of a rectangle $= l \times w$

$A = 6 \times 3$

$A = 18 \text{ cm}^2$

Area (A) of a triangle $= \left(\frac{1}{2}\right)b \times h$

$A = \left(\frac{1}{2}\right)6 \times 3$

$A = \left(\frac{1}{2}\right)18$

$A = 9 \text{ cm}^2$

Find the area of the triangle.

1.

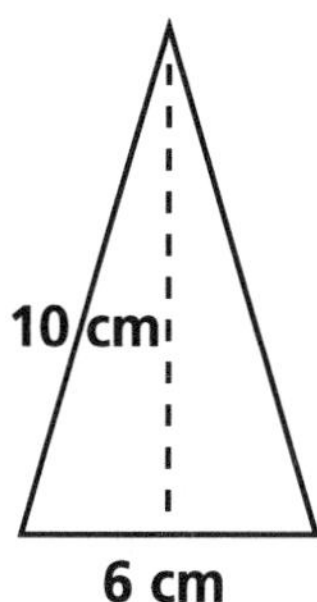

$A =$ __________

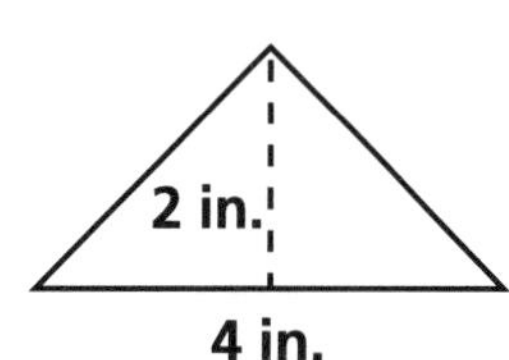

$A =$ __________

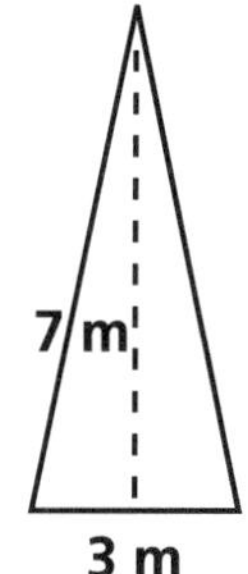

$A =$ __________

2.

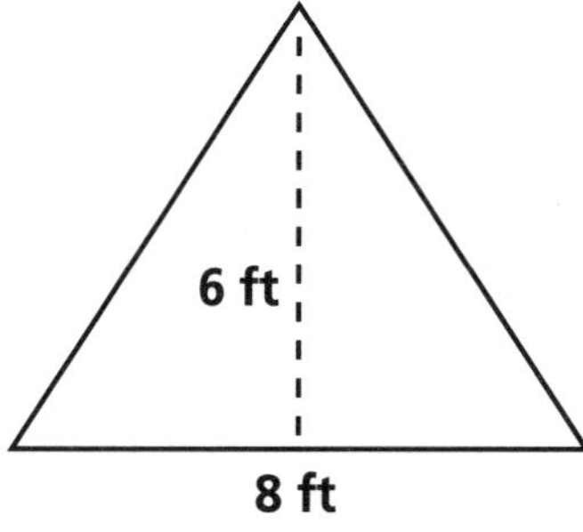

$A =$ __________

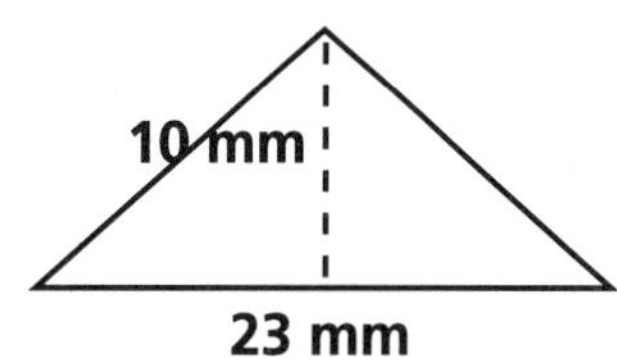

$A =$ __________

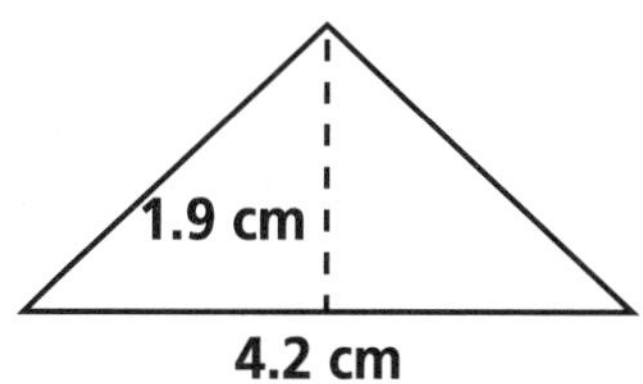

$A =$ __________

STANDARD

Look at the triangle and parallelogram shown below. The parallelogram is made from two congruent triangles. The area of the parallelogram is equal to the sum of the area of one triangle and the area of the other triangle, or **2** times the area of the triangle.

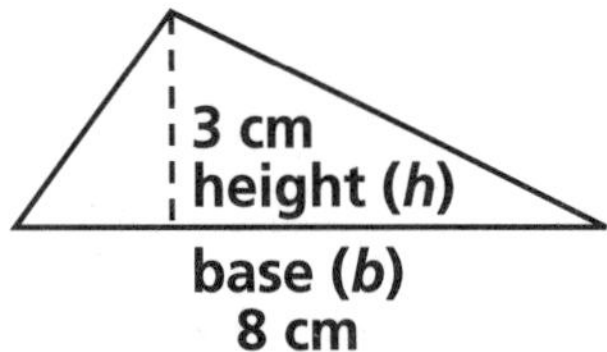

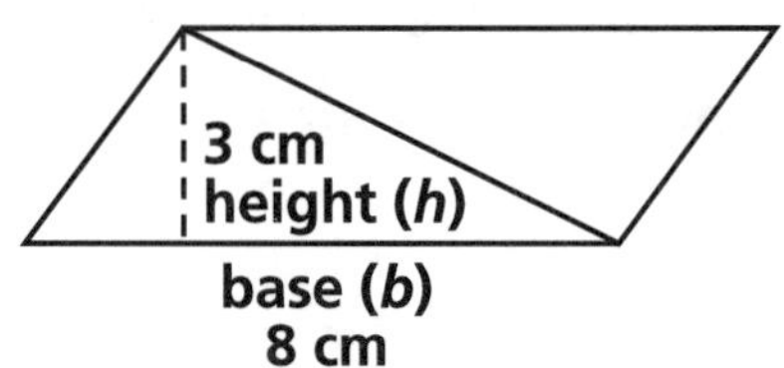

$$A = \left(\frac{1}{2}\right) b \times h$$
$$= \left(\frac{1}{2}\right) 8 \times 3$$
$$= \left(\frac{1}{2}\right) 24$$
$$= 12 \text{ cm}^2$$

$$\text{Area } (A) \text{ of parallelogram} = \left(\frac{1}{2}\right) b \times h + \left(\frac{1}{2}\right) b \times h$$
$$= \left(\frac{1}{2}\right) 8 \times 3 + \left(\frac{1}{2}\right) 8 \times 3$$
$$= \left(\frac{1}{2}\right) 24 + \left(\frac{1}{2}\right) 24$$
$$= 12 + 12$$
$$= 24 \text{ cm}^2$$

In simplest form, the formula $A = \left(\frac{1}{2}\right)b \times h + \left(\frac{1}{2}\right)b \times h$ is $A = b \times h$.

So to find the area of a parallelogram, use $A = b \times h$.

Find the area of each parallelogram.

3.

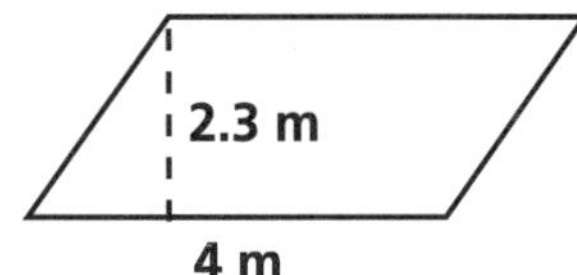

$A =$ ________

4.

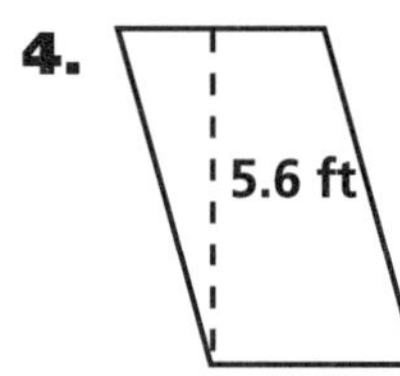

$A =$ ________

Problem Solving Reasoning **Solve.**

5. Choose the formulas you need and use those formulas to find the area of this figure.

____

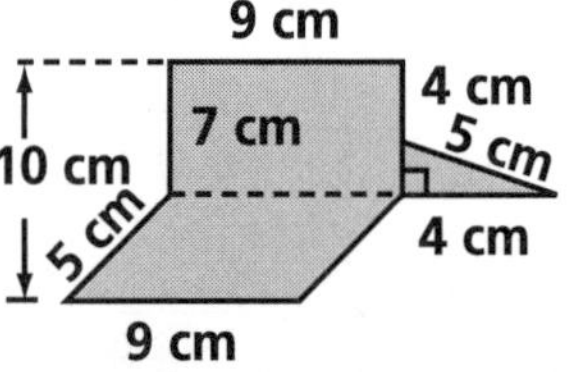

Test Prep ★ Mixed Review

6 Use the proportion to answer the question.

$$\frac{276}{12} = \frac{184}{x}$$

Mr. Lin drove 276 miles on 12 gallons of gas. At that rate, how many gallons of gas would he need to drive 184 miles?

A 23 gal **C** 8 gal
B 12 gal **D** 4 gal

7 **Reyna bought $\frac{2}{3}$ yard of blue ribbon, $\frac{3}{8}$ yard of green ribbon, and $\frac{2}{3}$ yard of red ribbon. How much ribbon did she buy in all?**

F $1\frac{17}{24}$ yd **H** $1\frac{1}{24}$ yd
G $1\frac{1}{3}$ yd **J** $\frac{17}{24}$ yd

Name ______________________

Circumference

The distance around a circle is its **circumference.**

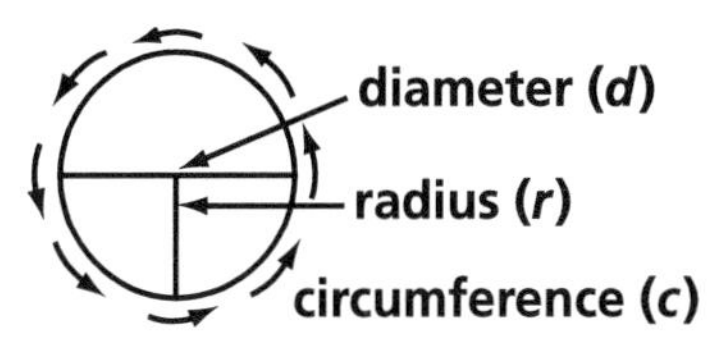

The **diameter** is the distance across a circle through its center. The **radius** is the distance from the center of a circle to a point on the circle.

Use a string and a centimeter ruler to measure the circumference and diameter of each object. Find the ratio of the circumference to the diameter to the nearest **0.01** cm.

	Object	Diameter	Circumference	$\frac{\text{Circumference}}{\text{Diameter}}$
1.	quarter			
2.	clockface			
3.	top of drinking glass			

Your answers in the last column should be about **3.14**. The Greeks used their letter π (**pi**) to name this ratio.

You can use a formula to find the circumference of a circle.

> The circumference (C) of any circle with diameter d is $C = \pi d$.
> or
> The circumference (C) of any circle with radius r is $C = 2\pi r$.

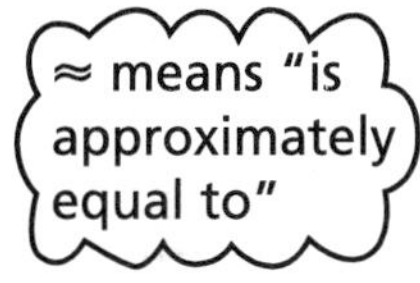

The decimal **3.14** and the fraction $\frac{22}{7}$ are two accepted approximations for π.

radius = **8** m

$C = 2\pi r$

$\approx 2 \times 3.14 \times 8$ m

≈ 50.24 m

radius = $\frac{3}{4}$ ft

$C = 2\pi r$

$\approx 2 \times \frac{22}{7} \times \frac{3}{4}$ ft

$\approx \frac{33}{7}$ or $4\frac{5}{7}$ ft

diameter = **10** yd

$C = \pi d$

$\approx 3.14 \times 10$ yd

≈ 31.4 yd

Find the circumference for each circle. Use 3.14 for π.

4. radius = **18** m — $C \approx$ ________ diameter = **5** cm — $C \approx$ ________ radius = **7** dm — $C \approx$ ________ diameter = **20** mm — $C \approx$ ________

Find the circumference for each circle. Use $\frac{22}{7}$ for π.

5. radius = $\frac{1}{2}$ ft — $C \approx$ ________ diameter = $\frac{7}{8}$ mi — $C \approx$ ________ radius = **14** yd — $C \approx$ ________ diameter = **49** in. — $C \approx$ ________

STANDARD

Find the circumference for each circle. Use 3.14 or $\frac{22}{7}$ for π.

6. radius = **12** yd | diameter = $1\frac{3}{8}$ in. | radius = **25** cm | diameter = $9\frac{1}{3}$ ft

C ≈ ________ | C ≈ ________ | C ≈ ________ | C ≈ ________

Problem Solving
Reasoning

Solve.

7. How does the circumference of a circle change when its diameter is doubled?

____

____

8. How does the circumference of a circle change when its diameter is tripled?

____

____

9. The diameter of the earth at the equator is about **12,756** km. What is the circumference of the earth at the equator?

____

10. What is the circumference of circle *A*?

____

Quick Check

Find the area of the figure.

11. Square, side length: **3.2** cm ________

12. Rectangle, length and width: **6** in. and **4.7** in. ________

13. Parallelogram, base and height: **1.5** ft and **4.2** ft ________

14. Triangle, base and height **0.6** mi and **0.22** mi ________

Find the circumference of the circle.

15. diameter: **7** in. ________ **16.** radius: **10** in. ________

Work Space.

Name ______________________________

Area of a Circle

STANDARD

The formulas for circumference and area of a parallelogram can help you find the area of a circle.

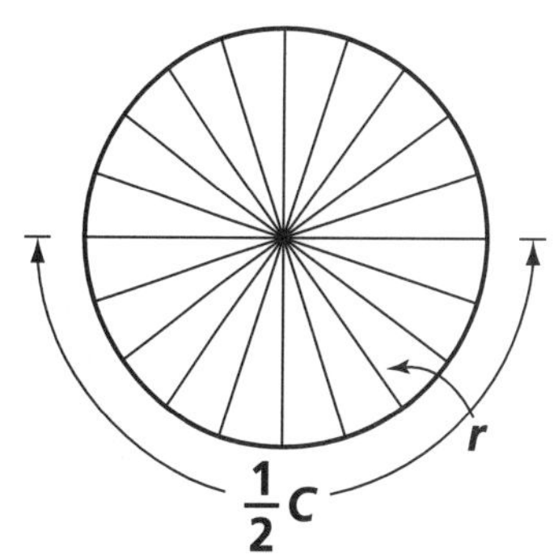

Circumference **(C)** = $2\pi r$

$$\frac{1}{2}(C) = \frac{1}{2}(2\pi r)$$

$$\frac{1}{2}(C) = \pi r$$

Divide a circle into **20** equal sections. Shade half of the sections. Separate the sections and arrange them in a side-by-side pattern as shown. This arrangement resembles a parallelogram.

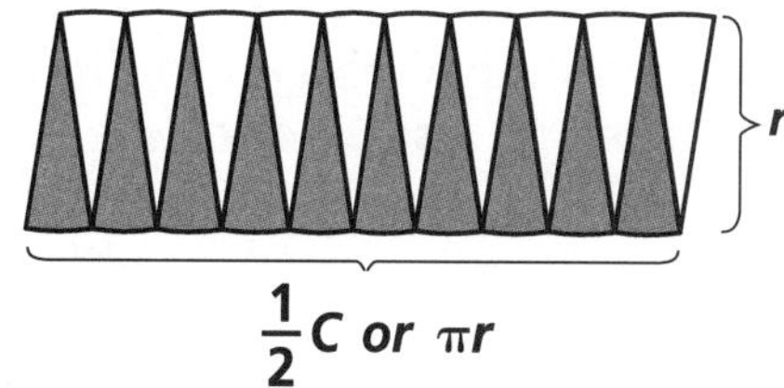

Area of a parallelogram = $b \cdot a$

Area of a circle = $\pi r \cdot r$ or πr^2

The **area (*A*)** of any **circle** with radius ***r*** is given by the formula $A = \pi r^2$.

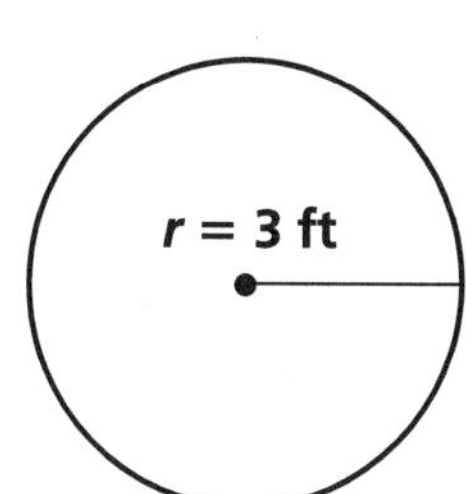

$$A = \pi r^2 \\ = \pi(3)^2 \\ \approx 3.14 \cdot 9 \\ \approx 28.26 \text{ ft}^2$$

or

$$A = \pi r^2 \\ = \pi(3)^2 \\ \approx \frac{22}{7} \cdot 9 \\ \approx \frac{198}{7} \text{ or, } 28\frac{2}{7} \text{ ft}^2$$

Find each area. Use 3.14 or $\frac{22}{7}$ for π.

1.

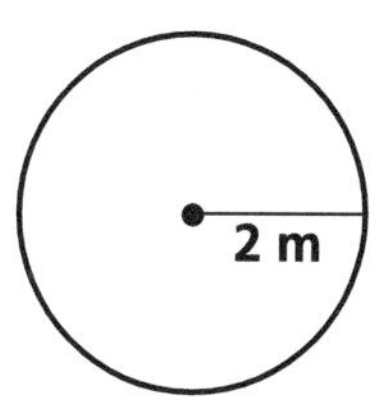

$A \approx$ __________

$3\frac{1}{2}$ in.

$A \approx$ __________

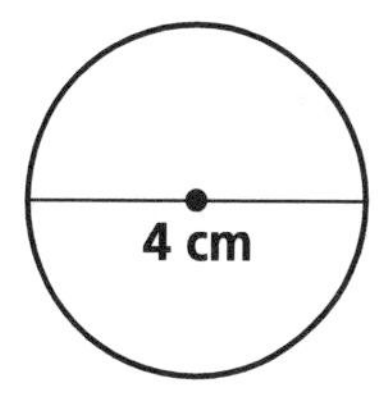

$A \approx$ __________

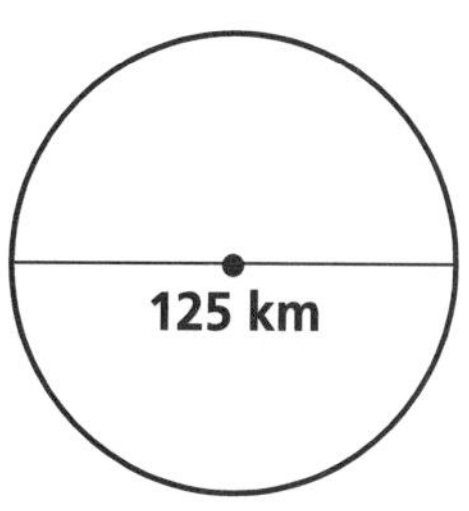

$A \approx$ __________

2. radius = $\frac{7}{3}$ yd

$A \approx$ __________

diameter = **30** mm

$A \approx$ __________

diameter = **7** ft

$A \approx$ __________

radius = **1.1** dm

$A \approx$ __________

STANDARD

Find the area of each circle. Use 3.14 or $\frac{22}{7}$ for π.

3. $r = 4$ yd | $d = 4$ yd | $r = 11$ cm | $d = 9$ m

$A \approx$ ______ $A \approx$ ______ $A \approx$ ______ $A \approx$ ______

4. $d = 3.4$ dm | $d = 21$ in. | $r = 50$ mm | $r = 4\frac{1}{2}$ ft

$A \approx$ ______ $A \approx$ ______ $A \approx$ ______ $A \approx$ ______

Given the circumference of a circle, find the radius and area rounded to the nearest tenth. Use 3.14 for π.

5. $C = 4$ yd | $C = 12$ cm | $C = 6.2$ km | $C = 1.25$ mi

$r \approx$ ______ $r \approx$ ______ $r \approx$ ______ $r \approx$ ______

$A \approx$ ______ $A \approx$ ______ $A \approx$ ______ $A \approx$ ______

Problem Solving Reasoning

Solve. Use 3.14 for π.

6. Divide this figure into a triangle, semicircle, and rectangle. Then find the area.

______

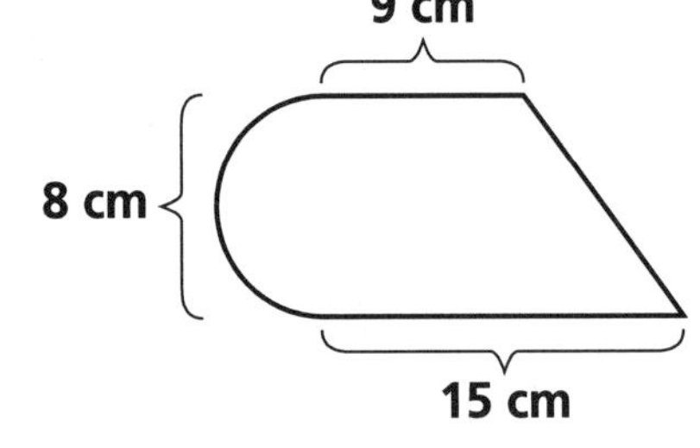

7. Use areas of circles, rectangles, and triangles to find the area of the figure at the right.

______

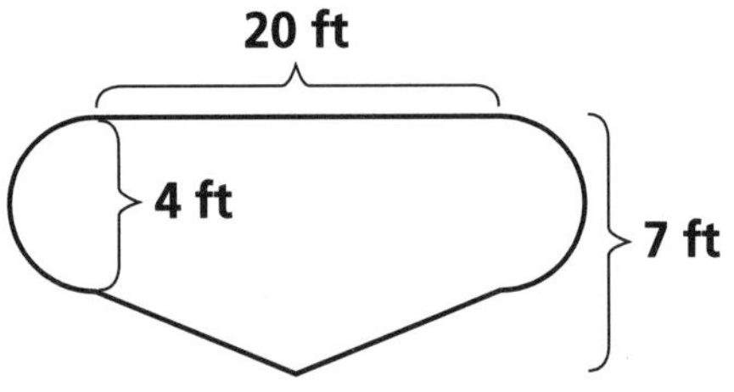

8. What is the area of the largest circle that can be cut out of a piece of paper **21** cm long and **23** cm wide?

______

Test Prep ★ Mixed Review

9 Hillary drew a chalk circle on the playground to use in a game. The circle had a diameter of 34 inches. What was the circumference?

A About 53 in.
B About 107 in.
C About 214 in.
D About 3,632 in.

10 Main Street School has 576 students. $\frac{1}{6}$ of the students are in sixth grade. How many students are in sixth grade?

F 3,456
G 576
H 96
J 86

Name ____________________

Prisms have two congruent bases.

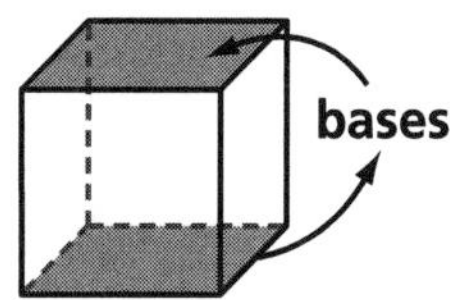

A **cube** is a special rectangular prism. It has 6 square faces, 12 edges, and 8 vertices.

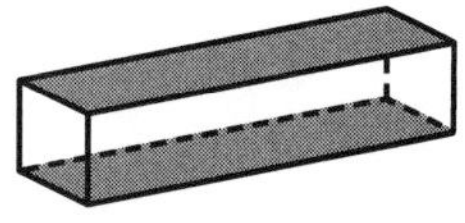

A **rectangular prism** has 6 faces, 12 edges, and 8 vertices.

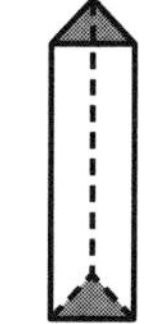

A **triangular prism** has bases that are triangles. It has 5 faces, 9 edges, and 6 vertices.

Pyramids have only one base. They are named for the shape of their base. The other sides have one point in common called the vertex.

triangular pyramid

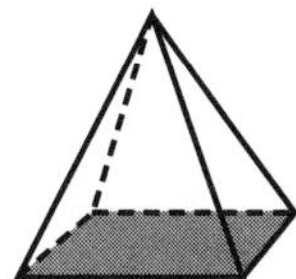

square pyramid

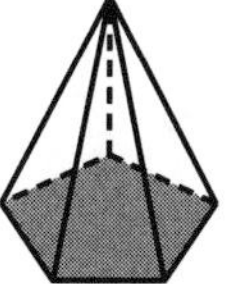

pentagonal pyramid

Other space figures have curved surfaces.

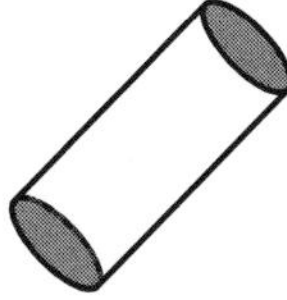

A **cylinder** has two bases that are circles. A cylinder has no vertices.

A **cone** has one base that is a circle. A cone has one vertex.

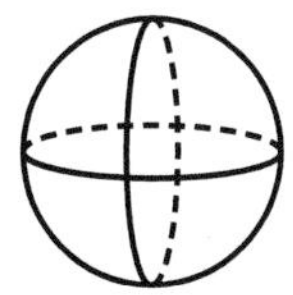

A **sphere** has a center that is the same distance from every point of the sphere.

Name one object that reminds you of the given space figure.

1. rectangular prism ____________ cylinder ____________ square pyramid ____________

Answer each question. Write *Yes* or *No*.

2. Can a pyramid have a triangle for a base? ______

3. Can a cone have a square base? ______

4. Does a prism always have congruent and parallel bases? ______

STANDARD

If a box shaped like a rectangular prism could be unfolded, it might look like this:

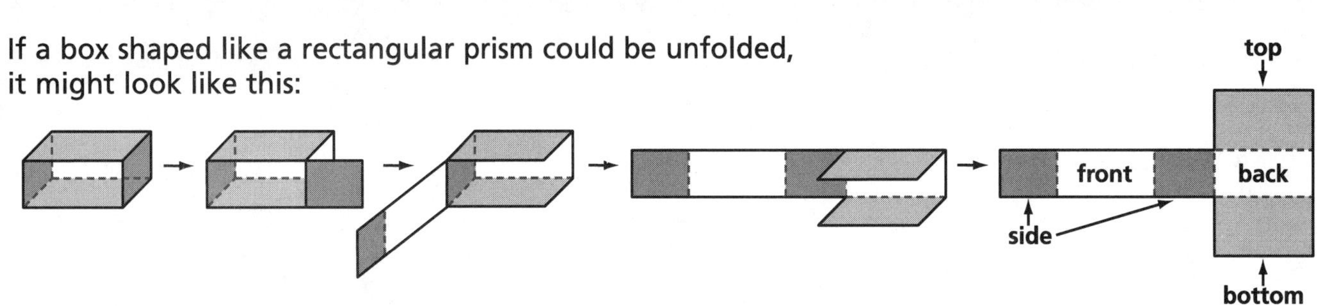

Circle the figure that can be made from each pattern.

5. 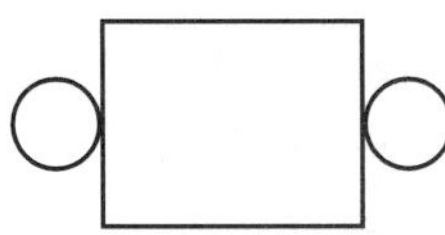

cylinder

sphere

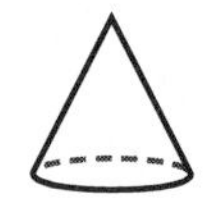

cone

6. 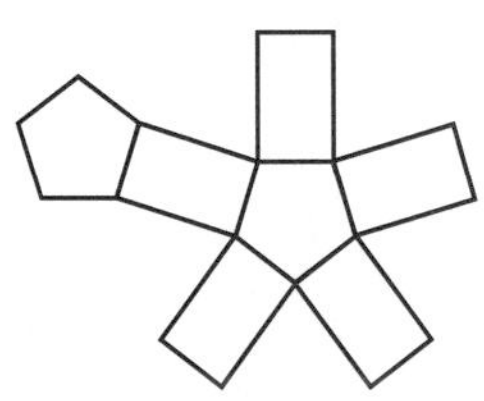

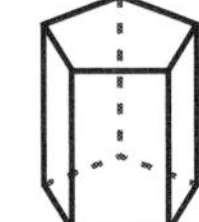

pentagonal prism

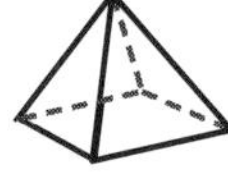

pyramid

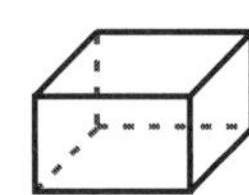

rectangular prism

7. 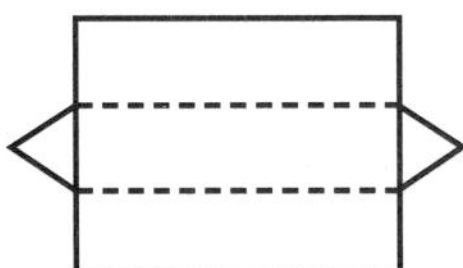

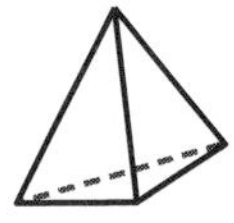

triangular pyramid

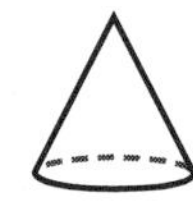

cone

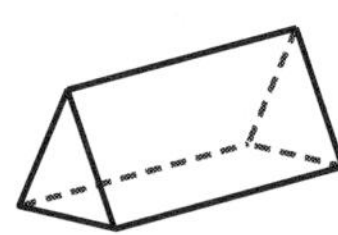

triangular prism

Can these patterns be folded into a cube? Write *Yes* or *No*.

8. 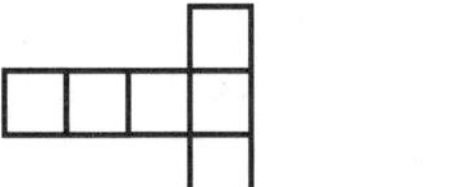 ______

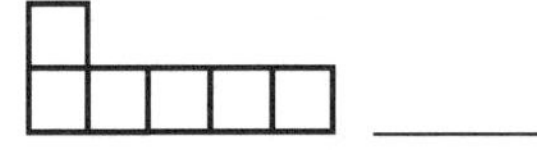 ______

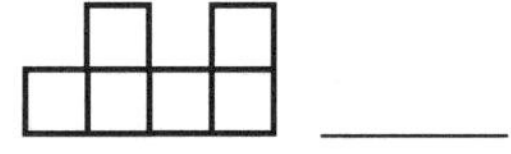 ______

Quick Check

Find the area of the figure. Use 3.14 for π.

9. Circle, radius **5** in. ____________________

10. Circle, diameter **6** cm ____________________

11. Semicircle, radius **21** m ____________________

Write the answer. You may want to sketch the figure first.

12. How many faces does a square pyramid have? ______

13. How many edges does a cube have? ______

14. Name a space figure that does not have any vertices.

____

Work Space.

Name ____

Surface Area

STANDARD

The **surface area** (*SA*) of a space figure is the sum of the areas of all of its surfaces. To find the surface area of a rectangular prism, first find the area of each pair of opposite faces and bases. Then find the sum of the areas.

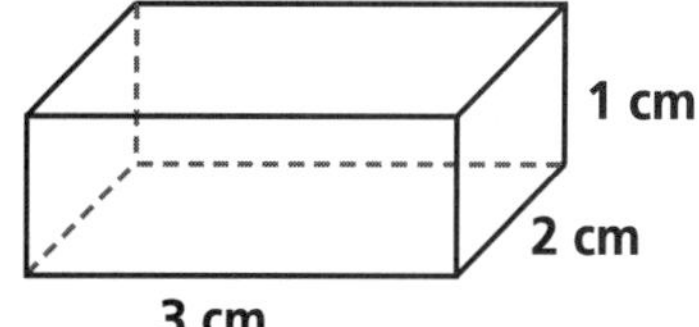

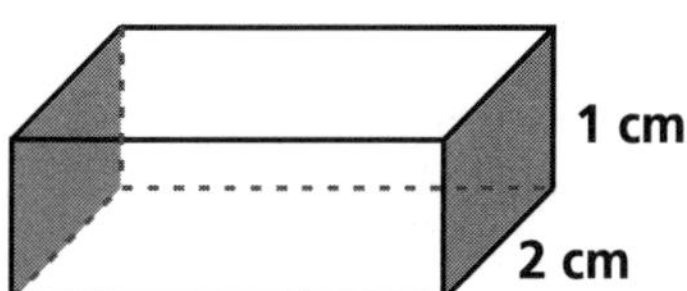

Sides

$A = 2(2 \text{ cm} \cdot 1 \text{ cm})$
$= 2(2 \text{ cm}^2)$
$= 4 \text{ cm}^2$

1 cm
3 cm

Front and Back

$A = 2(3 \text{ cm} \cdot 1 \text{ cm})$
$= 2(3 \text{ cm}^2)$
$= 6 \text{ cm}^2$

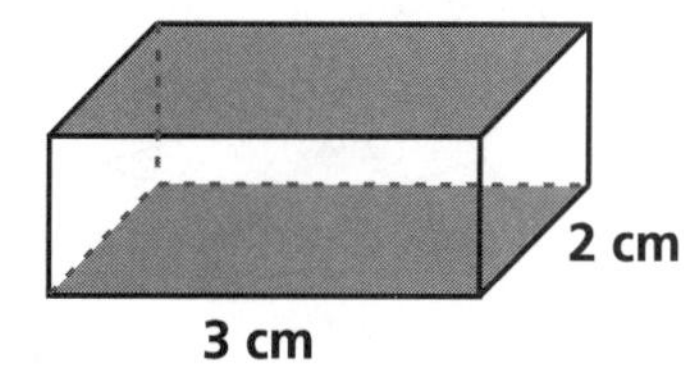

Top and Bottom

$A = 2(3 \text{ cm} \cdot 2 \text{ cm})$
$= 2(6 \text{ cm}^2)$
$= 12 \text{ cm}^2$

Surface Area (*SA*) = area of side + side + front + back + top + bottom
$= 4 \text{ cm}^2 + 6 \text{ cm}^2 + 12 \text{ cm}^2$
$= 22 \text{ cm}^2$

Find the surface area of each prism.

1.

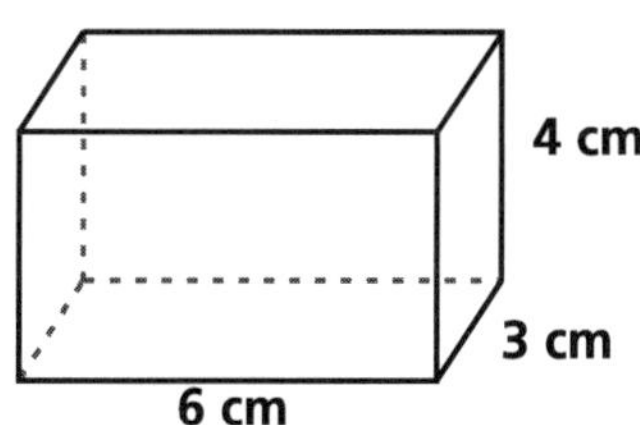

SA = _______ cm²

3 cm
3 cm
3 cm

SA = _______ cm²

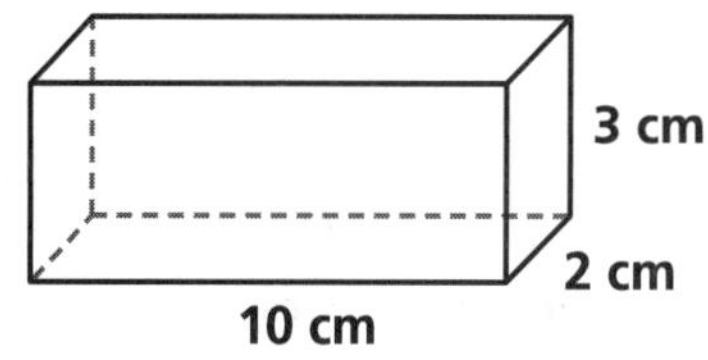

SA = _______ cm²

2.

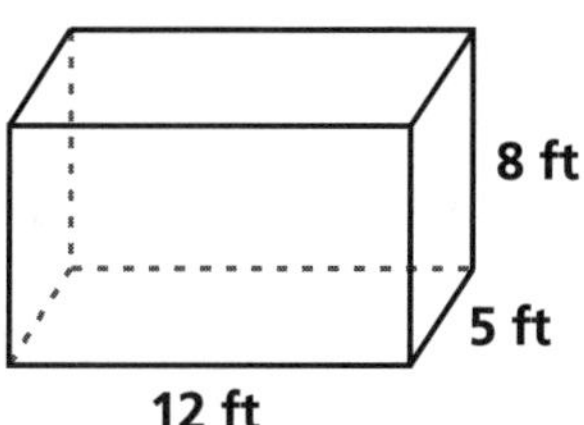

SA = _______ ft²

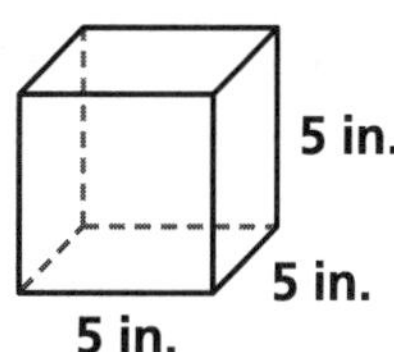

SA = _______ in.²

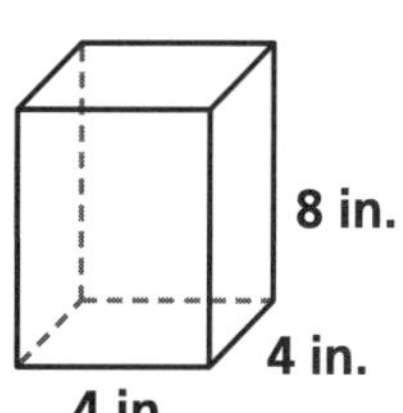

SA = _______ in.²

STANDARD

You can use a formula to find the surface area of a rectangular prism.

$$SA(\text{rectangular prism}) = 2(l \times w) + 2(l \times h) + 2(w \times h)$$

A rectangular prism is a cube when each face of the cube is a square.

$$SA(\text{cube}) = 6s^2$$

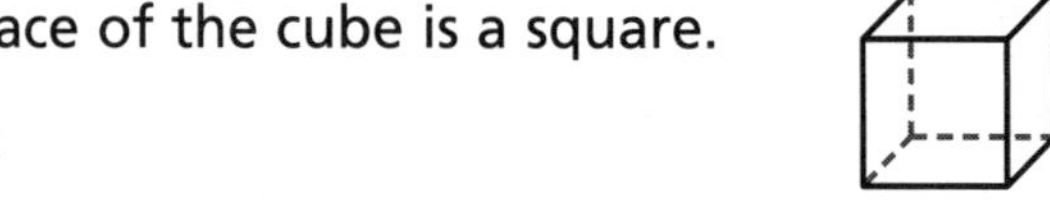

Use a formula to find the surface area of each figure.

3.

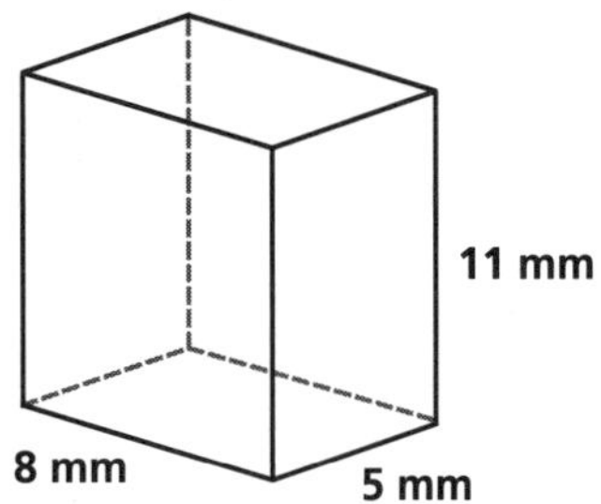

SA = __________ mm²

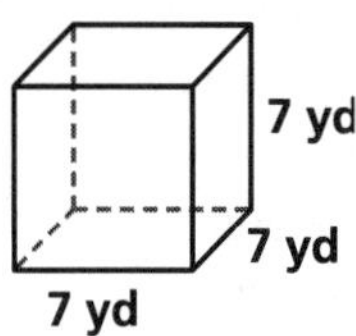

SA = __________ yd²

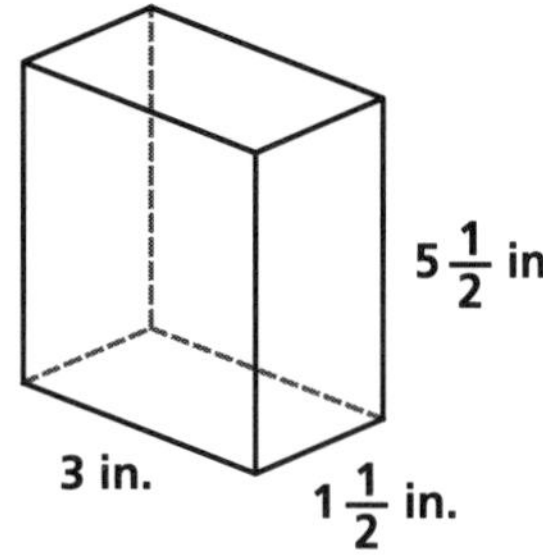

SA = __________ in.²

Problem Solving Reasoning Solve.

4. Karen wants to wrap a **10** by **8** by **5**-inch box with wrapping paper. She has one sheet of wrapping paper that measures **15** by **15** inches. Does she have enough wrapping paper?

Explain. ______________________________

____

5. Lorain has **2** quarts of paint. Each quart covers **100 ft²**. She is going to paint a stage prop that is the shape of a cube. Each edge measures **5** feet. If she gives it two coats, will she have enough paint? Explain. ______________________________

____

Test Prep ★ Mixed Review

6 Lorenzo bought 6 pounds of potatoes. The potatoes cost \$.86 for 2 pounds. How much did Lorenzo's potatoes cost?

A \$5.16 **C** \$1.72

B \$2.58 **D** \$.86

7 Ms. Lowry owns $85\frac{1}{2}$ acres of land. She plants soybeans on $\frac{2}{3}$ of the land. How many acres does she plant with soybeans?

F $128\frac{1}{4}$ acres **H** 57 acres

G $86\frac{1}{6}$ acres **J** $56\frac{2}{3}$ acres

Name ______________________

Problem Solving Strategy: Find a Pattern

STANDARD

In this lesson, you will find a pattern and discover a mathematical relationship.

Problem

A polyhedron is a space figure formed by many polygons. A prism and a pyramid are examples of polyhedra. There is a mathematical relationship between the number of vertices, faces, and edges of a polyhedron. See if you can find this relationship.

1 Understand As you reread, ask yourself questions.

- What facts do you know?

  A polyhedron has vertices, faces, and edges.

- What do you need to find?

  ____

2 Decide Choose a method for solving.

Try the strategy Find a Pattern. Use the polyhedra in the table below.

Polyhedron	V	F	E	V + F

3 Solve Fill in the number of vertices, faces, and edges for each polyhedron in the table.

Compare the column labeled ***V*** + ***F*** with the column labeled ***E***. Describe the relationship.

____

____

4 Look back Write this relationship in formula form.

____

STANDARD

Solve. Use the Find a Pattern strategy or any other strategy you have learned.

1. A rectangular prism has **8** vertices and **12** edges. A triangular prism has **6** vertices and **9** edges. How many vertices and how many edges does a hexagonal prism have?

Think: How many sides does a hexagon have?

Answer ______

2. How many squares are there in the figure below?

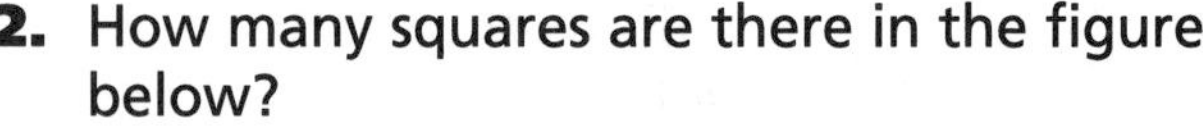

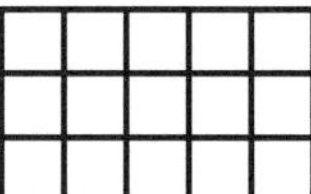

Think: How many **3** × **3** squares are there?

Answer ______

3. Based on your answer to problem **1**, how many faces does a hexagonal prism have?

4. How many faces does a pentagonal pyramid (base is a pentagon) have?

5. A cube has an edge that is **5** inches long. How many square inches of construction paper are needed to completely cover the cube?

6. The sides of a rectangle are in the ratio **1:4**. The perimeter of the rectangle is **60** inches. Find the length and the width.

7. Find the total number of unit cubes in the figure.

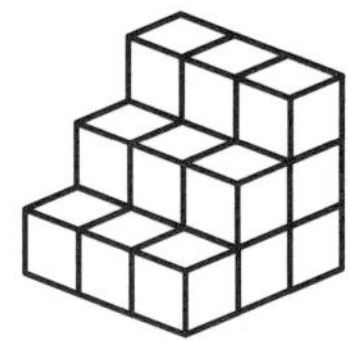

8. Draw the figure that comes next in this pattern:

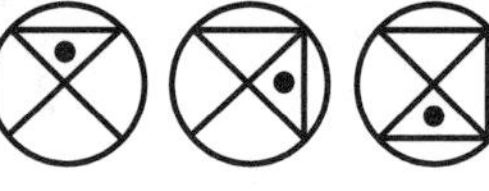

9. Marita and Alexandra have **63** marbles. Alexandra has twice as many as Marita. How many marbles does each have?

10. There are **12** posts equally spaced along the perimeter of a square patio. How many posts are on each side of the patio?

11. Your family phone bill is **$108**. This is $\frac{1}{3}$ more than last month's bill. How much was last month's bill?

12. Mitchell's driveway is **32** ft long. He plans to lengthen it so it will be $\frac{2}{5}$ longer. How long will the new driveway be?

Name ______________________________

Volume

STANDARD

The **volume** (*V*) of any object is the number of **cubic units** that can fit inside the object.

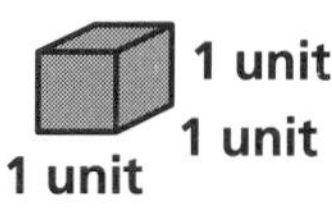

> The volume (***V***) of a **rectangular prism** with length ***l***, width ***w***, and height ***h*** is ***V = lwh.***

If you multiply the number of units of length (*l*) by the number of units of width (*w*), you find the number of cubic units on the base. Multiply this product by the units of height (*h*) to find the volume.

$$V = lwh$$
$$= 3 \text{ cm} \cdot 4 \text{ cm} \cdot 2 \text{ cm}$$
$$= 24 \text{ cm}^3$$

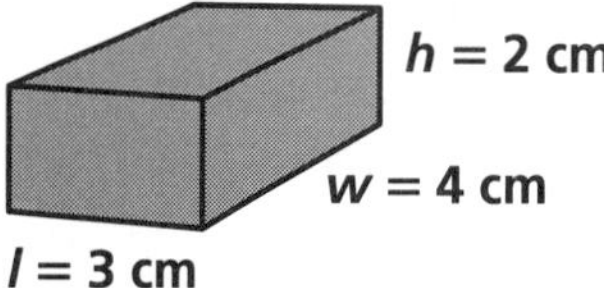

A cube is a rectangular prism in which every face is a square and every side (***s***) or edge is the same length.

> The volume (***V***) of a **cube** with side length ***s*** is $V = s^3$.

$$V = s^3$$
$$= (2 \text{ cm})^3$$
$$= 2 \text{ cm} \cdot 2\text{cm} \cdot 2 \text{ cm}$$
$$= 8 \text{ cm}^3$$

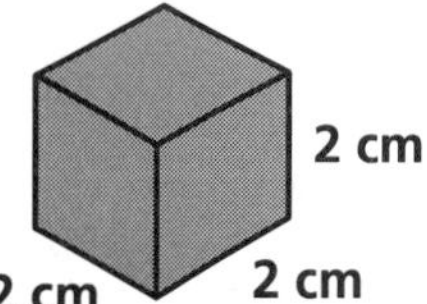

Find the volume of each figure.

1.

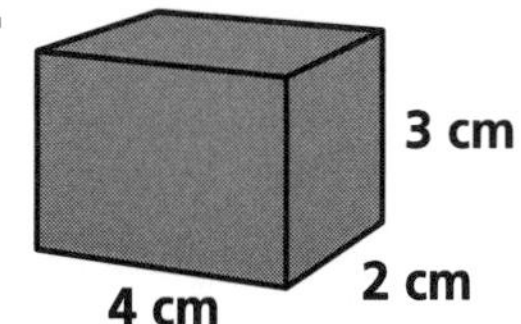

V = __________

V = __________

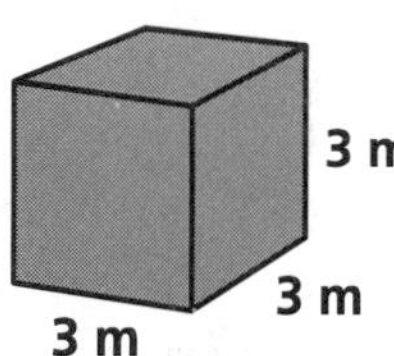

V = __________

2.

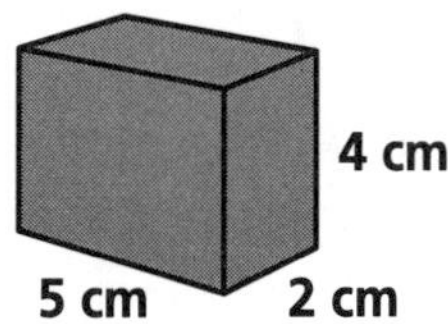

V = __________

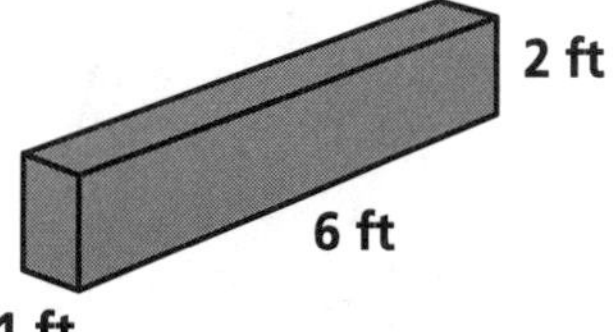

V = __________

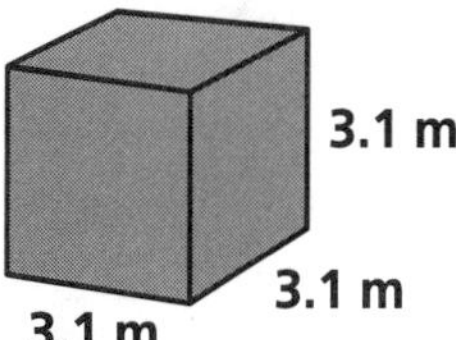

V = __________

STANDARD

You can find the volume of a triangular prism or a cylinder. You begin by finding the area of the base (*B*). Then you multiply by the height to find the volume.

The base of a triangular prism is a triangle. The base of a cylinder is a circle.

Volume of Triangular Prism

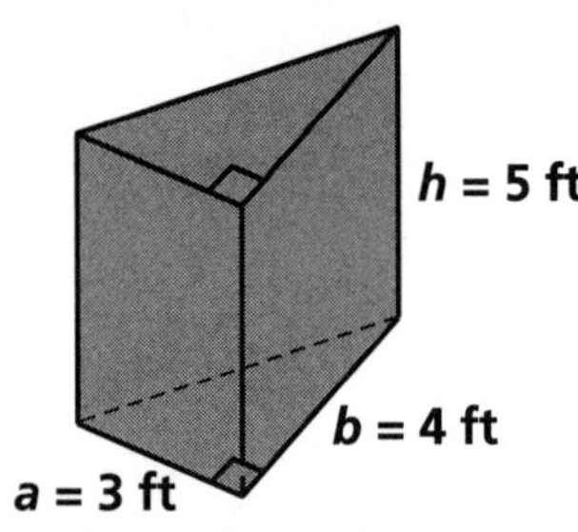

Triangular Prism

V = (Area of base) · height

$= \left(\frac{1}{2} \cdot a \cdot b\right) \cdot h$

$= \left(\frac{1}{2} \cdot 3 \text{ ft} \cdot 4 \text{ ft}\right) \cdot 5 \text{ ft}$

$= (6 \text{ ft}^2) \cdot 5 \text{ ft}$

$= 30 \text{ ft}^3$

The volume of the triangular prism is **30** ft³.

Volume of Cylinder

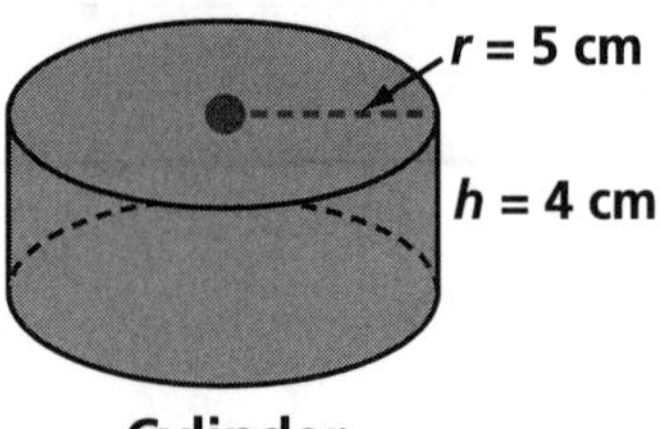

Cylinder

V = (Area of base) · height

$= (\pi \cdot r^2) \cdot h$

$\approx 3.14 \cdot (5 \text{ cm})^2 \cdot 4 \text{ cm}$

$\approx 3.14 \cdot 25 \text{ cm}^2 \cdot 4 \text{ cm}$

$\approx 3.14 \cdot 100 \text{ cm}^3$

$\approx 314 \text{ cm}^3$

The volume of the cylinder is about **314** cm³.

The volume (*V*) of a **prism** or **cylinder** with area of the base (*B*) and height *h* is ***V* = *Bh*.**

Find the area of the base (*B*) of each figure. Then find the volume (*V*).

3.

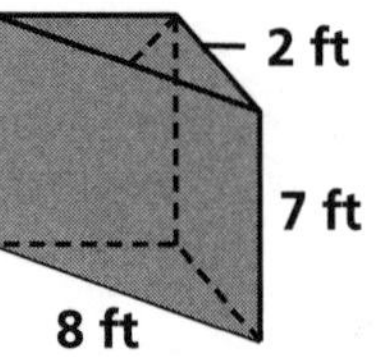

B = __________

V = __________

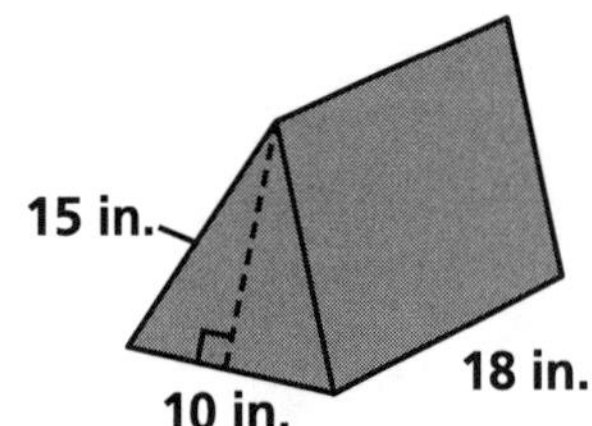

B = __________

V = __________

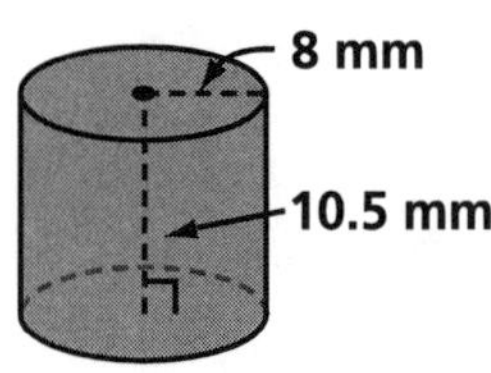

B ≈ __________

V ≈ __________

Name ______________________________

STANDARD

Find the volume of each figure.

4.

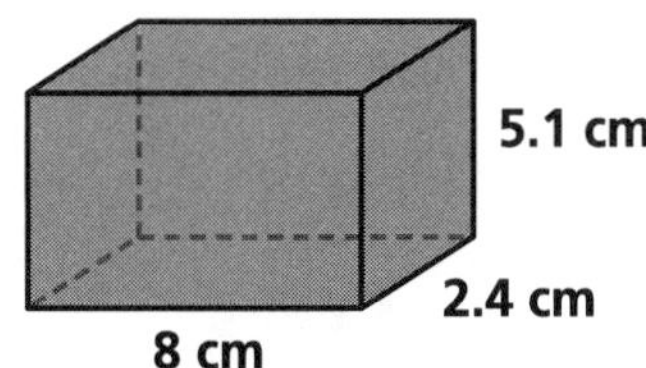

$V =$ ________

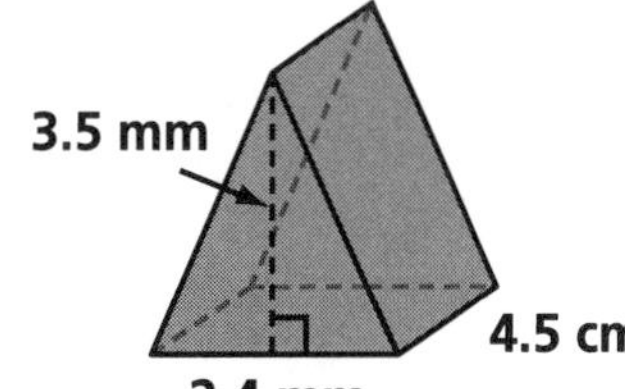

$V =$ ________

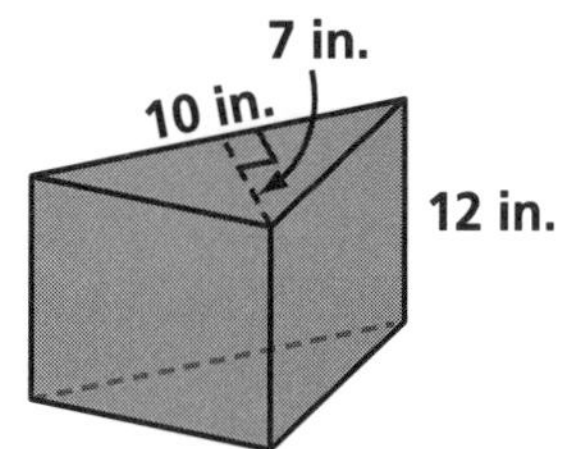

$V =$ ________

5.

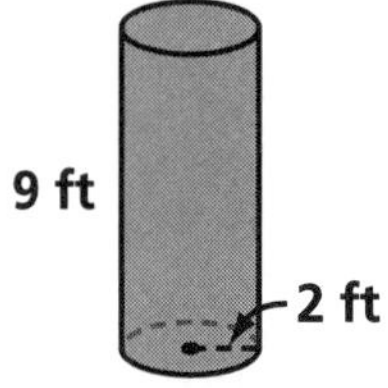

$V =$ ________

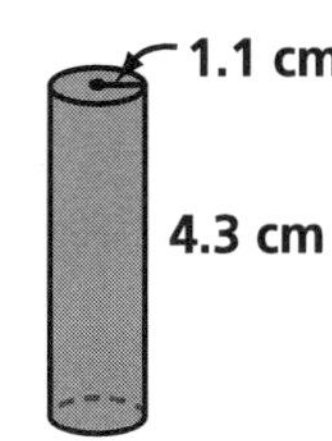

$V =$ ________

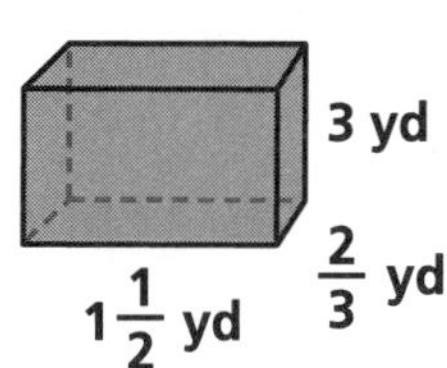

$V =$ ________

6.

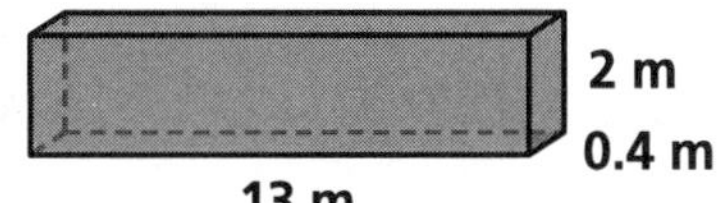

$V =$ ________

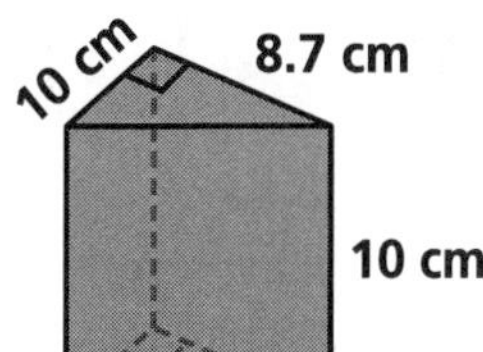

$V =$ ________

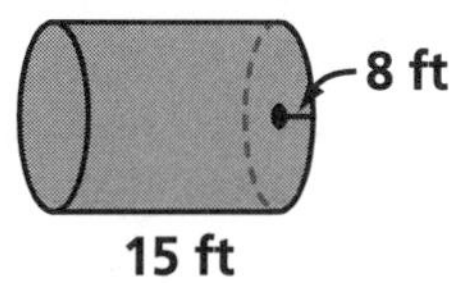

$V =$ ________

7.

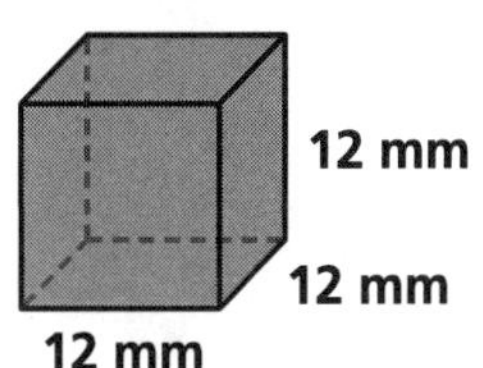

$V =$ ________

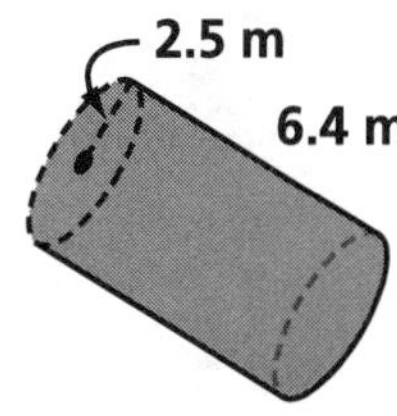

$V =$ ________

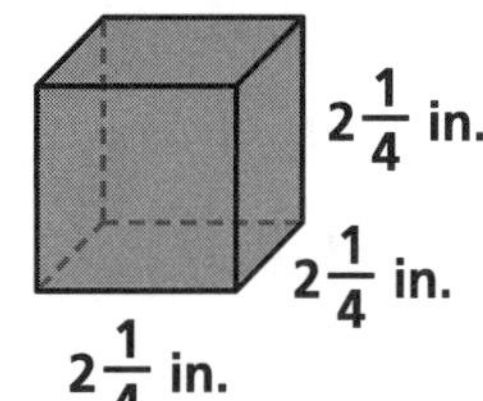

$V =$ ________

8.

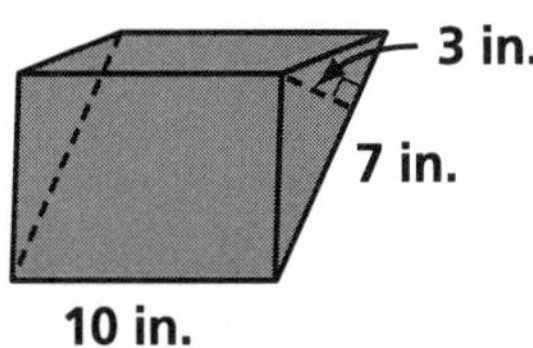

$B =$ ________

$V =$ ________

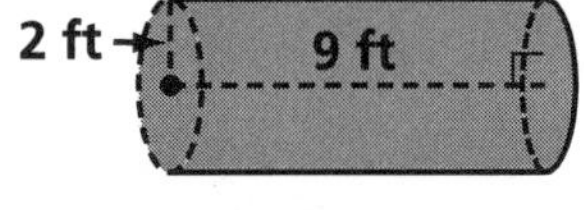

$B \approx$ ________

$V \approx$ ________

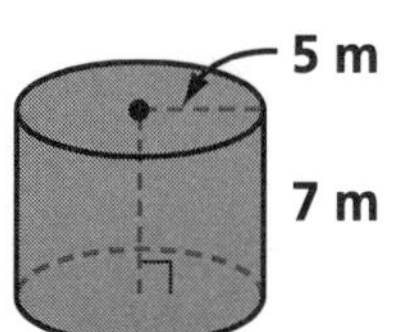

$B \approx$ ________

$V \approx$ ________

STANDARD

Complete.

9. hexagonal prism: $B = 30$ cm^2

$h = 25$ cm

$V =$ __________

triangular prism: $B = 20$ cm^2

$h =$ __________

$V = 250$ cm^3

10. pentagonal prism: $B =$ __________

$h = 18$ ft

$V = 414$ ft^3

octagonal prism: $B = 13$ in.^{2}

$h = 11$ in.

$V =$ __________

Problem Solving
Reasoning

Solve.

11. What is the volume of the prism at the right? __________

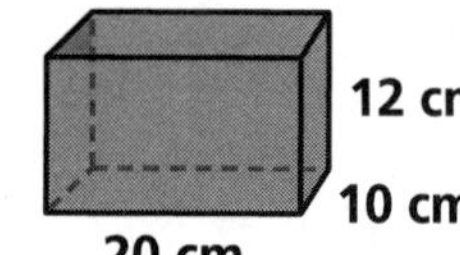

12. What would the volume of the prism be if the length, width, and height were halved? __________

13. By what number is the volume of the original prism divided when the length, width, and height are halved? ______

Quick Check

Find the surface area of the space figure.

14. A cube with edges of length **5** cm __________

15. A rectangular prism with length **2.5** m, width **6** m, and height **2** m __________

16. A cylinder, radius of base **5** in., height **8** in. __________

Find the volume of the space figure.

17. A rectangular prism with length $3\frac{1}{2}$ in., width **5** in. and height $2\frac{1}{2}$ in. __________

18. A cylinder whose base has an area of **45** m^2 and a height of **20** m __________

19. A triangular prism whose base has an area of **8.7** mm^2 and whose height is **15** mm __________

Work Space.

Name ______________________

Problem Solving Application: Use a Formula

STANDARD

To solve some problems, you need to know a formula.

In this lesson, you will use the appropriate formula to find the perimeter, area, surface area or volume of plane or solid figures.

Tips to Remember:

1. Understand 2. Decide 3. Solve 4. Look back

- Think about what the problem is asking you to do. What information does the problem give you? What do you need to find out?
- Picture the situation described in the problem. Draw a picture to show what is happening.
- Think about strategies you have already learned. Try using one of them to solve the problem.

Solve.

1. The Carson family measured the perimeter of their family room and found it to be **54** ft. If the room is **15** ft long, how wide is it?

Think: What is the formula for the perimeter of the room? What values can you substitute into the formula?

____

____

Answer ______________________

2. The Carsons want to order a pizza. A large pizza (**16** in. in diameter) is **$9.60** and a medium pizza (**8** in. in diameter) is **$4.80**. Which is the better buy? Explain your answer.

Think: What formula do you need to use to compare the size of the pizzas?

____

Answer ______________________

____

3. Beth wants to put a fence around a circular garden. The diameter of the garden is **5** feet. Fencing is **$1.25** per foot. How much fencing should she buy? How much will it cost?

Think: What formula do you need to use to find the distance around a circle?

____

Answer ______________________

4. Elijah is drawing a circle inside a square so that the circle touches each side of the square. If the area of the square is **16** in.^{2}, what is the area of the circle?

Think: What is equal to the diameter of the circle?

____

Answer ______________________

STANDARD

Solve.

5. On one wall of the a family room is a circular dart board with a radius of **20** cm. What is its circumference?

6. What is the area of the wall space covered by the dart board in problem **5**?

7. A gift box for a shirt is **12** in. long, **9** in. wide, and **1.5** in. high. What is the volume of the box?

8. How much wrapping paper would it take to cover the box in problem **7**?

9. A triangular sail has a base of **5** yd and a height of **8** yd. How many square yards of sail is that?

10. A lot is **22** yd long and **13** yd wide. If fencing costs **$1.25** a foot, how much will it cost to fence the lot?

11. A square has a side equal to the diameter of a circle. Which shape has the greater perimeter? Which shape has the greater area?

12. Square B has one side double the length of Square A. How do the perimeters compare? How do the areas compare?

13. The length, width, and height of a rectangular prism are multiplied by **3**. How is the volume of the prism changed?

14. The area of circle A is **12.56** in.^{2} The radius of circle B is one half of the radius of circle A. How does the area of circle B compare with the area of circle A?

15. A bookcase is **3** ft wide, **6** ft high, and **12** in. deep. How much floor space will it cover? How much wall space?

16. A car traveled **240** miles in **4** hours. What was the average speed of the car?

Extend Your Thinking

17. Look back at problem **7**. How many boxes would a roll of wrapping paper cover if the roll is **12** ft long and **30** in. wide?

18. Look back at problem **10**. Explain the method you used to solve the problem.

Name ______________________________

Unit 8 Review

Find the perimeter of each polygon.

1.

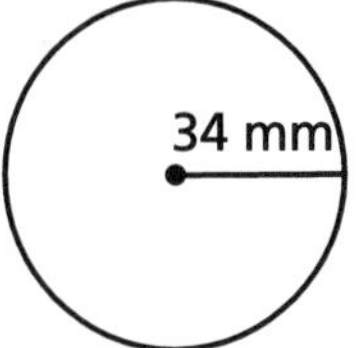

______

2.

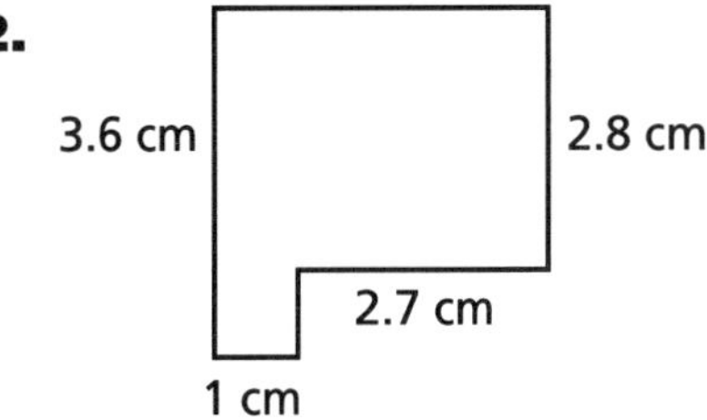

______

Find the circumference of each circle. Use $C = \pi d$ and 3.14 for π.

3.

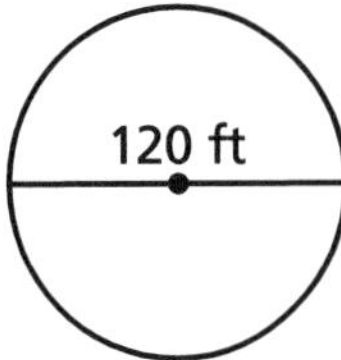

______

4.

120 ft

______

Find the area of each figure.

5.

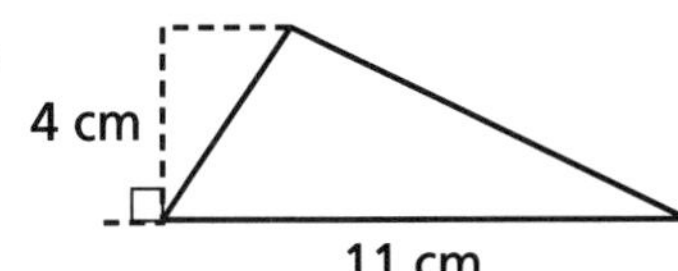

______

6.

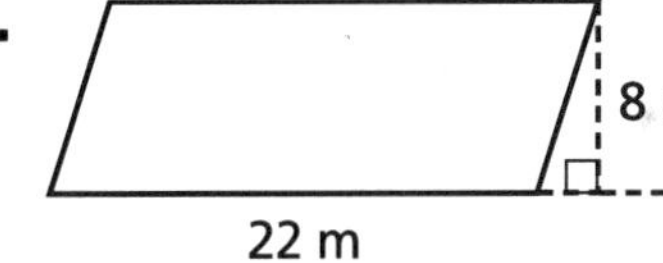

______

7.

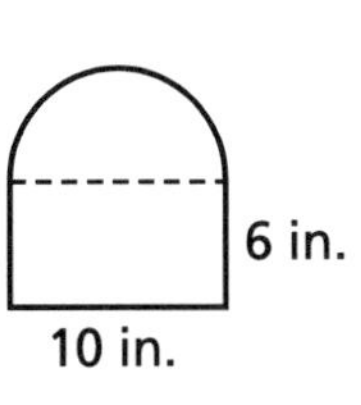

______

8.

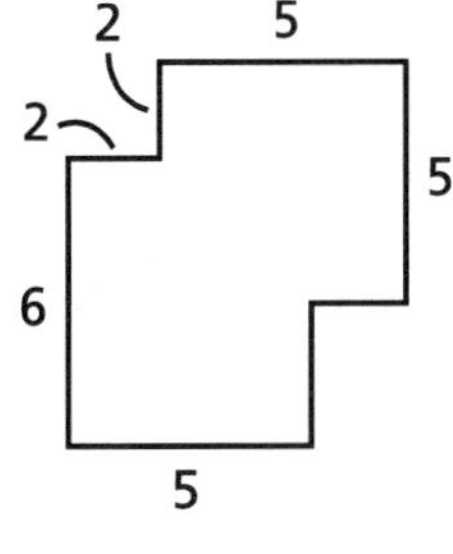

______

Find the volume of each figure. Use 3.14 for for π.

9.

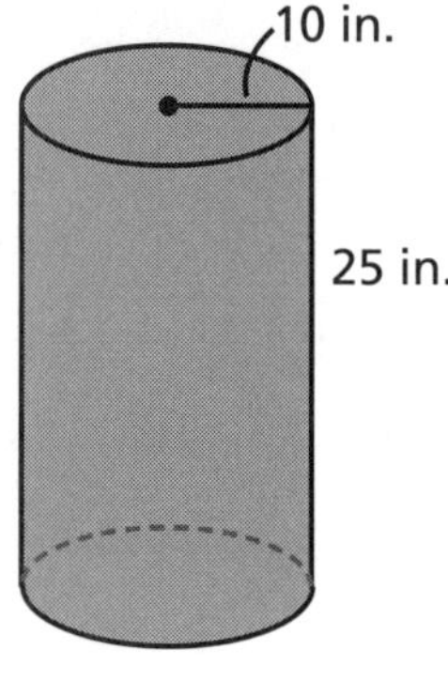

____

10.

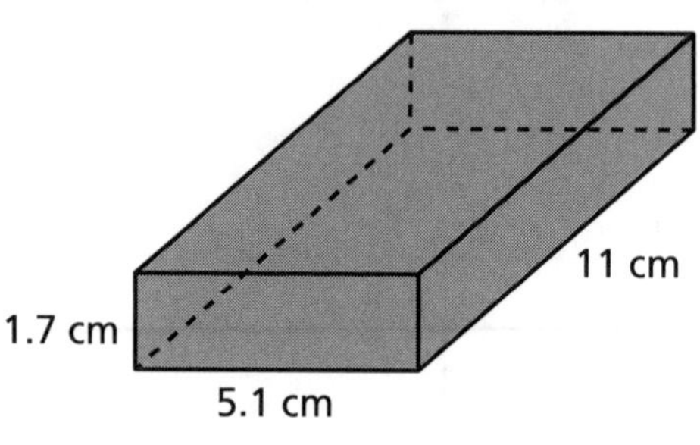

____

Find the surface area of each figure.

11.

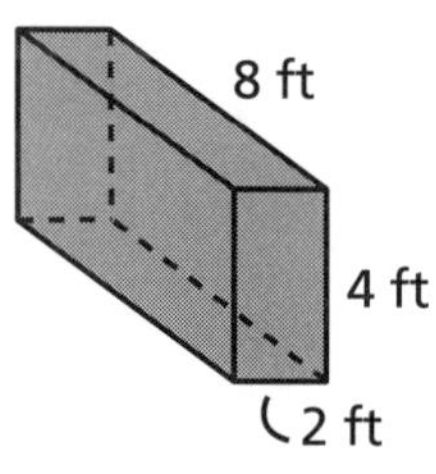

____

12.

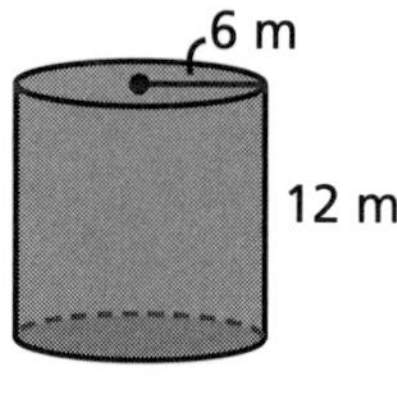

____

Solve.

13. What space figure has a base and a surface from the boundary of its base to its vertex? _______________

14. The floor of a room is rectangular and measures **10** ft by **16** ft. What formula would you use to determine the amount of wall-to-wall carpeting you would need to cover the floor of the room? Explain.

____

____

____

15. A square has a side that measures **16** in. If you cut from the square the largest circle possible, what would the circumference of the circle be? What formula did you use?

____

Name ______________________________

Cumulative Review
★ Test Prep

1 **Use the picture below.**

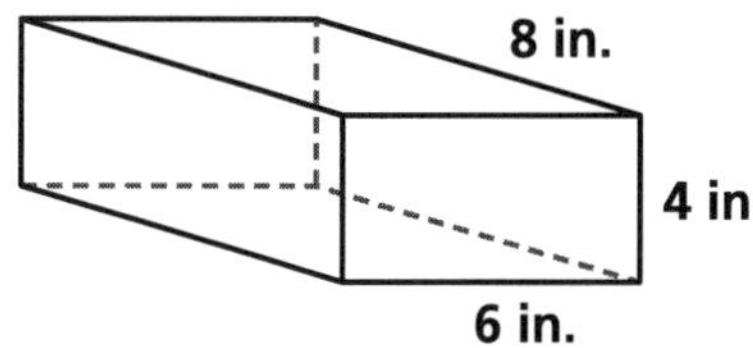

What is the surface area of the prism?

A 288 in.^{2} C 192 in.^{2}

B 208 in.^{2} D 144 in.^{2}

2 **Use the picture below.**

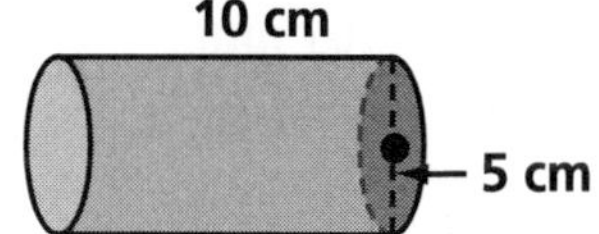

What is the volume of this cylinder?

F $\approx$ 62.5 cm^3 H $\approx$ 196.3 cm^3

G $\approx$ 157.1 cm^3 J $\approx$ 85.4 cm^3

3 **Use your inch ruler and the picture to answer the question.**

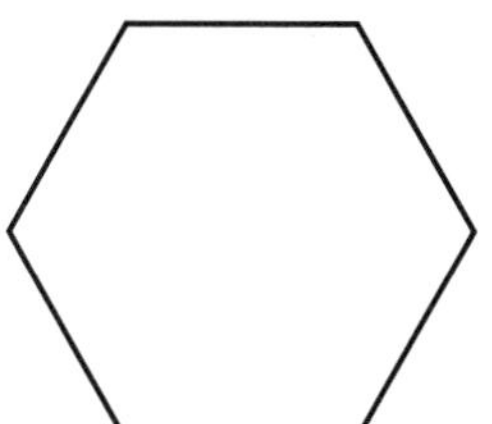

What is the perimeter of this figure?

A $1\frac{1}{4}$ in. C $7\frac{1}{2}$ in.

B $3\frac{3}{4}$ in. D 12 in.

4 **Use your centimeter ruler. Which figure has an area of exactly 3 cm^2?**

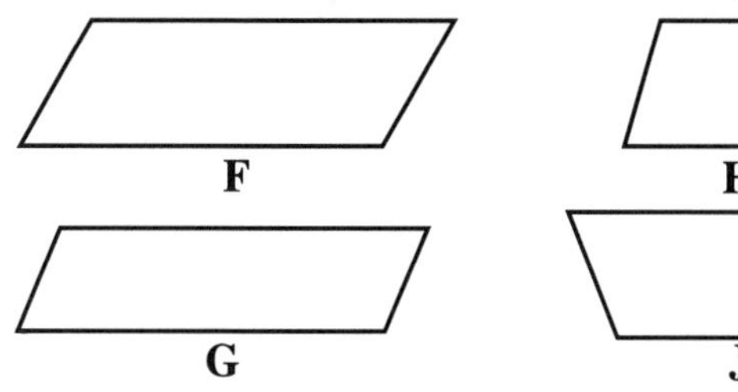

5 **Which figure is a triangular prism?**

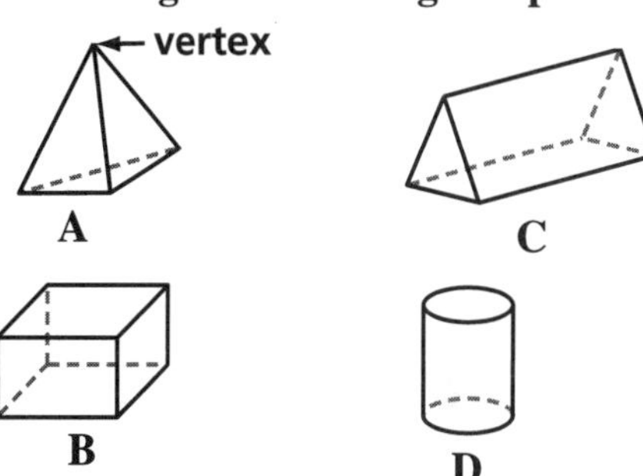

Use the picture to answer questions 6 and 7.

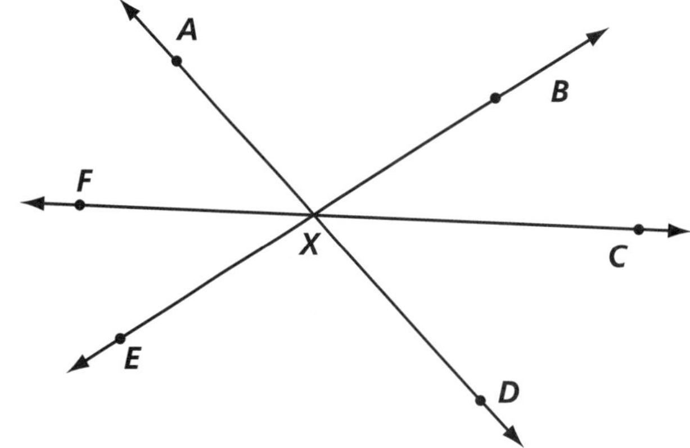

6 **Which two angles are vertical angles?**

F $\angle AXB$ and $\angle BXD$ H $\angle AXB$ and $\angle CXD$

G $\angle AXB$ and $\angle AXC$ J $\angle AXB$ and $\angle EXD$

7 **Which two angles are supplements?**

A $\angle AXB$ and $\angle AXE$ C $\angle AXB$ and $\angle EXF$

B $\angle AXB$ and $\angle AXF$ D $\angle AXB$ and $\angle EXD$

Use the figures to answer questions 8–10.

8 Which two figures are congruent?

F 1 and 4   H 3 and 8

G 2 and 6   J 5 and 7

9 Which two figures are similar but not congruent?

A 1 and 4   C 3 and 8

B 2 and 6   D 5 and 7

10 What is the name for figure 1?

F Pentagon   H Hexagon

G Octagon   J Quadrilateral

11 The rectangular gymnasium at the Kids' Club has an area of 800 square feet. Two opposite sides are each 40 feet long. How long are the other two sides?

A 360 ft   C 40 ft

B 200 ft   D 20 ft

12 Rick wrote a report that was $8\frac{2}{3}$ pages long. How is that number written as an exact decimal?

F 8.23   J $8.\overline{6}$

G $8.\overline{3}$ K NH

H 8.6

13 Use the picture to answer the question.

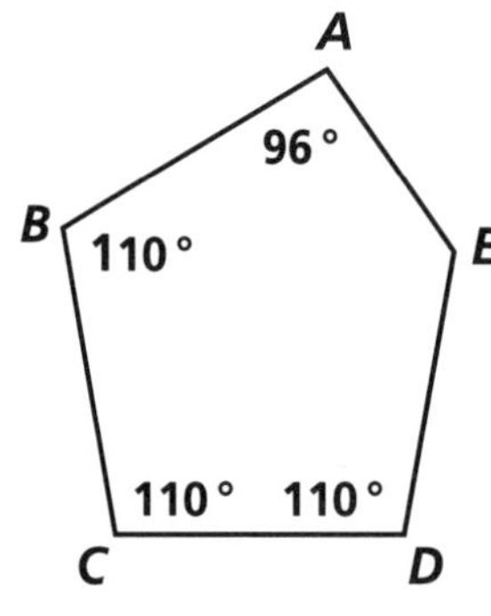

What is the measure of ∠AED?

A 96°   C 110°

B 108°   D 114°

14 Strawberries are selling at 3 pints for $2 at Super Shop and for $.79 a pint at Shop 'n' Save. Which is the better buy and how much less do these strawberries sell for?

F Super Shop by 2¢ per pint

G Super Shop by 9¢ per pint

H Super Shop by 12¢ per pint

J Shop 'n' Save by 20¢ per pint

K Shop 'n' Save by 71¢ per pint

15 One city has a real estate tax rate of $12 for each $1,000 of real estate value. What is this rate as a percent?

A 120%   D 0.12%

B 12%   E NH

C 1.2%

16 A length of 3.7 meters is to be divided into 8 equal pieces. How long will each piece be?

F 46.25 m   J 0.04625 m

G 4.625 m   K NH

H 0.4625 m

UNIT 9 • TABLE OF CONTENTS

Data, Statistics, and Probability

We will be using this vocabulary:

probability the number from 0 to 1 describing the chance of an event occurring

graph a pictorial representation of a point, function, or data

sample a subset of a set of data

Dear Family,

During the next few weeks, our math class will be learning about data, statistics, and probability.

You can expect to see homework that provides practice determining probability. Here is a sample you may want to keep handy to give help if needed.

Probability

Probability (***P***) is the chance of an event occurring and is expressed using the formula

$$P = \frac{\text{number of favorable outcomes}}{\text{total possible number of outcomes}}$$

Example: Suppose this spinner is spun once. What is the probability of the spinner pointing to **C**?

1. Determine the number of favorable outcomes. Since only **1** outcome or section of the spinner is labeled **C**, write **1** as the top number of the probability fraction.

2. Determine the total possible number of outcomes. Since the spinner can point to any of **8** outcomes or sections, the bottom number of the probability fraction is **8**.

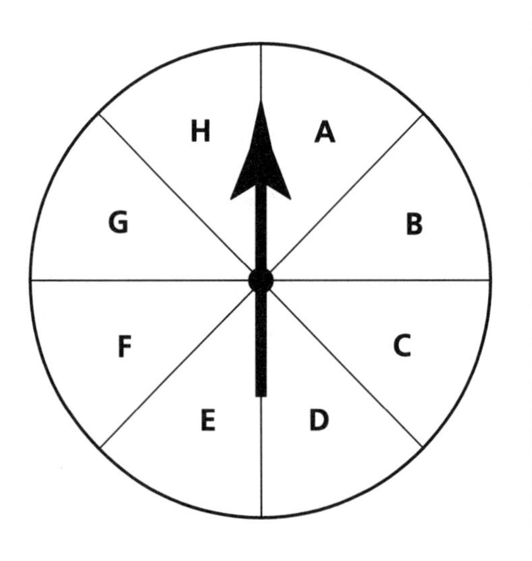

The probability that the spinner will point to **C** is $\frac{1}{8}$.

During this unit, students will need to continue finding probabilities and working with data and statistics.

Sincerely,

Name ______________________________

You can use a double-bar graph to compare two sets of data on one graph. Use the steps below to make a double-bar graph of this data.

Favorite Sport of 500 Students							
Sport	Football	Hockey	Soccer	Baseball	Basketball	Swimming	Track
sixth graders	45	25	40	50	35	15	40
seventh graders	25	15	20	50	55	45	40

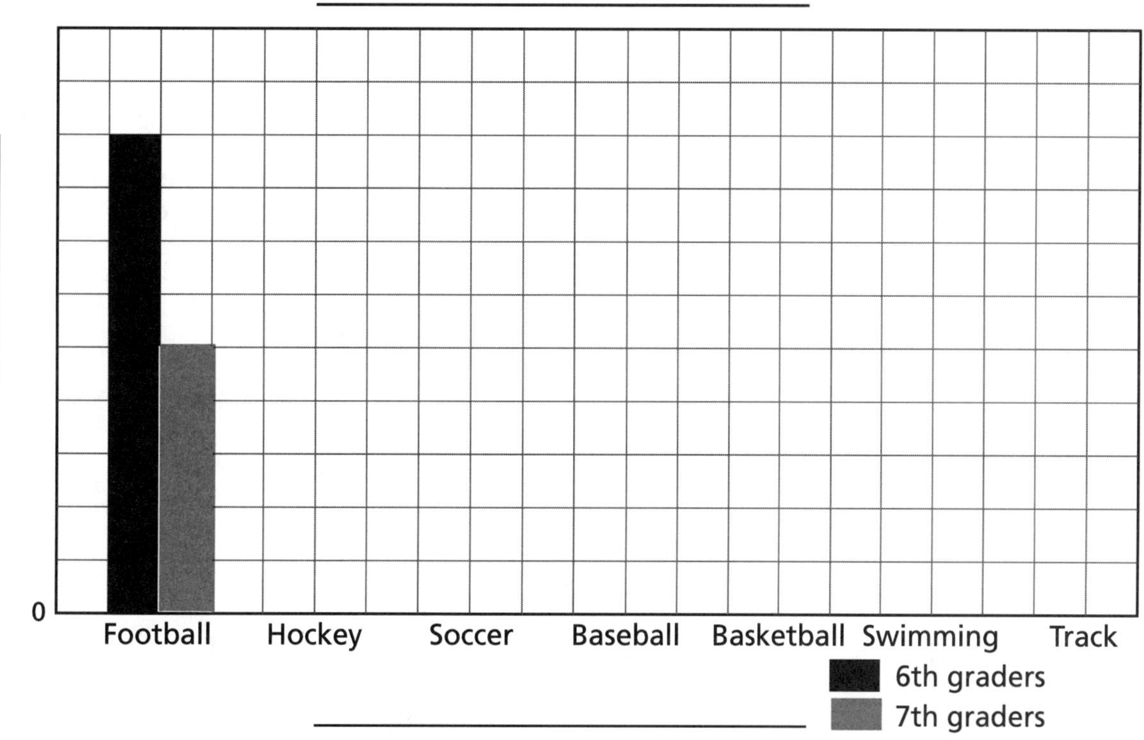

1. Label the axes and write a title.
2. What is the greatest number of votes for any sport? ______

   Which would be the best interval to use on the vertical scale: **2**, **5**, or **10**? ______

   Complete the vertical scale. Look at the bars for football. The black bar shows the number of sixth graders. The red bar shows the number on seventh graders.
3. How many sixth graders chose hockey? ______ Draw a black bar to show how many. How many seventh graders chose hockey? ______ Draw a red bar.
4. Finish the graph. Draw bars for the other sports.

STANDARD

You can use a double-line graph to compare change or growth over time. Use the steps below to graph this data.

Average Monthly Temperatures (°F) of Two Cities

	Jan	Feb	Mar	Apr	May	June	July	Aug	Sept	Oct	Nov	Dec
Boston	29	30	39	48	58	68	74	72	65	55	45	34
San Francisco	49	52	53	56	58	62	63	64	65	61	55	49

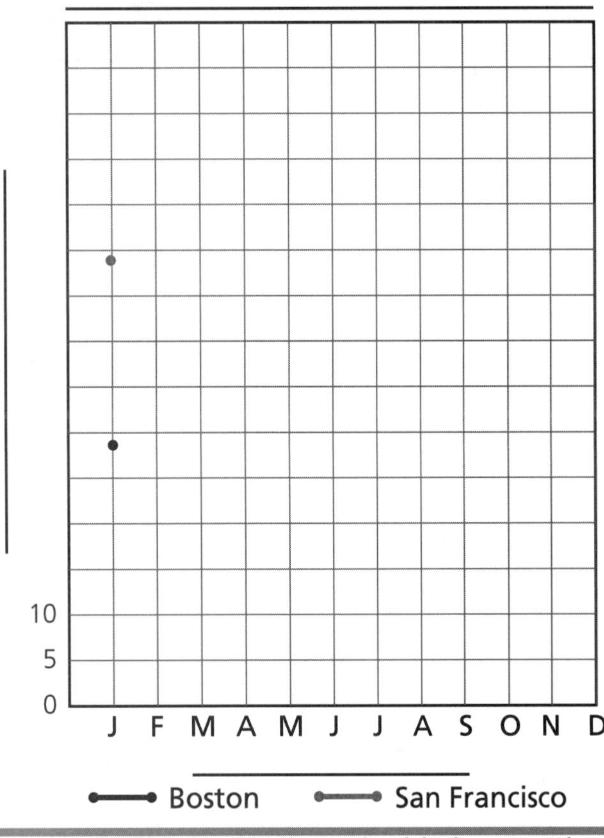

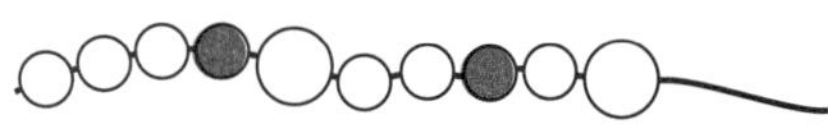

5. What is the highest temperature in the table? _______

6. Complete the scale. Make sure it extends far enough.

7. Label the axes. Write a title.

8. Find the line for February. What was the temperature in Boston? _______ Draw a black dot on the graph.

9. Continue placing black dots for Boston. Connect them with black lines.

10. Do the same steps for San Francisco, using red dots. Connect them with red lines.

11. Use grid paper. Make a double-bar graph using this data.

Time Spent on Activities (Hours)

	Sleep	Eat	Play	Study
School Days	8	2	1	2
Weekends	9	3	5	2

12. Use grid paper. Make a double-line graph using this data.

Number of Students Absent

	Mon	Tues	Wed	Thurs	Fri
Mrs. Kim's class	3	5	0	2	6
Mr. Lopez's class	2	1	3	3	3

Test Prep ★ Mixed Review

13 **Rosa is using beads to make a necklace. Every fourth bead is red. Every fifth bead is larger than the others. After how many more beads will Rosa need a large red one?**

A 6 **B** 8 **C** 10 **D** 15

14 **The diameter of a circle is 6 cm. About how many times longer is the circumference?**

F About twice as long

G About three times as long

H About four times as long

J About five times as long

Name ______________________

Clusters, Gaps, and Outliers

STANDARD

In one school, students can earn 5 points for each problem of the day they solve. The data below show the points earned by 25 sixth graders.

Points Earned by 6th Graders												
185	190	60	80	90	90	100	105	110	110	130	95	105
130	125	195	100	90	95	120	120	100	95	95	105	

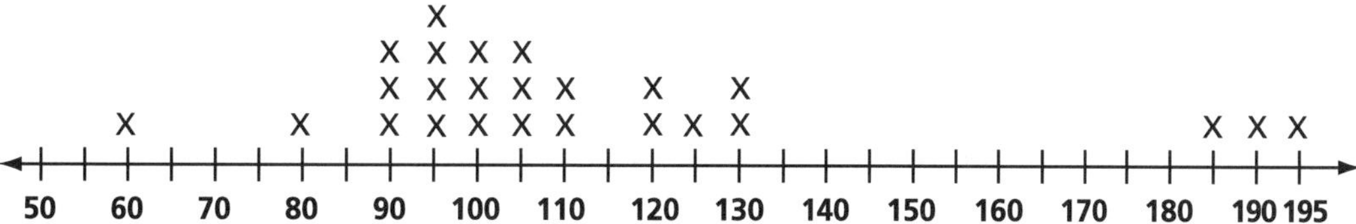

The line plot shows where there are groups of data points, called **clusters.** The number of points cluster around **100.** You can also see **gaps** on the line plot where there are no data points. There are also data points that represent values that are much greater or less than the other values. These values are called **outliers;** then, **60, 185, 190,** and **195** are outliers.

The mean of the data is **112.8**. The median is **105**. The mode is **95.**

To find out how the outliers affect the mean of the data, find the mean without the outliers:

The mean without **60, 185, 190,** and **195**:

$$\frac{2{,}190}{21} \approx 104.29$$

So, the mean without the outliers is **104.29.**

The outliers change the mean by more than **8** points. This indicates that the mean is not the best description of the data. Since the data clusters around **100,** the median of **105** is the better measure of central tendency to use.

Use the line plot to answer the questions.

Number of Words in First 20 Sentences of a Novel

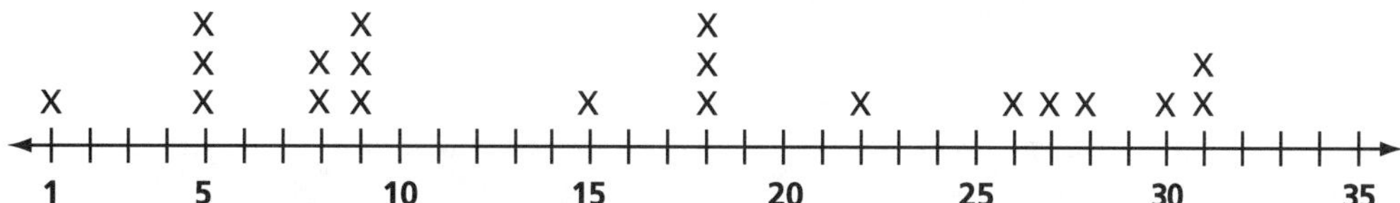

1. Does the data cluster or is it spread out? ______________________

2. Are there outliers? If so, where? ______________________

3. Find the mean, median, mode, and range of the data.

____

4. Which measure of central tendency best describes the data? Explain.

____

STANDARD

Use the line plot to analyze weekly salaries at the Toy Factory.

5. Where do the data cluster?

____

6. Are there outliers?

If so, where? _______

7. Find the mean, median, and mode.

____

Weekly Salaries at the Toy Factory (in Dollars)

8. What measure of central tendency best describes the data?

____

Use the line plot to analyze the number of hours preschoolers watch TV weekly.

9. Where do the data cluster?

____

Hours of Television Watched Weekly

X X X (1); X (7); X X (8); X (9); X (10); X (12); X (13); X X (14); X X (15); X X (16); X (18); X (20)

1 2 3 4 5 6 7 8 9 10 11 12 13 14 15 16 17 18 19 20

10. Are there outliers?

If so, where? _______

11. Find the mean, median, and mode. _______________

12. What measure of central tendency best describes the data? _______________

Problem Solving Reasoning Solve.

13. Karl's math quiz scores for nine weeks are: **95, 96, 65, 92, 98, 100, 55, 94,** and **95.** His teacher allows students to drop their two lowest quiz scores, then find the average. How much difference will this make in Karl's average?

____

Test Prep ★ Mixed Review

14 Jose bought $4\frac{1}{2}$ gallons of paint to paint the porch of his house. He has used $2\frac{2}{3}$ gallons. How much does he have left?

A $\frac{5}{6}$

B $1\frac{1}{6}$

C $1\frac{5}{6}$

D $2\frac{5}{6}$

15 The scale for a drawing of a shed is 1 inch = 4 feet. One wall of the shed is $2\frac{1}{4}$ inches in the drawing. How long is the actual wall?

F 9 ft

G 8 ft

H 6 ft

J 4 ft

Name ______________________________

Problem Solving Strategy: Conjecture and Verify

STANDARD

When a problem does not give enough information to solve it directly, you may need to begin with a conjecture about the answer.

To make your conjecture, use number sense, reasoning, and any information you have. Then test your conjecture to verify it or to see how you should revise it.

Problem

Steven scored 84 on his math test. What must he score on his next test so his average is 91?

 **Understand** As you reread, ask yourself questions.

- What do you need to find?

____

- What information do you have?

____

 **Decide** Choose a method for solving.

- Try the strategy Conjecture and Verify.

Is the number you need greater or less than 91? Explain.

____

____

- Is the number you need odd or even? How do you know?

____

____

- What will your first guess be? ______________

 **Solve** Verify your conjecture. Try again if you need to.

- Test your conjecture.

Conjecture	Test
96	$(84 + 96) \div 2 =$ ______

- Should your next try be greater or less? ______

 **Look back** Check your answer.

- Will the average be 91? ______

STANDARD

Solve. Use the Conjecture and Verify strategy or any other strategy you have learned.

1. Taryn's average on three science tests is **92**. She scored **87** on the first test and **100** on the second test. What did she score on the third test?

Think: If Taryn averaged **92** on **3** tests, what is the sum of the points she scored?

____

Answer ______________________

2. The mean of a set of numbers is **15**. There are **6** numbers in the set. What is the sum of the numbers in the set?

Think: Do you have to use addition to find the sum?

____

Answer ______________________

3. The numbers of track meets that each student in a class has attended are: **6, 3, 4, 4, 1, 0, 4, 0, 2, 2, 3, 1, 7, 6, 4, 5, 2, 0, 3**. Make a frequency table for the data.

4. Use the data in problem **3** to answer this question. What is the average number of track meets attended by each student?

____

5. Look back at problem 3. True or false: The mean and the median are the same?

____

6. The product of three consecutive whole numbers is **504**. What are the numbers?

____

7. A store had **3** brands of CD players. Each CD player came in **3** colors: black, white, and red. How many choices of CD players did the store have?

____

8. The length of a rectangle is **7** more than its width. The area of the rectangle is **120** cm^2. What are the dimensions of the rectangle?

____

9. For the set of numbers **96, 87, 95, 90, 85, 90**, and **94**, choose the correct statement.

a) The median is greater than the mode.
b) The mean is less than the mode.
c) The mean is greater than the median.

____

10. Lucy purchased **2** pairs of socks for **$2.95** a pair. She also purchased **2** sweaters for **$29.50** each. Tom purchased **3** sweaters for half the price Lucy paid. Who spent more money?

____

11. Three consecutive whole numbers have a sum of **114**. What are the numbers?

____

12. What time is **36** h, **30** min, **10** sec before **10:00** P.M.?

____

Name ______________________________

Surveys and Samples

STANDARD

Often TV newscasters report the results of surveys. Those results tell something about a large group or **population.** But the survey does not poll every person in the group.

A **sample** is a part of the population that is used to get information about the whole group. Poll-takers want the answers given by the sample to be similar to those of the whole group. Then it is a **representative sample.** A representative sample can be used to make predictions about the whole group.

Predicting a Number

A representative sample of **120** out of **1,200** students was used to see how many students would go to a basketball game. To predict how many students would go to the game, use a proportion.

Number Going (from sample) → 84; Total Sample Number → 120; n ← Number Going (from total population); 1,200 ← Total Population

$$\frac{84}{120} = \frac{n}{1{,}200}$$

$$120n = 84 \cdot 1{,}200$$
$$120n = 100{,}800$$
$$n = 100{,}800 \div 120$$
$$n = 840$$

From their sample, you can predict that about **840** students will go to the game.

Predicting a Percent

In a representative sample of middle school students, **72** out of **120** students said that they would run in the Fun Run.

Runners in Sample → 72; Total in Sample → 120; x ← Part; 100 ← Total Population

$$\frac{72}{120} = \frac{x}{100}$$

To predict what percent of all the students will run, use a proportion. Based on the sample, you can predict that **60** out of **100** students, or **60%,** of the students will run in the Fun Run.

$$120x = 72 \cdot 100$$
$$120x = 7{,}200$$
$$x = 7{,}200 \div 120$$
$$x = 60$$

Solve.

1. In a sample, **26** out of **50** sixth graders said they planned to go to the school dance. Based on this sample, how many of the **500** sixth graders would you predict will go to the dance?

____

2. In a sample of fifth graders, **18** said "yes" and **7** said "no" when asked if they planned to buy a yearbook. Based on this sample, how many of **250** fifth graders would you predict will buy a yearbook?

____

3. In a sample of seventh graders, **17** said "yes" and **13** said "no" when asked if they would enter a poster contest. Based on this sample, how many of **300** seventh graders will enter the poster contest?

____

4. In a sample of high school students, **120** out of **150** said they planned to go to college. Based on this sample, how many of the **1,500** would you predict will go to college?

____

STANDARD

Problem Solving
Reasoning

Solve.

5. A sample of **50** sixth graders were asked whom they planned to vote for in the election for class president. The results are shown at the right. Predict what percent of the vote each candidate will get.

Candidate	Number of Students	Percent of Vote
J. Rodriquez	8	
L. Johnson	13	
P. Hoffman	12	
K. Cheng	17	

6. Before an election, **1,000** registered voters were asked if they were in favor of building a new library. The results were Yes: **450**, No: **380**, No Opinion: **170**. Of **10,179** registered voters, about what percent would you expect to vote yes?

____

7. A representative sample of the sweatshirt sizes of **30** sixth graders was taken. The results were Small: **3**, Medium: **10**, Large: **17**. How many of each size should be ordered for **300** students in the sixth grade?

____

Quick Check

The data below shows the number of siblings and cousins that 8 friends had.

Name	Siblings	Cousins	Name	Siblings	Cousins
Elmer	0	6	Lamont	3	10
Gary	1	9	Rosa	0	2
George	2	15	Tyesha	1	5
Judy	1	7	Yoko	1	8

8. Use grid paper. Draw a double bar graph of the data.

9. On grid paper, Make a line plot of the number of cousins that the **8** friends had.

10. Do the data about the cousins have any outliers? Explain.

____

11. In a poll, **13** out of **25** students said they prefer pizza to spaghetti. If the sample were representative, about how many students out of **240** prefer pizza?

____

Work Space.

Name ______________________________

Selecting a Sample

STANDARD

A large school district wants to use a survey to find out how many families have a child who will be entering kindergarten in the fall. They need a representative sample if their poll is to be accurate. They considered the following samples.

Sample 1: Surveying 20 families from a voter registration list	**Sample 2:** Surveying one tenth of all families with children already in school	**Sample 3:** Surveying randomly one tenth of all families in the school district

The first sample is probably too small. A sample that is too small is likely to be biased. In this case, a sample size of about one tenth of the population is adequate.

The second sample is **biased.** Families without children will not be included.

A **random** sample is one in which every family has an equal chance of being chosen. For this survey, a random sample might be chosen by listing every family alphabetically and choosing every tenth family. A random sample will have the best chance of being representative.

Solve.

1. What is another way of choosing a random sample of the families?

____

2. Another method of choosing a sample is to mail every family a postcard to return. Do you think the people who return the postcards will form a random sample? Why or why not?

____

Suppose you survey 1 out of 10 people for a random sample. Tell how many of each group you would survey.

3. 1,240 drivers ______ 480 shoppers ______ 151 parents ______

4. 25,642 students ______ 37,848 account holders ______

5. 1.2 million teachers ______ 200,000 viewers ______

What is the population you would choose a sample from for each product?

6. pet food ______ school supplies ______

7. coloring books ______ baseball bats ______

8. horse blankets ______ baby strollers ______

STANDARD

The way a survey question is worded can also make the survey results biased. Compare these two questions.

Should bicyclists have the opportunity to use our town's excellent paths?

Should bicyclists be allowed to ride recklessly and endanger our citizens by using the paths that our city has built for walkers?

The first question makes it sound like letting bicyclists use the paths is a good idea. The second question makes it sound like a bad idea. People who would answer "yes" to the first question might answer "no" to the second. Either question leads to biased results.

A better question might be:

Should bicyclists be allowed to use city walking paths?

Problem Solving
Reasoning

Solve.

9. Crispy Crunch cereal company asked five children of employees to name their favorite cereal. Four out of **5** said Crispy Crunch was their favorite. What is wrong with this sample?

____

10. A radio station invites people to call in to vote yes or no for a new community pool. Will the results be representative of the entire community?

____

11. Diane wanted to know the most popular book of sixth graders. She surveyed **20** sixth grade girls out of **200** in the sixth grade. Is this a random sample?

____

12. Bob used this question in a survey; "Do you agree with the principal that homework is important?" Will he get unbiased results? If not, how would you rewrite the question?

____

Test Prep ★ Mixed Review

13 **Harry's test scores for one class were 90, 85, 0, 88, and 85. Which number will change the most if the outlier is disregarded?**

A The mean

B The median

C The mode

D The highest score

14 **Evaluate the expression $\frac{9a^2}{4}$ when $a = \frac{2}{3}$.**

F 1

G $2\frac{1}{4}$

H 4

J 9

Name ____________________

Evaluating Conclusions

STANDARD

Sometimes data is displayed in a way that readers will draw an incorrect conclusion.

The width of the bottles makes it appear that medical costs have quadrupled. By looking at the scale, you see that costs have only doubled.

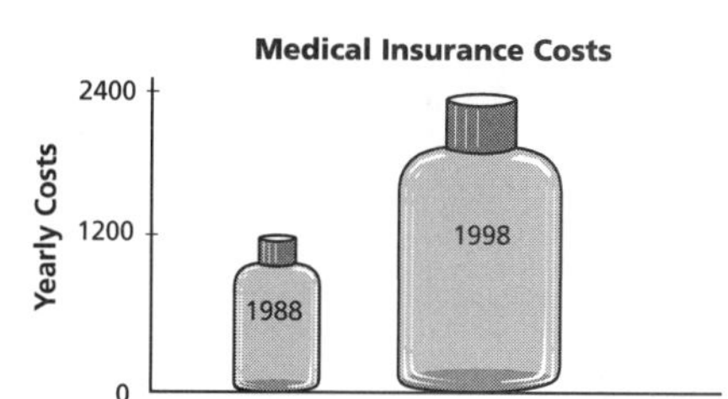

Conclusion: Medical costs were four times as much in 1998 as in 1988.

Tell what may have influenced the conclusion.

1. Incomes of Dentists and Doctors

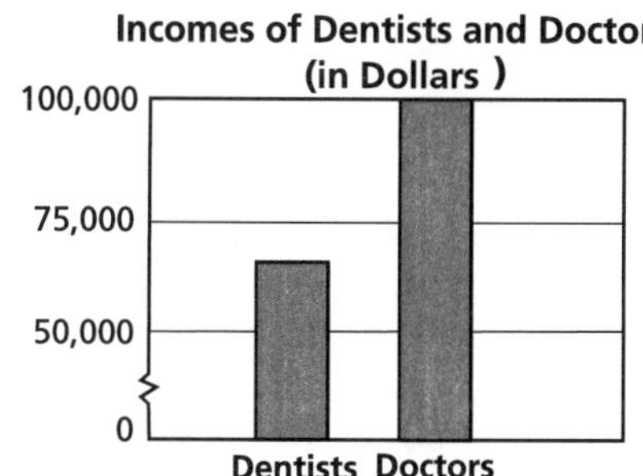

Conclusion: Dentists make only half as much as doctors. ____________________

____

2. Body Temperature for a **12**-hour Period

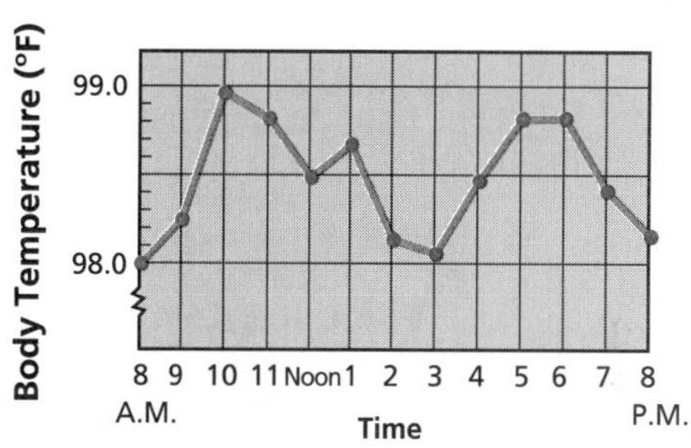

Conclusion: Body temperature varies a lot throughout the day. ____________________

____

Tell why these conclusions may be biased.

3. Four out of **5** dentists surveyed recommend Bubble Gum Toothpaste.

____

4. Ninety percent of the students prefer to watch T.V. ____________________

____

5. The best athletes and champions choose Zeebe running shoes. ____________________

____

6. Easy Fit jeans are everyone's choice.

____

____

STANDARD

7. Using the graphs below, which company appears to have increased its wages more over the years 1995–1998? ________

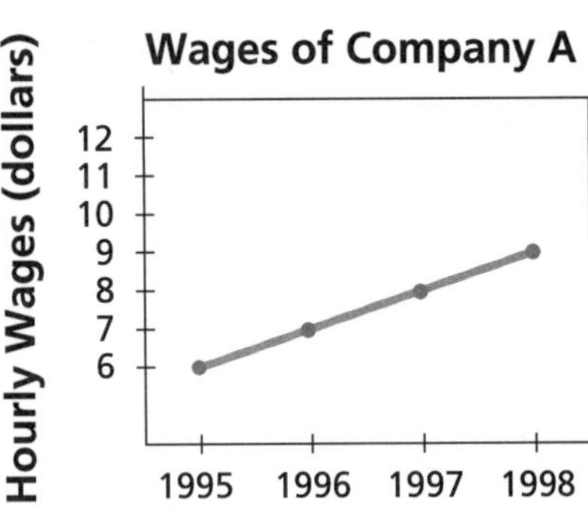

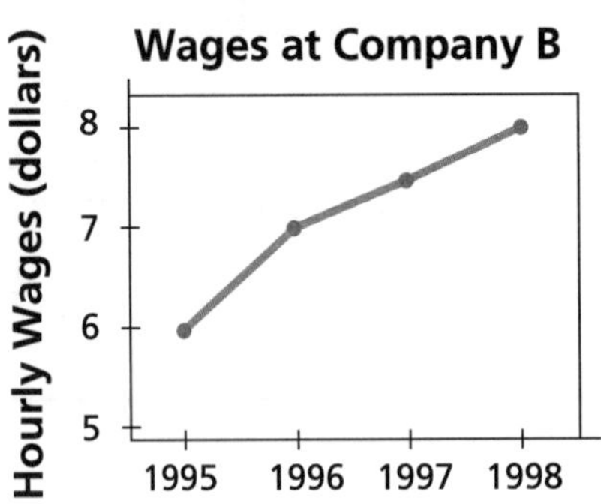

8. Which company actually increased its wages more? ________

9. What makes both graphs misleading? ________

Problem Solving
Reasoning

Solve. Use Graphs A and B.

Graph A

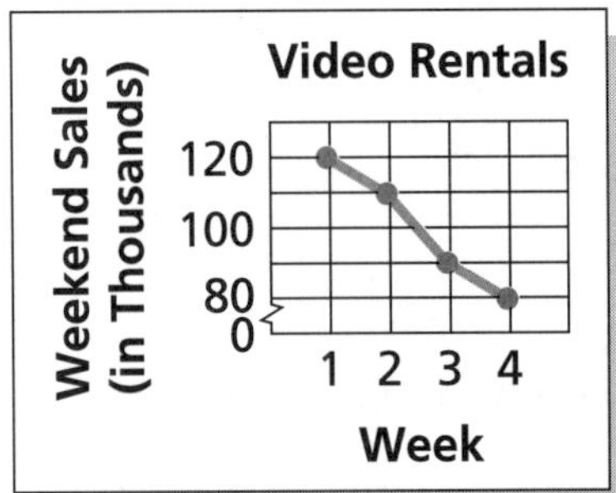

Graph B

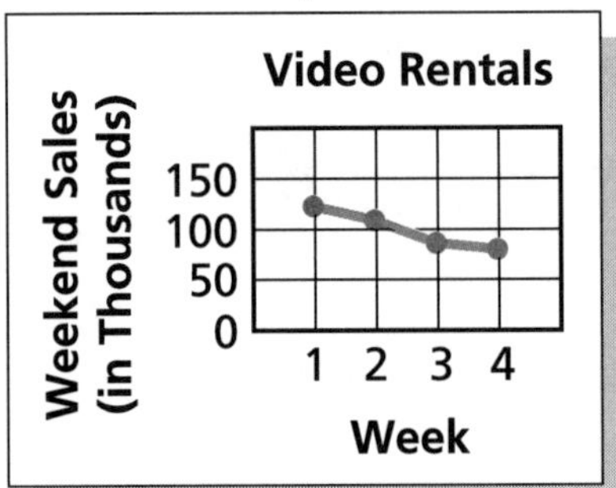

10. Which graph would you use to convince people that video rentals were staying about the same? Why?

____

____

11. Which graph gives a more accurate picture of the data? Explain.

____

____

Test Prep ★ Mixed Review

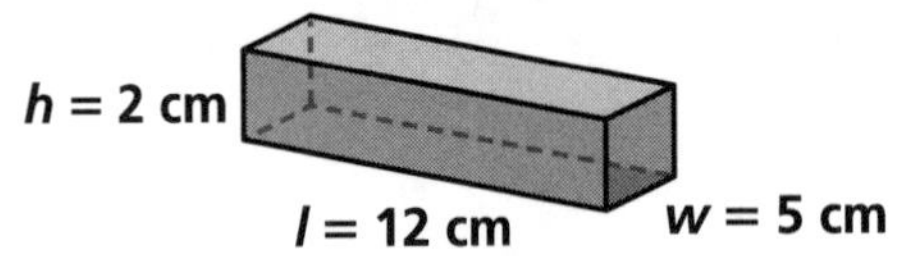

12 What is the surface area of the prism?

A 38 cm^2

B 94 cm^2

C 120 cm^2

D 188 cm^2

13 What is the volume of the prism?

F 38 cm^3

G 94 cm^3

H 120 cm^3

J 188 cm^3

Name ______________________________

Problem Solving Application: Use a Table

STANDARD

Sometimes you need to use the information in a table to solve a problem.

A baseball player player can determine his or her batting average if the number of hits and the number of times at bat (at bats) are known. In this lesson you will use tables such as the one shown to solve problems.

Player	Hits	At Bats
John	12	35
Marie	11	30
Taniqua	10	25
Sidney	14	36

Tips to Remember:

1. Understand 2. Decide 3. Solve 4. Look back

- Think about what the problem is asking you to do. What information does the problem give you? What do you need to find out?
- Compare the labels on the table with the words and numbers in the problem. Find the facts you need from the table.
- Predict the answer. Then solve the problem. Compare your answer with the prediction.

Solve. Use the table above.

1. Batting averages are rounded to the nearest thousandth. Find John's batting average.

Think: How do you find an average?

____

____

Answer ____________________

2. What is Marie's approximate batting average?

Think: $\frac{11}{30}$ is close to what fraction?

____

Answer ____________________

3. Does any player have a batting average of more than **0.5**?

Think: How can you decide without finding each average?

____

____

Answer ____________________

4. Which player had the greatest batting average?

Think: How do you find the player with the best batting average?

____

____

Answer ____________________

STANDARD

Solve.

Tennis players spin their racket and look at the logo on the end of the handle to see who serves first in a match. The opponent calls "up" or "down." A tennis team kept this tally for some of its players.

Player	Outcomes	
	Up	Down
Danielle	卌	卌 II
Julie	卌 III	IIII
Erica	卌 I	卌 I

5. Make a double-bar graph from the information in the tally.

6. In what fraction of all the outcomes was the logo "up"?

_____

7. Look at Table 1 below. Were there more deliveries during the week or on the weekend?

Table 1

Florist Deliveries						
M	T	W	T	F	S	S
8	3	12	7	6	18	16

_____

8. Look at Table 2 below. Roger and Beth each earn **$7.50** an hour. How much did each of them earn for the week?

Table 2

	Hours Worked				
	Day 1	Day 2	Day 3	Day 4	Day 5
Roger	2	2	6	8	7
Beth	6	3	8	5	8

_____

9. Look at the table in problem **7**. What was the average number of deliveries for each day? Is that number greater than the median?

_____

10. If Roger and Beth had to choose the mean, median, or mode to determine how much they would get paid for the week, what should each person choose?

_____

Extend Your Thinking

11. Look back at problem **10**. If Roger worked **8** hours on Day **1** instead of **2** hours, would that change his choice of mean, median, or mode?

_____

12. Look back at problem **6**. Explain how you found your answer.

_____

_____

Name ____________________

Probability

STANDARD

The **probability** of an event is a number between **0** and **1.** It expresses how likely the event is to happen. You can use a number line to represent probabilities.

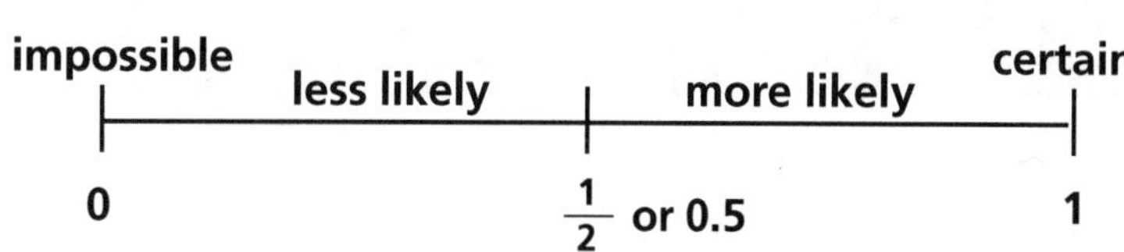

Probability is the ratio of the number of favorable outcomes to the total number of outcomes. Like any ratio, you can write it as a fraction, a decimal, or a percent. It can be found in two ways.

Experimental probability is the ratio of actual results. Suppose you spin this spinner **1,000** times and it lands on red **491** times. The experimental probability of landing on red is $\frac{491}{1,000}$ which is **0.491** or **49.1%**. You can also say it is about $\frac{1}{2}$.

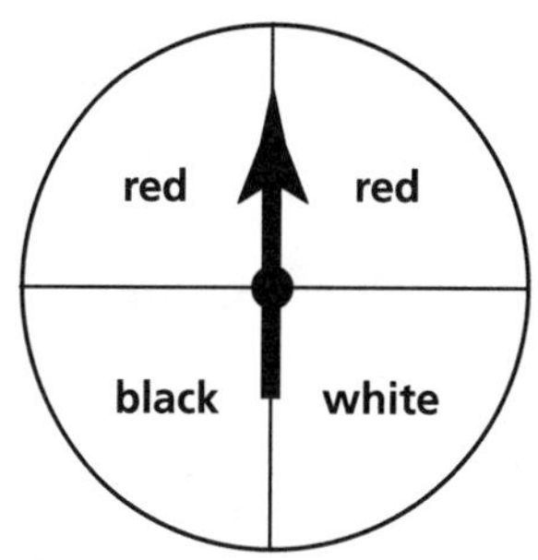

Theoretical probability is a ratio of equally likely outcomes. The spinner has **4** equally likely sections and two of these sections are red. So the theoretical probability is

$$P(red) = \frac{\text{number of favorable outcomes}}{\text{total number of outcomes}} = \frac{2}{4} \text{ or } \frac{1}{2}$$

So, the theoretical probability, written P(red), is $\frac{1}{2}$ or **0.5** or **50%**.

Other examples:

What is the probability of not spinning red?

$$P(\text{not red}) = \frac{\text{number not red}}{4} = \frac{2}{4} \text{ or } \frac{1}{2}$$

Spinning red and not spinning red are **complements** because any outcome must be one or the other.

Predict the number of times the spinner will stop on red in **5,000** spins.

Use the theoretical probability ratio and form a proportion.

Theoretical Probability →

$$\frac{1}{2} = \frac{x}{5,000}$$
$$2x = 5,000$$
$$x = 2,500$$

The spinner will probably stop on red about **2,500** times in **5,000** spins.

Find the theoretical probability for drawing a marble at random from the jar. Write the probability as a fraction, a decimal, and a percent.

1. P(white) ____________

2. P(black) ____________

3. P(not white) ____________

STANDARD

Complete. Do the activity at least 50 times to find the experimental probability.

Activity	Possible Outcomes	Event	Theoretical Probability	Experimental Probability
4. Tossing a coin		P(heads)		
		P(tails)		
		P(not heads or tails)		
5. Rolling a number **1**–**6** cube		P(**1**)		
		P(**2** or **5**)		
		P(even number)		
		P(not a prime number)		

6. Give an example of complements from the events above. ______________________

Problem Solving
Reasoning

Solve.

7. Light bulbs were tested randomly the day they were made. The results are shown at the right. If **10,000** bulbs were produced each day, how many bulbs would you expect to be defective each day?

Results	Monday	Tuesday
Defect	5	2
No defect	15	8

____

8. A batter has a batting average of **0.300**. This means the probability that he will get a hit is **0.3**. How many times would you expect him to get a hit out of **10** times at bat?

____

Quick Check

Work Space.

9. Describe a method of choosing a random sample of the entire sixth grade class at your school.

____

____

10. The populations of three cities are **1,250,000** people, **1,330,000** people, and **1,180,000** people. Describe how you could make the differences between the populations of these cities show up clearly on a vertical bar graph.

____

Find the probability of rolling the number or numbers on a number cube.

11. *P*(**3**)　　**12.** *P*(**2** or **4**)　　**13.** *P*(not **1**)

Name ______________________

The Counting Principle

An event that is made up of **2** or more events is called a **compound event.** Study the **tree diagram** below that shows the possible outcomes when you spin the spinner and then pick a card.

Event

Spin this spinner.

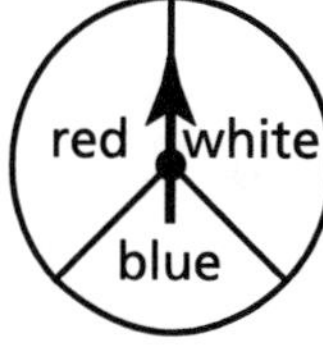

Then pick a card.

Tree Diagram

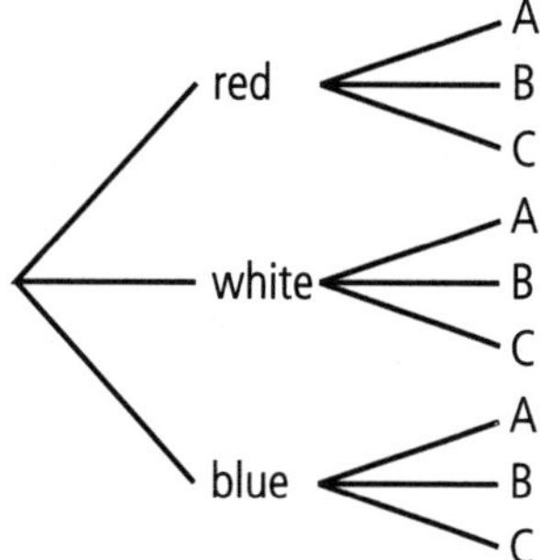

Outcomes

red, A
red, B
red, C
white, A
white, B
white, C
blue, A
blue, B
blue, C

There are **9** possible outcomes.

You can also multiply the number of outcomes for each event to find the total number of possible outcomes. This is called the **counting principle.**

First Event		**Second Event**	
red, white, or blue		A, B, or C	possible outcomes
3	×	**3**	= **9**

Make a tree diagram to show all the outcomes.

1. Spin this spinner.

Then flip a coin.

2. Roll this number **1–6** cube.

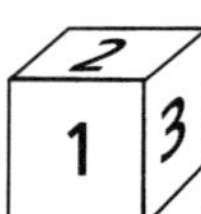

Then flip a coin.

3. Pick a card.

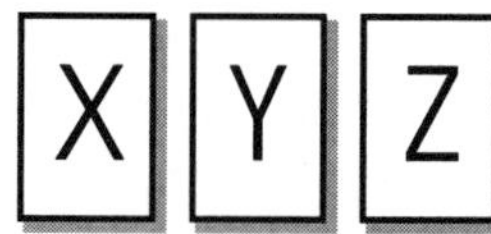

Then spin this spinner.

4. Toss a nickel.

Then toss a dime.

Then toss a quarter.

STANDARD

Use the counting principle to find the number of possible outcomes.

5. Pick a card. Then spin a spinner.

1 2 3 4

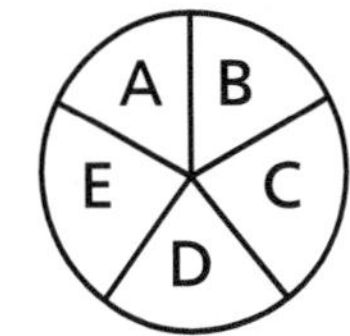

____

6. Pick a shirt. Then pick a pair of shorts.

____

7. Pick from **4** breads, then from **5** fillings.

____

Pick from **5** colors, then from **7** designs.

____

Pick from **3** crusts, then from **5** toppings.

____

8. Pick from **3** flavors, then from **2** sauces, then from **2** toppings.

____

Roll one **1–6** number cube, then roll another.

____

Pick from **4** entrees, then from **3** desserts, then from **2** beverages.

____

Problem Solving
Reasoning

Use mental math to solve.

9. How many ways are there to travel from Sun City to Big Mountain by way of Valleyville if Route 9A is closed for repairs? ______________

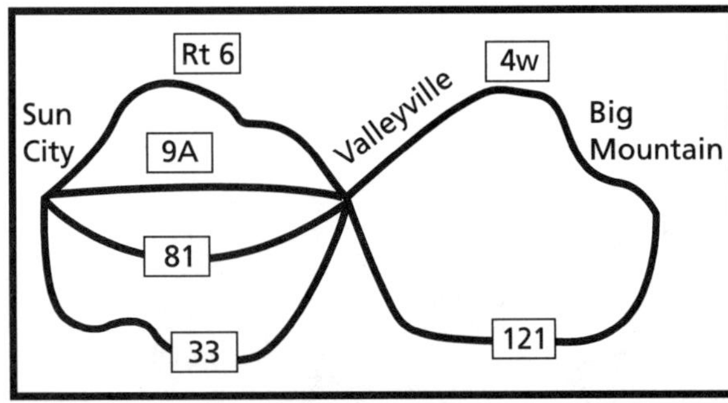

10. Sally's program this summer will be swimming, then drawing, then creative writing. What is probability of choosing this program at random? ________

Summer Park Activities
9:00–10:00
Swimming, Volleyball, Baseball
10:15–11:15
Drawing, Music
11:30–12.30
Creative Writing, Drama

Test Prep ★ Mixed Review

11 **A winter coat normally sells for $175. It is on sale for 20% less. What is its cost now?**

A $35 **C** $140

B $120 **D** $172.50

12 **Which of these methods would give a representative sample of the customers of a local drugstore?**

F Call every sixth person on the list of people who get their film developed there

G Put a questionnaire in the local newspaper and have people send it in

H Survey every tenth person that comes in the door

J Survey 20 people in the parking lot that have a bag from the drugstore

Name ________________________________

Independent Events

STANDARD

Rolling a number cube and tossing a coin are examples of **independent events** because the outcome of one event has no effect on the other.

What is the probability of rolling a **4** or **5**, then tossing heads? The tree diagram shows all the possible outcomes.

Roll a number cube

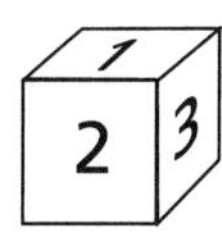

Then toss a coin

Tree diagram

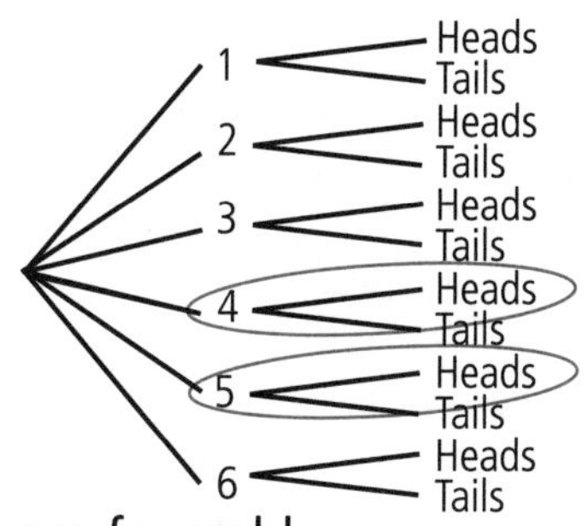

Outcomes

1, heads	(4, heads)
1, tails	4, tails
2, heads	(5, heads)
2, tails	5, tails
3, heads	6, heads
3, tails	6, tails

There are **12** possible outcomes. Two are favorable.

$$P(\mathbf{4} \text{ or } \mathbf{5} \text{ and head}) = \frac{2}{12} \text{ or } \frac{1}{6} \text{ or } 16\frac{2}{3}\%$$

You can also multiply the probability of each event to find the probability of two or more independent events.

$$P(\mathbf{4} \text{ or } \mathbf{5}) = \frac{2}{6} \qquad P(\textbf{head}) = \frac{1}{2}$$

$$P(\mathbf{4} \text{ or } \mathbf{5} \text{ and head}) = \frac{\overset{1}{\cancel{2}}}{6} \times \frac{1}{\underset{1}{\cancel{2}}} = \frac{1}{6} \text{ or } 16\frac{2}{3}\%$$

> The probability of two independent events occurring is the product of their probabilities.
>
> $$P(A \text{ and } B) = P(A) \times P(B)$$

Make a tree diagram to find each theoretical probability. Write each as a fraction and a percent.

1. Pick a card.

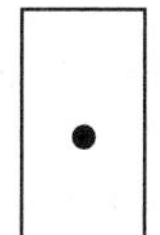
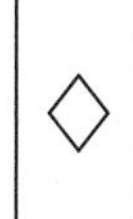

Toss a coin.

P(☆, heads) = ______ P(not ◇, tails) = ______ P(▬, heads or tails) ______

STANDARD

Use multiplication to find the theoretical probability. Write each as a fraction and a percent.

2. Pick a marble.

Roll a **1–6** cube.

P(gray, **3**) = ________

P(red, even) = ________

P(not red, odd) = ________

P(gray, **1** or **6**) = ________

3. Spin this spinner.

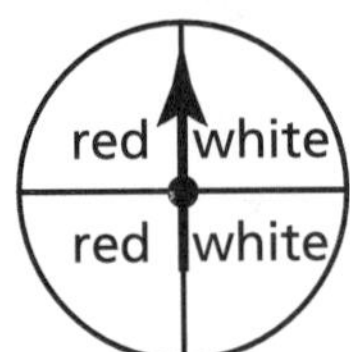

Then spin this spinner.

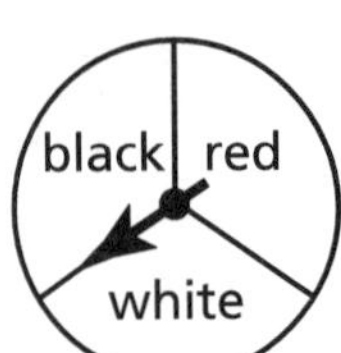

P(red, black) = ________

P(white, white) = ________

P(not white, black) = ________

P(red, black or white) = ________

4. Spin the spinner three times.

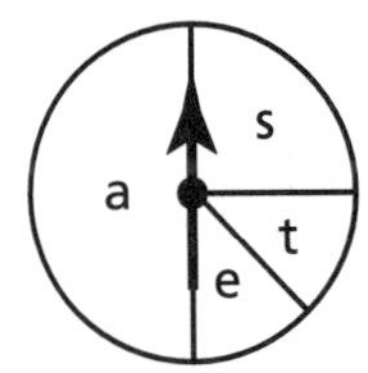

P(sea) = ________ *P*(ate) = ________

P(sat) = ________ *P*(tea) = ________

Problem Solving
Reasoning

Solve. Write each probability as a fraction and a percent.

5. Suppose you toss two number cubes numbered 1–6. What is the probability that neither cube is a 6?

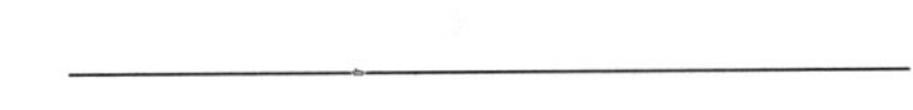

6. You are visiting Sydney, Australia, in January. Your guidebook says that the probability of rain on any day that month is 45%. What is the probability of rain two days in a row?

7. A survey found that 60% of one high school's students worked during the summer. Of the students who worked, 25% babysat. If a student from the high school is chosen at random, what is the probability that he or she babysat during the summer?

____

Test Prep ★ Mixed Review

8 **Julia wants to know which store in a mall shoppers visit most often. Which is the best method for selecting a sample for this survey?**

A Ask 100 people in the center of the mall at random

B Ask 50 people in the largest department store in the mall at random

C Put a questionnaire in the flyer that is mailed to people's homes and have them return it

D Ask 1 out of every 10 women she meets in the mall

9 **The numbers 1 through 10 are written on separate pieces of paper of equal size and dropped into a bag. What is the probability of drawing an 8 or a 5?**

F $\frac{1}{10}$ **H** $\frac{2}{5}$

G $\frac{1}{5}$ **J** $\frac{9}{10}$

Name ______________________________

Dependent Events

Compound events are **dependent events** when the outcome of the first event affects the outcome of the second. Picking a sock out of a suitcase and then picking another sock out of the suitcase are dependent events. After the first pick, there is one fewer sock in the suitcase.

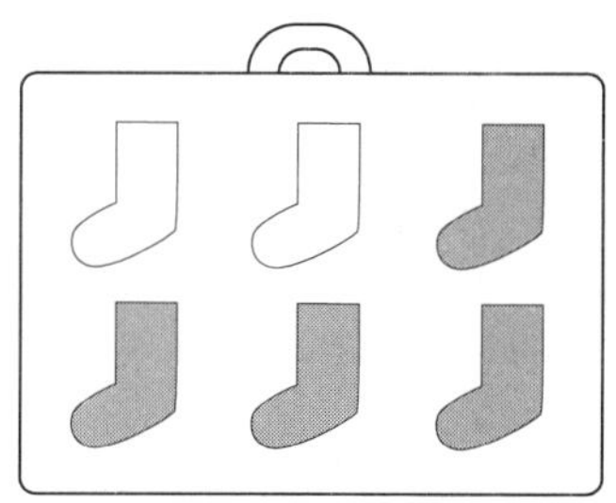

What is the probability of picking **two** white socks?

You can use the same formula you did for independent events to find the probability of dependent events.

$$P(\text{A and B}) = P(\text{A}) \times P(\text{B})$$
$$P(\text{white and white}) = P(\text{white}) \times P(\text{white})$$

First pick: P(white) $= \frac{2}{6} = \frac{1}{3}$

After the first sock is picked, there are only **5** socks left. If the first sock was white, only **1** of the remaining socks is white.

Second pick: P(white) $= \frac{\text{number white}}{\text{total number}} = \frac{1}{5}$

The probability of picking **two** white socks is $\frac{1}{3} \times \frac{1}{5}$, or $\frac{1}{15}$.

Use the socks above to find the probability.

1. P(gray and gray) ____________ P(gray and white) ____________

2. P(white and gray) ____________ P([white or gray], [gray or white]) ____________

3. P(red and red) ______ P([gray, gray] or [white, white])

____

Are the events independent (I) or dependent (D)? Write I or D.

4. Pick a name from a hat, then pick another name. ______

5. Pick a name from a hat, put the name back in the hat, then pick another name. ______

6. One player picks a card from a deck of cards and keeps it, then another player picks a card. ______

7. One student chooses a sticker without looking and keeps it. The next student chooses a sticker. ______

8. A number cube is rolled. A **4** lands up. The cube is rolled again. A **4** lands up. ______

9. You take a math test. Then you take a science test. ______

STANDARD

Complete.

10. Pick one card, then another.

☆	☆	☆	☆
▬	•	•	•

P(☆, •) = ______

P(☆, ▬) = ______

P(▬, ☆) = ______

P(▬, •) = ______

P(•, •) = ______

11. Pick a name, then another name.

Cathy, Charles, Rita, Mario, Christie

P(girl, girl) = ______

P(boy, girl) = ______

P(Charles, Cathy) = ______

P(Christie, Christie) = ______

P(Mario, girl) = ______

12. Pick a marble, then pick another marble.

P(◎, ●) = ______

P(⦶, ⊛) = ______

P(●, ⦶) = ______

P(⊛, ⊛) = ______

13. Pick one ball, then another.

① ② ③ ④ ⑤ ⑥ ⑦

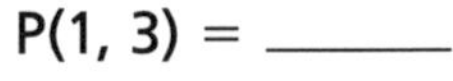

P(1, 3) = ______

P(6, not 2) = ______

P(5, 6 or 7) = ______

P(2, 2) = ______

Problem Solving Reasoning **Solve.**

14. Four horses, Prince, Botie, Patches, and Beauty, are chosen at random for horseback riding lessons. Two people take a lesson. What is the probability they will get Prince and Botie? ______

15. A game has 3 bonus cards and 6 chance cards. A player draws a card, then another card. What is the probability both will be bonus cards? ______

Quick Check

Solve.

Work Space.

16. At a sandwich restaurant, you can choose of **1** of **7** breads, **1** of **3** meats, **1** of **4** extras, and **1** of **4** sauces. How many different sandwiches can be made? ______

One number cube is numbered from **1** to **6** and another is numbered from **7** to **12**. Write the probability of rolling

17. a **1** and a **7** ______.

18. two even numbers ______.

A dresser drawer contains **5** white socks, **4** blue ones, and **9** black ones. First one sock and then another is drawn without looking. Find the probability of getting

19. **2** white socks ______.

20. **two** black socks ______.

Name ________________________________

Unit 9 Review

Solve. Use the graph to answer each question.

1. Which store increased its sales steadily from July to September? ______

2. During which month did Store B have the same amount of sales as the previous month? ______

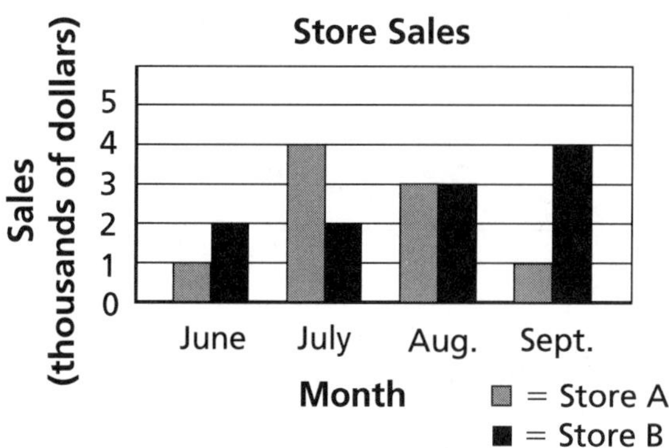

Solve. Use the line plot.

3. Which measure—mean, median, or mode—best describes the data?

Explain. ________________________________

____

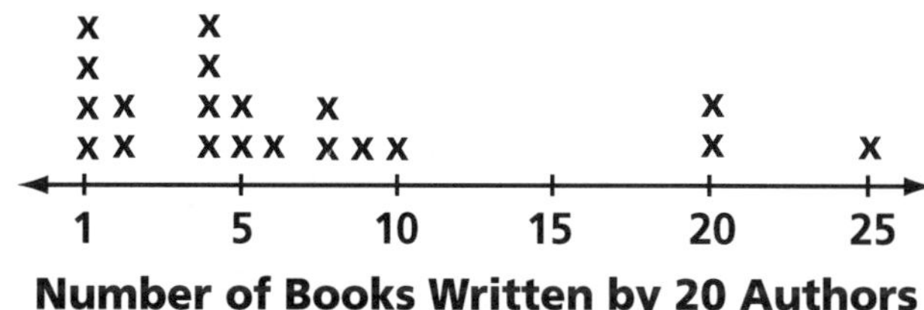

Solve.

4. Charles wants to learn the favorite color of the students in his school. He plans to survey the first **25** people he meets in the hallway. Would this be a representative sample? Explain.

____

5. A **1–6** number cube is tossed twice. What is the probability of tossing two fours? ______

6. If the experiment in exercise **5** was repeated **100** times, about how many times would you predict two fours would be tossed?

____

7. Sue has **3** pairs of socks—red, blue, and brown. She has two pairs of shoes—black and brown. What is the probability she could choose at random brown socks and shoes? ______

8. The table shows the outcomes of **10** coin tosses. In percent form, what were these experimental probabilities: **P** (heads), **P** (tails), and **P** (heads or tails)? ________________

heads	tails
IIII	卌 I

9. Write **3** different mixed numbers that have a mean of $3\frac{1}{4}$.

____

Name ___________________________

Cumulative Review
★ Test Prep

Use this diagram for exercises 1–3. $\Delta ABC \cong \Delta AED$.

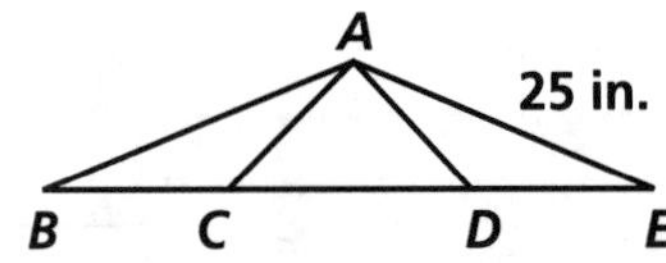

1 What is the length of $\overline{AB}$?

A Longer than 25 inches

B Equal to 25 inches

C Shorter than 25 inches

D Cannot be determined from the information

2 If $\angle E = 45°$ and $\angle EAD = 25°$, what is the measure of $\angle ADC$?

F 35°

G 70°

H 110°

J Cannot be determined from the information.

3 Which angle is supplementary to $\angle ADB$?

A $\angle B$

B $\angle BAC$

C $\angle ACB$

D $\angle CAD$

The results of a survey of 15 boys and 25 girls are shown in the bar graph below. Use the graph to answer questions 4 and 5.

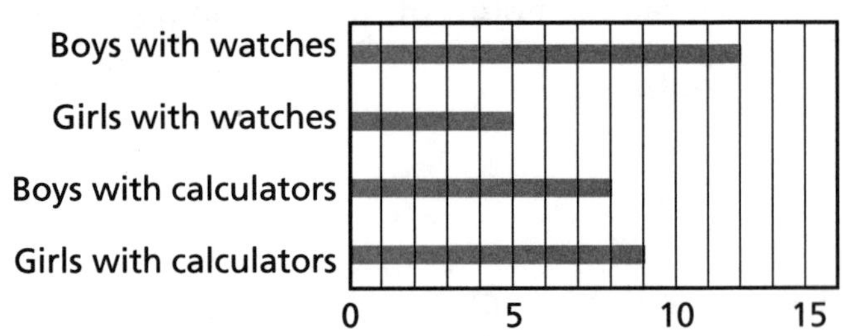

4 Which conclusion is true about the data?

F All the boys with calculators had watches

G Calculators are more popular with boys than with girls

H Watches are more popular with boys than with girls

J Some girls that did not have a calculator had a watch

5 Assume that the sample is representative of 360 students in a school. About how many of these students would you expect to have calculators?

A About 50 students

B About 100 students

C About 150 students

D About 200 students

6 A newspaper reported that one holiday weekend, 75% of all families would be cooking outdoors on a grill. Of these families, 80% would be grilling beef. What percent of all families would be grilling beef?

F 60%

H 45%

G 50%

J 40%

UNIT 10 • TABLE OF CONTENTS

Integers and Equations

We will be using this vocabulary:

integer any number in the set {. . . , $^-3$, $^-2$, $^-1$, 0, 1, 2, 3, . . .}

equation a mathematical sentence in which the values on both sides of the equal sign (=) are equal.

numerical expression a combination of one or more numbers and operations

algebraic expression a combination of one or more variables, numbers, and operations

Dear Family,

During the next few weeks, our math class will be learning about integers and equations. You can expect to see homework that provides practice with evaluating expressions. Here is a sample you may want to keep handy to give help if needed.

Evaluating Expressions

To evaluate an expression means to substitute given numbers into the expression, then simplify.

Example: Evaluate $2a + \frac{b}{3} + c$ when $a = {}^-4$, $b = {}^-6$, and $c = 3$.

$2a + \frac{b}{3} + c$	**1.** Write the expression.
$2(^-4) + \frac{^-6}{3} + (3)$	**2.** Substitute for *a*, *b*, and *c*.
$2(^-4) + \frac{^-6}{3} + (3)$	**3.** Follow the order of operations. Multiply and divide from left to right.
$(^-8) + (^-2) + (3)$	**4.** Add and subtract from left to right.
$^-7$	

The value of $2a + \frac{b}{3} + c$ when $a = {}^-4$, $b = {}^-6$, and $c = 3$ is $^-7$.

During this unit, students will need to continue practicing adding, subtracting, multiplying, and dividing integers.

Sincerely,

Name ________________________________

Positive and Negative Numbers

STANDARD

You can use a number line to show whole numbers and their opposites. Whole numbers and their opposites are called **integers**.

Negative integers, written with a negative sign ($^-$) are numbers *less than* ***0***. The number negative **5** is written $^-$**5**.

Positive integers, written with or without a positive sign ($^+$) are numbers *greater than* ***0***. The number positive **5** is written $^+$**5** or **5**.

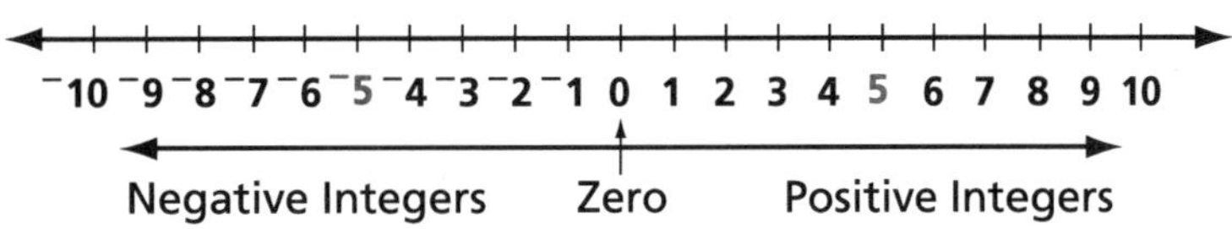

Zero is an integer that is neither positive nor negative.

Opposite numbers are the same distance from zero but are in opposite directions. Numbers such as $^-$**5** and **5** are opposites because they are both **5** units from **0**.

Write the integer. Include the word *positive* or *negative* in your answer.

1. Five units to the right of **0** is __________. Three units to the left of **0** is __________.

2. __________ is written $^-$**7**. __________ is written $^+$**10** or **10**.

3. Two units to the right of $^-$**3** is __________. Eight units to the left of **3** is __________.

4. Seven units to the left of $^-$**6** is __________. Nine units to the right of $^-$**2** is __________.

Write *Yes* if the number is an integer. Write *No* if it is not.

5. **360** ______ $^-$**1,400** ______ $4\frac{1}{2}$ ______

6. **16** ______ **5.8** ______ $^-$**6.58** ______

7. $^-$**0.3** ______ **9.6** ______ $^-$**1,101** ______

8. $^-17\frac{2}{5}$ ______ $\frac{5}{2}$ ______ $^-$**6.25** ______

Write the opposite of the integer.

9. **8** ______ $^-$**7** ______ **4** ______ $^-$**10** ______

10. **6,112** ______ $^-$**515** ______ **11** ______ **160** ______

11. $^-$**102** ______ **365** ______ **47** ______ $^-$**99** ______

12. **999** ______ **0** ______ $^-$**11** ______ **1,200** ______

STANDARD

Integers have many applications. Temperatures can rise or fall. The number of dollars in a bank account can increase or decrease. A height or elevation can be above or below sea level. All these situations can be expressed with integers.

Examples:

A **5°** rise in temperature → **5°**

A checking account is **$10** overdrawn → **⁻$10**

A shipwreck **1,300** feet below sea level → **⁻1,300** ft

Model the situation with an integer.

13. 30°C above freezing ________ A boat at sea level ________

14. **$10** earned ________ **$35** in debt ________

15. 5,280 feet above sea level ________ A kite **40** meters up ________

16. The opposite of **50°F** ________ A gain of **4** yards ________

Problem Solving Reasoning Solve.

17. Three divers are investigating a shipwreck at the bottom of the ocean. The first diver is waiting on a boat at the surface. The second diver is at **10** m below sea level. The third diver is **6** m below the second. Use integers to describe the position of each diver.

____

18. Marcus keeps a record of the money he has in his checking account. In January he wrote checks totaling **$45**. In February he made a deposit of **$100**. In March he did not deposit any money nor did he write any checks. Use integers to describe each month's activity in the account.

____

19. What number is its own opposite?

____

20. What is the opposite of the opposite of 5?

____

21. What is the sum of x and the opposite of x? ________

22. What is the difference between ^{-}x and its opposite? ________

Test Prep ★ Mixed Review

23 What is the value of $(x + 7)^2$ when $x = 4$?

A 11

B 22

C 53

D 121

24 The circumference of a circle is 22 feet. About how long is its diameter?

F 7 ft

G 9 ft

H 11 ft

J 13 ft

Name ______________________________

Comparing Integers

STANDARD

To compare two integers, you can think of how the integers are ordered on the number line. A lesser number is to the left of a greater number. A greater number is to the right of a lesser number.

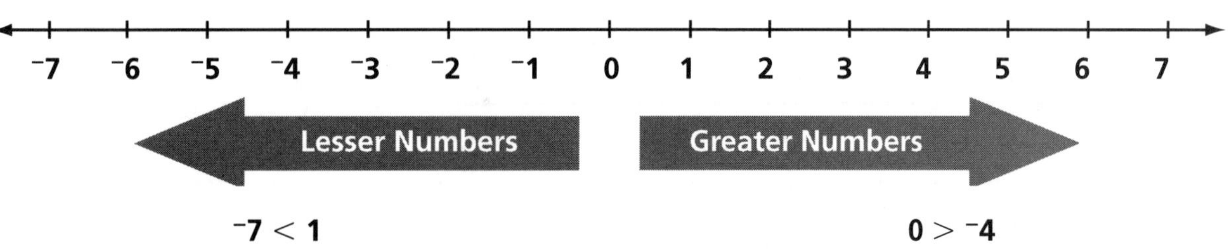

$^{-}7 < 1$

$^{-}7$ is less than 1

$0 > {^{-}4}$

0 is greater than $^{-}4$

Write $<$ or $>$.

1. $^{-}5$ ◯ $^{-}6$ 5 ◯ 6 $^{-}3$ ◯ 0 $^{-}9$ ◯ $^{-}6$

2. 8 ◯ $^{-}5$ $^{-}8$ ◯ 5 8 ◯ $^{-}8$ 5 ◯ 3

3. $^{-}16$ ◯ 16 0 ◯ $^{-}14$ $^{-}18$ ◯ $^{-}12$ 4 ◯ $^{-}2$

4. $^{-}8$ ◯ $^{-}12$ $^{-}9$ ◯ $^{-}7$ 4 ◯ $^{-}5$ 2 ◯ 6

5. 1 ◯ 6 $^{-}4$ ◯ 2 3 ◯ $^{-}1$ 0 ◯ $^{-}4$

6. $^{-}5$ ◯ $^{-}2$ 1 ◯ 3 $^{-}10$ ◯ 3 $^{-}5$ ◯ $^{-}1$

On the number line, graph the integer described.

7. the integer **1** less than **8**

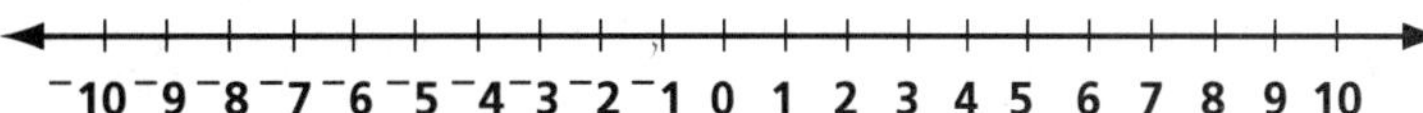

8. the integer **1** more than **8**

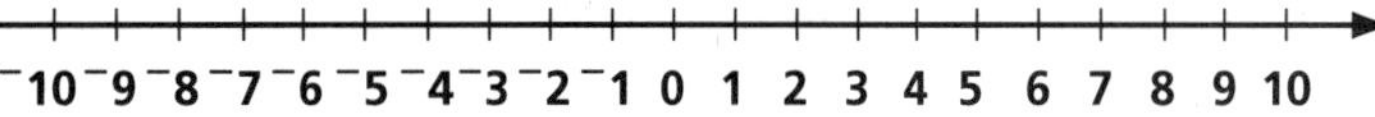

9. the integer **6** less than **$^{-}2$**

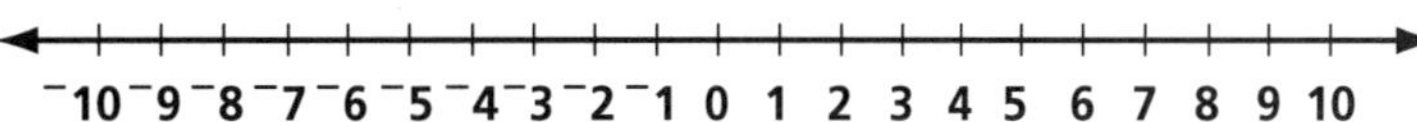

10. the integer **2** more than **$^{-}8$**

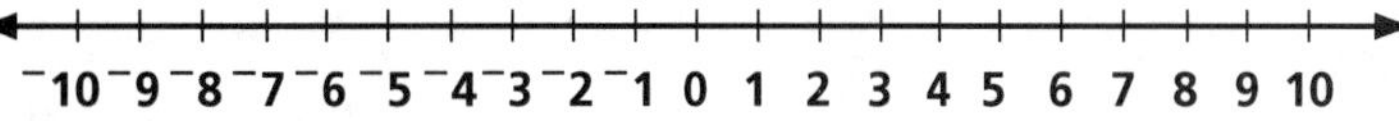

11. the integer **4** more than **$^{-}4$**

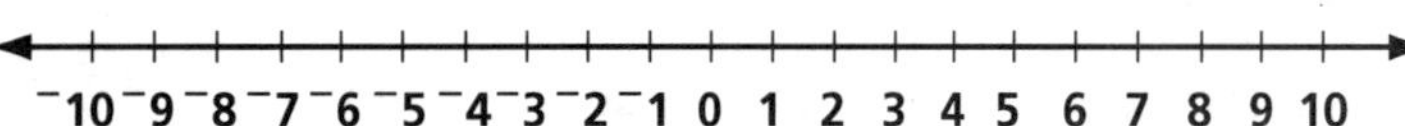

12. the integer **5** less than **3**

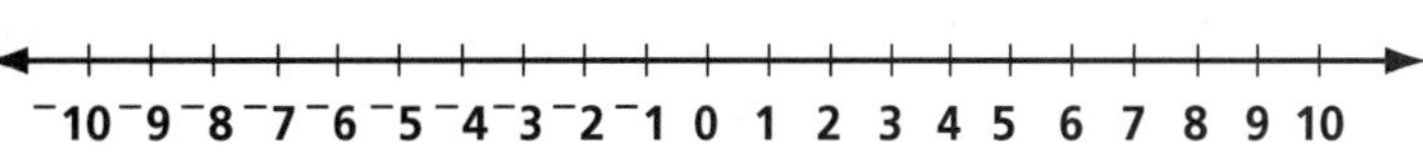

STANDARD

Any number that can be written in the form $\frac{a}{b}$, where ***a*** and ***b*** are integers and ***b*** is not zero, is a **rational number.** You can think of a rational number as a ratio. Every rational number occupies exactly one point on a number line.

Examples of rational numbers include $\frac{1}{2}$, $\frac{^-1}{5}$, $2\frac{1}{4}$, and $^-0.75$.

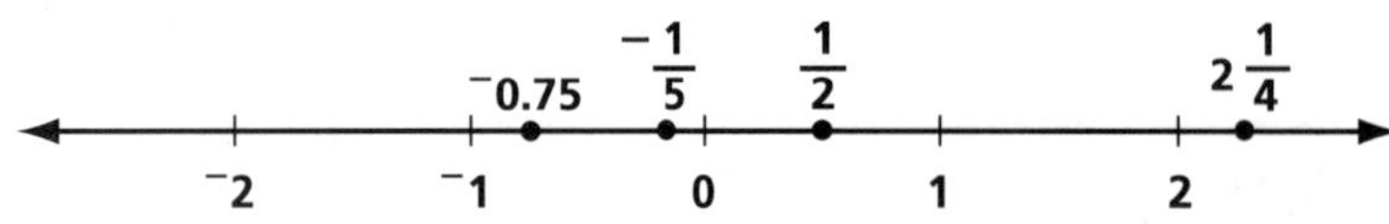

Write >, <, or =.

13.	$^-3\frac{1}{2}$ ◯ $^-5$	0.5 ◯ $\frac{1}{2}$	0 ◯ $^-0.5$	$^-.6$ ◯ $^-\frac{2}{3}$
14.	5 ◯ $3\frac{1}{2}$	$^-4$ ◯ $^-1\frac{1}{2}$	$^-1$ ◯ 3.7	0.001 ◯ $^-1{,}001$
15.	2 ◯ $\frac{3}{4}$	$^-8\frac{3}{5}$ ◯ 8	$\frac{1}{4}$ ◯ 0.25	1 ◯ $\frac{4}{3}$

Problem Solving
Reasoning

Solve.

16. Maria, Miranda, and Steven have the same grade average. For missing homework, Mr. Gicale deducted **2** points from Maria's average, **5** points from Miranda's average, and $1\frac{1}{2}$ points from Steven's average. Who ended up with the highest average?

Explain. ______________________

____

17. One night in February, the temperature dropped **1**°C every hour from **8** P.M. to **8** A.M. At **8** A.M. it was **⁻15**°C. Was the temperature at **8** P.M. the night before above or below **0**°C? Explain.

____

____

18. The following temperatures were recorded in **5** different places around the world on the same day in January: **⁻2**°C, **10**°C, **5**°C, **⁻1.5**°C, and **22**°C. Which temperature is closest to **0**°C? Explain.

____

____

19. A gain of **$4** followed by a loss of **$5** is the same as a gain or loss of what?

____

____

Test Prep ★ Mixed Review

20 Billy Joe had 96 CDs. Country and western artists recorded $\frac{11}{12}$ of them. How many CDs is that?

A 8 **C** 84

B 12 **D** 88

21 A rectangular prism measures 4 feet by 2 feet by 6 inches. What is its surface area?

F 11 ft^2 **H** 44 ft^2

G 22 ft^2 **J** 88 ft^2

Name ______________________________

Adding Integers

Suppose that Jim's house is located at **0** on a number line and that he left home and walked **3** blocks in a positive direction to his friend's house. Then he walked **8** blocks in a negative or opposite direction to the grocery store. Where is the grocery store located on the number line?

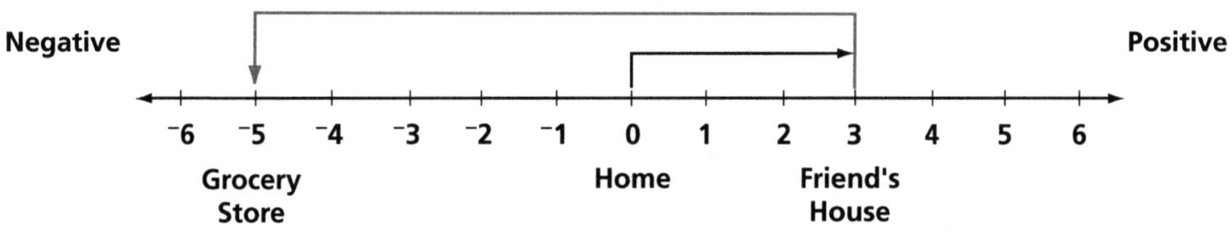

Complete the sentence by writing an integer. Use the number line above.

1. If you start at **0**, then go **5** blocks in the positive direction, you end at ______.
2. If you start at **2**, then go **5** blocks in the positive direction, you end at ______.
3. If you start at **$^-2$**, then go **5** blocks in the positive direction, you end at ______.
4. If you start at **0**, then go **3** blocks in the negative direction, you end at ______.
5. If you start at **2**, then go **3** blocks in the negative direction, you end at ______.
6. If you start at **$^-2$**, then go **3** blocks in the negative direction, you end at ______.
7. If you start at **$^-5$**, then go **5** blocks in the positive direction, you end at ______.
8. If you start at **3**, then go **8** blocks in the negative direction, you end at ______.

Let a positive number represent a trip in the positive direction and a negative number represent a trip in the negative direction. Complete by writing an integer.

9. Start at **0** and take a **4** trip. You end at ______.
10. Start at **3** and take a **4** trip. You end at ______.
11. Start at **$^-3$** and take a **4** trip. You end at ______.
12. Start at **0** and take a **$^-4$** trip. You end at ______.
13. Start at **3** and take a **$^-4$** trip. You end at ______.
14. Start at **$^-3$** and take a **$^-4$** trip. You end at ______.
15. Start at **6** and take a **$^-5$** trip. You end at ______.
16. Start at **$^-1$** and take **6** trip. You end at ______.

STANDARD

You can use a number line to add two integers.

$^{-}5 + 3 = ?$

Start at **$^{-}5$**. Then move **3** units in the positive direction.

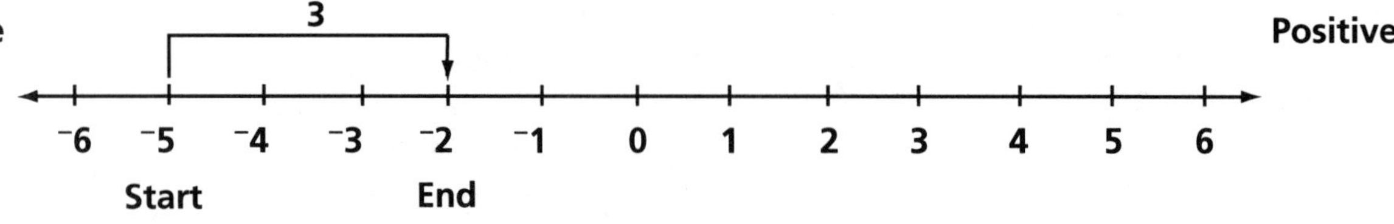

$^{-}5 + 3 = {}^{-}2$

The sum of **$^{-}5$** and **3** is **$^{-}2$**.

Add. Use the number line to help you.

17. $^{-}7 + 6 =$ ______

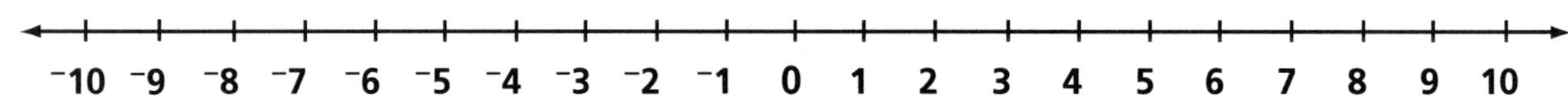

18. $^{-}4 + {}^{-}1 =$ ______

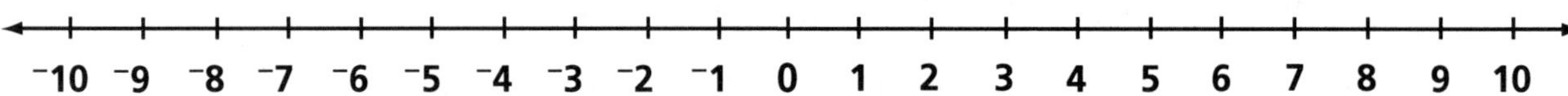

19. $5 + {}^{-}8 =$ ______

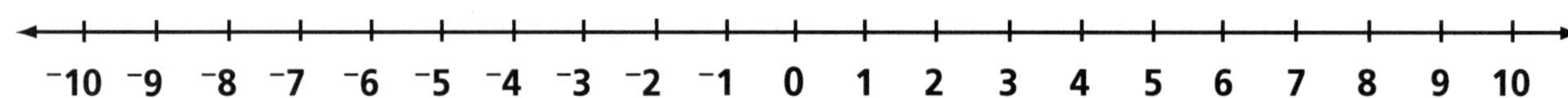

20. $6 + {}^{-}1 =$ ______

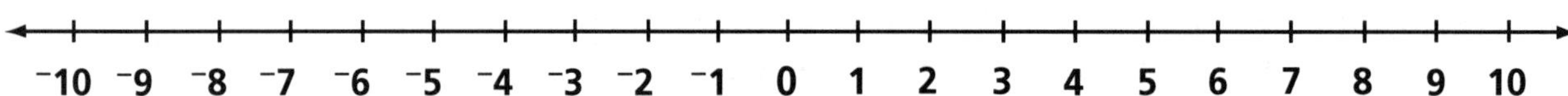

Add.

21. $^{-}5 + 8 =$ ______	$9 + 5 =$ ______	$6 + {}^{-}6 =$ ______	$6 + 7 =$ ______
22. $5 + {}^{-}5 =$ ______	$7 + {}^{-}9 =$ ______	$9 + {}^{-}8 =$ ______	$^{-}8 + 6 =$ ______
23. $^{-}7 + 7 =$ ______	$^{-}7 + {}^{-}8 =$ ______	$2 + 9 =$ ______	$5 + 6 =$ ______
24. $^{-}4 + 7 =$ ______	$^{-}8 + {}^{-}7 =$ ______	$8 + {}^{-}9 =$ ______	$9 + 9 =$ ______
25. $^{-}7 + {}^{-}5 =$ ______	$8 + 8 =$ ______	$^{-}4 + {}^{-}9 =$ ______	$^{-}9 + 6 =$ ______
26. $9 + 7 =$ ______	$6 + {}^{-}9 =$ ______	$^{-}4 + {}^{-}8 =$ ______	$^{-}7 + 0 =$ ______

STANDARD

Write the missing addend.

27.	$^-4$ + ______ = 2	$^-3$ + ______ = $^-5$	2 + ______ = $^-3$	5 + ______ = 0
28.	$^-7$ + ______ = $^-4$	6 + ______ = 6	7 + ______ = 9	$^-8$ + ______ = 0
29.	8 + ______ = 7	0 + ______ = $^-6$	$^-9$ + ______ = 1	$^-1$ + ______ = 1
30.	1 + ______ = $^-7$	8 + ______ = 5	1 + ______ = $^-8$	$^-2$ + ______ = 9
31.	$^-9$ + ______ = 0	9 + ______ = $^-4$	$^-4$ + ______ = 1	$^-6$ + ______ = 8
32.	$^-4$ + ______ = $^-1$	3 + ______ = 0	$^-12$ + ______ = $^-15$	5 + ______ = 2
33.	14 + ______ = 2	$^-6$ + ______ = $^-3$	$^-3$ + ______ = 6	8 + ______ = $^-8$
34.	$^-7$ + ______ = $^-4$	$^-6$ + ______ = $^-20$	1 + ______ = 7	10 + ______ = 5
35.	12 + ______ = 10	$^-10$ + ______ = $^-2$	$^-2$ + ______ = 12	7 + ______ = $^-9$

Problem Solving Reasoning Solve.

36. Will the sum of two negative integers be negative or positive? Explain.

____

____

37. How can you tell if the sum of a positive integer and a negative integer will be positive or negative? ______________________________

____

Quick Check

Write the opposite of the integer.

38. 7 ______ **39.** $^-16$ ______ **40.** 0 ______

Write the greatest integer of the three given.

41. $^-6$, $^-2$, 0 ______ **42.** $^-5$, $^-3$, $^-1$ ______ **43.** 2, 1, $^-5$ ______

Write the sum of the integers.

44. $^-5$ + $^-4$ ______ **45.** 12 + $^-6$ ______ **46.** $^-16$ + 7 ______

Work Space.

STANDARD

Name ______________________________

Subtracting Integers

You know how to subtract whole numbers by finding a missing addend.

$9 - 3 = \boxed{?}$

This number is the sum of these numbers.

$9 = 3 + \boxed{?}$

What number added to **3** equals **9**?

$9 = 3 + 6$

So, $9 - 3 = 6$

You can also subtract integers by finding a missing addend.

$^-8 - 2 = \boxed{?}$

This number is the sum of these numbers.

$^-8 = 2 + \boxed{?}$

What number added to **2** equals **$^-8$**?

$^-8 = 2 + {^-10}$

So, $^-8 - 2 = {^-10}$

Subtract. (Hint: Find the missing addend.)

1.	$7 - {^-2} =$ ______	$^-9 - 5 =$ ______	$^-3 - 7 =$ ______
2.	$5 - 2 =$ ______	$1 - {^-5} =$ ______	$6 - 9 =$ ______
3.	$^-4 - 7 =$ ______	$0 - {^-5} =$ ______	$12 - {^-8} =$ ______
4.	$15 - {^-4} =$ ______	$12 - 8 =$ ______	$^-19 - 7 =$ ______
5.	$^-9 - 3 =$ ______	$7 - {^-6} =$ ______	$12 - 7 =$ ______
6.	$8 - 17 =$ ______	$^-16 - {^-3} =$ ______	$^-9 - {^-9} =$ ______
7.	$9 - {^-4} =$ ______	$^-9 - 1 =$ ______	$^-22 - {^-11} =$ ______
8.	$13 - 24 =$ ______	$7 - 7 =$ ______	$^-7 - {^-7} =$ ______
9.	$0 - {^-26} =$ ______	$0 - 20 =$ ______	$^-5 - 10 =$ ______
10.	$^-5 - {^-10} =$ ______	$0 - {^-12} =$ ______	$^-6 - 0 =$ ______
11.	$10 - 10 =$ ______	$^-15 - {^-15} =$ ______	$^-20 - 30 =$ ______

Name ____________________________

STANDARD

Addition and subtraction of the same quantity are inverse operations. Every subtraction sentence is related to an addition sentence.

Notice how each pair of sentences are related:

$6 - 2 = 4$	$^-7 - 2 = {}^-9$	$3 - {}^-4 = 7$
$6 + {}^-2 = 4$	$^-7 + {}^-2 = {}^-9$	$3 + 4 = 7$

Complete each pair of related sentences.

12. $5 - {}^-2 =$ ______ $^-4 - 7 =$ ______ $7 - 6 =$ ______

$5 + 2 =$ ______ $^-4 + {}^-7 =$ ______ $7 + {}^-6 =$ ______

13. $8 - {}^-6 =$ ______ $^-9 - 3 =$ ______ $^-6 - {}^-5 =$ ______

$8 + 6 =$ ______ $^-9 + {}^-3 =$ ______ $^-6 + 5 =$ ______

14. $^-12 - {}^-5 =$ ______ $^-12 - 8 =$ ______ $9 - 6 =$ ______

$^-12 + 5 =$ ______ $^-12 + {}^-8 =$ ______ $9 + {}^-6 =$ ______

15. $^-5 - 7 =$ ______ $8 - 8 =$ ______ $10 - {}^-3 =$ ______

$^-5 + {}^-7 =$ ______ $8 + {}^-8 =$ ______ $10 + 3 =$ ______

16. $^-3 - 4 =$ ______ $^-7 - {}^-6 =$ ______ $5 - 2 =$ ______

$^-3 + {}^-4 =$ ______ $^-7 + 6 =$ ______ $5 + {}^-2 =$ ______

Use the related sentences in exercises 12–13 to help you complete the statement.

17. The opposite of $^-$**2** is ______. Subtracting $^-$**2** is the same as adding ______.

18. The opposite of **7** is ______. Subtracting **7** is the same as adding ______.

19. Subtracting **6** is the same as adding ______.

20. Subtracting $^-$**6** is the same as adding ______.

21. Subtracting **3** is the same as adding ______.

22. Subtracting $^-$**5** is the same as adding ______.

23. Subtracting **0** is the same as adding ______.

24. Subtracting **50** is the same as adding ______.

STANDARD

Subtracting any integer is the same as adding the opposite of the integer.

$7 - {}^-3 = 10$	${}^-9 - 3 = {}^-12$	$4 - 8 = {}^-4$
$7 + 3$	${}^-9 + {}^-3$	$4 + {}^-8$

Subtract.

25. $4 - {}^-5 =$ ______ $\quad {}^-3 - {}^-7 =$ ______ $\quad 10 - {}^-6 =$ ______

$4 + 5 \qquad {}^-3 + 7 \qquad 10 + 6$

26. $0 - 9 =$ ______ $\quad {}^-8 - {}^-7 =$ ______ $\quad 7 - 5 =$ ______

$0 + {}^-9 \qquad {}^-8 + 7 \qquad 7 + {}^-5$

27. $6 - {}^-4 =$ ______ $\quad 8 - {}^-3 =$ ______ $\quad 9 - 2 =$ ______

28. $2 - 8 =$ ______ $\quad {}^-9 - {}^-3 =$ ______ $\quad {}^-5 - {}^-9 =$ ______

29. $3 - {}^-9 =$ ______ $\quad 7 - {}^-4 =$ ______ $\quad {}^-9 - 7 =$ ______

30. $5 - {}^-6 =$ ______ $\quad 6 - 0 =$ ______ $\quad 3 - 4 =$ ______

31. $6 - {}^-8 =$ ______ $\quad {}^-9 - {}^-5 =$ ______ $\quad 5 - 2 =$ ______

32. ${}^-7 - 1 =$ ______ $\quad 6 - 9 =$ ______ $\quad 0 - {}^-5 =$ ______

Problem Solving
Reasoning

Solve.

33. At **6** A.M. the temperature was **⁻6**°F. Between **6:00** A.M. and **3:00** P.M., the temperature rose **11** degrees. Between **3:00** P.M. and midnight, the temperature fell **7** degrees. Write a number sentence that shows how to find the temperature at midnight. Then write the midnight temperature. ______________________

Test Prep ★ Mixed Review

34 **A book has 320 pages of text. It also has an additional 16 pages of photographs. What is the ratio of text pages to photo pages in simplest terms?**

A 320 to 16 **C** 80 to 4

B 160 to 8 **D** 20 to 1

35 **In a random sample of students at Jericho Middle School, it was found that 30% of the students bought a school lunch three or more days each week. There are 570 students in the school. About how many students in the whole school buy school lunch on three or more days each week?**

F About 17 students **H** About 171 students

G About 57 students **J** About 400 students

Name ______________________________

Problem Solving Application: Choose the Operation

STANDARD

Positive and negative integers are used to represent elevation, temperature, financial matters, and many other things.

In this lesson, you will have to decide whether to use addition or subtraction when solving problems with integers.

Tips to Remember:

1. Understand **2. Decide** **3. Solve** **4. Look back**

- Reread the problem. Circle important words and numbers.
- Find the action in the problem. Which operation shows this action better: addition or subtraction?
- Predict the answer. Then solve the problem. Compare your answer with your prediction.

Solve.

1. The temperature at midnight was $^{-}$**2**°F. Twelve hours later the temperature had increased by **5**°. What was the temperature at noon?

Think: What does the word "increase" indicate? What number sentence can you use to solve the problem?

____

Answer ______________________________

2. The high temperature one day was **3**°C and the low temperature for the day was $^{-}$**7**°C. What was the change in temperature for the day?

Think: What does the word "change" indicate? What number sentence can you use to solve the problem?

____

Answer ______________________________

3. The temperature on the shore has been dropping **3**°F per hour since **5:00** P.M. It is now **9:00** P.M. How has the temperature changed?

Think: Why don't you need to know the temperature to answer the question?

____

____

Answer ______________________________

4. The temperature was **60**°F at **5:00** A.M. By noon it was **88**°F. Suppose the temperature increases by the same number of degrees each hour. How many degrees per hour did the temperature increase?

Think: Are you looking the total amount of change in this problem?

____

Answer ______________________________

STANDARD

Solve.

5. The highest point on the continent of Africa, Mt. Kilimanjaro, is **5,895** m above sea level. The lowest surface point, Lake Assal, is $^-$**156** m , or **156** m below sea level. How much higher is Mt. Kilimanjaro than Lake Assal?

______

6. The lowest surface point in South America is on the Valdes Peninsula at $^-$**40** m. The lowest point of Lake Eyre in Australia is **24** m higher than the Valdes Peninsula. How low is the lowest point of Lake Eyre?

______

7. The highest recorded air temperature of **58**°C was in Al-Aziziyah, Libya. The lowest recorded air temperature of $^-$**89**°C was in Vostok Station, Antarctica. What is the difference between these two temperatures?

______

8. The greatest depth of Lake Huron is **229** m. The greatest depth of Lake Michigan is **52** m deeper than Lake Huron. What is the greatest depth of Lake Michigan?

______

9. A stock opened the week at a price of **$51**. The changes in the closing value of the stock for the next five days were $^-$**1**, $^+$**3**, $^-$**4**, $^-$**2**, $^+$**1**. What was the closing price of the stock at the end of the week?

______

10. The lowest surface point in North America is in Death Valley, at $^-$**280** ft below sea level. Denver, Colorado, referred to as the Mile High City, is **5,280** ft above sea level. How much higher is Denver than Death Valley?

______

11. In central Asia, the winter temperature ranges from $^-$**6**°C to $^-$**16**°C. What is the range in temperature for the winter?

______

12. A scuba diver is **4** meters below sea level. He descends **5** more meters. How far below sea level is he?

______

Extend Your Thinking

13. Look back at problem **6**. The lowest surface point of the Caspian Sea in Europe is halfway between the lowest surface points of Lake Eyre and the Valdes Peninsula. What is the lowest surface point of the Caspian Sea?

______

14. Look back at problem **8**. The greatest depth of Lake Superior is **104** m less than the sum of the greatest depths of Lake Huron and Lake Michigan. What is the greatest depth of Lake Superior? Which lake has the greatest depth?

______

15. Look back at problem **5**. Explain how you found your answer.

______

16. Look back at problem **7**. Explain how you found your answer.

______

Name ___________________________________

Multiplying Integers

STANDARD

Multiplication is repeated addition. $3 \times 5 = 5 + 5 + 5$, or 15

Knowing that multiplication is repeated addition can help you find the product of integers. $3 \times {}^{-}5 = {}^{-}5 + {}^{-}5 + {}^{-}5$, or ${}^{-}15$

A number line can also be used to find the product $3 \times {}^{-}5$.

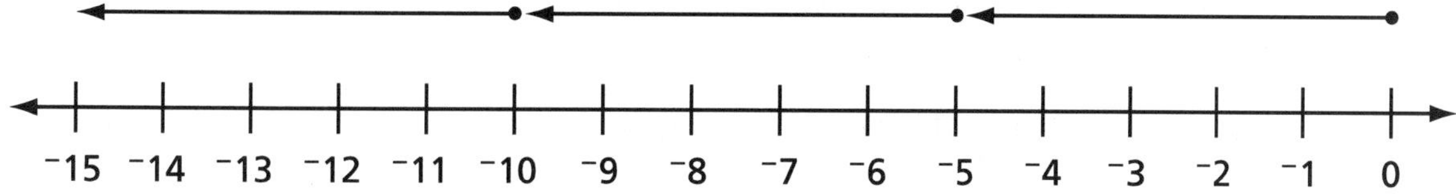

Multiplication with integers is a commutative operation. $3 \times {}^{-}5 = {}^{-}5 \times 3$

The product of two numbers with **different signs** is **negative**.

positive × negative = negative $3 \times {}^{-}5 = {}^{-}15$

negative × positive = negative ${}^{-}5 \times 3 = {}^{-}15$

Write the addition problem as a multiplication problem. Then solve.

1. $3 + 3 + 3 + 3$ ____________ ${}^{-}4 + {}^{-}4 + {}^{-}4 + {}^{-}4 + {}^{-}4 + {}^{-}4$ ____________

2. ${}^{-}6 + {}^{-}6 + {}^{-}6 + {}^{-}6 + {}^{-}6$ ____________ $1 + 1 + 1 + 1 + 1 + 1 + 1$ ____________

Find the product.

3. ${}^{-}2 \times 8$ = ______ $3 \times {}^{-}7$ = ______ ${}^{-}4 \times 5$ = ______

4. $9 \times {}^{-}2$ = ______ $6 \times {}^{-}6$ = ______ ${}^{-}3 \times 9$ = ______

5. $9 \times {}^{-}9$ = ______ ${}^{-}8 \times 4$ = ______ $10 \times {}^{-}11$ = ______

6. $13 \times {}^{-}4$ = ______ $20 \times {}^{-}8$ = ______ ${}^{-}51 \times 7$ = ______

Complete the pattern.

7. 3×1 = ______

2×1 = ______

1×1 = ______

0×1 = ______

${}^{-}1 \times 1$ = ______

${}^{-}2 \times 1$ = ______

${}^{-}3 \times 1$ = ______

8. $3 \times {}^{-}1$ = ______

$2 \times {}^{-}1$ = ______

$1 \times {}^{-}1$ = ______

$0 \times {}^{-}1$ = ______

${}^{-}1 \times {}^{-}1$ = ______

${}^{-}2 \times {}^{-}1$ = ______

${}^{-}3 \times {}^{-}1$ = ______

STANDARD

The product of two numbers with the **same sign** is **positive**.

positive × positive = positive $3 \times 2 = 6$

negative × negative = positive $^-3 \times {}^-2 = 6$

Write *negative* or *positive*. Use the patterns you found in exercises 7 and 8.

9. The product of a positive number and a positive number is a __________ number.

10. The product of a negative number and a negative number is a __________ number.

11. The product of a negative number and a positive number is a __________ number.

12. The product of a positive number and a negative number is a__________ number.

Find the product.

13.	$^-2 \times {}^-5$ = ________	3×7 = ________	$^-4 \times {}^-9$ = ________
14.	$^-9 \times {}^-5$ = ________	$^-6 \times {}^-6$ = ________	$^-3 \times {}^-9$ = ________
15.	$^-9 \times {}^-9$ = ________	7×4 = ________	$^-11 \times {}^-11$ = ________
16.	13×7 = ________	22×2 = ________	31×5 = ________
17.	$^-3 \times 11$ = ________	$7 \times {}^-7$ = ________	$^-4 \times {}^-5$ = ________
18.	$2 \times {}^-2$ = ________	$9 \times {}^-6$ = ________	$^-13 \times 6$ = ________
19.	9×8 = ________	$^-8 \times {}^-10$ = ________	$25 \times {}^-4$ = ________
20.	$^-15 \times {}^-4$ = ________	$12 \times {}^-6$ = ________	100×5 = ________

Problem Solving
Reasoning

Solve.

21. Suppose the height of a mountain is decreasing at a rate of 3 inches per year. What integer can be used to represent the yearly change in the height of the mountain? ______ What is the change in height after 9 years? ______________ How many years ago was the mountain 10 feet taller than it is now? ______________

Test Prep ★ Mixed Review

22 **At 8 A.M. one morning, the temperature was $^-8$°F. The high temperature for the day was warmer by 10°F. What was the high temperature?**

A $^-10$°F

B $^-2$°F

C 2°F

D 10°F

23 **A company is taste-testing a new type of potato chip. Which would be the best population to choose a sample from?**

F shoppers at a grocery store

G potato farmers

H kids who like corn chips

J everyone in the United States

Name ______________________________

Dividing Integers

STANDARD

Multiplication and division of the same quantity are inverse operations. You can use a related multiplication equation to solve a division problem.

$12 \div 2 = ?$ Think: $6 \times 2 = 12$, so $12 \div 2 = 6$

This number is the product of these numbers.

Other examples

$^-14 \div 2 = ?$

Think: $^-7 \times 2 = {}^-14$, so $^-14 \div 2 = {}^-7$

$^-24 \div {}^-4 = ?$

Think: $6 \times {}^-4 = {}^-24$, so $^-24 \div {}^-4 = 6$

Use related multiplication sentences to help you complete each sentence.

1. $18 \div {}^-2 =$ ______

______ $\times {}^-2 = 18$

$^-12 \div 3 =$ ______

______ $\times 3 = {}^-12$

$^-15 \div {}^-3 =$ ______

______ $\times {}^-3 = {}^-15$

2. $^-24 \div {}^-6 =$ ______

______ $\times {}^-6 = {}^-24$

$66 \div {}^-11 =$ ______

______ $\times {}^-11 = 66$

$56 \div 7 =$ ______

______ $\times 7 = 56$

3. $^-63 \div 9 =$ ______

______

$^-9 \div {}^-3 =$ ______

______

$28 \div {}^-4 =$ ______

______

4. $60 \div 10 =$ ______

______

$^-19 \div {}^-19 =$ ______

______

$38 \div {}^-2 =$ ______

______

5. $^-64 \div {}^-8 =$ ______

______

$^-25 \div 5 =$ ______

______

$36 \div {}^-9 =$ ______

______

Write *positive* or *negative*. Use the related sentences in exercises 1 and 2 to help.

6. A positive integer divided by a positive number is a ______________ number.

7. A negative number divided by a negative number is a ______________ number.

8. A negative number divided by a positive number is a ______________ number.

9. A positive number divided by a negative number is a ______________ number.

STANDARD

Follow these rules when dividing integers:

The quotient of two numbers with the **same sign** is **positive**.

positive ÷ positive = positive $\quad 6 \div 2 = 3$

negative ÷ negative = positive $\quad {}^-6 \div {}^-2 = 3$

The quotient of two numbers with **different signs** is **negative**.

positive ÷ negative = negative $\quad 6 \div {}^-2 = {}^-3$

negative ÷ positive = negative $\quad {}^-6 \div 2 = {}^-3$

Remember: The rules for dividing integers are similar to the rules for multiplying integers.

Multiplying Integers

The product of two numbers with the **same sign** is **positive.**

The product of two numbers with **different signs** is **negative.**

Find the quotient.

10. $16 \div {}^-2 =$ ______ $\quad {}^-15 \div 3 =$ ______ $\quad {}^-28 \div {}^-2 =$ ______ $\quad {}^-21 \div {}^-7 =$ ______

11. ${}^-24 \div {}^-3 =$ ______ $\quad 36 \div {}^-9 =$ ______ $\quad {}^-50 \div 5 =$ ______ $\quad 35 \div {}^-5 =$ ______

12. ${}^-63 \div 9 =$ ______ $\quad {}^-9 \div {}^-3 =$ ______ $\quad {}^-20 \div {}^-4 =$ ______ $\quad {}^-16 \div {}^-4 =$ ______

Problem Solving
Reasoning

Solve.

13. Which has the greatest quotient: ${}^-25 \div {}^-5$; $25 \div {}^-5$; ${}^-25 \div 5$; or $25 \div 5$? Explain. ______

______

______

Quick Check

Find the difference.

14. $4 - 8$ ______ **15.** ${}^-6 - {}^-10$ ______ **16.** ${}^-9 - 4$ ______

Find the product or quotient.

17. $4 \cdot ({}^-8)$ ______ **18.** ${}^-12 \cdot 6$ ______ **19.** $({}^-10)({}^-15)$ ______

20. $\frac{48}{{}^-3}$ ______ **21.** $\frac{{}^-91}{7}$ ______ **22.** $\frac{{}^-120}{{}^-15}$ ______

Work Space.

Name ______________________

Integers and the Order of Operations

STANDARD

When a numerical expression contains more than one operation, simplify the expression by following the order of operations.

1. Complete operations inside parentheses.
2. Simplify exponents.
3. Multiply and divide from left to right.
4. Add and subtract from left to right.

Simplify. $^-3 + {}^-5(^-10 - {}^-6) \div 2$

$^-3 + {}^-5\,(^-10 - {}^-6) \div 2$	**1.** Complete operations inside parentheses.
$^-3 + {}^-5(^-4) \div 2$	**2.** Multiply and divide from left to right.
$^-3 + 20 \div 2$	
$^-3 + 10$	**3.** Add and subtract from left to right.
7	

Simplify each pair of expressions.

1. $^-2 - (8 - 9)$ ______ $4 - (5 + {}^-3)$ ______ $^-1 - (^-3 + {}^-6)$ ______

$^-2 - 8 - 9$ ______ $4 - 5 + {}^-3$ ______ $^-1 - {}^-3 + {}^-6$ ______

2. $33 - (15 \div {}^-5)$ ______ $24 - (^-3 \cdot {}^-2)$ ______ $4 - (5 \cdot {}^-1)$ ______

$33 - 15 \div {}^-5$ ______ $24 - {}^-3 \cdot {}^-2$ ______ $4 - 5 \cdot {}^-1$ ______

3. $^-3 \cdot (4 + {}^-1)$ ______ $5 \cdot (^-2 - 5)$ ______ $^-2(^-4 - 6)$ ______

$^-3 \cdot 4 + {}^-1$ ______ $5 \cdot {}^-2 - 5$ ______ $^-2(^-4) + {}^-6$ ______

4. $(3)^2$ ______ $(3 + 2)^2$ ______ $^-(3 + 2)$ ______

$(^-3)^2$ ______ $(^-3 + {}^-2)^2$ ______ $^-3 + (^-2)$ ______

5. $^-6 + (4)^2$ ______ $^-4 + (4 + 2)^2$ ______ $7 - (5 + 9)$ ______

$^-6 + (^-4)^2$ ______ $^-4 + (^-4 - 2)^2$ ______ $7 + (^-5) - 9$ ______

6. $(2) - (1)^2$ ______ $(3) - (3 + 1)^2$ ______ $15 \div (3 + 2)$ ______

$(2)(^-1)^2$ ______ $(3)(^-3 - 1)^2$ ______ $15 \div 3 + 2$ ______

STANDARD

To **evaluate** an expression means to substitute given values for variables.

Evaluate $^-(x^2)$ for $x = 8$.

$^-(x^2)$

$^-(8^2)$

$^-64$

Evaluate $(^-x)^2$ for $x = 8$.

$(^-x)^2$

$(^-8)^2$

64

Evaluate $^-(a + 3)$ for $a = 6$.

$^-(a + 3)$

$^-(6 + 3)$

$^-9$

Evaluate $^-a + 3$ for $a = 6$.

$^-a + 3$

$^-6 + 3$

$^-3$

Evaluate the expression.

7. $^-(x^2) =$ ______ for $x = 4$ $\qquad$ $(^-x)^2 =$ ______ for $x = 4$

8. $^-(y + 5) =$ ______ for $y = 4$ $\qquad$ $^-y + 3 =$ ______ for $y = 4$

9. $(7)(^-a) + 3 =$ ______ for $a = 2$ $\qquad$ $7 - (a + 3) =$ ______ for $a = 2$

10. $9(^-y - 6) =$ ______ for $y = 1$ $\qquad$ $9 - (y - 6) =$ ______ for $y = 1$

11. $7 - x^2 =$ ______ for $x = 2$ $\qquad$ $(7)(^-x)^2 =$ ______ for $x = 2$

12. $^-y^2 + 2$ for $y = 2$ ______ $\qquad$ $5 - (x + 2)$ for $x = {}^-2$ ______

13. $8(a - 3)$ for $a = {}^-3$ ______ $\qquad$ $9 - b^2$ for $b = {}^-1$ ______

14. $3 + (x - 4)$ for $x = 2$ ______ $\qquad$ $y^2 - 4$ for $y = {}^-2$ ______

Problem Solving Reasoning

Solve.

15. Which two expressions have the same value for $x = 2$, $^-(x - 3)$, $(^-x - 3)$, or $^-x - (^-3)$? Explain.

____

Test Prep ★ Mixed Review

16 What is $\frac{4}{5}$ of 20?

A 15

B 16

C 17

D 18

17 What is the value of $^-8k^2$ when $k = {}^-3$?

F $^-72$

G $^-48$

H 48

J 72

Name ______________________

Integers and Expressions

STANDARD

You can use the rules for adding and subtracting integers to evaluate an algebraic expression with integer values.

Evaluate $x - y + z$ for $x = {}^-3$, $y = {}^-8$, and $z = 5$.

Substitute $^-3$ for x, $^-8$ for y, and 5 for z. Follow the order of operations to simplify.

$$x - y + z = ({}^-3) - ({}^-8) + (5) = 5 + (5) = 10$$

You can use the rules for multiplying and dividing integers to evaluate an algebraic expression with integer values.

Evaluate $3x + ({}^-2y)({}^-3z)$ for $x = {}^-2$, $y = {}^-1$, $z = 3$.

Substitute $^-2$ for x, $^-1$ for y, and 3 for z. Follow the order of operations to simplify.

$$3x + ({}^-2y)({}^-3z) = 3({}^-2) + ({}^-2)({}^-1)({}^-3)(3) = {}^-6 + ({}^-18) = {}^-24$$

> Multiplication and division can be shown in several ways.
>
> $3xyz \rightarrow$ 3 times x times y times z
>
> $3(x + y) \rightarrow$ 3 times the sum of x and y
>
> $({}^-2y)({}^-3x) \rightarrow {}^-2$ times y times $^-3$ times x
>
> $\frac{r}{^-3} \rightarrow r$ divided by $^-3$

Evaluate for $r = {}^-2$, $s = 4$, and $d = {}^-3$.

1. $r + s + d$ ______ $r - s - d$ ______ $r + (s + d)$ ______

2. $r - (s - d)$ ______ $r - d - s$ ______ $r + s - d$ ______

3. $r - s + d$ ______ $r - d + s$ ______ $r - (s + d)$ ______

Evaluate for $x = 2$, $y = {}^-1$, and $z = {}^-4$.

4. $3xyz$ ______ $2x - 3y + z$ ______ $^-5(x + y) - z$ ______

5. $\frac{x}{2} + y - z$ ______ $2x + y + \frac{z}{^-2}$ ______ $z(x - 3)$ ______

STANDARD

Evaluate for $x = 4$, $y = {}^-5$, and $z = {}^-1$.

6. $x - y + z$ ______ $\frac{xy}{^-2} + z$ ______ $2(x + y) + \frac{z}{^-1}$ ______

7. $2x - (3y + z)$ ______ $xy - xz$ ______ $x(y - z)$ ______

8. $\frac{xyz}{5}$ ______ $\frac{^-4}{x} - ({}^-2y) - z$ ______ $4x - 2(y + z)$ ______

9. $2xy - 3y$ ______ $y(2x - 3)$ ______ $2xy - 3$ ______

10. $\frac{xy}{({}^-2z)}$ ______ $\frac{^-4}{z} + ({}^-2y)$ ______ $\frac{15}{y} + ({}^-3yz)$ ______

11. $\frac{^-5}{y} - xz$ ______ $x(2y - 3z)$ ______ $\frac{(x - 2y)}{2z}$ ______

12. $\frac{8z}{x + y}$ ______ $y + z \div \frac{x}{z}$ ______ $xyz - 2xyz$ ______

13. $2xyz - xyz$ ______ $(3y + 10z - 6x) \times 0$ ______ $\frac{xyz}{4}$ ______

14. $\frac{4x - 4z}{2y}$ ______ $(x + y)(x + z)$ ______ $(x + y + z) \div 2z$ ______

Problem Solving
Reasoning

Solve.

15. Which expression has the greater value for $a = {}^-1$ and $b = 1$: $3a - 2b$ or $3(a - 2b)$? Explain.

______

______

16. Which expression has the greater value for $a = {}^-1$ and $b = 1$: $3 - (a - 2b)$ or $3 - a - 2b$? Explain.

______

______

Test Prep ★ Mixed Review

17 **Two number cubes, numbered 1, 2, 3, 4, 5, and 6, are rolled. What is the probability of rolling two 4's?**

A $\frac{1}{36}$

B $\frac{1}{12}$

C $\frac{1}{6}$

D $\frac{1}{3}$

18 **One winter evening the temperature decreased by 4°F for each of the next 8 hours. What measure best indicates the change in temperature during those 8 hours?**

F 4°F

G 32°F

H ⁻4°F

J ⁻32°F

Name ______________________________

Integers and Equations

STANDARD

The addition property of equality allows you to add opposites to solve equations involving integers.

Addition Property of Equality: Adding the same number to each side of an equation results in an equation with the same solution.

Solve: $x + 3 = {}^-12$
Add the opposite of **3** to each side of the equation.
Simplify.

$$x + 3 = {}^-12$$
$$x + 3 + ({}^-3) = {}^-12 + ({}^-3)$$
$$x + 0 = {}^-15$$
$$x = {}^-15$$

Recall that subtracting an integer is the same as adding the opposite of the integer.

$7 - ({}^-2) = 9$ means the same as $7 + (2) = 9$

You can use this idea to solve equations involving subtraction of integers. Rewrite all subtraction problems as addition problems.

Solve: $y - ({}^-2) = 9$
Rewrite subtraction as addition.
Add the opposite of **2** to each side of the equation.
Simplify.

$$y - ({}^-2) = 9$$
$$y + (2) = 9$$
$$y + (2) + ({}^-2) = 9 + ({}^-2)$$
$$y + 0 = 7$$
$$y = 7$$

Solve: $y - 9 = {}^-3$
Rewrite subtraction as addition.
Add the opposite of **$^-9$** to each side of the equation.
Simplify.

$$y - 9 = {}^-3$$
$$y + ({}^-9) = {}^-3$$
$$y + ({}^-9) + (9) = {}^-3 + (9)$$
$$y + 0 = 6$$
$$y = 6$$

Complete the steps to find the solution.

1. $x + ({}^-8) = 3$
$x + ({}^-8) + (\_\_\_) = 3 + (\_\_\_)$
$x + (\_\_\_) = (\_\_\_)$
$x = \_\_\_$

2. $x + 3 = {}^-5$
$x + 3 + (\_\_\_) = {}^-5 + (\_\_\_)$
$x + (\_\_\_) = \_\_\_$
$x = \_\_\_$

3. $x + ({}^-5) = {}^-2$
$x + ({}^-5) + (\_\_\_) = {}^-2 + (\_\_\_)$
$x + (\_\_\_) = (\_\_\_)$
$x = \_\_\_$

4. $x - ({}^-8) = 3$
$x + (\_\_) = 3$
$x + (\_\_) + (\_\_) = 3 + (\_\_)$
$x + (\_\_) = \_\_$
$x = \_\_$

5. $x - 3 = {}^-5$
$x + (\_\_) = {}^-5$
$x + (\_\_) + (\_\_) = {}^-5 + (\_\_)$
$x + (\_\_) = \_\_$
$x = \_\_$

6. $x - ({}^-5) = {}^-2$
$x + (\_\_) = {}^-2$
$x + (\_\_) + (\_\_) = {}^-2 + (\_\_)$
$x + (\_\_) = \_\_$
$x = \_\_$

STANDARD

Complete the steps to find the solution to each equation.

7. $x - (^{-}1) = 15$

$x + (1) + (\_\_) = 15 + (\_\_)$

$x + \_\_ = \_\_$

$x = \_\_$

8. $x + 2 = {^{-}25}$

$x + 2 + (\_\_) = {^{-}25} + (\_\_)$

$x + (\_\_) = \_\_$

$x = \_\_$

9. $x + (^{-}8) = 13$

$x + (^{-}8) + (\_\_) = 13 + (\_\_)$

$x + \_\_ = \_\_$

$x = \_\_$

Solve.

10. $x - 8 = 3$ $x =$ ____ $x + (^{-}6) = 7$ $x =$ ____ $x + 9 = 2$ $x =$ ____

11. $x - (^{-}8) = {^{-}13}$ $x =$ ____ $x - 4 = {^{-}9}$ $x =$ ____ $x + (^{-}2) = 10$ $x =$ ____

12. $x + (^{-}2) = {^{-}10}$ $x =$ ____ $x - 7 = {^{-}4}$ $x =$ ____ $x - (^{-}6) = 17$ $x =$ ____

13. $x + 20 = {^{-}20}$ $x =$ ____ $x - (^{-}14) = 1$ $x =$ ____ $x + 8 = {^{-}23}$ $x =$ ____

Problem Solving
Reasoning

Solve.

14. Claudia wants to solve $x - (^{-}5) = {^{-}3}$. What should she do first?

____

15. Gordon rewrote $x + (^{-}2) = 1$ as $x - (2) = 1$. Did he change the solution of the equation? Explain.

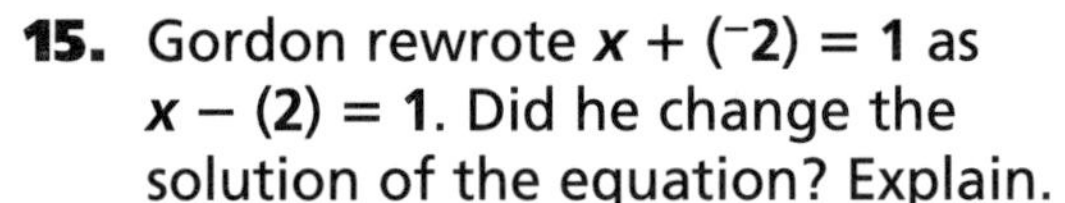

____

____

Quick Check

Evaluate the expression for $x = {^{-}3}$, $y = {^{-}5}$, and $z = {^{-}1}$.

16. ${^{-}x} - 4$ ____ **17.** ${^{-}(x^2 - 4)}$ ____ **18.** ${^{-}7y} + 5$ ____

19. $x^2 + y^2$ ____ **20.** ${^{-}3x} + 9z$ ____ **21.** ${^{-}2x} + y - 8z$ ____

Solve.

22. ${^{-}6x} = 156$ ____ **23.** ${^{-}y} = 17$ ____ **24.** $k - {^{-}3} = {^{-}18}$ ____

Work Space.

Name ______________________________

Problem Solving Strategy: Write an Equation

STANDARD

In this lesson, you will write equations to solve word problems.

You will use a variable in the equation to represent what you want to find.

Problem

After 3 ft had been cut from a piece of lumber, there are 9 ft left. How long was the original piece of lumber?

1 Understand

As you reread, ask yourself questions.

- What information do you have?

  3 ft were cut from a piece of lumber. **9** ft are left.

- What do you need to find?

  ____

2 Decide

Choose a method for solving.

- Try the strategy Write an Equation.

  Pick a variable to represent what you need to find.

- What variable did you select?

  ____

- Write an equation using the variable.

  ____

3 Solve

Solve the equation.

- Will you add or subtract to solve the equation? ______
- What is the solution of the equation? ______

4 Look back

Check your answer.

- Answer ______________________________
- Could you have written a different equation?

  ____

STANDARD

Solve. Use the Write an Equation strategy or any other strategy you have learned.

1. After a football team had a gain of **5** yd, they were on their **27** yd line. On what line were they before the gain?

Think: Did the play start or end at the **27** yd line?

____

Answer ______________________

2. The range of a set of scores is **29**. If the lowest score is **69**, what is the highest score?

Think: Will you add or subtract to find the range?

____

Answer ______________________

3. One day the temperature was **15°** above the average December temperature. If the temperature on this day was **56°F**, what is the average temperature for December?

____

4. Jo borrowed **$18** from her mother to buy a sweater. Now she owes her mother **$23**. How much did she owe her mother before she bought the sweater?

____

5. Marisa is twice as old as Chris. Chris is **4** years older than Keith. If Marisa is **24**, how old is Keith?

____

6. If the time in New York City is **1:15** P.M. and it is **3** hours earlier in San Diego, what time is it in San Diego?

____

7. I'm thinking of a number. If I divide it by **⁻7**, the quotient is **⁻9**. What number am I thinking of?

____

8. I'm thinking of a number. If I multiply this number by **3**, the product is **⁻24**. What number am I thinking of?

____

9. Find the next number in this pattern: **11, 7, 3, ⁻1**

____

10. The sum of two numbers is **⁻12**. One number is **2** more than the other. Find the lesser number.

____

11. A recipe calls for $\frac{1}{4}$ cup of sugar for a dozen cookies. How much sugar is needed for **6** dozen cookies?

____

12. Emma invited $\frac{1}{2}$ of her **24** classmates and $\frac{1}{3}$ of her **6** cousins to a party. How many people did she invite?

____

13. Todd earns **$8** an hour. If he gets paid $1\frac{1}{2}$ times that on Saturday, how much does he make per hour on Saturday?

____

14. One gallon of paint covers **18** square yards. How many gallons are needed to cover **54** square yards?

____

Name ______________________________

Unit 10 Review

Compare. Write >, <, or =.

1. $\frac{5}{3}$ ◯ 2

2. $^{-}3\frac{1}{2}$ ◯ 0

3. $\frac{^{-}2}{10}$ ◯ $\frac{^{-}1}{5}$

4. 3 ◯ $\frac{^{-}3}{1}$

5. On the number line below, plot point *A* at $^{-}4$, point *B* at $\frac{^{-}3}{2}$, and point *C* at $\frac{^{-}1}{2}$.

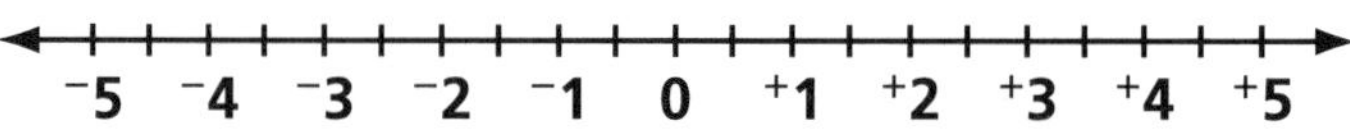

Add, subtract, multiply, or divide.

6. $^{-}2 + 5$ ______

7. $^{-}8 - (^{-}8)$ ______

8. $8 \cdot (^{-}6)$ ______

9. $^{-}12 \div {}^{-}3$ ______

Simplify each expression.

10. $^{-}18 - 6 \div 3$ ______

11. $^{-}5 + (^{-}2)^2$ ______

12. $4 - 6 \cdot 2$ ______

Solve for *n*.

13. $n - 3 = {}^{-}9$

$n =$ ______

14. $n + (^{-}7) = 11$

$n =$ ______

15. $n - (^{-}4) = 9$

$n =$ ______

Solve.

16. The temperature was $^{-}$**4**°C two hours ago. Since that time, it decreased **3**°C. To find the temperature now, would you add or subtract? Explain.

____

17. Marc is **8** years younger than his brother Richard. The sum of their ages is **22** years. What equation could be used to find Marc's age? How old is Marc?

____

Name ______________________________

Cumulative Review
★ Test Prep

Use the diagram below for exercises 1–3.

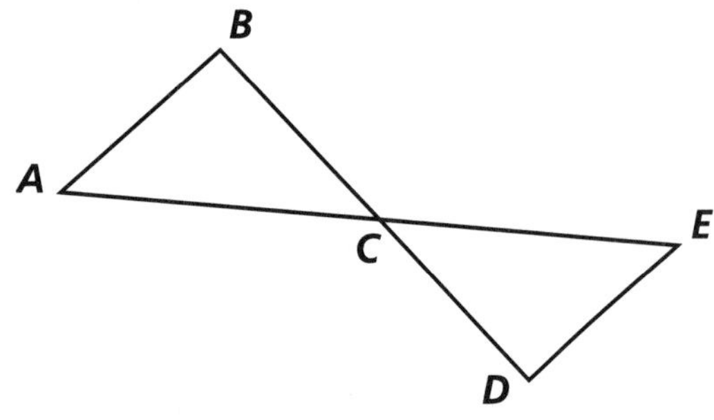

1 Which angle is congruent to $\angle ECD$?

A $\angle ECB$ C $\angle CBA$

B $\angle BCA$ D $\angle BAC$

2 If $\Delta ABC \cong \Delta EDC$, which segment is congruent to $\overline{DE}$?

F $\overline{AB}$ H $\overline{AC}$

G $\overline{BC}$ J $\overline{CD}$

3 If $\angle BAC = 52°$ and $\angle ABC = 90°$, what is the measure of $\angle BCA$?

A 218° C 48°

B 52° D 38°

4 If $\frac{n}{21} = \frac{7}{14}$, what does n equal?

F $\frac{1}{2}$ H $9\frac{1}{2}$

G 7 J $10\frac{1}{2}$

5 What is the least common multiple of 6 and 9?

A 12 C 24

B 18 D 54

6 There is a 35% probability that each student at Jackson Middle School plays a musical instrument. About how many of the 240 sixth-grade students at the school would you expect play an instrument?

F About 6 H About 100

G About 80 J About 120

7 What is the value of $^{-}g^2$ when $g = {}^{-}5$?

A $^{-}10$ C $^{-}25$ E NH

B 10 D 25

8 What is the solution of the equation $\frac{k}{^{-}6} = {}^{-}9$?

F $^{-}54$ H $^{-}1\frac{1}{2}$ K NH

G 54 J $1\frac{1}{2}$

9 A rectangular prism has sides $2x$, $3x$, and $4x$. Which equation gives the volume of the prism?

A $V = (2 \cdot 3 \cdot 4)x$

B $V = (2 \cdot 3 \cdot 4)x^2$

C $V = (2 \cdot 3 \cdot 4)x^3$

D $V = (2 + 3 + 4)x$

E NH

10 $\frac{2}{3} \times \frac{6}{5} = ?$

F $\frac{12}{8}$ H $\frac{8}{15}$ K $\frac{4}{5}$

G $\frac{18}{10}$ J $\frac{12}{5}$

UNIT 11 • TABLE OF CONTENTS

Coordinate Graphing and Rational Numbers

End of Book Materials

We will be using this vocabulary:

rational number any number that can be expressed in the form $\frac{a}{b}$ where a and b are integers and $b \neq 0$

x-coordinate designates distance along the horizontal or x-axis of a coordinate system

y-coordinate designates distance along the vertical or y-axis of a coordinate system

origin the point where the x-axis and y-axis of a coordinate system intersect

Dear Family,

During the next few weeks, our math class will be learning about rational numbers and coordinate graphing. You can expect to see homework that provides practice with evaluating rational expressions. Here is a sample you may want to keep handy to give help if needed.

Rational Numbers and Expressions

To evaluate an expression means to substitute given numbers into the expression, then simplify.

Example: Evaluate $\frac{4a^2}{8} + \frac{3}{b^3} + \frac{2}{2c}$ when $a = \frac{1}{2}$, $b = 2$, and $c = 4$.

$\frac{4a^2}{8} + \frac{3}{b^3} + \frac{2}{2c}$	**1.** Write the expression.
$\frac{4(\frac{1}{2})^2}{8} + \frac{3}{(2)^3} + \frac{2}{2(4)}$	**2.** Substitute for a, b, and c.
$\frac{4(\frac{1}{4})}{8} + \frac{3}{8} + \frac{2}{8}$	**3.** Follow the order of operations. Simplify exponents.
$\frac{1}{8} + \frac{3}{8} + \frac{2}{8}$	**4.** Multiply and divide from left to right.
$\frac{6}{8} = \frac{3}{4}$	**5.** Add and subtract from left to right. Simplify if possible.

During this unit, students will need to continue practicing adding, subtracting, multiplying, and dividing rational numbers.

Sincerely,

Name ______________________________

Graphing in the Coordinate Plane

STANDARD

This is a **coordinate plane**. The horizontal number line is the **x-axis,** and the vertical number line is the **y-axis**. The point where the axes intersect is the **origin.** The two axes divide the plane into four **quadrants**, numbered **I, II, III, IV**.

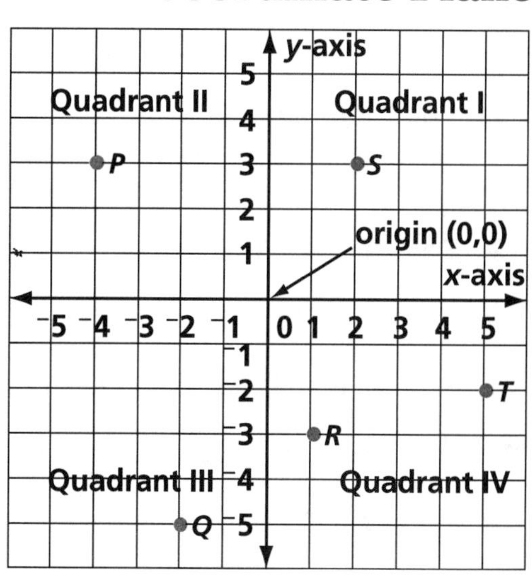

The point ***P*** shown is the **graph** of the ordered pair (⁻4, 3). To graph, or plot, point ***P***, begin at the origin and count **4** spaces to the left. Then count up **3** spaces.

The ordered pair (⁻**4, 3**) gives the **coordinates** of point ***P***.

Write the coordinates of each point.

1. *S* ______ *Q* ______

R ______ *T* ______

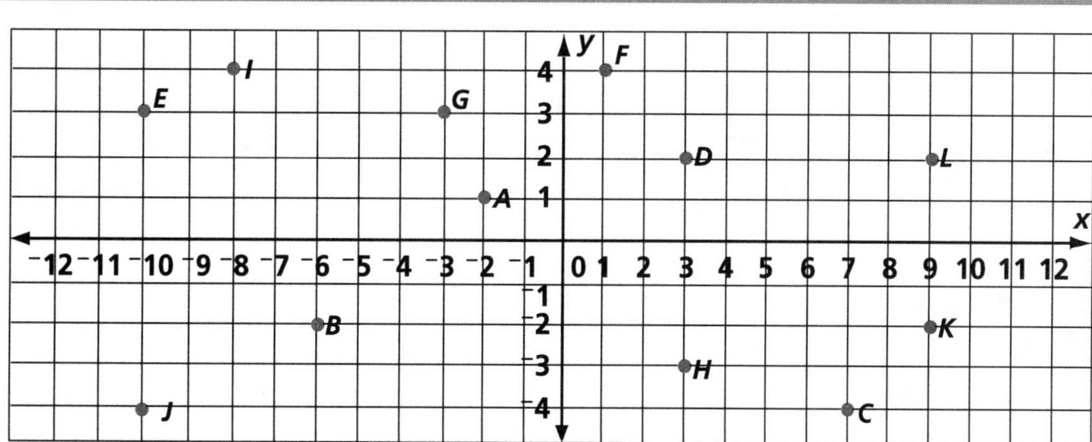

Use the graph above. Write the coordinates of each point.

2. *A* ______ *B* ______ *C* ______ *D* ______ *E* ______ *F* ______

3. *G* ______ *H* ______ *I* ______ *J* ______ *K* ______ *L* ______

Use the graph at the right.

In the ordered pair (2, ⁻1),

4. which number tells you the distance from the origin on the horizontal axis? ______

5. which number tells the distance from the origin on the vertical axis? ______

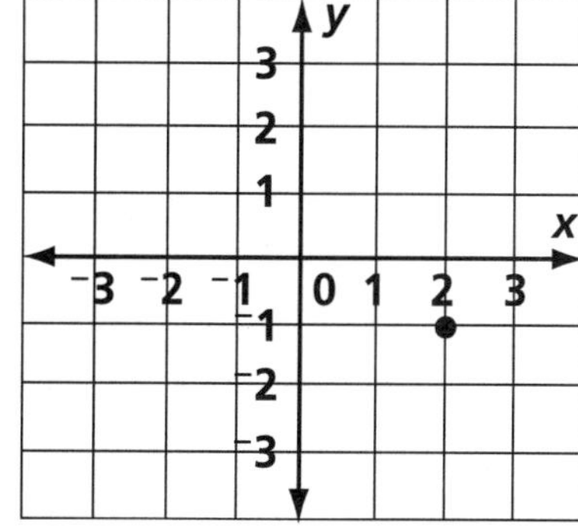

STANDARD

Graph each ordered pair. Label the point with its letter. Tell in which quadrant or on what axis the point lies.

6. Point *A* (3, 2) ______________

7. Point *B* (0, 3) ______________

8. Point *C* (2, $^-4$) ______________

9. Point *D* ($^-4$, $^-2$) ______________

10. Point *E* (4, 0) ______________

11. Point *F* ($^-3$, 4) ______________

12. Point *G* (1, 1) ______________

13. Point *H* ($^-1$, $^-1$) ______________

14. Point *I* (5, $^-3$) ______________

15. Point *J* (0, 0) ______________

16. Point *K* ($^-6$, 0) ______________

17. Point *L* (8, 6) ______________

18. Point *M* (0, $^-7$) ______________

19. Point *N* (7, 7) ______________

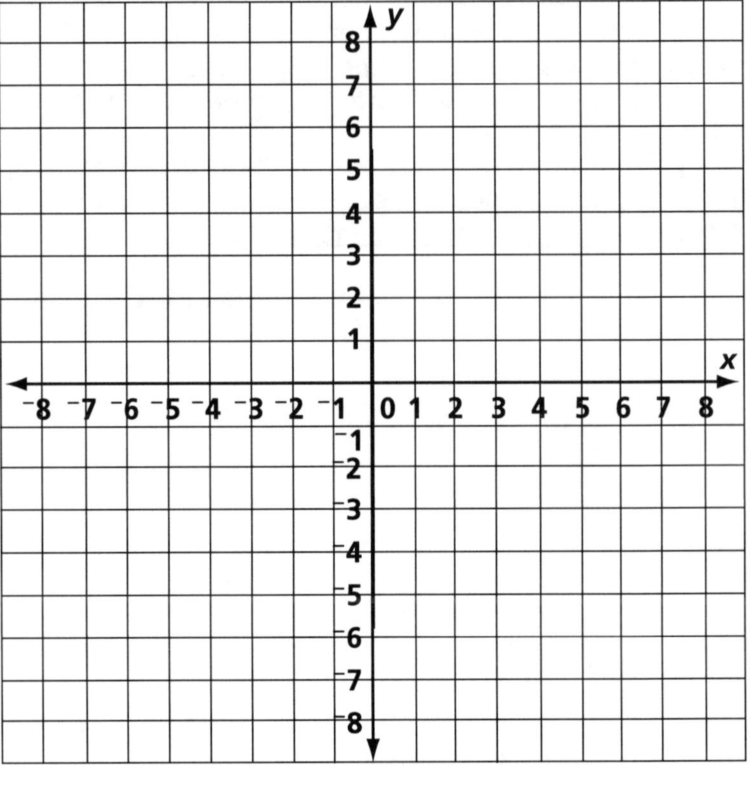

Problem Solving Reasoning Solve.

20. Gregory drew a square on a coordinate plane. One vertex is at (**0, 0**), another is at (**5, 0**) and another is at (**5, 5**). Where is the fourth vertex?

____

21. Carina graphed a rectangle, then added **5** to the *y*-coordinate and graphed a second rectangle. How far is the second rectangle from the first?

____

Test Prep ★ Mixed Review

22 **Which numbers are listed from least to greatest?**

A $^-5$, $^-3$, $^-1$, 1

B $^-5$, $^-3$, 1, $^-1$

C 1, $^-1$, $^-3$, $^-5$

D $^-1$, 1, $^-3$, $^-5$

23 **Which product is the prime factorization of 54?**

F $6 \cdot 9$

G $2 \cdot 27$

H $2 \cdot 3 \cdot 9$

J $2 \cdot 3^3$

Name ___________________________

Equations with Two Variables

STANDARD

You learned that the solution of an equation with a variable is a value that you can substitute for the variable that makes the sentence true. You can find the solution of an equation by using an inverse operation or by using mental math.

Inverse Operation:

$$x + 4 = 13$$
$$x + 4 - 4 = 13 - 4$$
$$x = 9$$

Mental Math:

$$x + 4 = 13$$
$$x = 9$$

The solution of an equation with two variables is the set of all ordered pairs that make the sentence true. It is helpful to organize a few of the ordered pairs in a table of values. The set of numbers that the variables may represent is the **replacement set.** The replacement set for the equation below will be the set of whole numbers.

Create a table of values for the equation $x + y = 5$.

$3 + 2 = 5$, so $x = 3$ and $y = 2$ →

$2 + 3 = 5$, so $x = 2$ and $y = 3$ →

$1 + 4 = 5$, so $x = 1$ and $y = 4$ →

$4 + 1 = 5$, so $x = 4$ and $y = 1$ →

$5 + 0 = 5$, so $x = 5$ and $y = 0$ →

$0 + 5 = 5$, so $x = 0$ and $y = 5$ →

Table of Values
$x + y = 5$

x	y
3	2
2	3
1	4
4	1
5	0
0	5

Complete the table of values.

1. $x + y = 8$

x	y
4	
	5
6	
7	
	8
	3

$y = x - 5$

x	y
6	
5	
7	
	5
	4
	3

$y = 2x$

x	y
0	
	2
	4
3	
4	
	10

STANDARD

You can also use the set of integers as the replacement set for an equation. This will give ordered pairs in all quadrants.

Create a table of values for the equation $x + y = 9$

$4 + 5 = 9$, so $x = 4$ and $y = 5$

$^-1 + 10 = 9$, so $x = {^-1}$ and $y = 10$

$^-6 + 15 = 9$, so $x = {^-6}$ and $y = 15$

$^-3 + 12 = 9$, so $x = {^-3}$ and $y = 12$

$12 + {^-3} = 9$, so $x = 12$ and $y = {^-3}$

$3 + 6 = 9$, so $x = 3$ and $y = 6$

Table of values
$x + y = 9$

x	y
4	5
⁻1	10
⁻6	15
⁻3	12
12	⁻3
3	6

Complete each table of values using the set of integers as the replacement set.

2. $x + y = 10$

x	y
1	
3	
	12
⁻3	
	15

$x + y = 7$

x	y
	4
0	
	8
⁻2	
	11

$x + y = 0$

x	y
3	
0	
	1
⁻3	
	5

3. $y = x + 3$

x	y
1	
0	
	2
	1
⁻6	

$y = x - 2$

x	y
5	
2	
	⁻4
	⁻5
⁻7	

$x - y = 0$

x	y
	⁻4
0	
	3
	2
	1

4. $= 3x$

x	y
1	
	0
	⁻3
⁻2	
⁻4	

$y = -x$

x	y
	⁻6
0	
	5
	2
	1

$y = {^-3}x$

x	y
	⁻3
	3
2	
⁻3	
	15

Complete each table of values using the set of fractions or mixed numbers as the replacement set.

5. $x + y = 10$

x	y
$4\frac{1}{2}$	
$3\frac{1}{3}$	
	$2\frac{4}{5}$
$8\frac{1}{6}$	
$\frac{1}{2}$	

$x + y = 7$

x	y
$3\frac{1}{2}$	
	$4\frac{2}{3}$
$1\frac{1}{6}$	
$5\frac{1}{7}$	
	$6\frac{2}{3}$

$y = \frac{1}{2}x$

x	y
1	
	$1\frac{1}{2}$
	$1\frac{2}{3}$
$2\frac{1}{2}$	
$1\frac{1}{5}$	

6. $y = x + 3$

x	y
$\frac{1}{2}$	
$1\frac{1}{3}$	
$5\frac{2}{3}$	
	$3\frac{1}{6}$
	$3\frac{2}{3}$

$y = x - 2$

x	y
$3\frac{1}{3}$	
	$3\frac{1}{6}$
$6\frac{1}{6}$	
	$\frac{1}{2}$
$3\frac{1}{5}$	

$y = \frac{2}{3}x$

x	y
	$\frac{2}{3}$
	$\frac{1}{2}$
$1\frac{1}{2}$	
2	
	2

Problem Solving
Reasoning

Write an equation with two variables. Then solve.

7. A number increased by another number is **8**. Which ordered pairs in the solution set have a difference of **2**?

____

8. A submarine descended **y** meters. It was then **900** m below sea level. If **y = 200**, how far below sea level was the submarine to start with?

____

Test Prep ★ Mixed Review

9 **Which sum and difference are equivalent?**

A $5 - (^-3)$ and $^-5 + (^-3)$

B $5 - (^-3)$ and $^-5 + 3$

C $5 - (^-3)$ and $5 + (^-3)$

D $5 - (^-3)$ and $5 + 3$

10 **Rebecca is wrapping identical gifts. Each gift uses $3\frac{1}{3}$ feet of ribbon. The roll of ribbon is 25 feet long. What is the greatest number of gifts she can wrap with the ribbon?**

F 5

G 7

H 8

J 9

STANDARD

STANDARD

Name ______________________________

Graphing Equations

You can use a table of values to graph an equation.

1. To graph the equation $y = x + 2$, first make a table of values. List three or four values for x. Choose easy numbers to work with such as **0, 1,** and **⁻1.**

2. Use the table of values to form three or four ordered pairs.

$y = x + 2$

x	y	
0	2	→ (0, 2)
1	3	→ (1, 3)
⁻1	1	→ (⁻1, 1)
⁻2	0	→ (⁻2, 0)

3. Plot the point for each pair of (x, y) values on a coordinate plane.

4. Draw a line through the points. This line represents all the ordered pairs you could have as solutions to the equation. This includes all fractional values for either x or y.

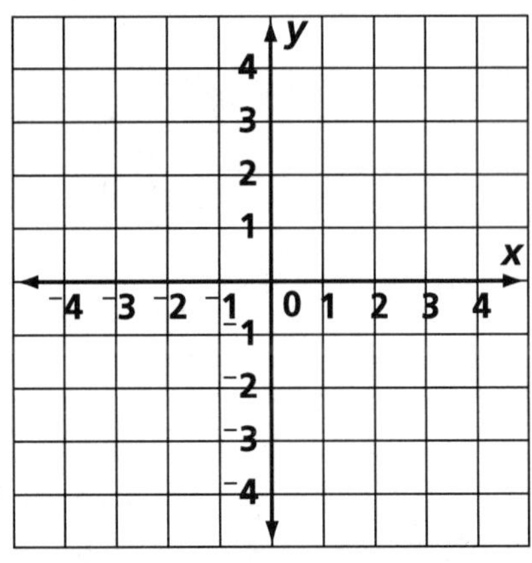

Complete the table of values and graph the equation.

1. Graph the equation $y = x - 3$.

$y = x - 3$

x	y	
⁻1		→ (⁻1, ____)
0		→ (0, ____)
1		→ (1, ____)
2		→ (2, ____)

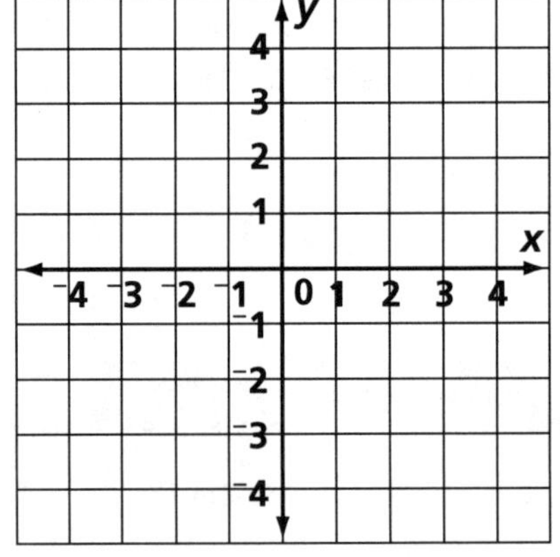

2. Graph the equation $y = {}^{-}2x$.

$y = {}^{-}2x$

x	y	
⁻1		→ (⁻1, ____)
0		→ (0, ____)
1		→ (1, ____)
2		→ (2, ____)

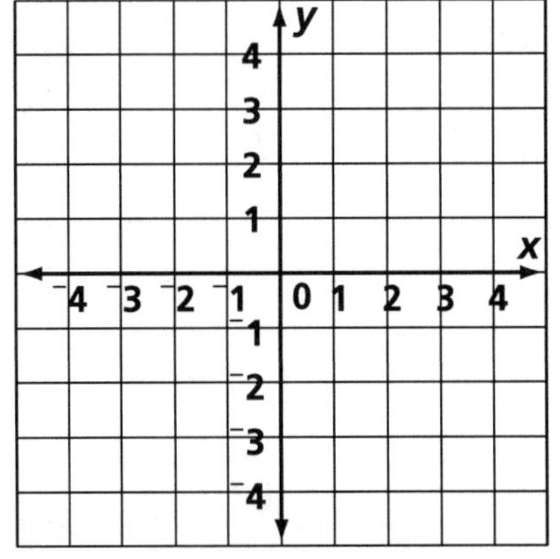

Name ___________________________

Graph the equation.

3. Graph the equation $y = 2x$.

$y = 2x$

x	y
$^-1$	
0	
1	
2	

→ ($^-1$, ____)
→ (0, ____)
→ (1, ____)
→ (2, ____)

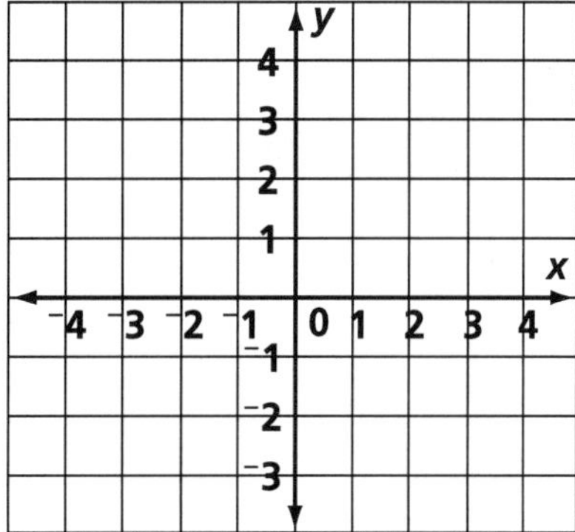

4. Graph the equation $y = 3 - x$.

$y = 3 - x$

x	y
$^-1$	
0	
1	
2	

→ ($^-1$, ____)
→ (0, ____)
→ (1, ____)
→ (2, ____)

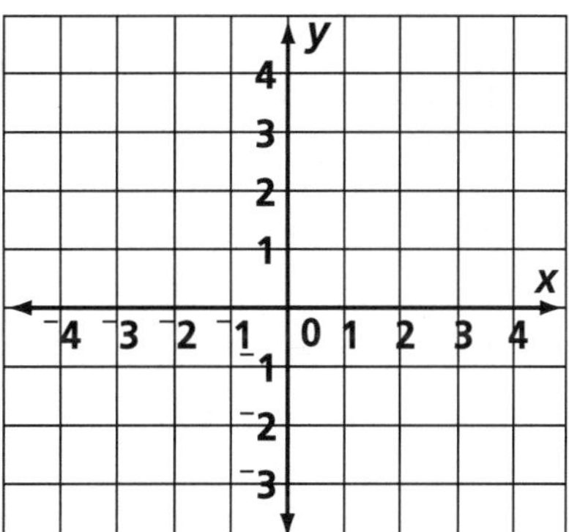

5. Graph the equation $y = {}^-1x$.

$y = {}^-1x$

x	y
$^-1$	
0	
1	
2	

→ ($^-1$, ____)
→ (0, ____)
→ (1, ____)
→ (2, ____)

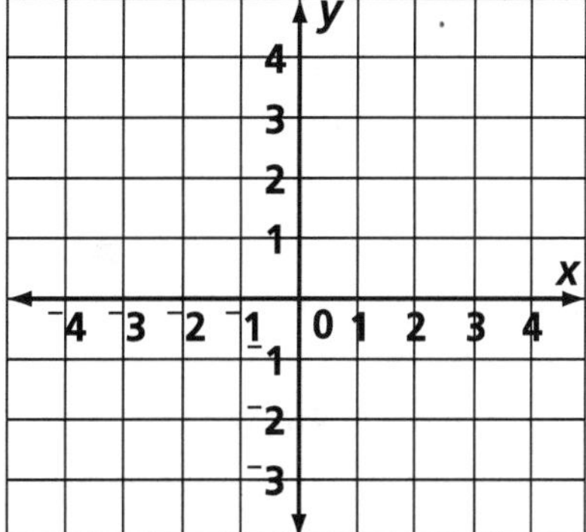

6. Graph the equation $y = x + 2$.

x	y
$^-1$	
0	
1	
2	

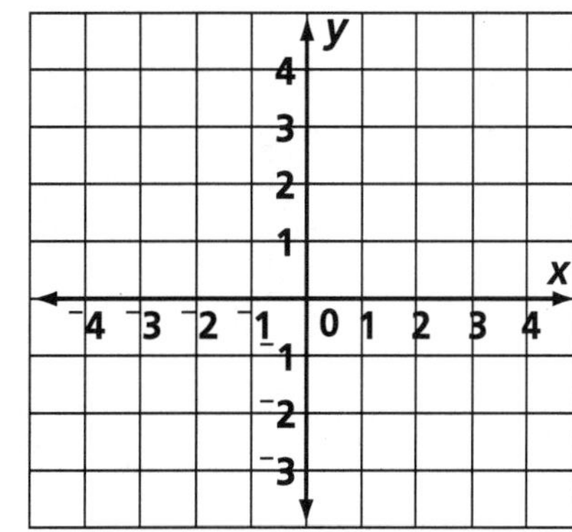

STANDARD

STANDARD

Problem Solving Reasoning Solve.

7. Graph each equation on the coordinate plane. Write the ordered pairs.

$y = x + 1$

x	y
⁻1	
0	
1	
2	

(⁻1, ____)
(0, ____)
(1, ____)
(2, ____)

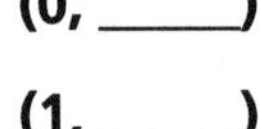

$y = x + 0$

x	y
⁻1	
0	
1	
2	

(⁻1, ____)
(0, ____)
(1, ____)
(2, ____)

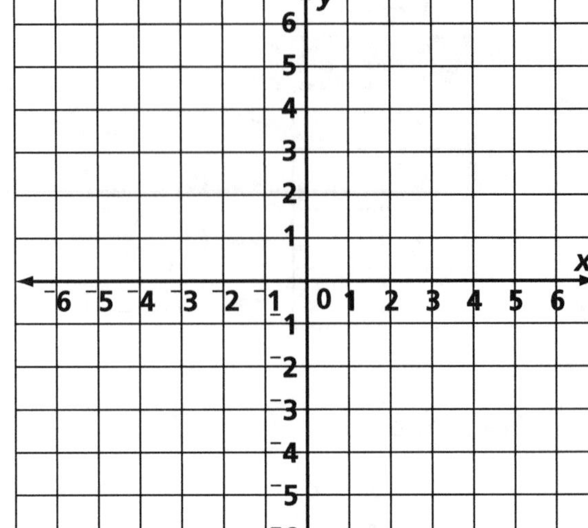

$y = x + 3$

x	y
⁻1	
0	
1	
2	

(⁻1, ____)
(0, ____)
(1, ____)
(2, ____)

$y = x + 2$

x	y
⁻1	
0	
1	
2	

(⁻1, ____)
(0, ____)
(1, ____)
(2, ____)

8. Describe any pattern you see. ____________________

Quick Check

The directions for moving on a coordinate plane starting from (0, 0) are given. Write the coordinate for the point at the end of the move.

9. Left 4, up 1 ________

10. Right 3, down 6 ________

11. Left 7, down 2 ________

12. Complete the table of values for the equation $y = \frac{x}{2}$.

x	y
4	
2	
0	
⁻4	

13. Graph the equation $y = \frac{x}{2}$. Use the solutions from the table in exercise 12.

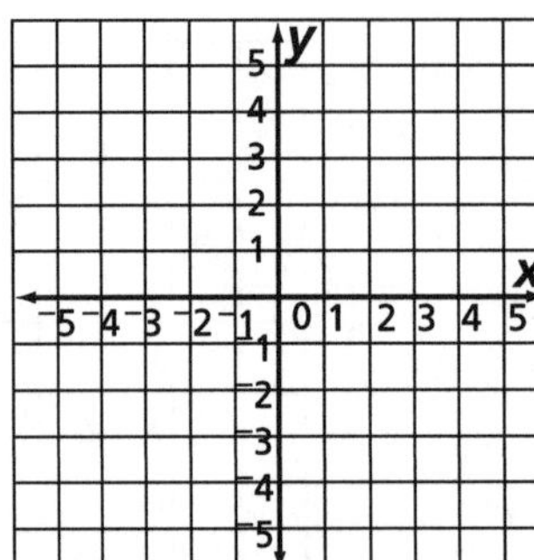

Work Space.

Name ______________________

Problem Solving Application: Using a Graph

STANDARD

The graph at the right shows the relationship between the number of chirps made by a cricket in one minute and the Fahrenheit temperature. This is the graph of a **linear equation**. This graph is a straight line.

In this lesson you will use graphs of linear equations to solve problems.

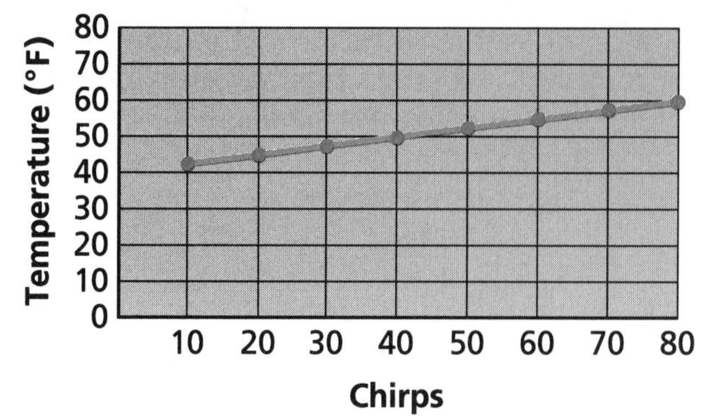

Tips to Remember:

1. Understand 2. Decide 3. Solve 4. Look back

- **Try to remember a real-life situation like the one described in the problem. What do you remember that might help you find a solution?**
- **Compare labels on the graph with the words and numbers in the problem. Find the facts you need from the graph.**
- **Predict the answer. Then solve the problem. Compare your answer with the prediction.**

Use the graph above to solve.

1. If a cricket chirps **40** times in one minute, what is the temperature?

Think: On which axis is the number of chirps?

____

Answer ______________________

2. If the temperature is **60°F**, how many times will a cricket chirp in one minute?

Think: On which axis is the temperature?

____

Answer ______________________

3. If a cricket chirps **50** times in one minute, what is the temperature?

Think: How much does the temperature increase when the chirps increase by **10**?

____

Answer ______________________

4. If the temperature is **100°**, how many times will a cricket chirp in one minute?

Think: What pattern do you see as the chirps increase by **20**?

____

Answer ______________________

STANDARD

Use the graph below to solve.

The graph at the right shows the number of calories in a certain number of crackers.

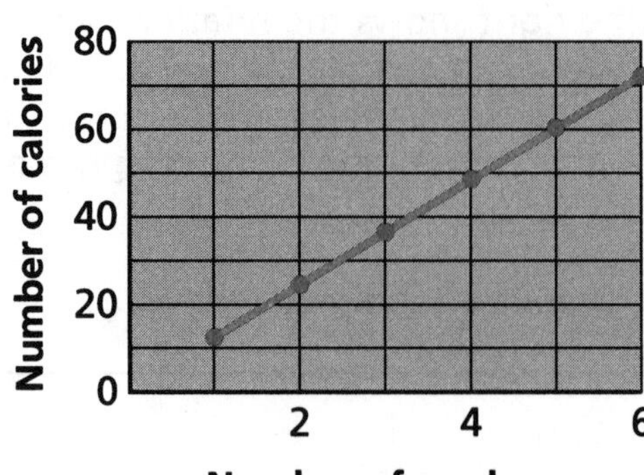

5. The suggested serving size for this cracker is **5** crackers. How many calories are in a suggested serving?

____

6. The number of crackers Suzy ate had a total of **36** calories. How many crackers did Suzy eat?

____

7. How many calories are in **1** cracker?

____

8. Rachel only wants to add **48** calories to her diet. How many crackers can she eat?

____

9. One week, George had **1** serving of crackers each day. How many calories did he get from these crackers?

____

10. Jody scooped **12** crackers from the box. How many calories were in them?

____

11. How many calories are in $2\frac{1}{2}$ crackers?

____

12. Predict the number of calories that would be in **15** crackers.

____

Extend Your Thinking

13. Look back at problem **5**. How can you check that the graph shows **12** calories for one cracker?

____

____

14. Look back at problem **6**. Explain the method you used to solve the problem.

____

____

15. Look back at problem **7**. Explain the method you used to solve the problem.

____

____

16. Look back at problem **8**. Explain the method you used to solve it.

____

____

Name ______________________________

Rational Numbers

STANDARD

On this number line, points ***A*** and ***B*** are between the whole numbers.

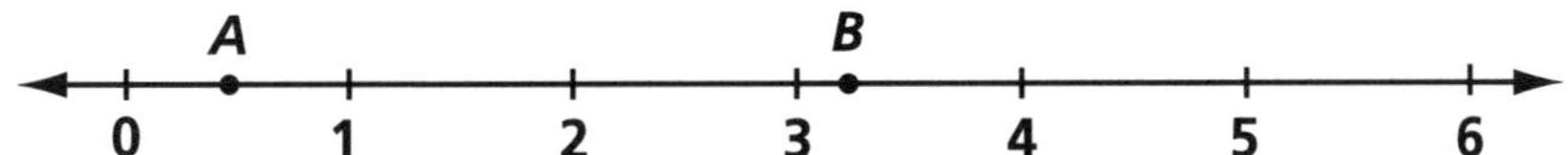

If point ***A*** is halfway between **0** and **1**, then point ***A*** represents the fraction $\frac{1}{2}$. The number $\frac{1}{2}$ is not a whole number, but belongs to a set of numbers called the **rational numbers.** Point ***B*** is one-fourth of the distance from **3** to **4**. The rational number represented by point ***B*** is $3\frac{1}{4}$.

> A rational number is any number that can be expressed in the form $\frac{a}{b}$, where ***a*** and ***b*** are integers and ***b*** is not **0.**

The set of rational numbers includes the following:

The set of positive and negative fractions such as $\frac{7}{12}$ and $-\frac{2}{3}$

The set of mixed numbers such as $6\frac{3}{4}$ and $^-1\frac{1}{2}$, because $6\frac{3}{4} = \frac{27}{4}$ and $1\frac{1}{2} = \frac{3}{2}$

The set of percents such as $12\frac{1}{2}\%$, because $12\frac{1}{2}\% = \frac{25}{200}$ or $\frac{1}{8}$

The set of decimals such as **0.13**, because $0.13 = \frac{13}{100}$

The set of whole numbers and integers such as **5** and $^-7$, because $5 = \frac{5}{1}$ and $^-7 = -\frac{7}{1}$

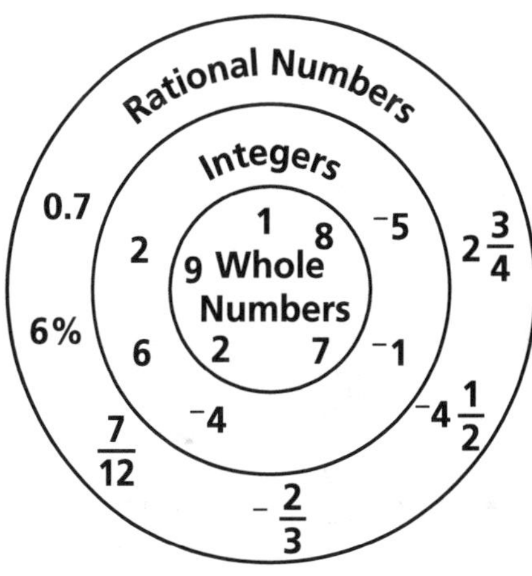

Write in the form $\frac{a}{b}$.

1. 0.31 ______ $1\frac{1}{2}$ ______ 76% ______ 2.5 ______ $^-3\frac{1}{4}$ ______

2. $^-0.79$ ______ $3\frac{1}{2}$ ______ 20% ______ 4.7 ______ 50% ______

Write the rational numbers on the number line. Then write >, <, or =.

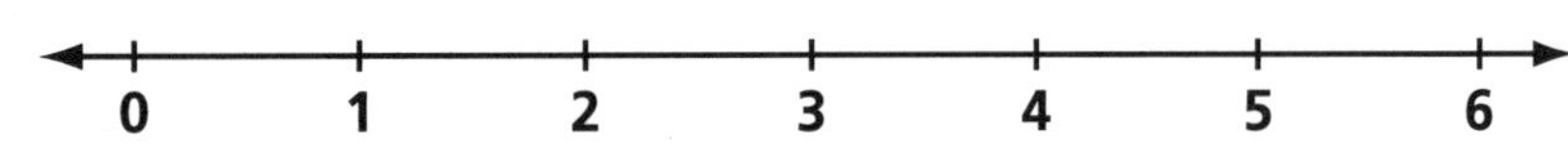

3. 90% ______ $\frac{3}{4}$ $2\frac{1}{2}$ ______ 2.25 3.5 ______ $3\frac{1}{2}$ $1\frac{2}{5}$ ______ 1.4

4. 60% ______ $\frac{1}{2}$ $1\frac{1}{3}$ ______ 1.8 4.75 ______ 450% 2.3 ______ $2\frac{3}{100}$

STANDARD

Which subset of rational numbers would you use in the given situation?

5. To tell the amount of money in your bank account. ______

6. To tell the amount of pepper in a recipe. ______

7. To tell your shoe size. ______

8. To tell a temperature below 0. ______

Write true or false.

9. Every rational number is an integer. ______

10. Every integer is a rational number. ______

11. Every whole number is a rational number. ______

12. All terminating decimals are rational numbers. ______

13. Mixed numbers such as $^{-}5\frac{1}{4}$ are not rational numbers. ______

14. A rational number cannot be a whole number. ______

15. Zero is not a rational number. ______

16. $\frac{\frac{1}{2}}{\frac{1}{8}}$ is a rational number. ______

17. The square root of 16 is a rational number. ______

18. Every fraction is a rational number. ______

Problem Solving Reasoning

Solve.

19. Can you write all the possible fractions equivalent to $\frac{1}{2}$?

Explain. ______

20. What is the rational number $\frac{1}{3}$ of the distance from **2** to **4**? ______

Test Prep ★ Mixed Review

21 Kishor is playing a card game. His scores for the last three hands were 55, $^{-}25$ and $^{-}60$. What was his average score for the three hands?

A $46\frac{2}{3}$

B 10

C $^{-}10$

D $^{-}46\frac{2}{3}$

22 Which ordered pairs are solutions of the equation $y = x - 5$?

F (25, 0), (24, 1), and (23, 2)

G (5, 0), (4, 1), and (3, 2)

H (5, 10), (4, 9), and (3, 8)

J ($^{-}5$, $^{-}10$), ($^{-}4$, $^{-}9$), and ($^{-}3$, $^{-}8$)

Name ______________________________

Rational Numbers and Their Properties

STANDARD

The properties of whole numbers and integers are also true for rational numbers.

Property	Examples	Using Variables
Commutative Property of Addition	$\frac{1}{2} + \frac{3}{4} = \frac{3}{4} + \frac{1}{2}$	$\frac{a}{b} + \frac{c}{d} = \frac{c}{d} + \frac{a}{b}$
Commutative Property of Multiplication	$\frac{2}{3} \times \frac{5}{8} = \frac{5}{8} \times \frac{2}{3}$	$\frac{a}{b} \times \frac{c}{d} = \frac{c}{d} \times \frac{a}{b}$
Associative Property of Addition	$\left(\frac{1}{3} + \frac{4}{5}\right) + \frac{1}{5} = \frac{1}{3} + \left(\frac{4}{5} + \frac{1}{5}\right)$	$\left(\frac{a}{b} + \frac{c}{d}\right) + \frac{e}{f} = \frac{a}{b} + \left(\frac{c}{d} + \frac{e}{f}\right)$
Associative Property of Multiplication	$\left(\frac{5}{8} \times \frac{1}{4}\right) \times \frac{1}{2} = \frac{5}{8} \times \left(\frac{1}{4} \times \frac{1}{2}\right)$	$\left(\frac{a}{b} \times \frac{c}{d}\right) \times \frac{e}{f} = \frac{a}{b} \times \left(\frac{c}{d} \times \frac{e}{f}\right)$
Identity Property of Addition	$2\frac{1}{2} + 0 = 2\frac{1}{2}$	$\frac{a}{b} + 0 = \frac{a}{b}$
Identity Property of Multiplication	$3\frac{3}{4} \times 1 = 3\frac{3}{4}$	$\frac{a}{b} \times 1 = \frac{a}{b}$
Distributive Property	$2\left(\frac{3}{4} + \frac{1}{2}\right) = 2 \times \frac{3}{4} + 2 \times \frac{1}{2}$	$a\left(\frac{b}{c} + \frac{d}{e}\right) = \frac{ab}{c} + \frac{ad}{e}$
Zero Property of Multiplication	$4\frac{5}{8} \times 0 = 0$	$\frac{a}{b} \times 0 = 0$

Integers and rational numbers have a property that whole numbers do not have. Every integer and every rational number has an **additive inverse.** The additive inverse is another name for the opposite of a number.

$^-6$ is the additive inverse of **6**, because **$^-6 + 6 = 0$.**

$\frac{4}{5}$ is the additive inverse of **$^-\frac{4}{5}$**, because **$\frac{4}{5} + \left(^-\frac{4}{5}\right) = 0$.**

Use the properties to write in the missing rational numbers.

1. $\left(\frac{1}{2} + \frac{4}{9}\right) +$ ______ $=$ ______ $+ \left(\right.$ ______ $\left. + \frac{3}{10}\right)$ $\qquad$ $^-\frac{4}{5} \times {^-\frac{2}{3}} =$ ______ $\times {^-\frac{4}{5}}$

2. $6\frac{7}{8} \times$ ______ $= 6\frac{7}{8}$ $\qquad$ $^-3\frac{3}{4} +$ ______ $= {^-3\frac{3}{4}}$ $\qquad$ $^-\frac{3}{2} \times$ ______ $= {^-\frac{3}{2}}$

Write the additive inverse.

3. 7 ______ $\qquad$ 15 ______ $\qquad$ $^-\frac{2}{3}$ ______ $\qquad$ $\frac{5}{4}$ ______ $\qquad$ $^-3\frac{1}{3}$ ______

4. 0 ______ $\qquad$ $^-\frac{4}{9}$ ______ $\qquad$ $\frac{17}{6}$ ______ $\qquad$ $5\frac{1}{7}$ ______ $\qquad$ $^-10\frac{2}{5}$ ______

STANDARD

The rational numbers have a property that neither the integers nor the whole numbers have. Every rational number, except **0**, has a **multiplicative inverse.** A multiplicative inverse is another name for a reciprocal.

$\frac{4}{3}$ and $\frac{3}{4}$ are multiplicative inverses, because $\frac{4}{3} \times \frac{3}{4} = 1$.

The rational numbers have another property that the integers and the whole numbers do not have. Between any two rational numbers there is another rational number. This is called the **density property.**

To find a number between any two rational numbers, you can find the arithmetic mean (average) of the two numbers.

Find a number between $\frac{1}{2}$ and $\frac{2}{3}$.

$$\frac{\frac{1}{2}+\frac{2}{3}}{2} = \frac{\frac{3}{6}+\frac{4}{6}}{2} = \frac{7}{6} \times \frac{1}{2} = \frac{7}{12}$$

So, $\frac{1}{2} < \frac{7}{12} < \frac{2}{3}$

Write the multiplicative inverse.

5. $\frac{5}{6}$ ______ $\frac{9}{7}$ ______ $-\frac{3}{5}$ ______ $1\frac{1}{2}$ ______ $-2\frac{1}{3}$ ______

Write the arithmetic mean of the pair of numbers.

6. $\frac{1}{4}, \frac{3}{4}$ ______ $\frac{5}{6}, \frac{1}{2}$ ______ $\frac{1}{3}, \frac{1}{4}$ ______ $4\frac{1}{2}, 16\frac{1}{2}$ ______

Find two rational numbers between the pair of numbers.

7. $\frac{2}{3}, \frac{5}{6}$ ______ $\frac{7}{2}, \frac{8}{3}$ ______ $\frac{8}{9}, \frac{1}{3}$ ______ $5\frac{1}{6}, 5\frac{7}{18}$ ______

Problem Solving Reasoning Solve.

8. Amy's house is **7.8** km from school. On the way to school she meets Terry **2.6** km from her house. How much farther do they need to go to get to school?

______

9. The length of a rectangle is **48.8** cm. It is **1.6** times longer than its width. What is the width of the rectangle?

______

Test Prep ★ Mixed Review

10 To solve the equation $\frac{3k}{4} = 9$, which operation can be used on each side of the equation?

A Multiply by 9

B Divide by 9

C Multiply by $\frac{3}{4}$

D Multiply by $\frac{4}{3}$

11 What is the solution of the equation $^-3x = 12$?

F 36

G 4

H $^-4$

J $^-36$

Name ____________________

Rational Numbers and Expressions

STANDARD

You have learned that expressions with variables can be evaluated. You replace the variables with their values. Then perform the operations.

Evaluate the expression $m + w + f$ when $m = 2\frac{1}{2}$, $w = 4\frac{1}{3}$, and $f = 5\frac{1}{4}$.

$$m + w + f$$

$$2\frac{1}{2} + 4\frac{1}{3} + 5\frac{1}{4}$$

$$2\frac{6}{12} + 4\frac{4}{12} + 5\frac{3}{12}$$

$$11\frac{13}{12}, \text{ or } 12\frac{1}{12}$$

Evaluate each expression when $x = 3\frac{1}{4}$, $y = 5\frac{1}{2}$, and $z = 1\frac{3}{8}$.

1. $x + y + z$ ______ $x + 2y - z$ ______ $2x + y + 2z$ ______

2. $x + y - z$ ______ $4x + 2y - 8z$ ______ $3x - y - z$ ______

Evaluate each expression when $a = {}^{-}\frac{1}{2}$, $b = 2\frac{1}{2}$, $c = \frac{2}{3}$.

3. $a + b + c$ ______ $2a - b - c$ ______ $a - ab - 2c$ ______

4. $\frac{b}{a} + c$ ______ $a^2 + c$ ______ $b^2 - c^2$ ______

Evaluate the expression $\frac{x + y + z}{3}$ for the given values.

5. $x = \frac{1}{3}, y = \frac{2}{3}, z = 1\frac{1}{4}$ ______ $x = {}^{-}0.25, y = 0.75, z = 0.25$ ______

6. $x = {}^{-}\frac{4}{5}, y = \frac{3}{2}, z = {}^{-}2\frac{1}{2}$ ______ $x = 98, y = 84, z = 82$ ______

STANDARD

Which is greater?

7. x^2 when $x = {}^-\frac{1}{2}$ or $x = \frac{1}{3}$? ______

8. $2x^2$ when $x = {}^-\frac{1}{3}$ or $x = {}^-3$? ______

9. $\frac{x^3}{2}$ when $x = {}^-2$ or $x = 2$? ______

10. $\frac{x^3}{3}$ when $x = {}^-1$ or $x = 1$? ______

Problem Solving Reasoning

Solve.

11. Find the perimeter of this rectangle by evaluating the expression $2(w + l)$ for $w = 2\frac{1}{2}$ and $l = 4\frac{1}{3}$. ______

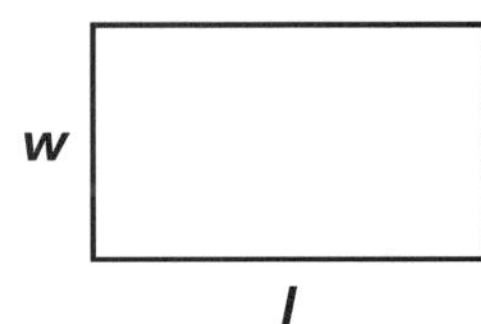

12. Find the perimeter of this equilateral triangle by evaluating the expression $3s$ for $s = 4\frac{1}{6}$. ______

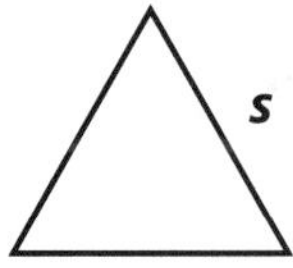

13. The expression to find the area of a rectangle is $l \times w$. How do the areas of two rectangles compare when $l = 3\frac{1}{3}$, $w = 2\frac{1}{2}$ for rectangle A, and when $l = 6\frac{2}{3}$ and $w = 1\frac{1}{4}$ for rectangle B?

______

14. The perimeter of a rectangle is **20** in. What is the area of the rectangle if all its sides are congruent?

______

Quick Check

Write the rational number as a ratio of two integers.

15. ${}^-2\frac{3}{4}$ ______ **16.** ${}^-1.72$ ______ **17.** 0 ______

Write a rational number that is between the two rational numbers.

18. 1.002 and 1.003 ______

19. ${}^-1\frac{7}{8}$ and ${}^-1\frac{3}{4}$ ______

20. $9\frac{1}{3}$ and 9.33 ______

Evaluate the expression for $x = \frac{2}{3}$ and $y = {}^-1\frac{1}{2}$.

21. ${}^-3x + 2y$ ______ **22.** $y^2 - 2x$ ______ **23.** $3x^2 - 4y$ ______

Work Space.

Name ___________________________

Problem Solving Strategy: Find a Pattern

STANDARD

A pattern does not always involve numbers or a series of figures.

In this lesson, you will find patterns on coordinate graphs.

Problem

When you look in the mirror, you see your reflection or mirror image. What are the coordinates of the reflection of △*ABC* over the *y*-axis?

1 Understand

As you reread, ask yourself questions.

- What facts do you know?

  The coordinates of point ***A*** are ______

  The coordinates of point ***B*** are ______

  The coordinates of point ***C*** are ______

- What do you need to find?

  ____

  ____

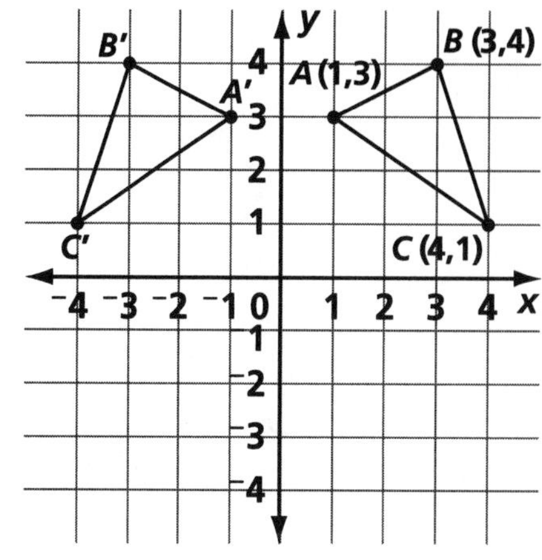

2 Decide

Choose a method for solving.

- Try the strategy Find a Pattern.

POINT	REFLECTION
A **(1, 3)**	***A′***
B **(3, 4)**	***B′***
C **(4, 1)**	***C′***

3 Solve

Fill in the coordinates of the reflection image, △*A′B′C′*, in the table.

- What is the relationship between the *x*-coordinate of each of the points in △***ABC*** and △***A′B′C′***?

  ____

- What is the relationship between the *y*-coordinate of each of the points in △***ABC*** and △***A′B′C′***?

  ____

4 Look back

State a rule to find the reflection of a figure over the *y*-axis.

____

STANDARD

Solve. Use the Find a Pattern strategy or any other strategy you have learned.
Use the graph for problems 1 and 2.

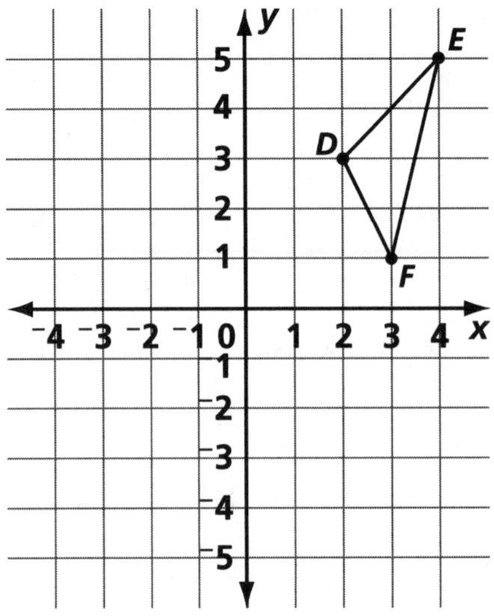

1. What are the coordinates of the reflection of △***DEF*** over the *y*-axis? Draw the image.

____

2. What are the coordinates of the reflection of △***DEF*** over the *x*-axis? Draw the image.

____

3. A palindrome is a number or word that reads the same in both directions. The number **2,002** is a palindrome. What is the next higher number that is a palindrome?

____

4. Draw the next figure in this sequence.

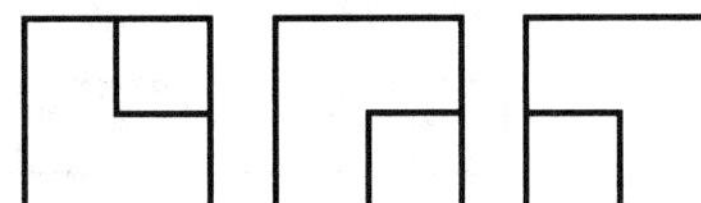

5. In a survey at Grant Middle School, $\frac{3}{5}$ of the students said they play a sport. If **120** students were surveyed, how many of them play a sport?

____

6. A taxi ride costs **\$2** for the first mile and **\$.75** for each additional $\frac{1}{2}$ mile. How much will it cost to go **5** miles?

____

7. Find the pattern and complete the table.

Point	Reflection
(⁻3, 2)	(⁻3, ⁻2)
(1, ⁻4)	(1, 4)
(0, 3)	(0, ⁻3)
(⁻2, ⁻1)	

8. Find the pattern and complete the table.

Point	Reflection
(2, ⁻5)	(⁻2, 5)
(⁻4, 2)	(4, ⁻2)
(⁻3, ⁻1)	(3, 1)
(1, 5)	

Name ____________________

Unit 11 Review

Complete a table of values and write ordered pairs for the given equation. Then graph the equation.

1. $y = x + 4$

x	y	Ordered Pairs
		(,)
		(,)
		(,)
		(,)
		(,)

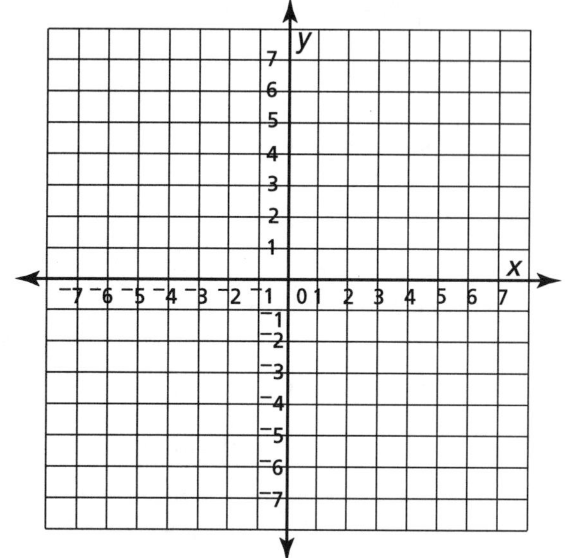

Write the letter that names each number on the number line.

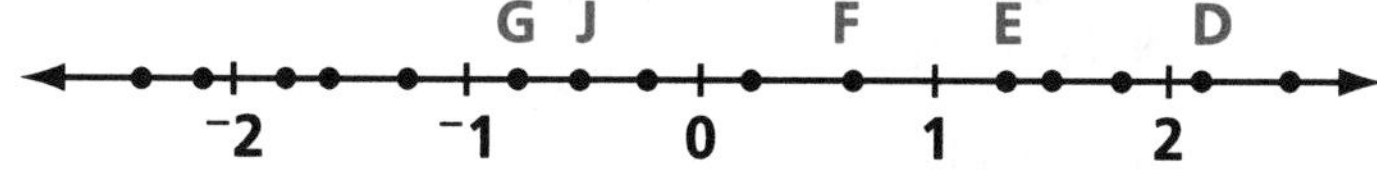

2. 1.3 ______ 3. $2\frac{1}{8}$ ______ 4. $\frac{2}{3}$ ______ 5. $-\frac{3}{4}$ ______ 6. ⁻0.5 ______

Order each group of numbers from least to greatest.

7. $\frac{1}{3}, \frac{4}{5}$, 0.66, 0.25 ____________

8. 2.20, $3\frac{1}{2}$, 2.50, $2\frac{1}{4}$ ____________

Evaluate each expression for $x = \frac{3}{4}$, $y = \frac{1}{2}$, and $z = 4$.

9. $2x + 4y \cdot \frac{1}{8}z$ ______

10. $3x \div y$ ______

Follow these steps to create a symmetrical design.

11.
- Use the ***x***-axis as a line of symmetry and graph the reflection of point ***R*** and the reflection of point ***T***. Label the first point ***B*** and the second point ***A***.
- Use the ***y***-axis as a line of symmetry and graph the reflection of point ***R*** and the reflection of point ***T***, Label these points ***C*** and ***D***.
- Use the ***x***-axis as a line of symmetry and graph the reflection of point ***C*** and the reflection of point ***D***. Label these points ***F*** and ***G***.
- Connect points ***D, T, A, G,***and ***C, R, B, F***.

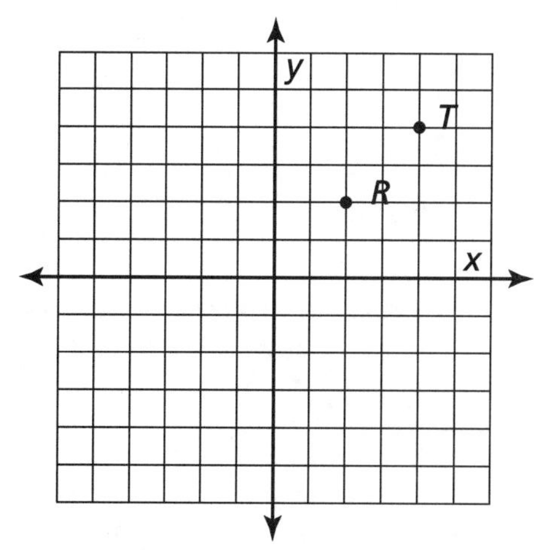

Name ________________________________

Cumulative Review
★ Test Prep

1 **What is the surface area of the triangular prism?**

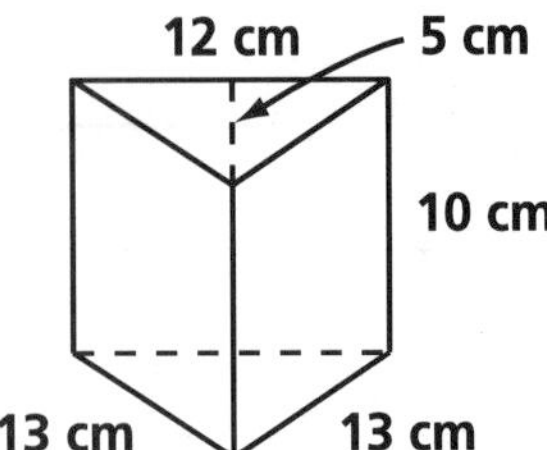

A 300 cm^2

B 306 cm^2

C 336 cm^2

D 440 cm^2

2 **Greg read the first 110 pages of a book in $2\frac{1}{5}$ hours. At this rate, how long will it take him to read all 325 pages?**

F 5 hours

G $5\frac{1}{2}$ hours

H 6 hours

J $6\frac{1}{2}$ hours

3 **A bakery makes a batch of 150 chocolate chip cookies. The table shows the number of chips that are in each cookie.**

Number of chips	Number of cookies
10 chips	20 cookies
11 chips	25 cookies
12 chips	25 cookies
13 chips	30 cookies
14 chips	30 cookies
15 chips	20 cookies

What is the probability that a cookie from this batch will have more than 12 chips?

A $\frac{1}{6}$

B $\frac{3}{10}$

C $\frac{7}{15}$

D $\frac{8}{15}$

4 **Which rational number is indicated by the arrow?**

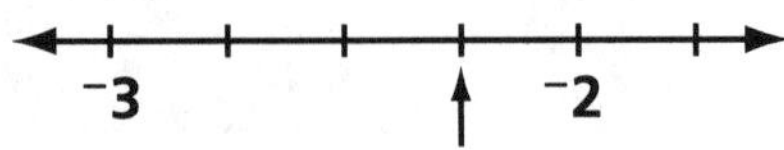

F $^-3\frac{3}{4}$

G $^-2\frac{3}{4}$

H $^-2\frac{1}{4}$

J $^-1\frac{3}{4}$

5 **Four companies sell their stocks in the same market. The table shows the amount by which the 4 stocks gained (positive) or lost (negative) value during one day.**

Company Name	Gain (+) or Loss (−)
ABC Inc.	$2\frac{3}{8}$
FGH Ltd.	$^-2\frac{1}{8}$
LMN Co.	$^-2$
TUV Assoc.	$^-2\frac{1}{2}$

Which answer choice shows the companies listed from the greatest loss to greatest gain?

A TUV, FGH, LMN, ABC

B LMN, FGH, TUV, ABC

C ABC, LMN, FGH, TUV

D ABC, TUV, FGH, LMN

6 **What is the value of the expression $3 - y$ when $y = {}^-4.5$?**

F 7.5

G 1.5

H $^-1.5$

J $^-7.5$

Tables of Measures

Metric System

Prefixes

kilo (k)	=	1,000		
hecto (h)	=	100		
deka (da)	=	10		
deci (d)	=	0.1	=	$\frac{1}{10}$
centi (c)	=	0.01	=	$\frac{1}{100}$
milli (m)	=	0.001	=	$\frac{1}{1,000}$

Length

1 kilometer (km)	=	1,000 meters (m)
1 hectometer (hm)	=	100 meters
1 dekameter (dam)	=	10 meters
1 decimeter (dm)	=	0.1 meter
1 centimeter (cm)	=	0.01 meter
1 millimeter (mm)	=	0.001 meter

Capacity

1 kiloliter (kL)	=	1,000 liters (L)
1 hectoliter (hL)	=	100 liters
1 dekaliter (daL)	=	10 liters
1 deciliter (dL)	=	0.1 liter
1 centiliter (cL)	=	0.01 liter
1 milliliter (mL)	=	0.001 liter

Mass

1 kilogram (kg)	=	1,000 grams (g)
1 hectogram (hg)	=	100 grams
1 dekagram (dag)	=	10 grams
1 decigram (dg)	=	0.1 gram
1 centigram (cg)	=	0.01 gram
1 milligram (mg)	=	0.001 gram

Area and Volume

1 square cm (cm^2)	=	100 square mm (mm^2)
1 square km (km^2)	=	10,000 square m (m^2)
1 cubic cm (cm^3)	=	1,000 cubic mm (mm^3)
1 cubic m (m^3)	=	1,000,000 cubic cm

Customary System

Length

1 foot (ft)	=	12 inches (in.)
1 yard (yd)	=	3 feet
1 yard	=	36 inches
1 mile (mi)	=	5,280 feet

Capacity

1 cup (c)	=	8 fluid ounces (fl oz)
1 pint (pt)	=	2 cups
1 pint	=	16 fluid ounces
1 quart (qt)	=	2 pints
1 gallon (gal)	=	4 quarts

Weight

1 pound (lb)	=	16 ounces (oz)
1 ton (T)	=	2,000 pounds

Area and Volume

1 square foot (ft^2)	=	144 square inches ($in.^2$)
1 square yard (yd^2)	=	9 square feet
1 acre (A)	=	4,840 square yards
1 square mile (mi^2)	=	640 acres
1 cubic foot (ft^3)	=	1,728 cubic inches ($in.^3$)
1 cubic yd (yd^3)	=	27 cubic feet

Other Measures

Time

1 minute (min)	=	60 seconds (s)
1 hour (h)	=	60 minutes
1 day (d)	=	24 hours
1 week (wk)	=	7 days
1 month (mo)	≈	4 weeks
1 year (yr)	=	12 months
1 year	=	52 weeks
1 year	=	365 days
1 leap year	=	366 days
1 decade	=	10 years
1 century	=	100 years

Counting

1 dozen (doz)	=	12 things
1 score	=	20 things
1 gross (gro)	=	12 dozen
1 gross	=	144 things

Geometric Formulas

Rectangle

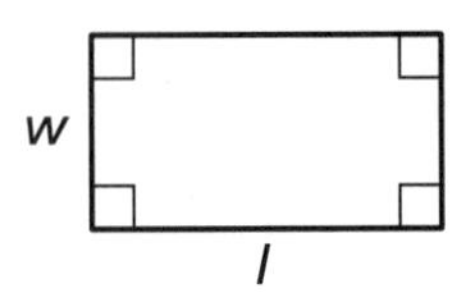

Perimeter:
$P = 2(l + w)$

Area:
$A = lw$

Square

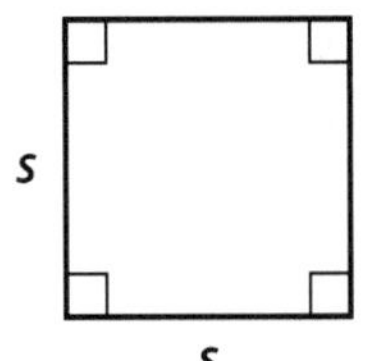

Perimeter:
$P = 4s$

Area:
$A = s^2$

Parallelogram

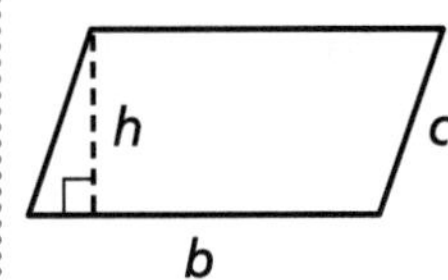

Perimeter:
$P = 2(b + c)$

Area:
$A = bh$

Triangle

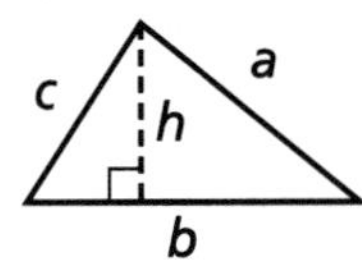

Perimeter:
$P = a + b + c$

Area:
$A = \frac{1}{2}bh$

Circle

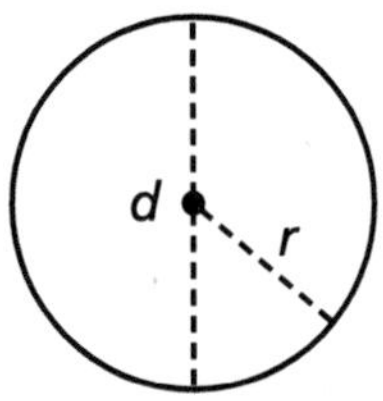

Circumference:
$C = \pi d$ or
$C = 2\pi r$

Area:
$A = \pi r^2$

Cube

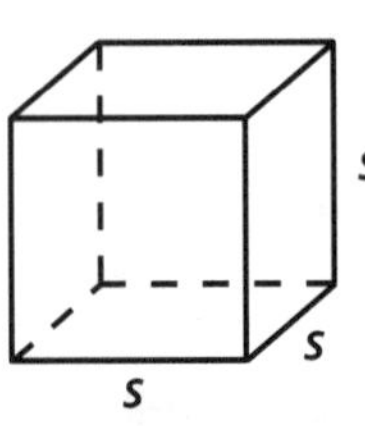

Surface Area:
$SA = 6s^2$

Volume:
$V = s^3$

Rectangular Prism

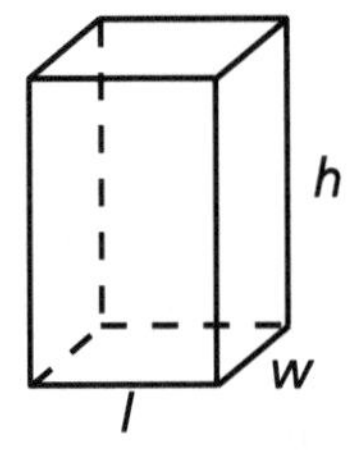

Surface Area:
$SA = 2(lw + wh + lh)$

Volume:
$V = lwh$

Cylinder

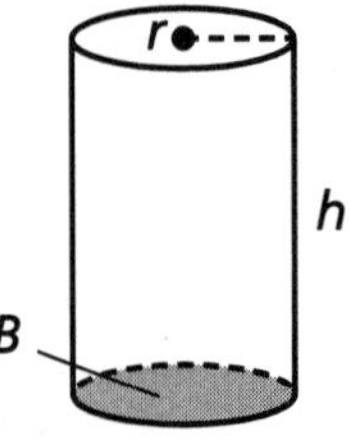

Volume:
$V = \pi r^2 h$
or $V = Bh$

Triangular Prism

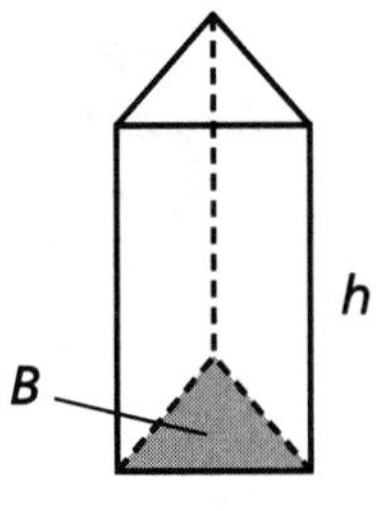

Volume:
$V = Bh$

Euler's Formula

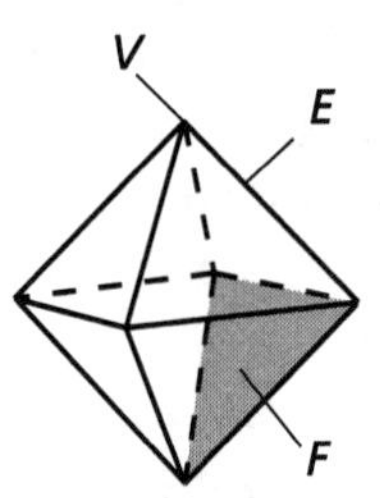

$V + F - E = 2$
V = number of vertices
E = number of edges
F = number of faces

Symbols

Symbol	Meaning
$=$	is equal to
$\neq$	is not equal to
$<$	is less than
$>$	is greater than
$\approx$	is approximately equal to
n, x	variables
$0.\overline{37}$	0.37373737 . . . (repeating decimal)
$a:b$	the ratio of *a* to *b*
%	percent
°	degree
$\angle A$	angle *A*
$\overline{AB}$	line segment *AB*
$\overrightarrow{AB}$	ray *AB*
$\overleftrightarrow{AB}$	line *AB*
$\triangle$	triangle
$\parallel$	is parallel to
$\perp$	is perpendicular to
$\sim$	is similar to
$\cong$	is congruent to
5^4	5 to the fourth power $(5 \cdot 5 \cdot 5 \cdot 5)$
π	pi
$^{+}5$	positive 5
$^{-}5$	negative 5
$P(A)$	the probability of *A*

Equivalent Fractions and Percents

$50\% = \frac{1}{2}$

$33\frac{1}{3}\% = \frac{1}{3}$

$66\frac{2}{3}\% = \frac{2}{3}$

$25\% = \frac{1}{4}$

$75\% = \frac{3}{4}$

$20\% = \frac{1}{5}$

$40\% = \frac{2}{5}$

$60\% = \frac{3}{5}$

$80\% = \frac{4}{5}$

$16\frac{2}{3}\% = \frac{1}{6}$

$12\frac{1}{2}\% = \frac{1}{8}$

$10\% = \frac{1}{10}$

$30\% = \frac{3}{10}$

$70\% = \frac{7}{10}$

$90\% = \frac{9}{10}$

$5\% = \frac{1}{20}$

$4\% = \frac{1}{25}$

$2\frac{1}{2}\% = \frac{1}{40}$

$2\% = \frac{1}{50}$

Glossary

A

acute angle An angle whose measure is less than 90°

acute triangle A triangle whose largest angle is an acute angle

addend (see *addition*)

addition The arithmetic operation that combines two numbers

Example:
$$\begin{array}{r l} 23 & \leftarrow \text{addend} \\ +\ 13 & \leftarrow \text{addend} \\ \hline 36 & \leftarrow \text{sum} \end{array}$$

addition property of equality If two expressions are equal, then adding the same number to each forms two more equal expressions. *Example:* If $n - 7 = 10$, then $n - 7 + 7 = 10 + 7$

algebraic expression An expression that contains variables such as x or n

altitude A segment of a triangle or parallelogram that is perpendicular to the base. In a triangle one endpoint is the vertex opposite the base.

angle A geometric figure formed by two rays with a common end point. The angle shown can be named either $\angle ABC$ or $\angle B$.

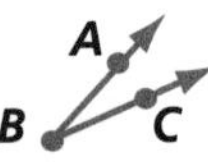

area A measure of the number of square units in a region.

associative property of addition Changing the grouping of addends does not change the sum. *Example:* $(37 + 95) + 5 = 37 + (95 + 5) = 137$

associative property of multiplication Changing the grouping of factors does not change the product.
Example:
$(25 \cdot 5) \cdot 2 = 27 \cdot (5 \cdot 2) = 270$

average A measure of central tendency. It is computed by adding all the items of data and dividing by the number of items.

B

bar graph A pictorial representation of data that uses lengths of bars to show the information

base (of a power) The number that is used as a factor when evaluating powers
Example: $3^4 = 3 \cdot 3 \cdot 3 \cdot 3$. The base is 3.

base (of a space figure) (see *cone, cylinder, prism, pyramid*)

bias A property of a sample that allows a characteristic to consistently be over- or under-represented

C

capacity The maximum amount of liquid that a container can hold

center (see *circle, sphere*)

central angle An angle whose vertex is the center of a circle

central tendency The most representative numbers of a set of data.

certain event An event that will always occur.
Example: If you toss a coin, it is certain that you will get either heads or tails.

chord A segment joining any two points on a circle

circle A plane figure composed of all of the points the same distance from a given point called the center

circle graph A pictorial representation of data that uses sections of a circle to show the information

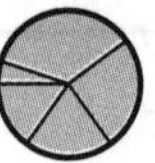

circumference The distance around a circle. It is about 3.14 times the diameter.

cluster Several items of data grouped into a small interval

common denominator A denominator common to two or more fractions. Any common multiple of the given denominators can be used to write equivalent fractions.
Example: Some common denominators of $\frac{1}{2}$ and $\frac{1}{3}$ are 6, 12, 18, 24, ...

common factor A number that is a factor of two or more whole numbers
Example: 1, 2, 3, and 6 are common factors of 12 and 18.

common multiple A number that is a multiple of two or more whole numbers
Example: Common multiples of 3 and 4 are 12, 24, 36, ...

commutative property of addition The order in which you add two numbers does not change the sum.
Example: $3 + 4 = 4 + 3 = 7$

commutative property of multiplication The order in which you multiply two numbers does not change the product.
Example: $3 \cdot 5 = 5 \cdot 3 = 15$

compatible numbers Numbers used to make estimates that are easy to work with mentally and are close to the given numbers

complementary angles Two angles whose measures have a sum of 90°

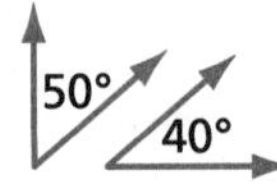

complementary events Two independent events whose probabilities total 1
Example: Rolling a number greater than 2 on a number cube and rolling a number less than or equal to 2.

composite number A number with three or more factors
Example: 9 is composite, because its factors are 1, 3, and 9.

compound event The combination of two or more single events
Example: Rolling a "4" on one number cube and then rolling a "6" on another.

cone A space figure with one flat, circular surface and one curved surface

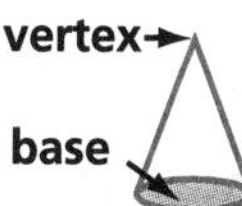

congruent figures Figures that have exactly the same size and shape. In congruent polygons, corresponding angles are congruent and corresponding sides are congruent.

coordinate Each number of an ordered pair
Example: (4, 6) has a first coordinate of 4 and a second coordinate of 6.

coordinate plane A grid with number lines used to locate points in a plane. It is divided into 4 quadrants by its axes.

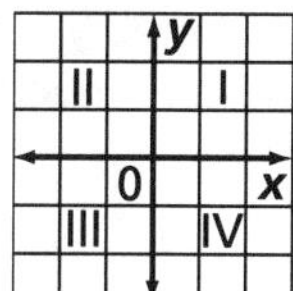

counting principle The number of possible outcomes of a compound event is equal to the product of the number of possible outcomes of the individual events

cube A rectangular prism whose faces are all congruent squares

customary system of measurement The system of measurement currently used in the United States

cylinder A space figure with two congruent circular bases joined by a single curved surface

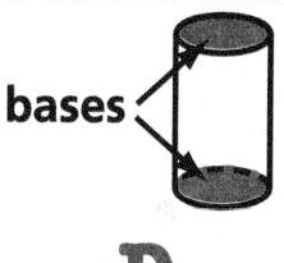

D

data Numerical information

decimal A number that uses place value to indicate parts of a whole. The decimal point separates the whole number digits from the digits representing parts of a whole.
Example: The decimal

3.67
decimal point

represents the number three and 67 hundredths.

decimal point (see *decimal*)

denominator The numeral below the fraction bar in a fraction. It tells how many parts are in the whole.

dependent events Two or more events such that the outcome of one influences the outcome of the others
Example: Suppose the numbers 1, 2, and 3 are each written on a slip of paper. Choose one number, and without putting it back, choose a second number.

diagonal A segment joining two vertices of a polygon that is not a side

Diagonals: $\overline{AC}$ $\overline{AD}$ $\overline{BD}$ $\overline{BE}$ $\overline{CE}$

A B C D E

diameter A chord of a circle that contains the center

difference (see *subtraction*)

digit Any of the symbols used to write numerals. In the base 10 system, they are 1, 2, 3, 4, 5, 6, 7, 8, 9, and 0.

distributive property The product of a number and the sum of two numbers is equal to the sum of the two products
Example:
$3 \cdot (2 + 7) = 3 \cdot 2 + 3 \cdot 7$

dividend (see *division*)

divisible A number is divisible by another number if it can be divided by that number with no remainder.
Example: 4, 16, and 640 are all divisible by 4.

division An operation that divides a set, region, or number into equal parts.
Example:
quotient → 10 R5 ← remainder
divisor → 6)65 ← dividend

division property of equality If two expressions are equal, then dividing each by the same nonzero number forms two new equal expressions.
Example: If $a = b$ and $n \neq 0$, then $a \div n = b \div n$

divisor (see *division*)

double-bar graph A bar graph that compares two sets of data by using two sets of bars

double-line graph A line graph that compares two sets of data by using one line for each set

E

edge (see *polyhedron*)

endpoint (see *ray, segment*)

equally likely Outcomes that have an equal chance of occurring.
Example: A spinner is divided into 6 congruent sections. Each section is an equally likely outcome of a spin.

equation A number sentence that says that two expressions have the same value.
Example: $3 + 7 = 10$

equilateral triangle A triangle with three congruent sides

equivalent fractions Two or more fractions that represent the same number.
Example: $\frac{1}{2} = \frac{2}{4} = \frac{3}{6} = \frac{4}{8}$

estimate To find an approximate solution mentally by using rounded numbers

evaluate To find the value of an expression

even number A whole number that is divisible by 2

event Any outcome or set of outcomes of an experiment

expanded form A number written as the sum of the value of its digits
Example:
The expanded form of 316 is

300 + 10 + 6

experimental probability An estimate of the probability of an event based on the results of an experiment

exponent A number that tells how many times a base is to be used as a factor.
Example: $3^4 = 3 \cdot 3 \cdot 3 \cdot 3$.
The exponent is 4.

exponential form A number expressed as a power
Example: Exponential forms of 64 are 2^6 and 8^2.

expression A combination of numbers, symbols of operation, grouping symbols, or variables that represents a mathematical quantity
Examples: $(7 + 3) \div 5$ or $6 \cdot n$

face (see *polyhedron*)

factor (see *multiplication*)

factor tree A diagram used to help factor a composite number into its prime factors

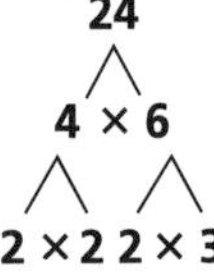

fraction A number such as $\frac{1}{2}$ or $\frac{3}{4}$ that is used to express a part of a region or set or a rational number

gap A significant interval that contains no data.

graph A pictorial representation of a data set or equation

greatest common factor The greatest number that is a factor of each of two or more numbers
Example: The greatest common factor of 24 and 30 is 6.

heptagon A polygon that has 7 sides

Regular heptagon **Irregular heptagon**

hexagon A polygon that has 6 sides

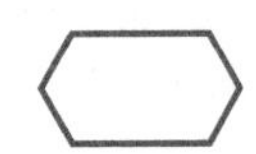

Regular hexagon **Irregular hexagon**

histogram A type of bar graph. The categories are consecutive intervals along a number line. The intervals are all the same size with no gaps between them.

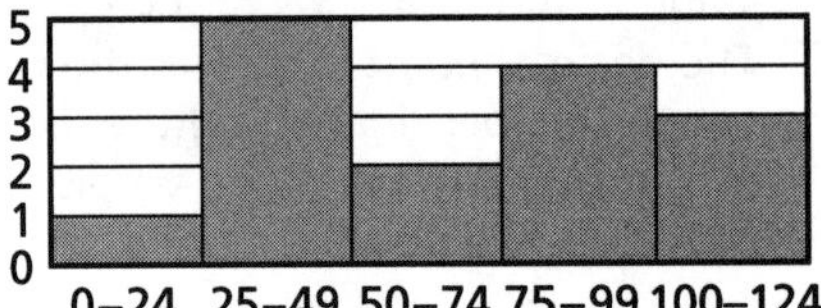

I

identity property of addition The sum of any number and zero is the number itself.
Examples: $7 + 0 = 7$ and $n + 0 = n$

identity property of multiplication The product of any number and 1 is the number itself.
Examples: $10 \cdot 1 = 10$ and $n \cdot 1 = n$

impossible event An event that cannot occur
Example: If you roll a 1–6 number cube, it is impossible to get a 7.

independent events Two or more events whose outcomes do not affect each other.
Example: Two tosses of a coin when you are recording "heads" or "tails"

inequality A number sentence that states that two expressions are not equal.
Examples:
$3 + 6 < 10$ read "Three plus six is less than 10."
$5 + 7 > 10$ read "Five plus seven is greater than 10."

integer The set of numbers containing all the whole numbers and their opposites

$\ldots {}^{-}3, {}^{-}2, {}^{-}1, 0, 1, 2, 3, \ldots$
negative integers, zero, positive integers

inverse operation An operation that undoes the results of another operation
Examples:
$(n + 5) - 5 = n$ The inverse of adding 5 is subtracting 5.
$(n \cdot 3) \div 3 = n$ The inverse of multiplying by 3 is dividing by 3.

isosceles triangle A triangle with at least two congruent sides

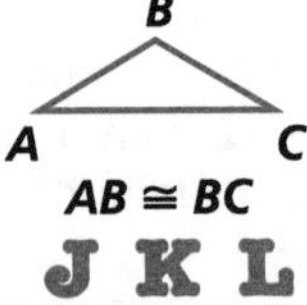

J K L

least common denominator The least number that is a common denominator of two or more fractions. It is the least common multiple of the denominators of each of the fractions.
Example: The least common denominator of $\frac{1}{2}$ and $\frac{2}{3}$ is 6.

least common multiple The least number that is a common multiple of two or more numbers
Example: 12 is the least common multiple of 3 and 4.

line A set of points that extends without end in two opposite directions

A B AB

line graph A pictorial representation of data that shows changes over time using line segments

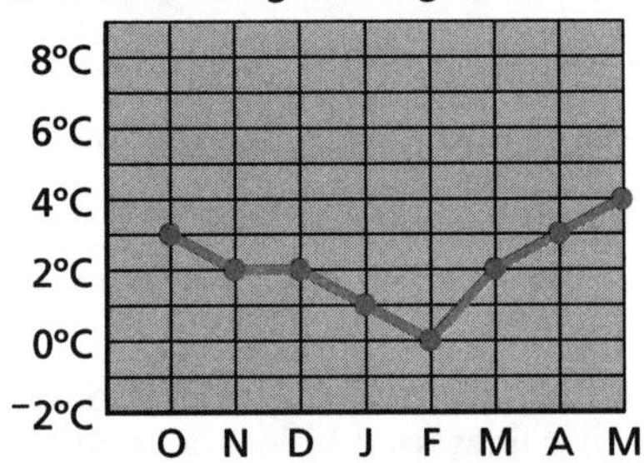

line plot A pictorial representation of a small set of data. Each data item is represented with an "x" placed above a number line.

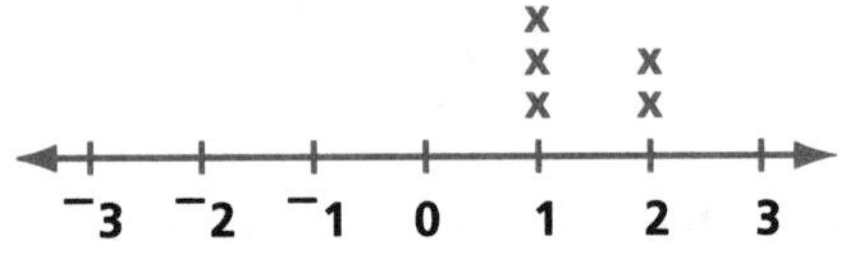

M

mean The average of a set of data. It is found by adding each item of data and dividing by the number of items.
Example: 4 is the mean of 2, 4, 5, 5.

median The middle point of the data when they are arranged from least to greatest. It is either the middle number or the mean of the two middle numbers.
Example: 4.5 is the median of 2, 4, 5, 5.

metric system of measurement An international system of measurement that uses the meter, liter, gram, and degrees Celsius as the basic units of measure

mixed decimal A decimal, such as $0.83\frac{1}{3}$, that ends with a fraction

mixed number A number, such as $2\frac{2}{3}$, that is made up of a fraction less than one and a whole number

mode The number (or numbers) that occurs most often in a set of data. If no number occurs most often, the data set has no mode.
Example: 5 is the mode of 2, 4, 5, 5.

multiple of a number The product of the number and any whole number.
Example: The multiples of 4 are 0, 4, 8, 12, 16, . . .

multiplication An operation that expresses repeated addition of the same number

Example:
$$\begin{array}{r l} 12 & \leftarrow \text{factor} \\ \times\, 4 & \leftarrow \text{factor} \\ \hline 48 & \leftarrow \text{product} \end{array}$$

multiplication property of equality If two expressions are equal, then multiplying each by the same number forms two new equal expressions.
Example: If $a = b$, then $a \cdot n = b \cdot n$.

negative integer (see *integer*)

number line A line that has its points labeled with numbers (called coordinates) such as whole numbers, integers, fractions, and so on

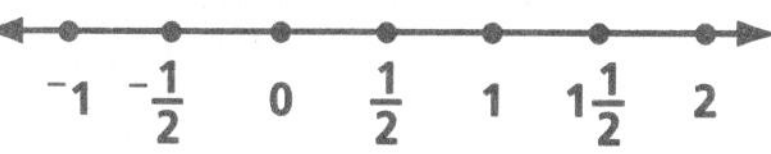

numeral A name or symbol for a number

numerator The number over the bar in a fraction. It tells how many parts of the whole are under discussion.

numeric expression An expression that does not contain variables
Example: $(7 + 4) \cdot 6$

obtuse angle An angle whose measure is greater than 90° and less than 180°

obtuse triangle A triangle whose largest angle is obtuse

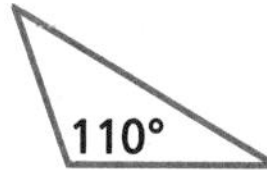

octagon A polygon that has 8 sides

Regular octagon Irregular octagon

odd number A whole number that is not divisible by 2

opposites Two numbers whose sum is 0; also called additive inverses
Examples: 2 and ⁻2 are opposites; so are $-\frac{2}{3}$ and $\frac{2}{3}$.

order of operations The rules that define the order in which the operations in an expression are to be evaluated. They are:

1 Work within parentheses.
2 Evaluate powers.
3 Multiply and divide from left to right.
4 Add and subtract from left to right.

ordered pair A pair of numbers used to locate a point in a coordinate plane. The first number is the horizontal distance from the origin; the second number is the vertical distance.

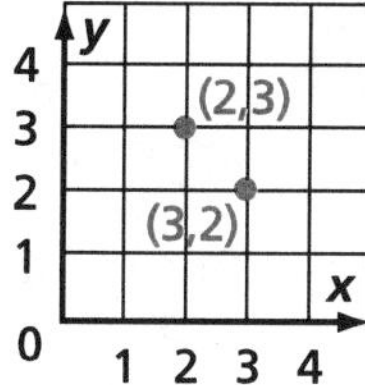

origin The point on a coordinate grid at which the two axes meet. Its coordinates are (0, 0).

outcome A result in a probability experiment

outlier An item of data that is significantly greater or less than all the other items of data

parallel lines Two lines in the same plane that do not intersect

parallelogram A quadrilateral with two pairs of parallel and congruent sides

pentagon A polygon with 5 sides

Regular pentagon Irregular pentagon

percent A ratio that compares a number to 100
Example: 39% is $\frac{39}{100}$.

percentage The result obtained by multiplying a quantity by a percent

perimeter The distance around a polygon. It is found by adding the lengths of all the sides.

period A group of three digits separated by a comma in a number written in standard form
Example: In the number 306,789, 245, the millions period is 306, the thousands period is 789, and 245 is the ones period.

perpendicular lines Two lines that intersect to form right angles

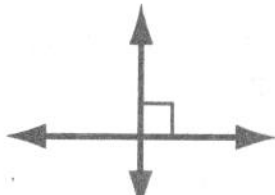

pi The ratio of the circumference of any circle to its diameter. Its value is about 3.14 or $\frac{22}{7}$.

pictograph A pictorial representation of data that uses a single symbol to represent multiples of a quantity

Muffins Sold in Cafeteria	
raisin	
cranberry	
Key Each = 10 muffins	

place-value system A system of numeration in which the value of a digit depends on its position in the numeral

plane A set of points that forms a flat surface that extends without end in all directions

plane figure A figure whose points are all in the same plane

point A location in space. It is represented by a dot.

polygon A closed plane figure composed of line segments that meet only at their endpoints.

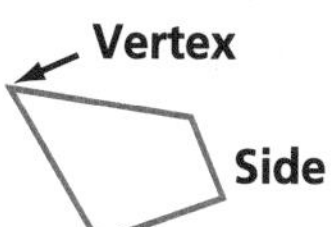

polyhedron A closed figure in space whose faces are all polygons

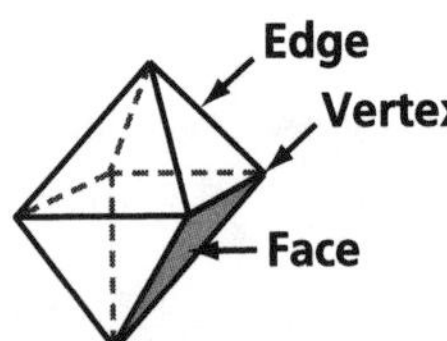

population The entire group of people or objects about whom information is wanted

positive integer (see *integer*)

power A number that can be expressed using a single base and exponent
Example: 32 is a power of 2; it is the fifth power of 2.

prime factorization A number expressed as a product of prime numbers
Example:
$36 = 2 \cdot 2 \cdot 3 \cdot 3$ or $2^2 \cdot 3^2$

prime number A whole number greater than 1 that has exactly two factors, itself and 1
Example: $2 = 2 \cdot 1$

prism A polyhedron that has two congruent, parallel bases that are joined by parallelograms. A prism is named by the shape of its bases.

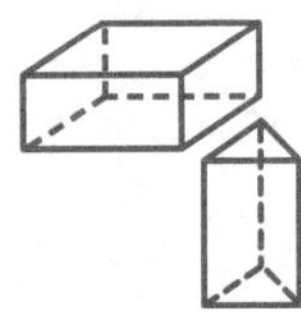

probability A number between 0 and 1 used to describe how likely an event is to happen; a measure of chance

product (see *multiplication*)

proportion A statement that two ratios are equal.
Example: $\frac{3}{4} = \frac{6}{8}$

protractor A tool used to measure angles

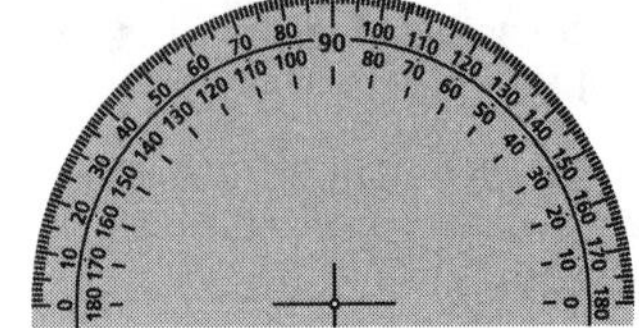

pyramid A polyhedron whose base is a polygon and whose other faces are triangles that share a common vertex. A pyramid is named by the shape of its base.

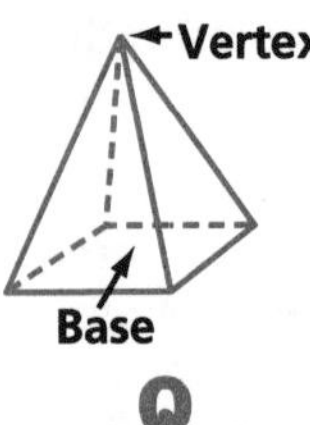

Q

quadrant (see *coordinate plane*)

quadrilateral A polygon that has four sides

quotient (see *division*)

R

radius A segment from any point on a circle to its center; also the length of this segment

random sample A sample chosen so that every person is equally likely to be chosen

range The difference between the least and greatest number in a set of data
Example: The range of the data 2, 4, 5, 5 is $5 - 2 = 3$.

rate A ratio in which unlike quantities are being compared, such as words per minute or feet per second

ratio A comparison of two quantities using division
Example: 3:4, 3 to 4, or $\frac{3}{4}$

rational number A number that can be expressed as the ratio of two integers
Examples:
$1.67 = \frac{167}{100}$ $\quad ^-5 = \frac{^-5}{1}$ $\quad ^-3\frac{3}{4} = \frac{^-15}{4}$

ray A part of a line that has one endpoint. When naming it, the endpoint is used first.

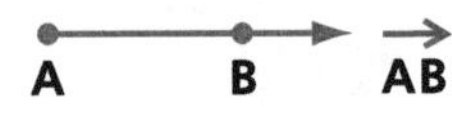

reciprocals Two numbers whose product is 1. They are also called multiplicative inverses.
Examples: 2 and $\frac{1}{2}$ $\quad ^-\frac{3}{4}$ and $^-\frac{4}{3}$

rectangle A parallelogram that has four right angles

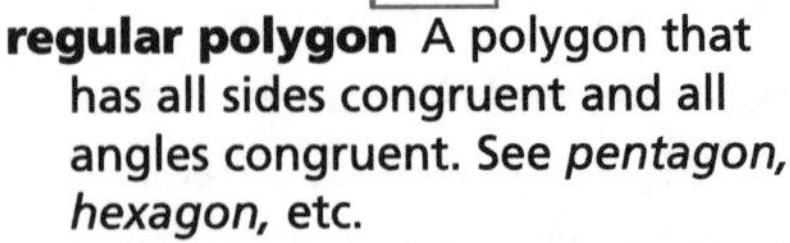

regular polygon A polygon that has all sides congruent and all angles congruent. See *pentagon, hexagon,* etc.

remainder (see *division*)

repeating decimal A fraction whose decimal expression shows a repeating pattern of digits.
Examples: $\frac{1}{3} = 0.333333\ldots$
$\frac{1}{11} = 0.09090909\ldots$

representative sample A sample whose results are proportional to the total population

rhombus A parallelogram that has all of its sides congruent

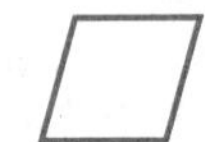

right angle An angle whose measure is 90°

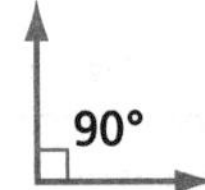

right triangle A triangle whose largest angle is a right angle

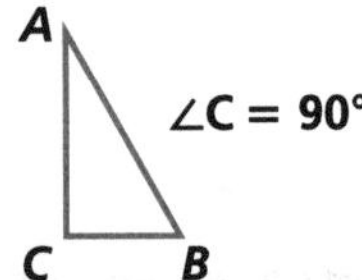

rounded number A number that is close to a given number in which the final digits have been replaced with zeroes
Examples: 12,501 rounded to the nearest hundred is 12,500.
12,501 rounded to the nearest thousand is 13,000.

S

sample A small group selected from a population. Data is collected from the sample and is used to make generalizations about the population.

scale drawing A picture or diagram that is an enlargement or reduction of another. Each distance in the drawing is in the same proportion as the corresponding distance in the original.

scale factor The ratio in a scale drawing or other similar figures that compares the scale drawing dimensions to the actual dimensions

scalene triangle A triangle that has no congruent sides

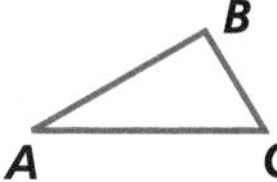

segment A part of a line that has two endpoints

semicircle Half of a circle

side (see *polygon*)

similar figures Two figures that have the same shape, but not necessarily the same size. In similar polygons, corresponding angles are congruent and corresponding sides are proportional.

simplest form A fraction less than 1 in which the numerator and denominator have no common factors except 1, or a mixed number in which the fractional part is in simplest form
Examples:
$\frac{5}{10} = \frac{1}{2}$ $\quad 2\frac{6}{9} = 2\frac{2}{3}$ $\quad \frac{12}{4} = 3$

solution A value of the variable that makes an open equation true

space The set of all points

space figure A figure that is not entirely in one plane

sphere A space figure that has all of its points the same distance from a point, called the center.

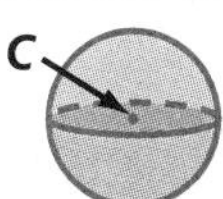

square A rectangle that has all its sides congruent

standard form A number that is expressed as a base 10 numeral
Example: 3,126 is the standard form of the number three thousand, one hundred twenty-six.

subtraction An arithmetic operation that takes away a given amount
Example:
$$\begin{array}{r} 345 \\ -\ 122 \\ \hline 223 \end{array} \leftarrow \text{difference}$$

subtraction property of equality If two expressions are equal and the same number is subtracted from each, then the two new expressions are equal.
Example: If $n + 7 = 10$, then $n + 7 - 7 = 10 - 7$.

sum (see *addition*)

supplementary angles Two angles whose measures have a sum of 180°.

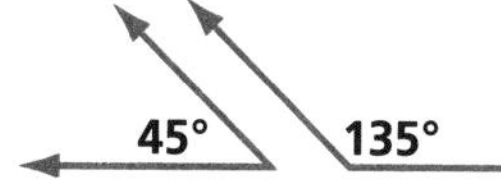

surface area The total area of all the faces or surfaces of a space figure

survey A method of gathering data about a population by recording the results of specific questions

T

term (of a ratio) Either of the two numbers of a ratio

terminating decimal The decimal expression of a fraction whose denominator can be written using only powers of 2 and 5.
Examples: $0.1 = \frac{1}{10}$ $\quad 0.675 = \frac{27}{40}$

theoretical probability The ratio of the number of favorable outcomes of an experiment to the number of possible outcomes. The possible outcomes must be equally likely.

trapezoid A quadrilateral that has exactly one pair of parallel sides

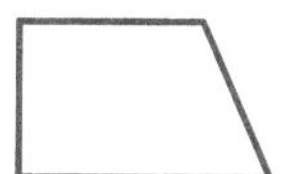

tree diagram An organized way of listing all the possible outcomes of an experiment

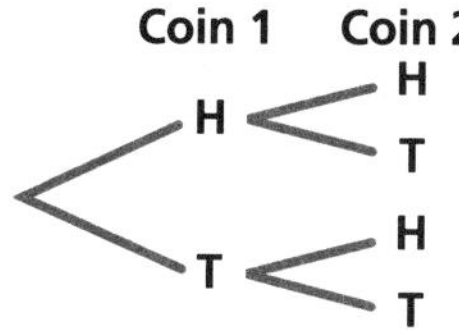

triangle A polygon that has three sides

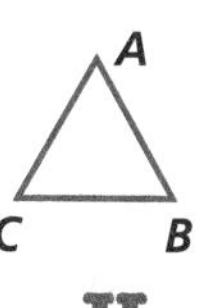

U

unit A fixed quantity used as a standard for length, area, volume, weight, and so on

unit price The cost of a single unit of an item
Example: $3 per pound for hamburger meat

unit rate A rate whose second term is a single unit, such as 50 miles per hour

variable A letter that is used to represent one or more numbers

variable expression (see *algebraic expression*)

vertex (see *polygon, polyhedron*)

vertical angles Two opposite angles formed by two intersecting lines

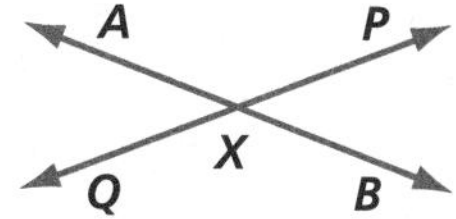

$\angle AXP$ and $\angle BXQ$ are vertical angles.

volume A measure of the space within a closed figure in space

W

whole number Any of the numbers 0, 1, 2, 3, . . .

***x*-axis** The horizontal number line on a coordinate plane

***y*-axis** The vertical number line on a coordinate plane

Z

zero property of multiplication The product of any number and 0 is 0.
Example: $6 \cdot 0 = 0$